John MacMillan, James Renwick

A Collection of Letters, Consisting of Ninety-Three

Sixty-one of which wrote by the Rev. Mr. James Renwick; the remainder, by the

Rev. Messrs. John Livingston, John Brown, John King, Donald Cargil, Richard

Cameron, Alex. Pedan, and Alex. Shields.

John MacMillan, James Renwick

A Collection of Letters, Consisting of Ninety-Three
Sixty-one of which wrote by the Rev. Mr. James Renwick; the remainder, by the Rev. Messrs. John Livingston, John Brown, John King, Donald Cargil, Richard Cameron, Alex. Pedan, and Alex. Shields.

ISBN/EAN: 9783337248550

Printed in Europe, USA, Canada, Australia, Japan

Cover: Foto ©Thomas Meinert / pixelio.de

More available books at **www.hansebooks.com**

COLLEC[...]
OF
LETTE[...]

Confifting of Ninety-[...]

Sixty-one of which wrote by [...] [...]r.
James Renwick; the rema[...] [...]e
Rev. Meffrs. *John Livingfton*, [...],
John King, *Donald Cargil*, [...] *Ca-
meron*, *Alex. Pedan*, and *Alex.* [...].

Alfo a few by Mr. *Michael Shields*, [...]
on of the General Corref[...]

From the years 1663 to 1[6...]

Containing many remarkable Oc[...]
to unknown in that Per[...]

Wherein is difcovered the true State [...]
and Teftimony at that [...]

[The moft of which never be[...]

EDINBURG[H]

Printed by DAVID PAT[...]
And fold by him at hi[s] Printing ho[...]
market, MDCCLXIV.
[Price Eighteen Pence bound]

Chriſtian Reader,

THOU haſt here preſented to thy view, ſome
of the valuable letters of the worthy and
now glorified Mr. *James Renwick,* whoſe memory
will be dear while reformation-principles are regarded in *Scotland;* together with ſome others,
all relative to the ſins and duties of that day, and
not at all impertinent in our day, wherein ſuch
duties are much ſlighted, and the ſame or like
defection, as keenly and effectually carried on
and corroborated, not only by profeſſed enemies to the covenanted intereſt of Chriſt, but
by profeſſed friends thereunto. It is certain that
Zion's King, did in a ſignal manner, diſplay his
banner in the Iſles of the ſea, and engaged them
to himſelf by ſolemn ſacred oaths and covenants:
he animated the ſpirits of his followers with zeal,
reſolution and faithfulneſs in their appearances
and contendings for him and his truths, and e-
ſpecially for the dignity of his kingly office;
he defeated the deſigns of enemies, and advanced
to himſelf a moſt glorious building, of a moſt
beautiful church, *founded upon the prophets and
apoſtles, Jeſus Chriſt himſelf being the chief corner
ſtone;* ſo that this church and nation was bleſſed
with a more glorious and perfect reformation
than any of her neighbour churches: The doctrine, worſhip, diſcipline and government, in all
points agreeable to the word of truth, was eſtabliſhed by eccleſiaſtic and civil laws, ſworn and
ſubſcribed to by the king's majeſty, and all ranks
and degrees in the land: but it is no leſs certain,
that this church and nation, which was once ſo

a 2   great

great a praife in the earth, is deeply corrupted, and hath turned afide quickly out of the way, into the moft fhameful defection, and heaven-provoking apoftacy, from the purity of a covenanted reformation ; fo that the Lord's controverfy againft *Britain* and *Ireland*, but efpecially harlot *Scotland*, is, as expreffed, *Jer.* ii. 21. *I had planted thee a noble vine, wholly a right feed: how then art thou turned into the degenerate plant of a ftrange vine?* Yet, as an evidence that our *Ifrael* hath not been forfaken, nor *Judah of his God, of the Lord of hofts; though their land was filled with fin againft the holy One of Ifrael;* it hath pleafed the covenanted God of the Ifles, for his own glory, and for keeping up the memory of his work in thefe lands, ever fince the national overthrow of reformation, and almoft univerfal defection of all ranks, to preferve a remnant, to witnefs and teftify for his kingly authority, caufe and covenants, many of which were animated with divine courage to triomph over the greateft difficulties and dangers, and feal their teftimony to his caufe with their blood, in the open fields, on fcaffolds and gibbets, to the confuting of enemies, and the ftrengthening and confirming of the faithful ; and ftill the Lord has left a very fmall remnant, whom he hath determined to declare and teftify againft the defections, evils and abominations of the times; endeavouring to follow the voice of the great Shepherd, and to go forth *by the footfteps of the flock,* and example of the faithful cloud of witneffes, feeding by the fhepherds tents, and to keep clofe by his ftandard who is *the chiefeft among ten thoufand,* and *to follow him,* upon all hazards, *through good report and bad report.*

As

As these Letters need not human commendation, so neither will the detraction of any who are so disposed blast their reputation; they are above the one, and despise the other. They will recommend themselves to all who have their senses exercised to discern good and evil, and can savour the things that are of God; whoever have any acquaintance with the sweet breathings of the Spirit of God, and have placed their satisfaction so intirely in the light of his countenance lifted up upon their souls, that they cannot enjoy themselves when they do not enjoy a God in Christ, will here find exemplified in an eminent manner, what a heaven the saints sometimes have, or may have, on this side of glory.

Perhaps some inaccuracies may be met with in the following Letters, which would not have been found in them, had the honoured writers either designed, or corrected them for the press; but, if any such are, it is hoped the candid reader will throw the mantle of love over them; as these Letters were never intended for the reflections of critics, but the instruction of Christians. As a fine stile or florid language is no great recommendation in itself; so the embellishments of oratory could not be expected to be met with in such an age, when men were continually harrassed, and in danger every moment of falling a prey to their enemies: but they are full of the language of heaven, which is many degrees more forcible than all artificial rhetoric. We indeed live in an age when men are generally more taken with the manner of address than with the matter spoken, at least, as to the concerns of God's glory, their own salvation, or what God hath done for us in these lands. *Israel* of old com-

memorated

memorated the wonders God had wrought for
them with an outstretched arm; saying, *I will
sing unto the Lord, for he hath triumphed gloriously; his right hand and his holy arm hath gotten
him the victory,* and calls all to *remember his
marvellous works that he hath done, his wonders,
and the judgments of his mouth.* Such was the
exercise of the church and people of God of old,
while we, in this age, are so far from saying,
What hath God wrought? that the most part desire not the knowledge thereof: We are at ease
in *Zion,* although Christ's crown is profaned,
his prerogatives royal trampled on, his ordinances
contemned, his church and people oppressed;
yet we, like *Gallio,* care for none of these things;
yea, our backslidings are justified, and what immediately brought on the national overthrow of
the Lord's work, *viz.* the admitting of malignants into places of power and trust, contrary
to the nations vows unto God; when now it is
done, is defended and pled for, as lawful and
right; and the memory of our renowned martyrs,
whose dying testimonies witness their explicit rejecting the pretended authority of the impious
brothers, who then tyrannized, is belied by professed witness-bearers for reformation truths.

The Reader, by the perusal of these letters,
may see by what a different spirit these worthies
were acted, what value they put upon truth,
what a lively sense they had of their vows and
obligations to Christ, personal and national, therefore they durst not deny his name, nor break
his bonds and cast away his cords, as the wicked
do; what hardships they underwent, rather than
part with a good conscience, or comply with e-
nemies

nemies in the least; and indeed, the smallest compliance would have been a yielding so far to the ruin of the work and people of God, which was undoubtedly the principal design of their oppressors, and what, even in their favours, as they called them, they intended; thereby verifying that scripture, *The tender mercies of the wicked are cruel.* They had such large discoveries of the love of Christ, especially under the cross, that their hardest trials were accounted light: But how unlike are we to them. They were zealous for the honour of Christ, and burnt in love to him, his truths, ordinances and people, but we are cold and lukewarm, have little concern for the cause of Christ; what they accounted their ornament and glory, we are ashamed of, and look upon it as a disgrace.

By these letters also the Reader may evidently discover what a false and invidious calumny it is to alledge, that an owning of the lawfulness of an Erastian authority is agreeable to the principles and practice of our Reformers, and of our Martyrs, in the bloody reigns of *Charles* II. and *James* VII. such an ignorant and lying aspersion is abundantly confuted from the contents of these valuable letters.

As the manuscripts, from which these letters are carefully printed, are still in the hands of the publishers, any who shall question their authenticity may easily be satisfied.

Thus much, Christian Reader, by the importunity of these concerned in the publication, I have been constrained to say. That the God and Father of our Lord Jesus Christ, who enabled his people to witness a good confession, for his

truths

truths and caufe, may make thefe Letters ufeful to unite all the lovers of truth in the way of duty, and animate them with the like refolution, in ftriving together for the valuable intereft of our reformed religion ; and that they may be bleft for awakening a fecure fleepy generation, to attend to the concerns of God's glory, the interefts of religion in themfelves, and in the world ; and to create in them a love to refor-mation principles, is the earneft defire of

Thine, to ferve thee,

PENTLAND,   *in the gofpel of Chrift,*
June 21. 1764

JO. M'MILLAN.

The

The CONTENTS.

LIV.

The following letters were wrote by Mr. *Michael Shields,* moſtly at the direſtion of the General meeting.

A

A
COLLECTION
OF
LETTERS.

LETTER I.

From Mr. James Renwick, *to the Honourable Mr.* Robert Hamilton.

Much honoured Sir,   Edinburgh, *July* 8 1682.

WE do not question your concernedness with us and our cause at the present; neither do we doubt of your desire to know how, and what the remnant here are doing, in reference to that which God is calling them to in this day. Upon that consideration, and out of obedience to your desire, intimate to me in a letter from our friend *And. Herd.* I have presumed, though unacquainted, which is to my great loss, to write this line (though confused) unto you. And as to matters before your brother S. his departure from us, whom we expect you shall see very shortly, God willing, we remit you to his information, as being more seen and perceiving than we ; and as to our procedure in matters since, I shall labour to give you a brief, yet true account. We do not question but ye know already, how that, by the

A   Lord's

Lord's special providence, there is a general correspondence, which, for a while by-past, hath been kept up among the societies of this land, who profess to own the way of God, and not to say a confederacy with this untoward generation; for which end there have commissioners from their respective societies met together, at least once a quarter, that they might treat and confer anent what is required in this day. And as to what was done the last meeting, the first thing after prayer, which was fallen about, was this: The commissioners names, together with the names of the shires from which they came, were written down; and out of these, fifteen were selected, because the whole would breed confusion, and these being thus selected went by themselves: then it was asked at every one of them, man by man, if they knew the mind of those with whom they were embarked in society; and how they and their society carried as to the owning of our public declarations, and if they any ways contributed brick to Babel, by actively strengthening the hands of the enemies of our Lord; and if they joined with these once ministers, who had now left their Master, and stepped aside from the way of the Lord. All professed that they and their societies were clear for our declarations; but there were some found, who joined with those who payed cess and locality, which we may observe in those who say they own our declarations, to be a confessing God with the mouth, but denying him in works; and though they were not guilty of those things themselves, yet being cloathed with the authority of these who were guilty, they were for that time casten, and desired, if the persons in their societies would not forbear these sinful courses, to separate from them; and

and though there were none to be found in that corner where they lived, who would forbear them, by keeping at a diſtance from them while ſo, they ſhould be received in the convention as particular perſons. There were alſo ſome there, who were found to have accepted the ſacrament of baptiſm and ordinance of marriage, adminiſtred by Mr. *Pedan*, who were for the time ſuſpended from ſitting, but this was after a long and ſtiff debate; for ſome ſaid, how could they upon Mr *Pedan*'s account be ſuſpended, before trial was made and he was found unfaithful? Then it was replied, that he had been many times tried, and practice had proved him unfaithful in this time bypaſt; ſo the moſt honeſt thought it only beſt, not to truſt implicitly, but after trial, to truſt according as he was found to be. Then their empty places being filled with commiſſioners ſelected, who were not found to be guilty of theſe things; it was pro-ceeded (as ordinary) Firſt, to ratify and approve what had been done by the foregoing convention; from which ſome receded, becauſe it had been en-acted, that your brother ſhould go abroad, and give true information of our caſe, and the heads of our ſufferings, to any godly Chriſtian deſirous to know, and unwilling to believe miſinformations and falſe calumnies, which enemies of all ſorts are very vi-gilant to caſt upon us. And ſome (though few) who were for his going abroad at firſt, and would approve of ſending, were not for his continuing any longer. But as to the illegal and diſorderly manner of their diſſentment, having at firſt agreed with the thing, we remit you to our friends, your brother, or *A. H.* Whereupon there was a great confuſion, and nothing could be done till, the diſ-ſenters drawing aſide, there was a new election of

A 2   thoſe

those who were both for his going abroad and continuance for a while   And the day being spent all that was gotten done was only a ratification of what had been done by the foregoing convention; another day when to meet appointed, and some fast days nominated.

Now Sir, you have here a brief account of our late confusions; but I think we ought to look upon them as the Lord's breaking us by these things, ay and while we break fully off from our sinful courses direct or indirect: But this is very observable, that those who dissented from that duty of sending our friend, your brother abroad, are the only pleaders for trusting Mr. *Pedan* before trial, and justify their joining with the abominators of the time, though they do not justify the abominations, which in them is a direct sinning, and an indirect following of their duty But O! Sir, wrestle much for the poor remnant, that they may be united in truth and holiness, which cannot be without separating from both the abominations and abominators of this time: for as the Lord hath said, *There is no peace to the wicked*, consequently there will be no peace to these who are at peace with the wicked as such. No more to trouble you at the time, but leaving you on him who hath kept you hitherto, that he may keep you to the end. I am,

SIR,

Your entire and obedient

servant in the Lord,

JAMES RENWICK.

LET.

LETTER II.

From Mr. James Renwick, *to Mr.* R. Hamilton.

Much honoured Sir,   *Edin. Sept.* 6. 1682.

THE confcioufnefs of my duty makes me prefume to write unto you; and alfo your honouring me with a particular line from your hand,
(being unworthy fo far as to be countenanced by
you) fuperadds a tie upon me thereunto. We received thefe foul-refrefhing letters of yours to our
friends, which to them are very encouraging, they
being defirous to be thankful to the Lord for what
he hath done, and to cry that he would carry on
what he hath fo nobly begun, and to be co-wreft-
lers with all that wreftle for Zion, upon the account of her defolation. And according to your
defire, all friends, having occafion to come to this
place, fee what ye wrote; and I alfo take fome
copies thereof and fend them to feveral corners of
the country: But indeed I cannot exprefs how all
that hear thereof are refrefhed and overjoyed.
But, O! Sir, pray that we may not be abufers of
mercies, and that we may get the Lord put and
kept in his room; and becaufe of thefe things, that
our hearts may only rejoice in the Lord. I cannot
indeed admire enough how fome behaved toward
you while here; but we may have peace, becaufe
it was upon the account of duty. But this I think
is obfervable in fuch cafes, that the Lord then lets
out himfelf to refrefh the fouls of his people; and
it is ordinary with him when there is leaft outward
encouragements to give moft inward encouragement from himfelf; *He flays his rough wind in the
day of his eaft-wind.* O! doth not this magnify his

A 3   wif-

wisdom and graciousness? who killeth, and yet
maketh alive : and does it not tell us that he is
unwilling to afflict? and should it not teach us only to look to himself for encouragement, with
whom there is no shadow of change? And as to
your call abroad, and especially your staying where
you are, surely the Lord's hand hath been only in
it, which his dispensations since hath confirmed.
But, O! labour to be thankful to the Lord, who
hath made you any ways useful where he casts your
lot: And, if my heart deceive me not, my soul
shall be thankful to him upon your account; and
whatever he does, or whoever he makes use of to
do any thing for him, let us only attribute the
praise thereof to his free grace and mercy that honours any so far.

When these refreshing news came to our hands,
my spirit was overjoyed with the hearing of them;
but immediately this thought struck into my mind,
that what if the Lord be now going to leave *Scotland*, seeing he is making his candle shine so clear
in another place; but this thought got no abode,
for it was greatly resented in the time; and the
thought of the many noble testimonies that he hath
honoured a remnant here to give for him, and the
precious blood that he had taken in fields and on
scaffolds, to seal his cause and quarrel. I say, the cries
of these, I thought, (though there were no more)
would not let him give up altogether with this
land, especially seeing it was married unto him,
and his keeping a remnant in it even to this very
day, speaking good unto us. Then again, I was
made to think that this rather might be the thing
which the Lord would do, because we have been
generally so treacherous a people, that he might
not possibly honour any of us to have any hand

in

in the delivery; yet he would deliver, and could command deliverance from afar. However I defire to believe, that he who hath preferved a remnant here to contend for him, will do fo ftill: But O! he is a fovereign God; well would it become us to put a blank in his hand, and to leave the filling up thereof to himfelf, and not to limit the Holy One of *Ifrael*, but rather believe in his word, who hath condefcended fo far as to fell us, *that all fhall work together for good to them that love and fear him*; he is wife and mighty, his end (which is his own glory, and the good of his people) cannot be fruftrate, and he can well make means work together for that end, when the contrary is intended by them. And what you wrote, Sir, among many things, I think, to me it fpeaks this, the making out of his word, that *he fhall fee the travel of his foul*, and that *he is able*, if it were, *out of ftones to raife up children to Abraham*, and that he will not want a teftimony; yea, that if thefe were filent *the ftones would cry out:* So this fhould learn us to credit him with the caufe who is the maintainer thereof, and will fhew himfelf to be the avenger thereof alfo.

Be pleafed to fhow Mr. *Brackel* that fome friends here, and I, have our fervices prefented to him; and that, when friends meet, I think, they will write to him in particular, from them in general, and fhow him that the laft day of the laft month was nominate by fome friends, having met in this place, a day of thankfgiving, for the noble teftimony the Lord had helped him to give, and for his enabling him fo fignally to ftand out, and not to quit any of his Mafter's rights. The relation of the whole bufinefs (which ye wrote) being in the entry of the day read in their hearing, that it might

prove

prove a mean to frame them for that duty, and
show that they are not omitters of what he defires
of them, they feeing it greatly their duty, and
rejoice in the Lord upon his account. And that
you, and friends with you, and friends here, may
be one in the Lord, and one in all our duties, I
thought fit to intimate here, that (as we reckon)
the laft Thurfday of this inftant, and the fecond
Thurfday of October are denominated days of public
fafting by the remnant here, and that the next general meeting of our friends is to be on the fecond
day of November. And as to what was done the
laft meeting, we refer you to the confuſed account
thereof in your brother's letter.

'You fhall receive from the bearer all our martyrs teſtimonies that are unprinted, but there are
written in with the   , two particular teſtimonies,
or rather letters, of James Skeen, which he never
intended to publifh as teſtimonies; fo, if you think
it fit (it being congruous with reafons) they need
not be printed, or at leaft, not as fuch; the one
whereof is directed to all profeffors in the fhire
of Aberdeen; the other, to all and fundry profeffors in the South! Receive alfo fome fermons of
Mr. Welwood's in a little book; but let the fermons, and alfo the teſtimonies, be well noticed;
for not having correct copies, though I write them,
I cannot anfwer for the correctnefs of them.—We
have fent you alfo a letter, with a paper written
by Mr. Donald's own hand, in anfwer thereunto:
but it is unperfected, he being taken away before
he got time to finifh it. But as for that book
which is in Glafgow, it is not as yet come to
our hand; but when corrected, it is promifed, and
when gotten it fhall be fent, with all the (fo
called) acts of parliament. So, leaving you and
all

all his people upon the Lord, lor counfel and direction, I am,

SIR,

Yours, to my full power

to ferve you in the Lord,

JAMES RENWICK.

LETTER III.

From Mr. James Renwick, *to the much honoured* R. Hamilton *at* Lewarden.

Much honoured Sir,   *Edin. October* 3. 1682.

WE received yours, which was very refreshful unto us, and also very feasonable, because of the many wholfome adv ces therein unto us, whereof we greatly ftand in need, efpecially in this juncture of time. But O that we could get the Lord acknowledged in all our ways, then he would direct our paths; for they are only well led and guided whom the Lord leads and guides. O noble guide! O fufficient guide! O true guide! and O conftant guide! he is nearer than a brother; though father and mother fhould both forfake, yet he will not; *he will not leave us, nor forfake us.* Tho' oftentimes we be fo unperceiving that we know not that it is the Lord who upholdeth, yet afterwards we will be made to fay, that *when our feet was flipping God's mercy held us up,* as the Pfalmift fpeaketh in another cafe, *Pfal.* xciv. 17. 18 and when we were as beafts and fools in many refpects, God held us by the hand, *Pfal.*

Pſal. lxxiii. 22, 23　O is not ſuch a guide well worth the following, with all joy and alacrity? Is not ſuch a matter well worth the ſerving, with all the ſoul, heart, mind, and ſtrength? He is not like other maſters; for there is an infinite diſproportion betwixt his work and his reward; and he gives no work, but he gives alſo a heart for the ſame, and all furniture ſuitable and requiſite for the doing thereof, which is the thing that other maſters cannot do. And, the more he gives, the more we may expect; for the more he gives, there is not the leſs behind; becauſe that which is infinite cannot be exhauſted, yea, not diminiſhed: O this is not after the manner of man! that the more he gives, the more we may expect. And doth he not many times lay abundantly whatever we need unto our hand, when we dare not ſay, that either we were right in ſeeking thereof, or exerciſing faith and dependence upon him for the ſame? O! does not this hold forth the freedom, freedom, of his free, free grace? And ſhould not this ſtop our mouths, and cauſe us be ſilent before him? and ſhould not this ſhame us out of our miſbelief, and cauſe us credit him fully and freely with all his matters, and our matters? for *bis foundation ſtandeth ſure, he knows who are his; and whom he loves, he loves unto the end.* There is no ſhadow of change with him. O let us follow him! O let us ſerve him! O noble Maſter! O noble ſervice! In ſerving of him, therein we ſhall get all our ambition ſatisfied. O let us follow him, and ſerve him in his own way: he cannot be found out of his own way; in his light we ſhall ſee light; in the light of his paths, and there only, we ſhall ſee the comfortable light of his countenance: O light! O comfortable light!

There

There be many that say, who will shew us any good? but let us say, *Lord lift thou up the light of thy countenance upon us.* He can, yea, doth gladden our hearts more than the enemies hearts in the time when their corn and wine were increased. O let us leave the world and follow him: Is he not saying, *Come with me from Lebanon, my spouse, with me from Lebanon.* O if his company will not allure us, surely nothing will; and both to ravish us therewith, and make us sure thereof, he says, *With me from Lebanon, with me from Lebanon.*

O worthy Sir, the Lord hath been kind unto you, and made you an instrument of much good; O ye are the more obliged to his free grace! Therefore, O be humble, and O be thankful; and my soul shall desire to be thankful to him upon your account: and the more he does for you, and by you, be ye the more engaged to be for him, and for him only.

We have no news to write unto you; but this is very observeable now, and clearly to be seen, That the fear and terror of the Lord is legibly written upon the consciences of malignants and backslidden professors: there is not so much heart and hand to be seen amongst any, as amongst the poor remnant. And how can it be otherways with these backslidden and backsliding professors? for they are suffering and sinning, sinning and suffering; and in their suffering they want the world's peace; and by their sinning, they want the sweet, sweet enjoyment of a peaceable conscience, and breaks and mars their peace with God. They are really deadened, their hearts are stricken with fainting, and their knees with feebleness: and any life or heart that is to be seen, is among the poor remnant, whom the Lord helps,

in

in any measure, to make *Moses* and *Joshua's* choice,
O! what means all this terror? Is it not the fore-
runner of sudden and sore judgments? He is on
his way, he is on his way; blessed are they, who,
when he comes, shall be found in his way, and
prepared to meet him. Worthy Mr. *Brackel's* letter was very refreshful to all who have heard it;
and there are copies thereof englished, and sent
to several corners of the country. He may-expect
a line from the remnant when they meet, which,
God willing, will be on the eleventh of this instant,
it being called sooner than expectation, for choosing out of these young men But go who will,
the work they are to go for is most weighty; and
their going in such a manner is also most weighty: but there is all furniture with him, who is
the life and the light of men. O that none
may go but these whom the Lord sends, and goes
along with; and whom he helps, and will help to
look to himself, and to himself only, for all frame
and furniture suitable. But we marvel greatly
what you mean in your letters, by speaking of
ordination against the Spring; for your worthy
brother knows assuredly, that we have none of
whom that, or any thing like unto it, can be expected.

The acts of the pretended parliament (according
to your desire) and the book ye wrote for, shall
come with the next occasion, God willing. Let
us know if you received these papers, and that
book, which we sent with your cousins. We know
it is the desire of the people, and we expect it
will be done at the meeting, that you should be
conjunct with your brother in his commission.
We hope we need not desire you, and friends
with

with you, to mind us. So, leaving you on him
who is wise, mighty, and gracious, with my
endeared love to yourself, and worthy Mr.
Brackel, and all our godly and concerned friends
in our Lord Jesus. I am,

Much honoured Sir,

Yours, to my full power

to serve you in the Lord,

JAMES RENWICK.

LETTER IV.

From Mr. James Renwick. *to Mr* Henry Jenkin-
son, *&c. at* Newcastle.

Endeared Friends,   *Edin. October* 3 1682.

WE wrote to you, and gave you notice of
our appointed public fast days, but we
never heard if it came to your hands; and our
still waiting to hear from you in answer to ours,
was the cause of our so long delay now: But,
however, at this time our concernedness with
you, and the great love we have unto you in
the Lord, puts us to it, that we can no longer
forbear; and that because we have heard, that
one Mr. *John Hepburn,* a preacher, was amongst
you; and we see it assuredly to be our duty to
desire you to beware of him; for he is one of
these who handles the word of God deceitfully:
and though he be not altogether so guilty of the
public defection, and of compliance, as some,

B   yet

yet he condemns the laudable practices of the godly party, who were helped to give testimony for truth, and against the enemies thereof: and he is incorporated with the rest in calumniating, reproaching and condemning these, who, in any measure, were kept faithful for their Lord and Master Jesus Christ; and his incorporation with them therein is enough to us, though there be other variances amongst themselves. Let us not own the way of God by halves, but wholly, fully, and in all things. And particularly, he is against our noble and faithful declaration published at *Sanquhar*, whereby that wretched tyrant *Charles Stewart*, and all his accomplices were cast off by us. as we ought; which, alas! was too long a doing: and by this he buries the blood, and condemns the faithful testimonies of so many worthies who have died upon that head, and therein have been eminently owned and assisted of the Lord. Indeed, herein he will run this subterfuge, and say, He acknowledges he ought to be rejected, and deposed; yea, possibly grant, that he deserveth death, both by the laws of God and the just laws of man; yet he cannot see how that can be done without another magistrate or magistrates: But we would answer, If he sees no otherways than so, he is but blind, and that is a deceitful and double dealing; for magistrates have no power but what is derivative from the people; and magistrates have not hing actually, but what the people have virtually; yea, and more than virtually, for they may actually confer it upon whom they think most fit, for the power of government is natural and radical to them, being unitely in the whole,

and

and singularly in every one : so whatever magistrates may do, the people may do the same,
either wanting magistrates, or the magistrates
failing or refusing to do their duty. We need
insist no further upon the lawfulness of the thing ;
for is not this most consonant to the law of
God, and the law of nature? and is sufficiently
cleared by all our most sound divines, particularly worthy Mr. *Knox*, who herein had the
approbation of *Calvin*, and other learned divines of his time, under their hand-writings : and
also is clear enough by the laudable practice of
our resolute and worthy Reformers. But as to
the necessity of the thing, to wit, of the rejecting *Charles Stewart*, as he is installed this day ;
hath he any power to govern, but what is established upon the ruins of the land's engagements?
and hath not the exercise thereof been still according thereunto? What then can we own in him,
if neither the establishment nor the exercise of
his authority? And does he not act in all things
by virtue of his blasphemous supremacy? And
the owning of him in less or in more, is the
owning thereof, because the supremacy is made
the essential of the crown ; and it is but one supremacy that he arrogantly hath both in matters civil and ecclesiastical, which is clear from
the Explanatory Act of the Supremacy : so that
it is essential to the crown, is the same with the
crown, and that which is one cannot be divided.

Now, dear friends, what ye have done in
this, to wit, in your joining with Mr *Hepburn*,
we do not impute it to your wilful stepping aside,
but to the insinuation, or reasonless recommendation of Mr. *Young*, who was hugely overseen
therein,

therein, and which is both a grief and an offence to the remnant. But, O! stand still, go not ye to them, but let them come to you: join with none out of the way of God, but labour to bring all into it that ye can, yet go not out of it yourselves to fetch them thither; and give not ear to the instruction that causeth to err.

We hope we need not bid you beware of Mr. *James Welch*, for he will soon kyth in his own colours. Labour to walk according to that paper sent by you unto us, and walk with none but these who will walk according thereunto. And we are sure if you would pole M. *Hepburn* upon these things in your paper, you should not find him to satisfy you. And if you will defend or continue in your joining with him, or any other who stands where he is, or where he was while he was here, we must deny correspondence with you: But, hoping for better things of you, and desiring an answer hereof we leave you on the Lord for light and life. I am,

Your friend and servant in the Lord,

JAMES RENWICK.

L E T T E R V.

From Mr. J. Renwick, *to the Rev. Mr.* William Brackel *minister of the gospel in* Holland.

Most Rev. Sir,   *Edin. October* 5. 1682.

Lthough our friends when met, are intended, with one consent, to write unto you, in token of thankfulness unto the Lord, for what he hath helped and honoured you to do for himself; and in token of their soul concernedness with, and real affection for all those whom the Lord helps and honours to follow himself in his own way, in owning of, adhering to, and contending for the faith once delivered to the saints: But especially, I say, in token of their soul concernedness with you whom the Lord hath so signally helped to advance in his own way, and contend for all his rights and privileges, being carried above the fear of frail mortal man. whose breath is in his nostrils, and only fearing him who is *Lord of lords, and King of kings*, the terrible Majesty of heaven and earth, the *high and lofty One who inhabiteth eternity:* Yet my soul is so unite unto you upon that account, and because of your real concernedness and soul-sympathy with all of us in *Scotland* who desire to be helped of the Lord, to espouse his quarrel to be only ours, and his concernments to be only ours; I say, so unite (tho' little or nothing I can say as I ought) that I cannot keep silent.

But, O! What shall I say? Is not the Lord God of hosts worthy and only worthy of all service, if we could serve him? May not that infinite and transcendent love (in the profound depth of the admiration whereof angels are drowned) which he bore unto man before the foundations of the world were laid, so ravish and fill our souls, as that we might say, Him only will we serve who loved us; nothing present or to come shall be able to separate us from the love of God that is in Christ Jesus? O! is not *his yoke easy, and his burden light?*

B 3

light? his cross is no cross, for he bears it himself, and also those who take it up. His will is holy, just, good and spiritual in all that he does. O! what is more desirable than to live and die *with* him, and for him? *for our light affliction which is but for a moment, worketh for us a far more exceeding and eternal weight of glory; while we look not at the things which are seen; but at the things which are not seen.* Let *us not weary in well-doing; for in due season we shall reap if we faint not. It is a faithful saying, if we be dead with him, we shall also live with him; if we suffer, we shall also reign with him; if we deny him, he will also deny us.* O! is not *Moses*'s choice very desirable? Are not *all his ways pleasantness, and his paths peace?* Where is peace to be found? is it not in his way? and when he gives peace, who can create trouble? He gives, and can give joy which no man can take from us. Now,

Most Reverend Sir, my soul desires, while I live, to praise the Lord, for what great things he hath helped you to do, in so nobly, faithfully and freely witnessing for his noble cause, and sweet *Scotland*'s cause: and my soul desires to honour you, because he hath so honoured you; and to love you, because he loves you, and hath caused you to love and own his cause, and receive his truths in love; and also to be afflicted in all the afflictions of his people, and to be such a sympathizer, and a burden-bearer with his poor remnant in this land, as that we may say of you, as *Paul* of the *Hebrews, Ye have had compassion on us in our bonds.* O Sir, go on in his way, and advance valiantly; be zealous for him and he shall animate you: *Cast not away your confidence, yet a little, and he that shall come, will come, and will not tarry: Now the just shall live by faith; but if any man draw back my soul shall have no pleasure in him, saith the Lord.* O! who is he that will harm you if ye be followers of that which is good. Therefore, *cease from man whose breath is in his nostrils for wherein is he to be accounted of?* Now, the Lord let you feed upon his all-sufficiency, and give all suitable frame and furniture unto you, for his work in your hands; and give you his Spirit whereby you may go on in his way, with all magnanimity, Christian boldness, and free speaking for him unto the sons of men.

O Sir! do not impute any thing said to you in this short and confused line to arrogance in me; for what may, if mistaken, give occasion thereof, flows only from my concernedness and soul-union with you. So, at the time I shall trouble you no further. But this I must tell you, and I think it is to be remarked, and may be clearly seen all this time, that the terrors of the Lord is greatly engraven and legibly written upon the consciences of all the compliers with the horrid abominations of this land. They are really deadened, and it is no wonder, for they have forsaken the Lord, and he hath forsaken them: He cannot be found out of his own way. A guilty conscience is bad company, and what means all this terror of sudden and sore judgments from the Lord? and there is not so much spirit, courage, and voidness of slavish fear among any, whether avowed malignants or compliers

pliers with them, as amongſt the poor remnant, who are deſiring to be helped of the Lord, in all things to make a right choice. O! pray for the Lord's return to poor *Scotland*, and for his appearance unto the rejoicing of his people, and confuſion of his adverſaries. And pray for him, who is,

Moſt reverend Sir,

Yours, to his full power

to ſerve you in the Lord,

JAMES RENWICK.

LETTER VI.

From Mr James Renwick, *to the honourable the Laird of* Earlſton, *at* Lewarden.

Much honoured Sir,   Rotterdam, *Nov.* 20. 1682.

IT is not a little troubleſome to me, that I ſhould be in this place ſo long; but I have occaſion to go away whenever the wind offers: and I hope, your Honour will be careful to get conveyed unto *Scotland,* with all expedition, an account of what you think fit to be contained in that letter which is to be written; for out of *Scotland* I cannot come, if once it pleaſed the Lord that I were there, untill that I get that letter with me. And it will be alſo very neceſſary that ſome ſhould be pitched upon for catechizing; and this muſt be recommended to the carefulneſs of ſome who will ſee it done at the general meeting.

And

And if *J. V.* be gotten reclaimed (for your honour knows, that he walked contrary to his own
duty, and our appointments, in joining with
Mr. *Hepburn* while out of the way of God; I
say, if he be gotten reclaimed, amongst others,
he may be one, as I think. It is reported in
the *Scottish* news, that the actually indulged (so
called) ministers are required, either immediately to take their test, otherwise to lay down their
charges at the feet of those men of whom they
took them up; and if it be so, let the world
think what they will. I dare not be sorry thereat, but on the contrary rejoice, because that indulgence hath been, and is yet a stumbling-
block unto the people of God; and is not the
removing of stumbling blocks a token of sudden
good to his people, how low soever they be
brought! It is also reported, that *Charles Stewart* hath ordained his council in *Scotland* to proceed against *Haltoun* in making him accountable
for the mint: *Haman's* rejoicing is short. O Sir,
I cannot get the thoughts of the weighted case
I left you in, when we parted, out of my mind:
But this I think, the Lord is taking several ways
with your honour, in discommending all other
things unto you, that so he may commend himself unto your soul, and that ye may be kept from
rejoicing in any thing but himself alone; and when
he is the matter of our joy, that is the joy that no
man can take from us. O! 'tis himself that is
the portion of his people, and the world cannot
deprive them thereof, and this is our comfort.

Remember me to your worthy brother, your
lady and her sister: and as I have been partly an
eye, but more an ear witness unto some of the
troubles ye have been put to upon our blessed
Lord's

Lord's account; so I hope also, to be a witness to the everlasting inconceivable joy ye shall be fill'd with, when these who overcome shall be sitting in white robes, upon thrones, with crowns upon their heads judging the world. O are ye not high up now! are ye not far ben in the king's palace, when ye are sitting upon thrones giving your *amen* to the sentence, which he will pass upon the world. Walk worthy of the name by which ye are called. So leaving you on him who is the Rock of ages, whose work is perfect, for perfecting what concerns you. I am,

Your Honour's servant in all Christian duty,

JAMES RENWICK.

LETTER VII.

From Mr. James Renwick, *to the much honoured Mr.* Robert Hamilton.

Much honoured Sir,   *Rott. Jan.* 18. 1683.

I Received your letter, but the interveening of some dispensations put me so that I was not in case for answering it. Our friend *G H.* having written to you; therefore, I shall not now speak, neither of our own progress, nor of what sad news otherwise we have heard. The Lord help us to patience, for we have need of it, and make us submissive to his will, who can do nothing but good. O they are happy who are well away! and they are happy who will be carried through, for there are sad days coming,

and

s shall not escape. I cannot express
impressions I have of it, especially
fast day that they had in this pro-
ie morning whereof I fell into a
hought, that I was preaching upon
Zech. vii. 5. at the end of the verse,
ill fast unto me, even unto me?
ie Lord) and thought that I brought
it, that they were hypocritical,
utside folk, or outward only in their
it did not fast unto the Lord. And
who fasted, and yet retained sin,
o let it go. And then, made appli-
iny particular sins in thir lands. I
if this as a dream, however it hath
sion upon me. O to be helped to
rd's command, and to exhort others
Luke xxi. 36. *Watch ye therefore, and*
that ye may be accounted worthy to
'se things that shall come to pass, and
e the son of man. O dear Sir! I can-
the case I am in, partly, with our
falling into the hands of our Lord's
d partly, with my being so long demy brethren. I cannot tell what
re my hand; but, my longings to be
I cannot express, I would spare no
ivel, and fear no hazard; only, I do
duty to go on deliberately in a seen-
ire there is no probability of safety.
iat the Lord would be pleased to pro-
iccasion which might be my duty to
id that he would order all things aright
rgement of his kingdom: O precious
ind O noble way that he is taking
inlarge it, by stretching out the bor-

ders

ders thereof with blood! His houſe is a coſtly houſe, and it is well worthy of coſtly cementing. I hope I need not bid you labour to ſubmit chearfully to the holy and wiſe will of the Lord, and be ſtrengthening unto theſe with you. The Lo d ſtrengthen, the Lord comfort and give himſelf inſtead of all things to them, and to you, is, and ſhall be the earneſt prayer of him who is,

Much honoured Sir,

Yours, to ſerve you in the Lord,

while he hath a being in time,

JAMES RENWICK.

LETTER VIII.

From Mr. J. Renwick, *to the much honoured Mr.* Robert Hamiltoun.

Rott. Jan. 22. 1683.

Right hon. and dear Sir,

THis afternoon I have received two letters from you, wherein ye call me unto you, by the deſire of that worthy lady and her family. I am very ſorry I cannot get you ſo ſoon anſwered as I would deſire ; for this day or to-morrow I cannot come, being detained here by a certain diſpenſation fallen out, of which I can-not now write ; but when met (if the Lord will) I ſhall give you an account of the matter and manner of it. However upon *Monday* I reſolve

to

to come away, and shall stay so long as I may and can be serviceable to any there. But O! that I could commend the Lord and his noble way to the world: and I must say this to his praise, that he is daily giving me confirmations of his way, and engaging me thereunto, and folding me in all circumstances with his own concernments. Being in haste I shall say no more; recommending you and that worthy family to the Lord, for all ye stand in need of. I am,

Yours to serve you in the Lord, while

JAMES RENWICK.

LETTER IX.

From Mr. J. Renwick, *to the much honoured Mr* R. Hamiltoun.

Much honoured Sir,   *Groningen, Feb.* 6. 1683.

O That now when I write to you there were for every drop of ink that falls from my pen, a tear falling from my eye: There is more than cause enough for it, yea, I cannot say but I am made to see the same; for, in some measure, I see and know the poor afflicted. tossing and wandering remnant, in such a case as the waters have overflowed their heads, the Lord having covered himself with a cloud. But for all this (woes me) my eye doth not rightly and thoroughly affect my heart. O! if we could confider, that the Lord doth not afflict willingly, nor grieve the children of men; and

C   then

then reflect upon our griefs and afflictions in this day, we would be put, with amazement, to wonder at the greatnefs of our fins: And inftead of coming to the Lord with this in our mouths and in our hearts, *That which we fee not, teach thou us: Wherein we have offended, we will offend no more,* we are ftill adding fin to fin, which are both the tokens and the caufes of the Lord's difpleafure. O! there is nothing, I think, fo fad as the fpiritual judgments of the Lord, and nothing betokens fo much of his difpleafure. O Sirs! cry and wreftle, and defire all that love *Zion,* to cry to, and wreftle with the Lord, that he would preferve a remnant from being fwallowed up by this weighty cloud of wrath hanging over our heads, ready to break forth, now when we are fo ripening for the fame.

I fhall let you know my mind in all our particulars; but as yet I can fay nothing : but as for my own prefent cafe, ye may know that from what I have faid; for thefe things that ought, and that I fee, do not rightly affect my heart: And by feeing this alfo, I am in a confufed, anxious, and difconfolate condition at prefent; yet I dare not fay but the Lord is kind, though I be froward: and, I think, that which my foul would take as the greateft proof of his kindnefs, would be a melting frame of fpirit from himfelf. But O! in all cafes, let us have our recourfe to that Rock that is higher than we, where we fhall find comfort for our hearts that are perplexed; and let us lay our All under the feet of all men, but quite a hoof of God's matters to no man. Let us be lions in God's caufe, and lambs in our own. Remember me to your brother

ther

ther *E* and fisters : I hope, God willing, to write to him fhortly. I am,

Much honoured Sir,

Your foul's fympathizer,

JAMES RENWICK.

LETTER X.

From Mr. J. Renwick, *to Mrs.* J. H. *at* Lewarden *in* Friefland.

Worthy Madam,   *Gron. Feb.* 13. 1683.

THE fenfe of my duty will not let me omit writing unto you; although, if it would pleafe the Lord, I would defire a clearer fight of fome things than I have at prefent, that fo I might be admitted to tell you my thoughts more diftinctly : but his way with me is in the depths. I cannot tell what method he would have me to take in things ; for I find my ordinary ftudies that are more directly for exercitation than for edification, put me out of a concerned frame with the afflictions of *Jofeph.* And then feeing this, when I fet upon other things, my thoughts begin to flight thefe ordinary means. What the Lord would have me to do therein, as yet I wot not. O that he that hitherto hath condefcended, would condefcend to let me know what courfe he would have me to take, and make me willing to follow the fame. O it is hard to carry within meafure, and to give any thing its own place. O let us

     earneftly

earneſtly labour to get a ſympathizing frame of ſpirit keeped up, with that poor, afflicted, chattered, and broken remnant in *Scotland*; for I obſerve this palpably, that I am never in any ſort of a good frame, but when they are lying near my heart, and when their afflictions are touching me. There are many things that are very diſcouraging like; but there is comfort, Jeſus Chriſt is a King, and ſeeing he is a King, he will have ſubjects; yea, he will reign till he put all his enemies under his feet. Shall not the pleaſure of the Lord proſper in his hand? *He will ſee the travel of his ſoul, and be ſatisfied.* And may not our ſouls feed upon the raviſhing thoughts of the pureneſs of that church which he will have in *Scotland?* What ſhall be the end of all theſe things? ſhall they not all tend to the purging *Jacob* from his ſin.

O Madam, live near the Lord, and labour to get him preſent with you; his preſence will make all trials ſweet. Who would not come off with him from *Amana*, I ſay with him from *Amana?* He is the chief among ten thouſand; his countenance is comely as Lebanon, excellent as the cedars; yea, he is altogether lovely. A ſight of the preciouſneſs that is in him will cauſe us to go through fire and water with him and for him: Will not the conſolations of his Spirit bear up the ſoul in all its difficulties? eſpecially when it is ay made to ſee in the end, that it could not want one dram weight of its cup. And O the great need that there is of the conſolations of his Spirit this day! for I have had theſe thoughts this long time, that many would be tryſted with ſuch diſpenſations, as would not ſo much call for

light

light to lead them, as for heart comforting grace to bear up their spirits in them. I think some of our difpenfations will be to fome more difcouraging than darkening. O mind fweet *Scotland*, and him who is

Your Ladyfhip's fervant

in all Chriftian duty,

JAMES RENWICK.

L E T T E R XI.

From Mr. J. Renwick, *to the much honoured Mr.* R. Hamiltoun.

Honoured Sir,　　　　　*Gron. Feb.* 22. 1683.

I Cannot exprefs my obligation to you for writing to me, a poor empty nothing; and confidering my prefent cafe, your letter was very feafonable: for my great exercife is, and was, how to know the motions of the Spirit, and what he would have me to do in the circumftances wherein I ftand; and ye have given fome marks thereof, which I think indeed are very holding. But in this I muft reverence a higher hand than yours. I have, fince I faw you laft, had as fad conflict, yea more fad than ever I had heretofore: but O that I could blefs and praife the name of the only holy and wife God. There is not one dram in the mixture of my cup that I can want; yea, I fee a neceffity for all that I meet with: and though I have had

C 3　　　　　　　　　　very

very fad conflicts, the Lord (O infinite conde-
fcendence!) hath made me to poffefs fweet
hours both in the night and day. And as to my
cafe, I may fay, *The Lord ftays his rough wind
in the day of his eaft wind;* for notwithftanding
that *deep calleth unto deep,* yet the Lord keeps
my fpirit, in fome meafure, ftayed and ftablifh-
ed as to that: but when I ponder other circum-
ftances, I am put to many ftrange thoughts; yet
the Lord makes me even feed many times upon this, and that even with great joy, that as
he is dealing with his church this day, fo is he
dealing with me; yea, I fee not one circum-
ftance in the one, but I muft fee it in the o-
ther: yea, and is not this matter of great joy.
The Lord forbid that I fhould defire to be otherwife dealt with than his church: O how unnatural
like would that defire be! When his way is in the
depths with his church, why fhould it not be
fo with us? But, O Sir, I fee a cloud of wrath
ready to fall out; and I fear, I fear that we will
not be found free of it. O may not any thing
be eafily born; but how can this be born? O
for grace to turn fpeedily and repent, it may be
the Lord would repent him of the evil. There
is mourning and humiliation that the Lord is
calling for; and the Lord will ay, I think,
give us ftroke upon ftroke, and blow upon blow,
until he get that effectuate If my heart deceive me not, I could fubmit (at leaft defire to
fubmit) to any thing in time, but to this, *viz.*
to have a deep hand in drawing more wrath
forth, I cannot fubmit, I ought not to fubmit:
O that the Lord would rather take me away in
the midft of my days. But I ought not to mifbe-
lieve; he can keep my feet from falling, he

can

can perfect strength in my weaknefs. But this
is the way that the Lord would have me to take;
yea, I think affuredly, this is the courfe he
would have me to fall upon, to feek all that I
need from himfelf by prayer: for, to the praife
of his free grace I muft fpeak it, when he helps
me either to pray or meditate, he is not wanting; but in other things I do not find him.
However, I think, this may be the caufe of it,
I cannot win to ufe them and keep them in
their own places. But there are fome things
good in themfelves, and good when made right
ufe of; but to me they are as *Saul's* armour to
David, I can put them on, but I cannot walk with
them: and I cannot fay but I could put them
on, unlefs I fhould lie of the Lord, who (bleffed be his name) hath given me, in fome meafure, a difpofition.

O Sir, as your letter was very refrefhful, on
the one hand; fo, upon the other, it was very
weighty unto me; becaufe you fay the trouble
you told me of is not yet away: But, O I fear
there may be much of a temptation in it, for
I cannot fee caufe for trouble upon that account.
But my hearing that you are troubled is no
furprizal unto me, for you were often brought
before me fince I parted with you, and you
was ay reprefented as one overwhelmed and
weighted, and this was fometimes troublefome
unto me; but when I thought upon the cafe of
the Lord's church, I was then made to think,
why fhould I wifh it to be otherways with you,
than it is with your mother: But is not the
Lord taking all ways with us, to fpean us from
all things; yea, even to make us denied to one
another? He will have us to take himfelf for
all

all our contentment and satisfaction: O noble contentment ! O sweet satisfaction ! Other airths may fail us, but the Lord will never fail any that put their trust in him : and whatever the Lord hath to do with you in any place, as he calls you forth, so he will also, in his own blessed time, lead you whither you should go; *Heb.* xi. 8. *By faith Abraham, when he was called to go out unto a place which he should after receive for an inheritance, obeyed; and he went out, not knowing whither he went.* O Sir, pray for sweet *Scotland* ; pray that zeal and tenderness may be kept there : and pray for him who is, .

Much honoured Sir, .

Your soul's-sympathizer,

and servant in the Lord,

JAMES RENWICK.

LETTER XII.

From Mr. James Renwick, *to Mr.* Robert Hamilton, *at* Lewarden.

Much honoured Sir,   Gron. March 6. 1683.

I Received your letter with worthy Mr. *Brackel's*, which were very surprising to me, in respect of the circumstance of the time ; and the sense of the work, together with my own unfitness, came so upon my spirit, that I began to give place to this resolution, that I would desire some more time ; but therein I could find no peace,

the

ing tortured and racked. And up-
hand, when I confidered the afflict-
ting cafe of the remnant, both in
e open adverfaries, and of treache-
t eafe, who ftand in the crofs-way;
I confidered how the glorious truths
wronged, by cruelty againt them,
hand, and perfidious treachery and
g on the other; I thought it would
able thing, the Lord calling me
fitting me therefoe, if it were but
public teftimony againft the fame:
jections arofe in the heart, flowing
enfe of my unfitnefs; but the Lord,
to his holy name!) anfwered them
letter, and with that word, *Pfal.*
I have laid help upon one that is
d also I thought, that it was fo like
s dealing with his church, and faw
orious wifdom and infinite love to-
, (for if I had any thing in me, I
ly to forget him, and not to refort
hauftible and precious treafure;
as put to run to himfelf, having
h to betake me to) that I could
for my objections more. But O!
rk indeed; I fee that we can never
get the weight of any thing taken
and laid on himfelf, till he let us
ewhat of the weightinefs thereof,
it were, laid heavy upon us. O!
ghty work indeed! who is fit for
e myfteries of falvation? Who is
ing our fweet Lord Jefus Chrift,
ft and king in *Zion*, without any
nd for opening up the fame? Who
is

is fit for dispensing these glorious benefits of the
covenant of redemption? O! who is sufficient
for these things? And why is he calling poor
unworthy nothing me out to such a great and
glorious work? I think that he is saying, that
the excellency of the power may be of himself,
and not of me. So, having the mouth of all
objections stopped, I offer myself in all trembling, fear and humility; yet having great reason to believe in him for all things, though I be
altogether unfit. O dear Sir, wrestle, wrestle,
and desire all true lovers of *Zion* to wrestle with
the Lord, that ye and we may be directed in this
great affair. O set time apart, and seek the
mind of the Lord there: ye will meet with
difficulties in it; but I hope the Lord will have
a care of his own work, and direct you wisely.
For my own part I desire nothing but what may
be for the advantage of the cause, and I hope
the Lord hath so framed my affections, that
whatever is seen not to be advantagious, I shall
not desire.

We desire humbly to thank you for your
books, the Lord he will repay you: and as for
your letter from *Scotland*, which ye sent to me,
it was very refreshful: I am sure the Lord moved
you to send it; for I was made therein to see a
great proof of the Lord's condescendency to poor
me. That which it contains of *Andrew Young*,
being the thing which I was expecting, for he was
still brought before me, and represented as a
man full of bitter passion; yea, he was so brought
still in my way, that the day, or two days before I received the letter, I said several times to
my neighbours, that I was sure I would hear
something of him. O! that I had the tongue of
the

he learned, to fet forth the praife of that fo glorious and excellent, yet fo condefcending a God. O! there is none that knows him but hey will love him. The many proofs of his kindnefs and condefcendency, make me many imes to cry out, *What is man that* he is *mindful f him, or the fon of man that he fhouldft vifit him?* But he loves, becaufe he loves; and there can be no other reafon given for it. I fhall rouble you no further at the time, but prefent ny love and fervice to your worthy brother; I hope he is not unconcerned at this time: and as for his going to *Scotland,* the Lord will direct him what to do: and I fhall labour, through the Lord's ftrength, to obey your anfwer hereof. O Sir! wreftle, wreftle, and defire all to wreftle with the Lord, that he would carry on his own work, and get glory to himfelf in fitting inftruments, and in making his people a zealous people, a holy people, a felf-denied people. I am,

Much honoured Sir,
Your fympathifing friend,
and fervant in the Lord,
J A M E S. R E N W I C K.

L E T T E R XIII.

From Mr. James Renwick, *to the much honoured Mr.* Robert Hamilton.

Much hon. Sir,   *Amfterdam, March 30. 1683.*

AFTER I had fent away your *French* mail, and a letter with it, I received yours, but
the

the poſt being juſt now going away, I have no
time to write. But O! what would I, or could
I ſay, but only deſire to be ſubmiſſive to the
Lord's will, who hath made a neceſſary ſeparation
betwixt us, that I cannot have the comfort and
advantage of your company: But, though you be
abſent from me as to bodily preſence, you are
not long out of my mind; I wiſh I may get you
kept in your own place, and be kept from murmuring and diſcontent at my want. I reſolve to
paſs for a while under the name of *James Bruce*.
I have no time now to write to theſe worthy ladies; but before I go to *Scotland* I ſhall ſee to
get it done, yet if once I were there, I think, I
would know better how to write of matters.
The Lord himſelf be with you. I am,

Much honoured Sir,

Yours to ſerve you in the Lord,

while I have a being in time,

JAMES RENWICK.

LETTER XIV.

To Mrs. J. H. *at* Lewarden *in* Frieſland.

Worthy Madam,   *Groningen, March* 31. 1683.

I have no time to write any thing to you, but
I hope you will not think me to be ſo far out
of my duty as to be unmindful of your caſe; for
I am very ſenſible of the circumſtances whe re-
in you ſtand: However, though your trials be
many,

many, and your fears not few, yet I think not your case strange, the like hath happened to the Lord's people. O take all well out of the Lord's hand; look to his purposes in his dispensations, and then you will be made to read love to you in the saddest of them. Away with scrimpit sense, which constructs ay God's heart to be as his face is: Faith is a noble thing, it soars high, and can read love in God's heart when his face frowns: Have you not reason to construct well of him? Bode good upon his hand: your evening of sorrow shall be turned unto an everlasting morning of joy. Let the faith of this sweeten your present case unto you. The Lord be with you all. Mind him who is,

Worthy Madam,

Your friend and servant in the Lord,

and a sympathizer with you in your trials,

JAMES RENWICK.

LETTER XV.

From Mr. James Renwick, *to the much honoured Mr.* Robert Hamilton.

Much honoured Sir,   *Gron. April* 23. 1683.

I Received the inclosed yesterday, but I have no time to write any thing for the occasion is now going; only I have written this day to Mr. *Br* at *Lee* and by the Lord's gracious free condescendence, was put and kept in a good frame all the while: O! that I could praife him for his free, free love. He lets me fee much fin, and yet lets me fee alfo, that he does not contend for the fame, which cannot but be great matter of wonder. O! no fight, I think, is fo fweet as that fight, for it is backed with admiration of his free love, and alfo with felf-loathing. Hoping that ye will be mindful of poor unworthy me, as with my whole heart I defire to be of you. I am,

Much honoured Sir,

Yours at command,

to ferve you in the Lord,

JAMES RENWICK.

L·ETTER XVI.

From Mr. James Renwick, *to Mrs.* Jean Hamilton *at* Lewarden.

Worthy Madam,   Gron. *April* 25. 1683.

I Thought it my duty to acquaint you with what great things the Lord hath done in this place, for his own noble caufe, and for us poor, weak, empty nothings: For when upon *Thurfday* laft; being the 19*th.* of this inftant, Mr. *J. F.* and I went in before the Synod, which was then fitting, and fought ordination from them; they, for the moft part not knowing us, after we had removed for a little fpace, began to aſk among themſelves what we were, and what

what we were feeking, having heard fomething thereof from ourfelves. Whereupon, firft *Dom. Philingius,* then *Dom. Albringha* rofe up and declared unto them fomewhat of the cafe of our church; at which, fome of them fell out with tears, and faid, Though the kings of the earth fhould be againft them, they would go on in our affairs. Whereupon, we were called in again unto them, and three men were appointed for our trials; and the tenth of the next month, for the day; the minifters of this town having undertaken for the expence which we ought to have been at. So, having many things to do, I fhall detain your Ladyfhip no further. But O! is not this great matter of praife, that the Lord fhould let his own hand be fo much feen, in procuring fuch teftimonies to his noble caufe; yea, before he want a teftimony, *the very ftones would be made to cry out:* Therefore, come and let us worfhip him, come and let us exalt his name together; he reigns, and therefore let his followers be glad. Recommending you to his fatherly care; hoping, that ye will not be unmindful of poor unworthy me, upon whom the Lord hath laid fo many obligations to be for him, and whom he is now calling forth to his vineyard in fuch a weak condition: But my fufficiency is of him, and to be found faithful is all my defire. My love and fervice to your worthy fifter, the Lady and her children.

> *Worthy Madam,*
>   *Yours, to my full power,*
>   *to ferve you in the Lord,*
>   JAMES RENWICK.

LETTER XVII.

To the Lady Earlſton *Younger.*

Worthy Madam,   Groningen, May 5. 1683.

I Received your Ladyſhip's letter; but I am
ſorry I had not the time to write ſooner back
to you: However, I hope you will excuſe me,
conſidering the circumſtances I ſtand in at this
time. Your letter repreſents to me a troubled
caſe; but, I think, not a bad caſe, becauſe ye
have the ſenſe of it upon your ſpirit. You ſay,
a hiding God, who can bear it? O that I could
ſee theſe pleaſant days, to hear many crying
that cry, to hear many ſignifying their deſire
after himſelf, by crying out, they could not want
him, that they could not be content without him;
yea, and that they could not be content with a-
ny thing elſe, being wilful in the matter. It is
true indeed, they who know what his ſenſible
preſence is, they will not get born up in his conceived abſence; and if I could, I would deſire to
mourn over their unperceiving temper, who can
equally bear up in both: But, when the ſoul,
not being filled with ſenſe, pants after him *as
the hart pants after the water-brooks*, and getting
up, and running through the whole fields, crying
out, *Saw ye him whom my ſoul loveth*; I cannot
but think, that the Lord is eminently preſent
with that ſoul, though not to its own apprehenſion; yea, and though there be no changes in
the Lord, nor in his love; yet of all times, as
to the outletting thereof, he is at ſuch a time,
moſt faſht to keep it in. And who knows not,
that

that love, the more it is covered, the more it burns; as fire, the more it be covered, the more it smokes, unless it be extinguished; for, *whom he loves, he loves unto the end.* O let us not misconstruct him, for he dow not abide it. And for mine own part, I am made many times to go and bless his holy name, because of his withdrawing; for I see much more of his love manifested therein, than if he were sensibly present; because then I am made to see many things in myself I saw not before; for, it is most difficult to carry aright upon the mount: Do we not find this, that in such cases, we forget ourselves many times? as *Peter*, when he was with our Lord on the mount and saw his glory, said, *It is good for us to be here; let us make three tabernacles, one for thee, one for Moses, and one for Elias;* which *Luke* notes with that, that *he knew not what he said.* O! let us study that noble life of faith, which the Lord is at so much pains to learn us; for it is faith followed with holiness that all the promises are made unto, not one unto sense.

Your Ladyship writes, that since you came unto this land, the Lord's way hath not been ordinary with you; and I think, it looks the liker his way that it is so: and though (possibly at the time) you cannot see what is the language thereof, I am sure that afterwards he will let you see it; we have the swellings of *Jordan* to pass thro' yet, and the Lord seems to be training you up for what is before your hand learning you only to live the life of faith. O let us wait upon him, for we many times loss our alms because we want patience to wait on a little. Let us ly near himself, that we may not be confused nor surprised in a day of firey trial. not knowing where to

run.

run. And as for that trouble which arifeth from the finding of friends like to take offence at your not going to the kirk; I confefs, in its own place, it is a matter of concernment; but we have one who is higher, whom we muft look to that we offend not; and to feek their countenance fuch a way, I dare not, nor will not counfel you to it. Labour to follow the Lord leading you, for I think, your cafe in that particular is from the Lord; and although that ye are humbled with your fabbath days being your worft days, be not too much troubled, for the Lord feems only to be trying you; and if Satan get in his foot, and make you to queftion duty for the want of fenfe, he will get his end mightily gained. O what is the matter though all the world fhould forfake us, and though all men fhould turn againft us, if he be for us we need not care. O fweet word, Though father and mother fhould forfake us, yet he will not: And though our heart and flefh faint and fail us, yet he never will fail us. O Madam! I have not time to fay what I would, but I fhall omit the reft until meeting, which, if the Lord will, fhall be fhortly. Our ordination is going on; but, for ought I think, Mr. J. F. will not go thorow. O! pray, pray that the Lord may let his hand be feen, with poor weak, unworthy me; without him I can do nothing; O what exceffive madnefs will it be for me to go on without himfelf. If he go not with me, I pray that he may not carry me up. My love and fervice to your worthy fifter and all your family. I am,

Your Ladyfhip's fervant
to ferve you in all things in the Lord,

JAMES RENWICK.

LETTER XVIII.

From Mr. James Renwick, *to the much honour-*
ed Mr. Robert Hamilton.

Much honoured Sir,   *Amst.* May 30. 1683.

YOU know what a great work the Lord hath
laid upon me, and how he hath laid so
many obligations upon me to be for him, and
him only : I hope that ye will be mindful thereof; praying that he will endow me with zeal,
courage, refolution, conftancy, tendernefs and
humility ; and give a door of utterance, that
with all boldnefs I may fpeak all his words, and
that he may follow the fame with his rich bleffing. I do not think, but tryals and difficulties
are abiding me, but if he be with me I fhall not
care. We muft not this day feek ourfelves
great things, when the Lord is bringing evil upon all flefh, and is breaking down what he hath
built, and plucking up what he hath planted. O!
I muft fay this indeed to the praife of his free
grace, that he is continuing and increafing his
kindly dealing with my foul. O that I could
praife him, and commend him to all flefh. Remember me to all our friends in the Lord, particularly to worthy Mr. *Brackel*, if ye have occafion ;
your worthy fifter, and the worthy lady *Van. Her.*
whom I am fingularly obliged to be mindful of, and
not only I, but the church of God. The Lord's
bleffing be with you, and the earneft good wifhes
of him who is,   *Much honoured Sir,*
             Yours to ferve you in the Lord,

             JAMES RENWICK.

From Mr. J. Renwick, *to the much*
Mr. Robert Hamilton.

Much honoured Sir,   *Amst. Ma*

HAving met with E. D. who is co
your fifter's fervant, I thought
to acquaint you, that your worthy br
fton is a long while ago come from
having met with friends there, and,
there are three papers drawn up; on
fome reafons why we have rejected
another, fome reafons of our fepar
thefe (fo called) minifters; and the
fays, is a call to, and a proteftati
them: I wifh it may be a bringing u
mire (and not a cafting us into it ove
I hope it will. But the reafon of yo
not coming hither ere this time,
ing by *London*: I hope he knows his
call thereunto, tho' I cannot fee it
alfo coming alongft with him; but
will not meddle with J. N. the L
him and lead him, for that land is
fnares, efpecially at this time. Ol
who were apprehended, four have
Teft; whereof one is *Alexander Mill*
man. O! *all flefh is grafs;* for I th
if there was a zealous man in *Scotla*
one: yet the Lord hath not left us
hath accepted a bloody facrifice off our
men being execute, *viz.* John Wilfo
a young gentleman, and *David* N

Galloway, of whom I hear nothing but what is matter of praise, and cause of encouragement. O! let us go on and run our race rejoicing, and with patience: The cup of the *Amorites* is fast filling, and their day is near at hand, when they shall get their own blood to drink, for they are worthy.. *Robert Lawson* is saying he will not die at this time, but I like not such prophecies as our case stands. *John Gib* and his companions are freed both from death and banishment, and have their liberty to go through all the prison, and large expence daily allowed unto them, by him whom they call the Chancellor. If the enemies had done otherways, thy would not act like themselves. Courage, dear Sir, they will drop ripe very suddenly.

I have sent you with the said *E D.* the exposition of the text which you desired, and shall take care to get a true copy of your letter secured unto you. I shall add no further at the time, but praying that the Lord may be unto you a present help in all times of need.; for I think difficulties and discouragements are many, but ye know where your strength lies, and what must comfort you. O! hitherto he hath not been wanting, neither will he be wanting, for he is a faithful God, who keepeth covenant; and he knows this, that if he had not now put another work in mine hand, and were calling me to another place, it would be my hearts desire to serve you (as indeed is my duty many ways) and to take part with you in all your troubles; but what I cannot do by bodily presence, I hope the Lord will help me to do it by heart sympathy and

willing-

willingnefs. Leaving you on your Mafter's hand,
I am,

       Much honoured Sir,

        Yours, to ferve you in the Lord,

         while I have a being in time,

          JAMES RENWICK.

LETTER XX.

From Mr. James Renwick, *to the honourable*
    Mr. Robert Hamilton.

Honourable Sir,   *Rotterdam, June* 18. 1683.

I Have received both your former and later
  letters: but you may fee an emblem of the
cafe I was in when I wrote laft unto you, by my
not anfwering fome particulars in your former
letter, which I ought to have done. However,
I have heard that our friend *G.* hath written to
you, wherein, I hope, he hath given you a full
account of his paffage at *Utrecht;* and alfo of
fome ftrange difapointments that have happened
unto us fince, which made me often remember
a word of yours to myfelf, That ye thought I
fhould meet with fome ftrange things in my going home. I have met with fome ftrange things
indeed, and have nothing to boaft of, but only
of the Lord, who is to be admired in all his
doings; for they are works of wonder: and O
that he would help me to fubmit to his holy,
and wife will, in keeping me fo long here;
yet I think the work is the liker his work
                      than

hat there fo many difficulties in the way of it.
lut as for Mr. *A. Cameron* I did not fee him, but
hear that he is come unto you. The Lord, I
ope, will let you know your duty, and will
lear that beft unto you, by converfing with
imfelf. O! add not drunkennefs to thirft;
int, if the Lord call, fee that you beftir your-
elf in it all that you can: he that hath had
iis hand fingularly with you in many pieces of
reat fervice, will not leave you in this. And
s for *A. H.* and *A. H.* they know indeed of my
irdination; and the way they came to know it
vas, by their peremptor queftions, to which I
ould not negatively anfwer; and then finding
bem gather the affirmative, I told them it was
e, but injoined filence upon them: but as for
ither particulars of our affairs they know none
iy me, fave that *James Ruffel* and we, when
ve met, could not agree.

You wrote aneut Mr. *Flint* and Mr. *Boyd*, their
ieftowing three hours each day upon *James Ruffel*
ind his comrade, in teaching of them; but as
matters ftand, I cannot approve of it, upon many
confiderations; for it is both encouraging and
hardening to them: I fay, encouraging to
them to hold on their courfes, for I fee very
little hope of what they pretend unto. I fear
that there be rather in it a faction feeking to
make a party. And as for Mr. *Binny*'s being
employed to teach our expectants, the Lord, I
hope, will give me to know my duty in it, ab-
ftracting from all perfons whatfoever

As for what you wrote of fairs and mercats on
faints days, I agree heartily with it; it was my
own thought before, but confufedly. However,
I defire to blefs the Lord, who hath made you a
mean

mean in that (as in some other things) to make me more distinct therein. O! I cannot express what I owe unto you; I say, I cannot express what I owe unto the Lord, whom I desire to bless while I live, that ever I saw your face. The Lord hath also made you to back what I was resolved on before, by your wholesome advice, in counselling me to take up an inventory of the Lord's way of dealing with friends and enemies in their persons and families, particularly and generally. And be assured, much honoured and dear Sir, that I shall, as I ought, keep nothing back from you; for, under the Lord himself, I have none that I can expect such counsel from as from you: therefore you must still be giving me your advice, and lay it out before the Lord ere you give it to me; for, indeed, I will lay much weight upon it: however, I desire to weigh it in the balance of the sanctuary. As for your going further away, I desire indeed to believe, that the Lord hath some work ado further abroad; but, I think, the change of dispensations calls you to stay still a while with our friends that are with you; for assuredly they will be much affected with the news of our dear friend Earlston, your dear brother's being taken: and also, I think, you cannot move until you hear what comes of him, (the Lord, I think, hath a great kindness for him, and will honour him) and till you receive letters from *Scotland*, both to yourself, to the presbytery of *Groningen*, and other friends.

I am not a little sorrowful at the very heart, that I am not in *Scotland*, to obey all your commands anent your dear brother. The Lord himself knows, that nothing that ever I was

trysted

tryfted with, was fuch an exercife to me, as my
being detained now out of it is. My longings
and earneft defires to be in that land, and with
that pleafant remnant, are very great. I cannot
tell what may be in it, but I hope the Lord hath
either fome work to work, or elfe is minded
prefently to call for a teftimony at my hand ;
and if he give frame and furniture, I defire to
welcome either of them. O ! dear Sir, mind
me, become of me what will. I have much ado,
many obligations lying upon me ; and the Lord
hath laid on not a few of them by your hands ;
and therefore you are the more engaged to be
mindful of me : and, I may fay it, your God lets
me not be unmindful of you ; and I am of the
mind, that fometimes he is very kind unto you,
putting mixtures of joy and rejoicing in himfelf. into your cup of forrow.

When I am writing this line, I received from
Scotland, a packet of letters, directed for your
fifter the Lady *Earlfton* ; but, expecting that there
were letters for myfelf therein, I prefumed to
break up the packet, but did not read her letter ; and found three for myfelf, but none from
fome that I moft expected a line from, *viz.*
M. B. neither hear I any word of news, for they
are not dated, but I expect it is long fince they
were written. However, I hear that all the
forces of *Scotland*, the rendezvous of hell, are
a-foot, becaufe there is one *Alexander Smith* one
of our focieties, and a godly youth, whom I
heard was apprehended, refcued from the enemy, who were taking him from *Edinburgh* to
Glafgow * to be executed, and one of their

E .guard

---

* Mr. *Wodrow*, in his Hiftory, p 219 thinks it was from
Glafgow to *Edinburgh*, at *Inch-belly Bridge*.

guard being flain. The Lord be thanked, that he is flirring up any to vex the *Midianites*, and to account their brother's cafe to be their own. I muft alfo tell you this, that I hear in one of my letters, that the Lord is making the increafing of the perfecution to blow up fome's zeal to a greater height than it was before. O good news! dear Sir, it minds me of *Paul's* words, *Phil.* i. 28. *And in nothing terrified by your adverfaries*, &c. It is not long till the cup of the *Amorite* and *Edomite* fhall be brim-full. Courage yet, for all that is come and gone; the lofs of men is not the lofs of the caufe: what is the matter tho' we fhould all fall, I affure all men that the caufe fhall not fall.

I thought fit alfo to fend you the Martyrs Teftimonies (not having gotten one of them read) altho' that my letters fpeak nothing of them, yet I know none elfe that they are ordained for, or that fhould have them but you. And as for the taking away of that every way abufed oath, if it be not already taken away, through the Lord's ftrength, I fhall fee unto it. But do not think, much honoured and dear Sir, that Mr. *Boyd* will get any thing done, as he vents himfelf; for no prefbytery will ordain him, unlefs he be called by the remnant of the church of *Scotland;* and it they fhall now write to the contrary, he will have no ground to plead upon from their fending of him hither, and giving him a commiffion; For, *Pofterior ult. evertere priorem.* I fhall fay no more, but my love and fervice to Mr. *Brackel*, and thefe ladies *V. H.* whom, I hope, the Lord will help to fympathize with you in your prefent condition. The blef-

ing of the God of *Jacob* be with you, and the
earneſt good wiſhes of him, who is,

Hon. and dear Sir,

Yours, to ſerve you in the Lord,

while he hath a being in time,

JAMES RENWICK.

L E T T E R XXI.

From the Rev. Mr. James Renwick, *to Mr.*
Robert Hamilton.

Hon. and dear Sir,   *Rott.* June 23. 1683..

I Thought it fit (ſuppoſing that poſſibly you
may not ſee it nor hear of it) to write to
you, that I have ſeen in the *Engiiſh* News Papers, that there was a company of granadiers
appointed to meet *Meldrum's* troop, that they
might receive from them our worthy friend
Earlſton, in order to the bringing him to *Edinburgh:* but it is alſo inſerted, that ſome ſay he
is eſcaped. O! if it hath pleaſed the Lord ſo
to order it, both his taking and his eſcape may
have many languages unto us: But what I think
I ſee is in the one, and will be in the other; if
it be true (as I would gladly hope it will, becauſe
they never uſe to inſert ſuch things but when
they are true) I forbear to mention until meeting, which, if the Lord will, ſhall be on *Monday* night, or *Tueſday* morning. O dear and
honourable Sir, we have many enemies, let us

ly

ly near our ſtrength: wicked men and backſlid-
ers will do more and more wickedly. I ſhall
ſay no more, having many things to tell you
when met; but think it fit that notice hereof be
ſent to your worthy ſiſter Mrs. *Jean*, if ſo be
that ye think ſhe will not otherwiſe hear. Leaving you on our Maſter. I am,

Honourable and dear Sir,

Yours to ſerve you in the Lord,

while I am

JAMES RENWICK.

LETTER XXII.

From the Rev. Mr. James Renwick, *to the honourable Mr.* Robert Hamilton.

Honourable Sir,: *Dublin, Aug.* 24. 1683.

I Am aſſured that ye will think it ſtrange that
ere this time I ſhould not have written unto
you, but many hinderances hath been caſt in my
way, by reaſon of the difficu ties and dangers of
this time; all thir lands being, in a manner, in an
uproar, by reaſon of challenging and ſuſpecting
all perſons, and the tranſmitting of any letters.
However, I can no longer forbear to write,
though it ſhould never come to your hand; having many things to ſay to the commendation of
the Lord's wiſdom and power in out witting and
reſtraining men. But O I think, the Lord hath
had a ſpecial hand in my coming to this place;

for

for he hath not suffered me to be idle; and bleſſed be his name, he hath kindled a fire which, I hope, Satan ſhall not ſoon quench: For all the people of this place were following men who did not follow the Lord, and thought theſe were right enough; yet now, ſome of them are ſaying, we have been miſled; we never knew before this, that we were ſtanding between the Lord's camp and the adverſary's. O! what ſhall I ſay? bleſſed be the name of the Lord, who lets me ſee that *he will ſee the travel of his ſoul and be ſatisfied*; and gives me many confirmations of his calling me to this work, wherein my deſire is only to be faithful. O rejoice in him who hath called me forth to fight againſt theſe who oppoſe themſelves, notwithſtanding of all their malice at me; and pretended friends their meeting to conſult upon my apprehending. I ſhall ſay no more, he hath found ſome who have engaged to do for me, in taking me home to *Scotland*. But I have the more patience here, becauſe of the Lord's doing great things. The Lord be with you, and all his *Iſrael*.

Honourable Sir,

  Yours, to ſerve you in the Lord,

  while I am

   JAMES RENWICK.

LETTER XXIII.

From the Rev. Mr. James Renwick, *to the* Honourable Mr. Robert Hamilton.

Hon. and dear Sir,   *Edin. Sept.* 26. 1683.

I Have been thinking much long for an opportunity of writing unto you, but I hope, your
goodnefs will not draw any wrong conftructions
from my neceffitate delay; for, bleft be the only holy and wife Lord, I am made to rejoice in
him thereanent, and have been kept, by his
grace, from murmuring and quarrelling againft
him, becaufe I faw much of himfelf, and his holy and wife purpofes, yea, even toward me, in
the circumftances I ftand in, in every ftep, fince
my departure from your Honour. For, being
kept fome days at the *Texel*, where I was, in
fome meafure, exercifed to know what might be
the language thereof, which I could not know
till afterwards; we launched forth into the fea,
where we were toffed for fome days with a violent contrary wind, and driven within uptaking
of the coaft of *France*, before that we could get
the *Englifh* coaft taken up; and all with very
great hazard, for the veffel was but little, and
not at all firm, which occafioned our fetting into
an harbour in *England* called *Rye;* where we
went afhore and were much noticed by the tyrant's waiters, it being upon the back of the difcovery of their plot; yet, the Lord fo reftrained
them that we were not challenged; however, we
thought it not fit (fearing fnares) to ftay afhore,
and therefore went aboard again. But after fome
days, the faid waiters in their paffing by, came

abroad

aboard of us, and aſked very rudely of the ſkipper, where we were; who repiied, that we were
aboard; and then aſking what men we were, was
anſwered by the ſkipper, that he knew not;
which I overhearing, thought that his anſwer
would make the ſaid waiters more inquiſitive:
However the Lord ſo reſtrained them, that when
they came unto us, they had no power to chal-
lenge us. · Now all this time, we ſtill concluded
that we were already apprehended, ſeeing no
probability of ſhunning it: But,-bleſſed be the
Lord, that was no way terrifying to me; for
notwithſtanding of his other ſpecial aſſiſtance, I
ſaw ſo much of his hand in it (we being driven
ſeven leagues back unto that place) that I could
not quarrel, but was much refreſhed with that
word, *It is the Lord, let him do what ſeemeth him
good.* Then, after this, the ſkipper did what he
could to enſnare us on the ſabbath-day, but the
Lord ſo ſtruck him with his own hand, that he
was not able to go forth to give any information of us; and in the *Monday* morning the
Lord ſent a fair wind, which was embraced, and
ſo brought us ſafe away, far beyond our expectation. O! all this ſhould learn us to credit him with his own cauſe, and with our caſe;
and may let us ſee, that enemies, further than
is permitted, ſhall not prevail. Then after this,
winning forward unto *Dublin*; from whence
there was no way of departing without a paſs;
but deſiring to wait the Lord's time, and to
commit our caſe unto him, he wonderfully provided an occaſion for our friend *G. Hill,* but in
no ways they would condeſcend to take me with
them, which was a piece of exerciſe unto me to
know what might be the language of it; yet in
                                            the

the time, I could not see it fully; but afterwards was made to see, that the Lord had some piece of work to do there. O! blest be his name, for he hath set some upon a search of their ways, and to know that they had not been right; who were so affected with my departure from them, (when the Lord had wonderfully provided an occasion, whereby I was cast out in the night-time at a hill-side, some few miles below *Greenock*,) that they entreated me with tears to stay; saying, that their necessity was greater than *Scotland's*; and would not part with me, until, that upon some suppositions, I promised to return again. But, as the Lord stirred up some people to all this, their (so called) ministers increased their malice, especially one Mr. *Jack*, the ring-leader of the rest, who sought to speak with me; which I would not, nor could, without stumbling of the people, refuse; who, when met, we reasoned upon several heads, particularly this, Whether or not a person attacked for duty might choose a punishment? whereof I held the negative. But, in a second conference, he having some of his companions trysted with him, fell on more briskly, and asked, How came I to draw away his congregation? To which I replied, That I denied him to have a congregation, and did only labour and desire to draw the people from sin unto their duty; and for accepting his call to preach, that I ought not, nor would not, because I could not own him as a faithful minister of Jesus Christ; for he had betrayed the cause of the Lord. And for satisfying him anent my ordination, I told, when I met with faithful ministers of Christ, I should subject myself to them, but him I declined as

com-

competent to require that of me; and also, that
I behoved first to be satisfied anent his entry to
that congregation; the exercise of his ministry
during 'his continuance therein; and now his
yielding it up at the enemies command; all
which was to be reconciled with the word of
God, our engagements, and the duty of a minister; which when he heard, he grew mightily
passionate, falling out in bitter reflections; and I
perceiving the dishonour done to God thereby,
told him, that I would speak no more to such
men in such a frame, and so departed. I had also
some battles upon your account; but the Lord
assisted in that, as in all other things; for I saw
it was not you, but the cause and party which
they reviled.   O! honourable and dear Sir,
What shall I say to all those things? It is good
keeping the Lord's way; for he will not leave
nor forsake.

. Now, since I came to my own land and people, I have seen several things which are encouraging and promising; as the Lord's helping
some, of whom little was expected, to shew both
zeal and stedfastness in his cause: And other
things which speak out wrath to be at the doors,
as the neutrality and lukewarmness, yea declining of many, who have been helped to be hitherto valiant. O! blessed be the Lord, who will
not give his glory to another, and blasts every
thing that our eyes are upon.

As for news, the Lord is wonderfully to be
seen in every thing, and assists in what he calls
us.   For in coming through the country, we
had two field-meetings, which made me to think,
that if the Lord could be tied to any place, it is
to the muirs and mosses in *Scotland*. O! he will
                                                        have

have a day of his power to be seen in this land.
I say, he is to be seen in hiding, preserving and
providing for his people in such a day of the enemies cruelty, and seems to have some strange
thing upon the wheels, especially in your Honour's dear brother's case, which we desire to
wait upon and behold; for enemies cruelty and
threatnings against him are great, and their snares
and subtilties no less; however, they are wonderfully restrained, and he strangely reproached,
but very causelesly. And as for *Robert Lawson,*
(so sad and sweet in several respects) he is suffered to cast all his former doings, to the hardening of backsliders, and the grieving of the godly.
But *Edward Aitken* is escaped, and intends to
come to you and follow his books: but his carriage in the public matters hath been very hurt-
ful to the cause, and in private, very unchristi-
an, opening mouths to reproach and blaspheme;
therefore, I hope ye will not move in it, without the general meeting's advice. Also, I expect that *Thomas Linning* will be sent to you,
and hope, ye will be satisfied with him, for
he hath been very satisfying, refreshing and encouraging to me since I came home.——

We are in some confusion now through the
want of time, and upon other accounts. However, as occasion offers, I will labour to get a full
information of every thing sent unto you; for I
am sensible of the advantage that it will be unto
the Lord's cause.

Now, the Lord be with your honour, making
you a brazen wall and iron pillar against all
enemies and forsakers of his truth as hitherto,
by his grace, he hath done; and point out unto
you your duty in every case, helping you to follow

low it. Write to friends, for your letter was
very refreshing, rejoicing, and strengthening
unto them, and to him who looks upon you as
his father and brother; and remains

Your Honour's assured friend,

sympathizer, and servant in the Lord,

JAMES RENWICK.

LETTER XXIV.

From the Rev. Mr. James Renwick, *to the honourable Society of strangers at* Lewarden *in* Friesland.

Nov. 13. 1683.

Honourable and dear Friends in our Lord,

I Have not only heard, but also, in the little
space I was amongst you, saw, many tokens
and evidences of your love to our lovely Lord,
and tender sympathy with his afflicted sufferers;
which was no small refreshing and encouragement to me, and also a great engaging and
endearing of my heart unto you; so that I know
not how to unfold my thoughts, nor unbosom
my ardent affections. But as my heart is much
with you, so, I may say, you are frequently with
me, and that in the times which you most require, when I desire to prostrate myself at the
footstool of the throne of grace. However, I
could not forbear, neither thought I it my duty
to omit writing unto you But, what shall I
say, but that which you yourselves know? the
Lord

Lord, being the only object whereupon all our desires can satisfyingly terminate, is worthy of all honour, fear, love, and service; yea, and at the mentioning of this, we may stand astonished, and wonder, that he in himself, supertranscendently and infinitely glorious, uncapable of receiving any additional glory from his creatures, should call such unworthy worms, self-destroyed creatures, to serve him; which, though he had not freely and graciously promised any reward after time, would be a reward unto its self. But, O! what can be his end in calling and drawing out such destroyed and unworthy creatures, as any of the lost posterity of *Adam*, to love and serve him? It is not that he may get good (of which he is uncapable) but that he may give good. O! praised be his free grace, he hath provided and laid open a way whereby we may have both access and right unto him, by the mediation of his Son, our Lord Jesus Christ: Therefore let us answer his call, and come unto him, where all, and only our happiness lies, with hearts so enlarged, and conceptions so framed and shapen out, as that nothing less than himself may satisfy; for more cannot be desired: Let us come unto him, follow him fully; take up his cross, and our engagements against the world, the devil, and the flesh; for he is a noble and glorious Captain whose banner we have to fight under, who not only bears his soldiers charges sufficiently here, all their stock being only in his own hand, but also makes them sure of the victory, and of the kingdom and crown in the end of their battle; they being to walk with him in glorious white robes, throughout all eternity. Let us espouse his quarrel for our

t be difcouraged for what oppofites
in all their iutended actings againft
e but pulling down themfelves, and
kingdom ; and neither be annoyed
ficulties in time, but look above
hefe, unto the rich recompence of
the day is near at hand, when thefe
of clay fhall fall down about our
fhall be fet at liberty; made un-
rieving his Spirit, or forrowing any
tted for the bleft, full and eternal
Father, Son, and Holy Ghoft. O
will that be, when the faints fhall
of him, incircling him with both
or rather being incircled by him ?
and look out for it, longing for the
iat fhall be heard in heaven ; O!
will it be fung ! *Arife, arife, arife,
dove, my fair one, and come away;
ur winter is paft, and your ever-
ier is come.* O let the thoughts
mer, and tafting of the firft-fruits
eten this our winter unto us ; mak-
fully to travel through the fame,
f our Beloved in our mouths, and
endure what travel or tribulations,
ur chaftifement or inftruction, he
l things well may be pleafed to let
    And as ye have been helped thro'
come companions with us in our
fo I would have you look out for
on yourfelves, for the Lord will
ake terribly the earth, and punifh
nts thereof for their iniquity, lay
    and defolate lands : for all na-
erfpread with a fupine and loath-
F   fome

some formality; yea, avowed profanity, and
dreadful blasphemy against the heavens. I say
not this, my honourable and dear friends, to
discourage you, but rather for the continuance
and encrease of your holy zeal, which ye manifest towards the Lord's cause and interest. O!
go on in it, for therein shall be your peace as
to duty, and he himself is your exceeding rich
reward.

Now, for your great kindness, love unto, and
sympathy with our bleeding and wounded mo-
ther-church, which I saw amongst you; and particularly for your heart love and tender respects
toward myself, though altogether undeserved,
I cannot express how I am engaged to the Lord,
and obliged unto you; yea, it passeth my apprehension. But I am singularly obliged indeed;
so I must beg further matter (though already
enough be had) by the continuance of your
mindfulness of our distressed and wounded church;
and of that exceeding great and weighty work,
which ye know the Lord hath laid upon me.
But why should I fear? the work is his own;
and he sends none a warfare on their own charges; and, ever blessed be his holy name, I may
say this from sweet experience; for I have
found him a present help in all my necessities,
and many ways beyond my expectation, confirming my call, and countenancing his work both at
home, and elsewhere were he was pleased to cast
and detain me. Now, the Lord be with you.
Again mind me, as I desire to do you. Remaining,

Honourable and dear Friends,

   Your hearty wellwisher,

     Assured and obliged friend and servant,

      to my full power in the Lord.

       JAMES RENWICK.

LETTER XXV.

*From the Rev. Mr. James Renwick, to the ho-
nourable Mr. Robert Hamilton.*

Honourable and dear Sir, Edin. Nov. 14. 1683.

THough I have many things that I would and
could fay, yet I am fo bufied, which I
think ye may know, that I cannot be fo large in
writing to you as I would : However, I fee many encouragements and difcouragements ; encouragements from the Lord's omnipotency,
condefcendency, and faithfulnefs ; yea, the glory that is to be feen in his noble way of managing his own caufe : and difcouragements from
feveral airths which I expected not ; for fince I
came home, I have found fome, of whom I expected better things, cleave to crooked and
perverfe ways ; yea, and turn very imbittered a-
gainft us : and at the prefent (oh fad ! but too
true) we are peftered with a company of
prejudiced evil perfons, who join hands and iffue
with backfliders, and make known every thing
unto them ; wherein I only defire and labour,
that the particular perfons may be found out,
that fo we may proceed againft them according
to the word of God, and our duty.

My coming home hath had fuch effects as I
expected indeed, for enemies are more cruel
and eager in perfecution than ever, and backfliders more imbittered with malice than heretofore ; but fome of whom I expected to be cordial with, I have not found it fo ; neither fhould
I in the ways that they are upon : and this hath

F 2   been

been chiefly occafioned by my tefti
as it hath, by the Lord's goodnefs,
ing, encouraging and ftrengthenin
it hath made others vent more wh
And herein I rejoice, yea, and
(there being not an article in it, t
more and more confirmed of) beca
tendency to the fiding of us, ei
gainft the Lord. But among all fr
helpful and ftrengthening unto me,
George Hill. However, I muft fa
the Lord countenancing and bleffi
yea, and giving teftimonies for h
ever bleffed be his holy name there

As for informations in other thi
little to give your Honour; only at
ing, all that we did was the reading
mony, fome papers for coming
fubfcribing them; laying afide th
of fecrecy; and ordaining *T. L.*
fcholars. At this meeting prefent
know of nothing to be done, bu
papers to be fubfcribed; our fcho
whom we are jealous of, examine
fought out to be fent unto your H
our letters and papers; and (that
our continual work) a way thou
finding out of thefe, whofe tongu
are fo againft the Lord. And a
in other things, fince I came h
been more pained and indifpofed o
thefe feveral years before: howeve
fweet unto me, for I faw two thing
when before I was cafting up, and
pieces of coft, I thought I faw m
Lord's hand, but only bodily ftreng

that there was enough of that in mine own; and
he takes that way with me, which, O! is glorious, that I may have the strength as well as
other furniture from his own hand, in more than
an ordinary manner, that so his name may get
the more praise therefore.   Secondly, I saw this
in it, that though I have been in some places of
the country, yet I have but win through little
of it: and where I have not been, I fear more
an anxiety after the ordinances, than a thirsting
after the Lord; so that, I think, the Lord is
seeking to get his people both to prize, and yet
to be denied to the means.

O! dear Sir, the thoughts of our long absence is frequently troublesome unto me; but
shall we not have a joyful, a joyful meeting in
heaven; and who knows, but we may meet in
time? In the mean time, only be mindful of
me, and the work which you know the Lord
hath laid upon me, as I am, and desire to be of
you, both in public and private.   The Lord be
with you.   I am,

Your Honour's hearty wellwisher,

real sympathizer, greatly endeared friend,

and most obliged servant in the Lord,

JAMES RENWICK.

LETTER XXVI.

From the Rev. Mr. James Renwick, to the Ladies Van. Heermaen, at Lewarden in Friesland, 1683.

Worthy Ladies, beloved in the Lord,

THough it hath pleased the holy God, in his
wise providence, to carve out my lot unto me, since my departure from you, that I
had no time and occasion of writing; yet the
Searcher of hearts knows (as I hope your goodness will construct it) that I have not been forgetful of you, nor of your heart-concernedness
with *Zion*'s case, and sympathy with her afflicted
children, particularly us in *Scotland ;* whereof
I have seen great tokens and evidences. O go
on in holy tenderness: go on in zeal, for therein shall ly your peace, as to duty. Follow the
Captain of Salvation fully, for he makes all his
followers to enjoy the prize; his soldiers he
makes them overcomers, and his servants kings,
to reign with him for ever more, in his inheritance, whereunto he, their elder Brother, hath
entered, to take possession in their names.
What shall we say of these unspeakable privileges
of his people? Shall we not stand still struck
with wonder and admiration, having our mouths
filled with the praise of him, who left the glory
of heaven, and the bosom of the Father, to
come down, and to take upon him our nature,
that therein he might interpose himself betwixt
the Father's wrath and us, both by his suffering,
and fulfilling of the law for us, that we might

not

not only be freed from sin and the consequents thereof, but be made partakers of such inconceiveable priviIeges, ard be restored to a more happy and sure estate than what we fell from. It is angels work to desire to look into this, and it will be our work throughout all eternity ; and should we not study to be more in it now, *viz.* in praising of him for his covenant of free grace, and *for his works of wonders done unto the sons of men;* who delighteth to manifest his mercy, his power, and his holy wisdom, and to let poor things find something of himself in all his attributes, in their own experience; so that they are made to say, *He is good, and does good.* And for mine own part I may say, that tho', when I had the occasion to see your Ladyships, he had done great things for poor unworthy me ; so that I had great reason to set forth his praise, if I could have done it ; yet now he hath done much more, which may furnish new matter of praise : for, since my departure from you, the Lord hath been pleased to tryst me with several difficulties, that he might have occasion of manifesting himself, in bringing me through the same. In fire or water I dare not say he hath left me or forsaken me ; and though perils by sea, and perils by land, and the snares of enemies to the cause and cross of Christ, have been many, yet he hath wonderfully brought me hitherto through the same, and frustrate the expectations of the wicked; and not only hath been at great cost and pains to lay obligations on me to be for him ; but also hath taken many ways to train me up for this work he has laid upon me, and the circumstances of the time wherein my lot is fallen. But the greatest of all, I think, is, the

many

many confirmations he hath given me of his own cause; and also, of his call to such a weighty business; and his letting me see what hath been a great part of his end in detaining me so long from my own land and people; which was, to cast me and keep me a little space in *Ireland*, where he hath kindled a fire, which I hope, he will not suffer to die out; and hath put some people upon a searching of their ways, wherein they had turned from him. O! blessed be his name, who will *see of the travel of his soul, and be satisfied*; and who is that good shepherd, out of whose hand none shall pluck his sheep; for *the gates of hell shall not prevail against his church*; and no wonder, for it is a rock, and built upon a rock. O! come, let us lift ourselves under his banner, and take his part against a lukewarm generation, and resolve upon trials; for, I think, he loves none whom he lets want them: But consider for whom it is, it is for his name's sake, who is *the chief among ten thousand*, who is *altogether lovely*.

Now, the Lord, who is not unrighteous to forget your labour of love, be all things unto you, and reward you for your sympathy and concernedness with the Lord's people in this land, who are very sensible of your becoming companions with them in their tribulations, and that ye have had compassion upon them in their bonds, and desire the help of your prayers for the desolations of the Lord's holy mountain. So, no more at the time, being assured of your concernedness with our much honoured friend *Robert Hamilton*, of whose courage, constancy, and zeal for the Lord's cause ye have proof; for, what is done to him is, as it were done to us all. Mind poor me,

and

and the great work the Lord hath laid upon me.
The Lord be with you.

MADAMS,

Your Ladyships affectionate servant,

and sympathizer in the Lord.

JAMES RENWICK.

LETTER XXVII.

From the Reverend Mr. James Renwick, *to the honourable Mr* Robert Hamilton.

Hon. and dear Sir,   *Jan.*   1684.

BEing by the Lord's providence with the Lady *Earlston,* when sending away her letters,
I behoved to salute you with this line, shewing
you, that (blessed be the Lord) I am well every
way, though my case be singular, and my trials
no less such; yet I may turn my complaints into
triumphant songs; for I have seen the Lord's
wonders in the land of the living, and he is still
increasing the number of his followers: for, tho'
I should go over and over again to any country-
side, at every time there come others ay out
who did not come out before. But enemies are
intending sad things against us; for they are now
leading out their forces to the West, threatning
to lay it desolate; saying, That we will never be
curbed till they make that country a hunting-
field. But, let them prat, a higher hand rules
all: and I am persuaded, that we shall thereby
be

be more affrighted than skaithed; though ou
fears be not great, whatever be the fears of th
apoftate party. Know alfo, that Mr. *Shields* i
brought to *Scotland :* I know that he and M^r. *An*
drew Cameron and Mr *Flint* were joined toge
ther in feeking after o.dination, that they migh
come home to *Scotland :* But when I heard it,
was not fatisfied that you was not owned in it
However, this hath a ftrange language: the Lor
hath cruthed it; for their papers anent the fame
and many books were caft away at fea. O! th
majefty of your God and my God, that fhines in
his management of affairs: Let you and me ftan
ftill and admire this. So, leaving you to hi
all-fufficiency; with my love to all my friend
with you. I am,

As formerly,

JAMES RENWICK

L E T T E R XXVIII.

From the Rev. Mr. James Renwick, *to the ho.*
able Mr. Robert Hamilton.

Hon. and dear Sir,　　　　*March* 29. 1684.

I Have very much to fay, but I have no time
to exprefs myfelf: However, though I had
ten thoufand times ten thoufand years, yea, the
faculty of angels, I could, in no ways, lay out
mine obligations to free grace; but behoved,
when I had babled my fill, to feal up all with
this, CHRIST IS MATCHLESS: O he is the
wonder of the higher houfe! and will he not be
your

ur wonder and my wonder throughout the
es of lasting eternity! Come away then, let us
)our to keep up that work now, wherein eter-
:y will not weary us: We cannot now think
;htly of him, but we shall get eternity to the
)rk: His beauty and excellency is so ravishing,
at a poor weak, doilt-fond soul will be made
turn its dazled eyes away from him, when yet
e heart will be melting in love's hand. O·!
t we be narrow vessels that can receive no-
ing; but hereafter we shall see him as he is.
what is he! Angels cannot define him, and
: must be silent; yet this I must say, he is
atchless: all perfections meet in him; he is
orious, and he is the only best of choices; O!
is glorious in himself, and manifests that in
l his actings; his doings are like himself, and
rry large characters of all his attributes engraven
on them. Why are such confusions upon his
urch, but that he may get occasion to make
s wisdom conspicuous in bringing order out
ereof? O! he will do it, and his carrying on
strange work of discovery is a pledge of it: his
ithfulness is engaged to do it. Let us not fear,
ough enemies cruelty, and steppers-aside's ma-
:e, be more than formerly, yet his word shall
ınd sure: And poor mad fools, what are they
)irg, but crushing themselves, and setting up
is throne? Now,

Right honourable and dear Sir, there are ma-
y particulars which I would write, but I cannot
;t it done; howbeit I shall wait to catch some
portunity for it. Our friend *George* having
jven you at the time, a brief touch of some
lings; the Lord helps him to give many evi-
ιuces of sincerity and stedfastness to the cause,

and

and affection to such in all places who are most
sorely shut at upon the cause's account. I thought
to have written something unto you anent *T. L.*
but *George* having spoken my mind, I shall forbear.   Yet there is one thing which is your duty,
and which is also my duty to mention unto you,
and that is, that you would take pains upon *J. F.*
to wear out that bad impression which *James
Russel* hath given him of us: O deal tenderly
with him, for he is but young, yet I hope, of
zealous intentions.   Be concerned with him in
that strange place, for he is a child of many
prayers; his relations bear a great affection to
the cause, and to all who own the same; and
your name is very savoury unto them. It is weighty
to me, that *James Russel* hath insinuate himself
so much upon him; for, his being sent abroad
was, in some measure, upon expectation that he
and I should be together.   Now,

   Right honourable and dear Sir, let not difficulties damp you; there is nothing that falls out
but what is in kindness both to the remnant and
to you: Regard not the reproaches of tongues;
are not these the badges of your honour? our
lot must not be thought strange, for the Lord's
people heretofore have met with the like.   Remember ye have need of patience: we have e-
nemies now upon all hands; and I must say, that
man *James Russel* hath been a costly *James
Russel* to the poor church of *Scotland*.   I shall
say no more; but as malice of opposites to the
cause increaseth, let our love thereunto and to
one another increase.

   Your assured friend and servant in the Lord,
     and your unworthy brother in afflictions
        and reproaches for his name's sake,
             JAMES RENWICK.

LETTER XXIX.

Worthy Madam,   *June* 20. 1684.

I Received your letter, which unbosomed to
me a troubled case, which in no small measure does affect my spirit ; but as I am affected
with the trouble of spirit which ye express ; so, I
am refreshed with my observing that you are not
insensible of your case, your great complaint being of the want of light and life : But I am persuaded, that a creature altogether wanting the
one and the other, cannot be troubled anent
their apprehended want of either ; for none miss
but which doth not belong unto them : a horse
hath no sense of his want of the wings of an
eagle, because these are not proper to him ; but
the want of his feet, he presently misseth the
same, when he is put to go : These who never
knew any thing of light and life cannot miss the
same. I grant indeed, many unregenerate have
a missing of common influences, which flashes are
far from that heart-sealing that the believer is
acquainted with. However I conceive, that as
common influences are not permanent, and tend
nothing to the changing of the heart ; so, the
poor creature gets leave to rest in them, seeking
no further ; and when missing them, is troubled
chiefly, if not only, because external duty then
is neither so easy nor pleasant There are depths
here that I dare not now launch out unto, least
time will not allow me to bring myself out a-

G   gain.

gain. But, O Madam! what shall I say unto you? Let no less than Christ himself satisfy you; study to dwell under the impression of his preciousness, for the contemplation thereof fills the heart with love to him; and love, you know, is a most active and lively thing: and judge not your state by what you find your case, as to your sense, sometimes to be; for a very fruitful tree will bear neither fruit nor leaves in the winter season, while as much sap will be in the root: Spend not time in debating, but in the sincere and serious use of these means that ye have of union and communion with Christ, and this is both the surest and the shortest way to win to fixedness; neither seek sense's satisfaction for the present, but a well grounded assurance for the future: Look to the infinite power, and infinite love of Christ; *there* is a two-edged sword to cut assunder all your Gordian knots. Infinite power, what can it not do? and infinite love, what will it not do! Never seek any thing in yourself to commend you to Christ, for that will keep you still staggering; so to his grace who is able to perfect what concerneth you, do I recommend you. But as to your troubled case, in not knowing well whether you be called to stay where you, are, or to come home; I confess, when I ponder all circumstances I find it very puzzling, and I may say, it hath given me some errands to God, and am in no small measure concerned therewith: But I would desire you, without anxiety, to wait on a little; for the Lord by his providential dispensations, or in a more extraordinary manner, will determine you: some concerned friends are also spoken to anent it, that they would ponder the case before the Lord, and see whether they

will

will defire the babies to come home or not; and their mind, I think, will be foon reported to your worthy brother, as this comes into your hands; fo at the time, I can write the lefs anent it, and therefore leave you upon the Lord, who is all in all; begging, worthy Madam, that you would not forget the cafe that ye know he is in, who remains

Your Ladyfhip's foul's wellwifher, fympathizer,

and obedient fervant in the Lord,

JAMES RENWICK.

LETTER XXX.

From the Rev. Mr. James Renwick, to the Honourable Mr. Robert Hamilton.

Hon. and dear Sir,   *July* 9. 1684.

YOur letter which I received was wonderfully fweet and refrefhing to me, and was made a mean, in fome meafure, to prepare me for what I was to meet with; for immediately there-after I was involved in fuch troubles as before I had not been tryfted with, but all indeed, to manifeft, in a wonderful manner, the Lord's love and power to and for his people. For, upon the fabbath, I fay, after your letter came to my hand, we met for public worfhip, near the *Whinn bog* in the *Monkland*; but that country being generally apoftatized into an open hoftility againft the Lord, fome went quickly away unto *Glafgow*, and gave notice unto the enemies

forces:

forces: Howbeit we heard thereof ere forenoon's sermon was ended, yet continued untill that part of the work was gone about: And thereafter, thought it fit to depart from that bounds, and that the armed men should keep together for their better defence and safety; which, through God's goodness, was a mean to keep the enemy from noticing and pursuing strangers, that being stricken into some confusion and terror, and keeping both their horse and foot in one body; yet they lodged all night, we not knowing of it, within a mile of some, and two miles of others of us, intending to set foreward toward these houses where we were. But the Lord, whose ways are wonderful, made use of a malignant gentleman to detain them, he asserting that none of us went toward that airth. Notwithstanding, this wakened up the adversaries more; so that, they kept up a pursuit and search, which proved very obstructive to our general meeting, which was upon that *Thursday* thereafter: For upon that very day, they came with horse and foot to search these muirs where we were, and came near upon upon us ere we got any thing concluded; which thing moved us (we suspecting that they, some way or other, had gotten notice of some of us being together) to remove from that place some way off into a little glen, where we resolved to keep ourselves obscure: but after we had rested and refreshed ourselves a little, we espied four of their foot marching toward us, whereupon it was thought fit, to send out so many to meet with them, who when they came together fired upon one another: but, the Lord's gracious providence so ordered it, that there was not the least skaith upon our side; there being

one

one of the enemies wounded so that he died
since. Howbeit the shots alarmed the rest of the
enemies which were upon the hill; and, when we
drew out to the open fields, we saw their foot not
very far from us, and got present advertisement
that the enemy was still upon the pursuit and
near unto us: We, in all haste, set foreward
through the moss, having no outward strength
to fly unto, but by crossing the way of the adversary; whereupon we expected an encounter with
them; yet committing ourselves into the Lord's
hand, we went on, until we came unto another certain moss, where we staid until night, and got much
of our business done. But in all this, the wonderful power of God was seen, both in spiriting
his people for that exigence, and preserving us
from falling amongst the hands of the adversaries:
yea, though he shewed us wonders therein, yet
he delighted to shew us more; for, upon the
Saturday night thereafter, there was a competent number of us met in a barn for worship, and
had not well begun until we heard both the
drums and trumpets of the enemies; but we
thought it most expedient to set watches without,
and continue at our work until we saw further.
Nevertheless, in all these tumults and dangers,
the Lord's goodness was so manifested to his
people, that he not only hid them under his
wings, and preserved them; but also, he kept
their spirits from the least fear, confusion or
commotion; yea, the very sight of some of
them, would have made resolute soldiers a-
mongst us. So, after this hazard was over, some
of us thought it convenient to stay where we
were (it being a woody place) until the sabbath
day were past: But, ere the middle of the day,

we got an alarm that the enemy was within two miles or thereabout, coming toward that airth; whereupon we went over *Clyde*; but so soon as that was, we being in number about six or seven, had almost rencountered with a party of the enemy's horse, who at the crossing of our way, had inevitably met with us, if that the Lord had not so ordered it, that a friend of ours had seen them ere they could see us, who thereupon came running toward us with a white napkin (because conspicuous to us) flourishing in his hand; whereupon we halted, and when he came to us, we lurked among some bushes until the enemy past by; and thereafter we setting foreward by two and two upon our journey, which was intended to be but short, some two of us met with one of the adversary's number upon horseback, who presently fled with all his might toward *Lanerk*, we being within three short miles thereof; which forced us to take a desperate course, in running through that plenished country unto *Darmead* Moss, still expecting to forgather with that hostile town of *Lanerk*, both horse and foot; but the Lord's power and goodness was such toward us, that we escaped all their hands; which thing was great matter of admiration unto us all, and made me to wonder no little. That scripture, *Psal.* cxxvi. 2, 3. being my companion, *Then said they among the heathen, The Lord hath done great things for them. The Lord hath done great things for us; whereof we are glad.* And also, that other *Psalm*, cxi. 6. *He hath shewed his people the power of his works, that he may give them the heritage of the heathen.* O! all these things that he did to us and for us, were matter of great rejoicing in himself: But as I thought I saw them

be pledges of greater things, whereby his at-
butes might be more manifested, they were
ade matter of double and greater joy unto me.
e hath given us proofs of what he can do for
s people in the day of their strait, and gives us
od cause to commit unto his faithfulness the
anagement and raising up of his seemingly bu-
ed work, and the carrying through of his peo-
e: and ever since, it hath been my chief exer-
se, yea, and a while before that, the deep and
biding impreffion, of his unexpected, sudden and
lorious appearing for his name and people.

I think we are like unto a poor helpless, de-
icable, dead-like company, lying deprefled
a valley; and he, as it were, by his word
nd works difcovering himself upon a hill top
n our view, ftretching out his arms, and all
ightering to be at us, calling unto us that we
would join our hearts and voices together, and
cry him down unto us; offering that his power
and love meeting together, fhall trade down
and diffipate unto nothing our dreaded obftructions of one fort and another; yea, I fay, if I
know any thing of the mind of the Lord, that
this is his fpecial call unto all his fincere followers this day, *Ifa.* lxii. 6, 7. *Ye that make mention of the Lord, keep not filence; and give him
no reft, till he eftablifh Jerufalem, and till he
make it a praife in the whole earth.* O! let us
all join together in this exercife, and let us be
fincere, fervent and conftant in it. Let us be
at no manner of eafe while *Zion* is in trouble:
for though we fhould be content with our calamity, yet we fhould in no ways be content with
our fin procuring the fame; nor with the prefervation of enemies in their infolence and rebel-
· lion

lion againſt the Lord, whereby his name is d[...]
ly blaſphemed; alſo procured by our back ſl[...]
ing. I ſay, let us join in this exerciſe, in cryi[...]
to the Lord for his appearing; for his peop[...]
delivery ſhall be ſo glorious, that it ſhall abu[...]
dantly make up all the coſt, wreſtling, a[...]
ſuffering that they can be at: and though ma[...]
of them with their bodily eyes may never ſee i[...]
and though ſome of theſe that, in their plac[...]
and ſtations, are employed about the buildin[...]
many never ſee the cape-ſtone put thereupo[...]
for as ſhort a work as the great Maſter-buil[...]
er will make of it, yet what's the matter[...]
they are about their duty; and their deliver[...]
ſhall be more complete and more glorious[...]
And, for mine own part, though the ene[...]
my ſhould not get me reached, ſeemingly thi[...]
tabernacle of clay will ſoon fall; for I am often[...]
times variouſly and greatly diſtempered in my[...]
body; but while the Lord hath any thing to[...]
do with me, I ſhall continue, and I deſire to[...]
continue no longer; though many live longer[...]
than the Lord hath work for them. Howbeit,[...]
I many times admire the Lord's kindneſs toward[...]
me, for I never find any diſtemper of my body[...]
but when I am ſo circumſtantiate, as, in many[...]
reſpects, I may diſpenſe with it; and, through[...]
his grace, this all my deſire, to ſpend and be[...]
ſpent for him in his work, until my courſe be[...]
ended: and for ſeeing better days with my bodily eyes (though I am perſuaded they are near[...]
hand) I am not in the leaſt anxious, neither[...]
was that deſire either ſoon or late my exerciſe;[...]
for though they will be a happy people who will[...]
be ſo privileged; yet I count them more happy

who

who are altogether without fear, care, sinning,
or sorrowing.

As for other news, Right honourable and dearly beloved in our Lord, very many of us, within these three quarters of a year, have fallen a-
mongst the enemies hands, and some they executed upon scaffolds ; but the Lord so owned
and countenanced such, especially these five at
Glasgow, that the sight of them took great effect
upon the generality of the people, and raised
such a frame amongst them, which was dreaded
by the enemy; yea, and a grand persecutor,
called Major *Windram*, had three children, who
within a little while of other died, one of them
a very young boy, and two daughters come to
the years of discretion, who died very sweetly
and satisfyingly ; declaring, that the Lord's
hand was stretched forth against them, because
of the hand their father hath in shedding the
blood of the saints; and obtested him before
God, that he would quite the course that he fol-
owed : which things had some, though no promising effect upon him. Whereupon, since the
enemy thought it most conducing to their purpose to banish them all; so many who carried
very stedfastly were sent away, they leaving faithful joint testimonies behind them; whereof one
was subscribed by twenty-two hands, twenty of
them having carried honestly; and the other
two acknowledging their fainting, in either seeking or consenting unto banishment : But, I think,
the Lord hath a special end in the exile of such,
sending them away to be witnesses against the
many complying ministers and professors, who
are going to that same place : and may not we
be content to want a company of our friends

out of our own land, that they may be a testimony for the Lord in another place. Howbeit the enemies hands are wonderfully bound up now from shedding of blood. I do not know what may be done, through the Lord's permission, by these new created powers, the Earl of *Perth* being called chancellor; but *York's* faction is discourted, there being a variance, at least pretended, betwixt his brother and him; but if real, I think, it may be a mean to shorten some of their days. And as for what we did at our last general meeting, after we had condescended to answer your desires, we laid it upon *T. Linning* to write his testimony, and shew it to the next meeting, which he engaged to do; and if the meeting be pleased therewith, I think he will go abroad unto you And, for my own part, if his testimony be satisfying, I can say nothing against it; for I think he is the most hopeful lad, by appearance, that we have; and hath kythed much willingness to serve the remnant any way. But at our last meeting we got not Mr. *William Boyd* spoken to, nor heard; nevertheless I am sadly afraid that he breed us work yet: but I pray the Lord may disappoint my fears.

Now, right honourable and dearly beloved in our sweet and precious Lord, what shall I say unto you? or how shall I express myself? The incomparableness of times trials and sufferings, with the loveliness of Christ, and the glory that shall be revealed thereafter, makes me sometimes I see neither trouble nor danger, mine eyes being shut thereat, and carried to behold a small glimpse of that which is beyond tribulation's reach; but in such a case silent wondering

ıg is most my exercise. O! what a life will it
e, when we shall neither sin nor sorrow! when
e shall lay down our arms, and take up the
alm of victory and triumph in our hands, and
ollow the Lamb with songs of praise in our
ouths! everlasting love and joy will be all the
ork that is there. O! what manner of work
that? The ardency of love, without abat-
ıg or intermissions arising. from the conti-
ual beholding of crowned Christ's supertranf-
endent loveliness and excellency, and the
ılness of joy, without intermissions and allay-
ıents, arising from the enjoyment of that so
ovely and beloved object; What manner of
ork is that? They that get a sight of that, will
e made to cry out, *We will spend no more la-*
our for that which satisfyeth not. O! the full
nd sufficient satisfaction that is in the matchless
earl, Christ: he is all things desirable. Let us
estow all our love, our whole affections upon
im: and when we have done, let us wonder
hat he should seek it, and take it off our hands.
While in these lists of justling, let us put all
ur weapons in love's hand: love is a resolute
oldier, love is an undaunted champion; love's
ye is so much taken up with contemplating
ıe Beloved, that it cannot see dangers in the
ay, but runs blindly upon them; and yet not
lindly, but knoweth for whom, and for what
t so ventureth. Love will never turn the wea-
ons against the Beloved; yea, will never turn
ıe back upon the Beloved's quarrel. O! what
champion is love? I confess good company,
nd abiding company, is much to be desired,
nd love is that. Faith at length will evanish
nto sight, and hope into possession; but love is
the

the Chriftian's continual companion, and a brave companion it is; for it is no burden to love, when there is the lafting enjoyment of the Beloved, and the full and continual affurance of immenfurable love again, as it is when love is made perfect.

Ah! if time would ftay, I would not weary to write unto your Honour; for, I do not know when, if ever, I may have the occafion again. But while I am, I defire to be concerned with you. O! go on, and fear not. The Lord, I hope, will fhew you a token for good, that they who hate you may fee it and be afhamed. Dread nothing in your intended journey, the Lord will be with you; and I pray again and again that fo it may be, and that he may blefs your labours, and make them contribute to the procuring an uniformity amongft churches, that fo he may be one, and his name one amongft us. I hope I need not defire you to mind me a poor thing, who have much to do, and nothing in myfelf to do with, and who remains,

Honourable and dear Sir,

Your real, conftant fympathifing friend

and fervant in the Lord,

JAMES RENWICK.

LET.

LETTER XXXI.

From the Rev. Mr. James Renwick, *to Mr.*
Robert Hamilton.

Honourable and dear Sir,   *August* 23. 1684.

I Thought once that your expectation of our
letters should have been more quickly answered than now it could be; but the holy
and wise God, who doth all things well, so ordered it that it is fallen out otherwise: for upon
the 30th day of *July*, when I was going, in
company with other three, to the general meeting, we espied two dragoons meeting us, and
not expecting any more to be following, we
went foreward, not dreading them; but when
we came within word and shot, we saw a party
of about twenty more very near upon us: whereupon, seeing there was no probability of resist-
ing them, we turned up to a hill called *Dun-
gavel*. But my three neighbours being on foot
and I on horse-back, they compassed about the
foot of the hill, but I took up to the height,
being hotly pursued by many of that party;
some whereof were at my right-hand to keep
me from the mosses, and others behind, who
always as they came within shot, discharged upon me: so being near unto the top of the
hill, and finding myself beset round about, and
seeing no visible door to escape, I thought fit to
quit the horse which I had, and to wait till I
saw what God did in it. But after I had lighted
from the horse, I saw before me a piece of good
equitable ground, whereupon I essayed to mount

H   again

again upon the horfe, but the beaft would not ftand unto me; whereupon I refolved to kill the horfe, left the enemy fhould be thereby ftrengthned; howbeit, having but one fhot, I thought fit to keep it for a greater extremity; finding the beaft fuch as would not ftand ftill, I reached it with a fhabble which I had, conjecturing, that poffibly (the place being uninhabited) the beaft might fave my wallet and the papers, together with Mr. *B*'s wallet. Thus I went up to the top of the hill upon foot, and feeing myfelf fo encompaffed that I could not run from them, and that I was in no ways able to fight with them, I judged it my beft to clap upon the ground: fo I went unto a caim, which by fituation was about fix or feven pace of ground out of all their eyes, thinking to ly down upon it; all the hill being green, and bare in that place, knowing that God could carry their fight over it; fo coming to the top of it, I efpied in it a pit, which when I faw, it entered into my mind, that it was ordained of God for hiding of me: Thus I lay down into it, winning by God's goodnefs, to a chearful fubmiffion to death, torture, or whatfoever his will might be. But I was, in no fmall meafure confident, that no evil at that time could happen unto me, the Lord giving me that fcripture, *Pfal.* vi. 8. *Depart from me, all ye workers of iniquity;*—which was fo powerful, that I was made, I think, a hundred times to repeat it over, ere I could get myfelf ftayed; together with that other *Pfalm,* xci. 11. *For he fhall give his angels charge over thee, to keep thee in all thy ways:* which was fuch unto me, that I lifted up my head to fee thefe angels; but, confidering my folly in

that

that particular, I was made to laugh at my own witlessness. So I lay still until the sun set, sometimes praying and sometimes praising God, tho' Oh! I can do neither to purpose. But all the joy that the Lord's works of wonder for me did afford, were swallowed up in sorrow, because of what befel my dear brethren, who (all that were with me) fell into the enemies hands, one of them receiving eleven wounds. Then, after all, when I thought upon drawing off the hill, not knowing the way to one friend's house in the whole country; I besought the Lord, that as he had hid me, so he would lead and guide me. Thus I set my face toward *Clyde*, and after I had travelled about four miles, I met with *Wind-hill*, with whom I stayed two days, and kept a meeting upon the second night, even while the militia was searching that side of the country; and twice that night I very narrowly escaped, as it had been even out of their very paws. O! time would fail me to relate the Lord's works of wonder for poor unworthy me: for even since, I have in one day escaped three or four signal hazards. O! what shall I say of the Lord's way with me? He will either have me taught, otherwise he will have me appear to be indocible. O for grace to answer his pains taken upon me. And as for the present case of our land, it was never such; enemies have issued forth a proclamation, calling all the militia be-north *Tay* to be in readiness against the fifteenth of this month with fifteen days provision; and it is thought, to spread over the west-land Shires; but the Lord knows what their purposes are. However, they have proclaimed, that all men in country habit, wherever they are seen, are to be challenged, and kept till it be

known

known what they are. Now, the adverfary is moft cruel, and apprehends not only all men, but even the women whom they can get their hands upon, and ufe them moft barbaroufly. O what meaneth this hot furnace? furely it is not to confume, it is to purge and refine. O for grace, for grace to endure unto the end. I think *Scotland* is now like a woman in hard labour, who muft either get a fpeedy help and delivery, elfe fhe will be in peril of dying in travel. But courage yet, her fharpeft fhower is at the minute of her delivery. Die, die fhe will not, for the Lord is but hafting through her travel. The more fore the pains be, the more joyful her delivery will be; yea, the Lord will make brave mirth at it; for he will have a feaft of many a man's carcafe at it. As for more particular news, *N. K.* will give you an account; I have not feen his teftimony, but I think, he is a good honeft lad. *R. G.* hath carried always very ftedfaftly, and is now fentenced with banifhment; a wonderful reftraint upon enemies indeed.

I faw your honour's letters which you wrote home anent Mr. *Flint*'s bufinefs; and I cannot pafs this, that I obferved in the ftrain of them much trouble, if not difcouragement to be held forth. O fy upon you, where is all your undaunted boldnefs and true magnanimity now? what fear you? what can he and his party do? they are incapable of doing harm here; they are but rendering themfelves fuch, as that their memories fhall be written over with contempt and ignominy to all after generations.

Now, the Lord be with you, and teach you to ufe your weapons rightly for him in this day

of

of rencounter. O ceafe not to pray for poor *Scotland*, now in travel, and for him who is,

Yours, as formerly,

JAMES RENWICK.

P. S. If time would permit, ilk day furnifhes me both with fad and refrefhful tidings to reprefent unto your honour; refrefhful, for our prifon houfes are filled with fongs of joy and praife, yea, they were never more refrefhful, for they are palaces indeed. But our fad cafe otherwife ftill increafeth; for many are apprehended; yea, women incarcerate, and fome of them banifhed, and men execute upon the very day when they receive the fentence of death.

JAMES RENWICK.

L E T T E R XXXII.

From Mr. James Renwick, *to the honourable Mr.* Robert Hamilton.

Hon. and dear Sir, 1684.

I Received yours, and was refrefhed to fee a line from your hand again; yet I am not a little troubled that our converfe by letters fhould not be more frequent; but continual hurrying and toffing ftops it on my part, together with fuch a multitude of bufinefs, that fometimes I would put a greater price upon an hour of time than upon much riches. O Sir! who knew my

H 3 work,

work, if they had not hearts harde
mants, they would be affected with
tion; but·why fhould I fay thus, foi
the Lord's Rindnefs to poor unworth
would make me the object of their er
fay this indeed, that the Lord fuff
work, however unfupportable to flefi
to he burdenfome unto me; for,
world think my cafe moft miferab
think, it is fo happy that I know no
day, upon the face of the earth w
would exchange my lot. O! it is
and pleafant to be fwiming in the
Jordan for Chrift and with Chrift, tl
ter in the pleafures of fin, and del
flefh; yéa, though Chriftians had n
hereafter, I cannot but judge theii
here, happy beyond all others; as
fayeth, *Thou haft put gladnefs in my*
than in the time when their corn and i
creafed, Pfal. iv. 7. And when the
moft, I know, it is the time where
fmiles moft upon his own: O therefc
of them fear a fuffering lot: enemies
felves fatisfied that we are put to wa
ftormy nights thro' moffes and moi
if they knew how we were feafted,
are fleeping, they would gnafh the
anger. O! I cannot exprefs, how
I have had when the curtains of heavi
drawn, when the quietnefs of all tl
filent watches of the night, has bri
mind the. duty of admiring the dee
unexpreffible ocean of joy and wond
the whole family of the higher hoi
laftingly drowned; each ftar leadin

ouder what he muſt be, who is the ſtar of Ja-
ob, the bright and morning ſtar, who maketh
ll his own to ſhine as ſtars in the firmament. In-
eed (if I may term it ſo) I am much obliged to
nemies, for, though they purpoſe my miſery,
et they are inſtrumental of covering many a fat
able to me; and while they are pining away in
uſk envy and pale fear, I am feeding in peace
od joy. O poor fools! what can they do? the
reateſt wrong they can do, is, to be inſtrument-
l in bringing a chariot to carry us to, that high-
r houſe, and ſhould we not think this the great-
ſt favour. Let enemies never think that they
an make the people of God's caſe miſerable,
hile he lives and reigns; and I wot well, he
ath that to give, and will give that which will
weeten all the ſours of his followers. And I
ay ſay this to his praiſe, that I have found ſo
uch of his kindneſs and ſupply in ſetting a-
out his work in ſuch hard circumſtances, that
hrough the prevailing of a body of death ſome-
mes, and deſire to be with himſelf, makes me
og for a diſſolution; yet, I think, I could be
utent to dwell if it were a thouſand years in
his infirm and weakened body of clay, with
ntinual toil and hazard, to carry his name to
s people.

Now, Right honourable, as to news here,
now, that the Lord is ſtill increaſing his peo-
le in number and ſpiritual ſtrength; and many
ſacrifice he is taking off their hands; for there
re not many days wherein his truths are not ſeal-
d with blood, and that in all places, ſo that, I
iuk, within a little, there ſhall not be a moſs
r mountain in the Weſt of Scotland which ſhall
et be flowered with martyrs. Enemies have
brought

brought down the *Highlanders* upon us, and the
with the forces do run through the countr
(Lord give direction and strength) and kill al
whom they meet with, if they do not say whatfo
ever they bid them. We are fearing maffacres
here is a maffacre indeed. *Oh that my head wer*
waters, and mine eyes a fountain of tears, that
might weep without intermiffion, *for the flain o*
the daughter of my people. Alfo, they have givei
out, by act of parliament and open proclamation
that all minifters and hearers who are to be foune
in the fields, are to be killed prefently; and i
found in houfes, the minifter is to be killed, anc
the people fined. The devil now is come dowr
in great wrath, becaufe he knoweth his time to
be but fhort. Mr. *Alexander Shields* is yet alive
and feems ay to be more and more right; he
indeed hath made a foul fall, but I think, he i
duly fenfible. All the reft of the prifoners are
very well encouraged. I have of late made a
hafty journey into *England* the length of *New-*
caftle, and (bleffed be the Lord) with much more
nor expected encouragement and fuccefs. I car-
not at this inftant grant your defire, but I fhall
keep your memorandum till I get it done, for I
have been thefe eight days fo hurried and chafed
with continual alarms, that I could not get fett'ed
to write any; and the Lord, to manifeft his
power, gave me a moft remarkable delivery.

Now, dear Sir, begging it of you and all friends,
that you will be bufy and inftant with God, that
he may be with us in the day of our extremity:
and commending you all to the grace of God,
with my love and fervice to yourfelf, and them
of whofe concernednefs with the Lord's caufe, we
are all fenfible, and that they are moft ftrengthening

ening to you against all your antagonists, particularly to the *En. V. H.* to whom I purpose, God willing, to write. I am ever,

As formerly,

JAMES RENWICK.

LETTER XXXIII.

From the Rev. Mr. James Renwick, *to* ———

Hon. and dear Sir,   *Feb.* 28. 1685.

I Received your letter, which was many ways refreshing unto me ; as also, the way of its coming to my hand, for when I was upon my travels, about the setting forth of my master's ware, there arose such a storm of weather, which forced me to turn off my journey a little, to the nearest great inns, and there I got your letter, and also my wares better received off my hand than ever before in that place. Hence I am made to see, that divine providence is a mysterious thing, and that I never lofs a whit more of a storm. Also, there is one thing in your letter which made me not a little to admire, to wit, your apprehension that I was sorely sick, that there was a great faith among traders, and that my sickness was a great mean of my preservation; a leel guess indeed. In reference hereunto, I must tell you a pretty passage. Upon a certain night, after the dismission of a market, there went about forty of our merchants foreward a little before me, upon the way that I was going, with whom I
                                          trysted

tryſted to meet the night following: But after a
little ſleep, ſickneſs ſo poſſeſt me that I was not
able to keep my tryſt; whereupon I ſent away
ſome merchants that were with me to go foreward with the reſt about their buſineſs; who
upon the day following, were aſſaulted with
a great multitude of our antagoniſts, who were
ſix for one, ſo that our merchants were
not able to ſtand; whereupon they took the
retreat, and outſtripped their antagoniſts without any ſkaith; ſave the loſs of one : Now,
before this came to paſs I dreaded it. But
what think you of my ſickneſs and your gueſs?
for if I had been with the reſt I had been taken
from all trading; for my body is ſo weakened
with much travel, that though I travel more
than any, yet I cannot come ſo good ſpeed as o-
thers, when need requireth: Alſo within two
days my ſickneſs left me. Now, I leave all this
to your thoughts, for it would be tedious for me
to write mine; and I think, you may gueſs at
them, as you did at that which was more dark.
But to come to the ſubſtance of your letter, you
have opened up the myſtery of our trade abroad,
which I dreaded, yet I underſtood it not; but I
agree with your advice, as to theſe men's ſubſcribing of our principal accounts. But my maſter
is taking the wiſeſt way in it; for now he hath
I oughed off our antagoniſt's chief factor; ſo that
I think, all merchants will now ſhortly ſide themſelves, and when at the puſh they declare themſelves willingly whoſe trade they are for, it will
ſreak forth the more ingenuity, and we will
know the better what to think of them; ſo we
need not be raſh in our propoſals, till we ſee how
theſe men ſettle, for now they muſt ſettle ſome
way

, This is my poor advice at the
ave not as yet met with any num-
ierchants to confult with anent it.
: fame myftery from abroad is alfo
ı us, but I find all our merchants
; for all forts are moft earneft that
ıd with them, and they with us. But
ı refpect not the advantage of our
, but of their own: Neverthelefs,
ın, makes them fo earneft to trade
ır wares go well off our hands at
; part of the reafon of it: Our mer-
ncreafe, this is another part: But
chief reafon be this, They look up-
ıturous merchants, that dow not a-
with naughty commodities, but fet
ıolefale; and that we are refolute,
ırm will keep us back from our in-
;e: Whereupon they think, if we
vith them, they would get us fet up-
rate traffic, and if we did won, it
heir hand; and if we loft, we would
ilves, which the moft part of them
gard much. Here, I think, lies the

ıy Sir, for your further fatisfaction
ion anent our trade at home, thefe
I think fit to tell you that I obferve,
e greateft part of the country give
ition to our trade, and the way there-
they have not hearts to give their
mey for our wares. (2.) That very
our wares fo worthy, that they fpare
w either gold or money upon them.
ery many, who, I thought, would
oked us in the face, refort to our
markets

markets in all places. (4.) Very many are feeking to be in our incorporations, who, I think, are downright for our trade; but I fear fome of them are feeking rather, that we fhould have a great ftock, and that they fhould fhare with us, than that my mafter fhould get credit; whereas he refpects his credit more than he doth all the gold and money in the world. (5.) None are received in amongft us, who either leave us, or rue their trading with us. (6.) Our merchants are all fearlefs, as if they could not lofe any thing. (7.) They are refolute, they will not flip a market for a foul day, or ly in the harbour becaufe of a ftorm. (8.) The waiters are fo angry at our goods, that ordinarily they do not bring them, when they catch them, to public roupings, or to be burnt by the hands of the common hangman, but deftroy them where they may find them: This is occafioned partly by the refolutnefs of our merchants, who will not let the waiters carry away any of our goods, fo they come to be deftroyed when the waiters are the ftrongeft party; and partly by the malicioufnefs of the waiters, who, unlefs our merchants renounce their trade, they prefently deftroy their goods. I may fay, my mafter hath gotten us fome brave refolute merchants, whom an hafty propofal never furprifeth. (9.) The waiters have gotten many of the beft of our goods deftroyed; yea, they have caped more from us within thefe two years, than I thought then we had; and the more they take, we have the more behind; but this is only through the wit of my mafter; yea, he is fo wife, that ere he want wares he will make ftones give filver. (10.) There is fome difference amongft our merchants

anent

anent the manner of seeking in our debts of the last accounts, which we gave in against our antagonists; but I do not fear that my master will suffer a breach among us upon that head, for we all agree in the matter.

Now, to come to what is your desire in your memorandum sent unto me.

1. As to that information anent Mr. *Lap.* I got it from young Mr. *Fisher*, who had it from his brother at *London*. As also, I know, that his brother hath left trading with the leading merchants at *London*, save with Mr. *Fife*, with whom I hear not that he trades much.

2. As to correspondence with *Groemvezyh,* (by whom I understand Mr. *Br.*) there hath been more since his flitting; and as for any letters betwixt him and Mr. *Fisher* Elder, is a thing unknown to me; neither have I any distinct notion of his seeking to trade with us, save by the apprentice you sent over.

3. As to our late accounts, we shall see to get them unto you; as also how that money may be received off your hand.

Now, Right honourable Sir, at the time, I shall trouble you no further, not knowing well how to get this conveyed to your hand; but leave you to my master's direction and counsel, who, I know, can make known unto you the secrets of our trade, and the engines of our opposers. My love to all friends who wish us a good market, and show them I forget them not. I am,

Yours, to serve you to my power
in my master's employment,

J. RENWICK.

LETTER XXXIV.

From Mr. James Renwick, *to Mrs.* Jean Hamilton *at* Lewarden *in* Friesland.

Worthy Madam,   March 2. 1685.

YOur letter was long in coming to my hand, and it hath been long in answering; but I had never the expectation of an occasion before this; as also your case was troublesome to me, and I knew not well what to say anent it; and the most that I can say yet, is, that I desire earnestly to sympathize with you, and to mind you before the Lord, for I know your burdens. However I dare not advise you to it;

1. Because of the many corruptions, which, I fear, are not so burdensome to them now, as once I apprehended they were to some of them.

2. Because of your own unclearness anent it: I say this, not that I make our clearness a sufficient warrant either to do or not do; for then the scriptures would not be the rule; yet to him that esteemeth any thing to be unclean, to him it is unclean: As also, I think, your unclearness is not groundless. But here ariseth the difficulties.

(1.) How shall this be reconciled with your worthy brother's practice? yet I do not see them jostle together; for though he heareth, yet I know, he withdraweth from what is corrupt, which you would not get so handsomely done.

(2.) How shall this be reconciled with the ordination? yet neither is there any contradiction here; for in the ordination they came to us, and acted according to *Scotland*'s reformation, and if
                                   these

thefe whom you were to hear, would do fo in all points of worfhip, you need not have any fcruple.

But as for your coming here with the children, I fee not how you can refolve upon it as yet, for though your cafe be fad there, as to many things, it would be more fad here. Therefore my poor advice is, that you would contentedly ftay a little, till you fee what the Lord doth, and wreftle through your difficulties the beft way you can; for we are expecting ftrange things fuddenly at home: Yet if you faw a general calamity coming upon that place, better to come home and fhare in *Scotland*'s calamity, in whofe fin we have all a fhare, than to fhare in the calamities of another place.

Now, Dear Madam, my dear and worthy friend, look to the Lord himfelf for your direction, upholding, encouragement, comfort, and upmaking; for come what will it will be well with the righteous, and all fhall end in public teftimony of divine favour to thefe who wait upon the Lord; though he fhould fhake heaven and earth yet he *will be the hope of his people, and the ftrength of the children of Ifrael,* Joel iii. 16. Now, to the word of his grace I commend you;

Worthy Madam,

Your Ladyfhip's

undoubted fympathifing friend

in the Lord,

JAMES RENWICK.

LETTER XXXV.

From the Rev. Mr. James Renwick, *to the honourable Mr.* Robert Hamilton.

Hon. and dear Sir,   *Edin. May* 13. 1685.

I Have been with your friend *Robert*, and got some account of affairs, which made me to wonder not a little; but *Andrew Cameron's* information hath made me to wonder much more; for I could not believe that policy could mask over temporal defigns with fo fair colours and pretences. ,Whereupon, we have great need of the wifdom of the ferpent, as well as the harmleffnefs of the dove. I find, *Andrew Cameron's* drift is to get in with *Argyle;* but to me his arguments are more diffuafive than perfuafive. But I dread *W. B.* greatly, having feen a paper from his own hand, where he yields to all their defire: I fear the hand of *Joab* hath been in it; and he, forfooth, would have it publifhed in our name; but, through grace, I will oppofe it with my whole vitals. I am likewife afraid of fome others amongft us, but of none fave of fuch as I had former jealoufies, but could not bottem fufficient reafons againft them. I have feen alfo your animadverfions upon the affociation, which I agree with; for I look upon it as a *Cromwelian* and *Bothwelian* compoud: But as for your animadverfions on our declarat on, I think, the comentaries of politics have made you look upon it after another fort than otherwife you would have done; for we defigned it to be taken jointly alongft with our other teftimonies and actings,

and

and so the door is not wider than it was: neither can any show any thing in that declaration but what I think may be easily reconciled with our other testimonies and actings; so, I think it a thing below you or me to trouble ourselves with the various expositions that persons, for their own ends, put upon it: for some represent it as the strictest thing that ever came from our hands, thereby to make us odious; some again, as the laxest that ever came from our hands, that thereupon they may get a door to enter; but there is none opened, and our wall is so well cemented, that, through our camp-master, they will not break thorough: If some shall jump over it, and go out from us, yet our wall shall stand inviolable. Wherefore trouble not yourself, O right honourable, about Logomachies, for our practice will comment upon it.

Hoping to meet with friends shortly, I will be, in a capacity to inform you fully. And praying that the Lord may give light and life. I am,

> *Right honoured,*
> *Yours as formerly,*

JAMES RENWICK.

LETTER XXXVI.

From the Rev. Mr. James Renwick, to the honourable Mr. Robert Hamilton.

Honourable Sir,   *July* 9. 1685.

IF I durst have ventured this with the post, or could have had another occasion, I would have

have written to you ere this time; for, I know
you will be anxious to hear how it is with us:
But it would take a great volume, and require an
accurate obferving capacity to write our cafe:
Howbeit this is no fmall comfort and encourage
ment, that the Lord fo vifibly takes our matters
in his own guiding; for, before *Argyle* brake,
many of our friends were greatly puzzled, whether the Lord was calling them to follow their
former methods, or to draw altogether by themfelves, and to emit a declaration of their own;
whereupon, there was a meeting appointed to
confider the matter, and alfo a day for prayer;
but the Lord difappointed our meetings, one after
another, until *Argyle* was apprehended and his
party fcattered; fo this was put out of our heads:
yet our fnares fince have been greater than heretofore; for Mr. *Barclay* and Mr. *Langlands* pafs
up and down the country, and have got themfelves too much infinuate upon feveral of our
wanderers, pretending no difference from us, but
a willingnefs to join.   Howbeit, I met with Mr.
Langlands, and found him no otherways than
when I was in *Holland*: He owned his writing
that letter to Mr. *Brackel*, but would grant with
no wrong therein; fo the main thing that they
drive at, is, to have us lay afide our challenges,
and they would be filent.   But it is clear to me,
that the Lord doth not fend them; for, if he
did, they would not cover their iniquity; alfo
their need, and not our need hath moved them;
but if they fhall, in fuch a ftrain, ftep to the fields
with public preaching, I think, they will not keep
them long, for he hath taken poffeffion of our
high places until he return to our temple again.
Howbeit, if it were the Lord's will you were a-
mongft

mongſt us, I think (through the Lord's grace
and aſſiſtance) that might be inſtrumental of very
much good; but for my ſoul, I dare not adviſe
you to come, conſidering what hazards you may
run in your coming; yet you may lay it out before the Lord, and if he do not open a door for
your journey, do not venture upon it; for, I
hope, he is reſerving you for ſome greater work.
O be not anxious, for the Lord will make a
ſtroke clear our controverſies.

As for our news, *Argyle's* party is wholly diſ-
ſipate; for they diſagreed amongſt themſelves,
not upon the ſtating of their quarrel, but upon
the way of proſecuting it. No conditions to
them were keeped, and this rendered them very
diſſatisfied *Argyle* is beheaded; *Rombold* execute, after the manner of worthy *Rathillet;* Sir
J. C. apprehended, and his ſon, with ſeveral o-
thers. But *Monmouth* is yet buſied in *England,*
whereby the *Scots* forces are marched right towards the border, which animates *William Cleland,* &c. to make a new ſtir, and ſo our difficulties are as formerly. As for your brother Sir
William, he was lieutenant to *Rombold;* he is
yet alive, with ſome of his friends. I reſolve to
ſpeer him out, and inform him I have ſeen *J.
N.* who ſaith, he is with us in all things, and
that he came with *Argyle* only for paſſage, being
under no engagements, and taking no place from
them. *Andrew Cameron* is a great agent for
them, and not ſimple in their buſineſs; he re-
fuſeth joining with no miniſters who were not
actually indulged, or defenders of ſuch. *G. H.;
R. Smith,* and *David Steel,* are well; but *R.
Smith* cannot find an open door to come unto
you.

you. *M. B.* is like to die in prison. Mr. *Alexander Shields* seem not to be of a right stamp *.
Now, I hope your Honour will pardon my confusion, occasioned by my hasty pen. I cannot
express my thoughts to you; but I say again, the
Lord will take our matters in his own hand: O!
let us be busy with himself, and commit all unto
him, who hath the government upon his shoulders. *Scotland's* day is coming; happy those
who are in their chambers. My love and service
to all friends with you, foreigners and others.
The blessing of him who is in the burning bush
be with you. I am,

Honourable Sir,

Your servant as formerly,

JAMES RENWICK.

LETTER XXXVII.

From the Rev. Mr. James Renwick, *to* Robert
Speir *at* Edinburgh.

Dear Friend,   *October* 23. 1685.

WHat past at our last meeting time will not
allow me to inform you of, neither need
I be careful about the same; for I know that the
bearer can do it as distinctly as I: however, I
thought fit to write unto you, shewing that the
meeting is no ways discontent with your purpose
of

---

* He took the Abjuration Oath the 6th of *August*
after this, as *Wodrow* testifies, vol. ii.

of going abroad at this time. And as to what I have writtten to my honourable and dear friend; which I did let you see, though I judged it not fit to communicate the same to other friends; as I was telling you by word, so I desire that you would signify to him, that he must take it only as my thoughts at that time, which, in a great measure, were undigested, and through the multitude of business and contendings, and various weights upon my spirit, not a little confused: also, as I was telling you my mind more fully anent these things than I have written it, so I desire that you would speak with him concerning the same, shewing my thoughts more conspicuously than my letter doth. Moreover, if I have written any thing which is unseasonable, or not right and equal, I am content to be informed and instructed by him: but it is my desire, if he will agree therewith, that after his reading and considering the same it may be destroyed; for I think it not any advantage to the cause, to keep any letter from friends, but what is written as their fixed and deliberate thoughts about matters.

Now, for your coming home, I think you have seen many depths of mercy and judgment manifested to the poor church of *Scotland*; you have seen the afflicted remnant brought unto, and through many difficulties; you have seen much matter of joy and sorrow; so, I hope, your travels hither have not been without fruit. So, praying that the Lord may make his own hand appear at his own work, and establish a remnant in his own way, in the midst of snares and damping difficulties, and commending you to his direction,

rection, affiſtance, protection, and proviſion,
am,

Dear Sir,

Your aſſured friend,

and ſervant in the·Lord,

JAMES RENWICK

LETTER XXXVIII.

From the Rev. Mr. James Renwick, *to Mrs.* J
Hamilton, *at* Lewarden *in* Frieſland.

Worthy Madam,   *Nov.* 18. 1685.

YOU doubtleſs think it ſtrange of my long
ſilence, and it is far contrary to my own
reſolution ; but the abounding. of inward **care,**
and the continuing of outward toſſing, blocketh
me up from doing many things which I would :
and it is no great wonder that a man under ſuch
variety of providences as I am, cannot be maſter
of his own purpoſes. Howbeit, I may ſay, your
caſe, and the caſe of the family, lieth in ſuch a
meaſure upon my heart, that I cannot get the
ſame forgotten ; and though this be an inſignifi-
cant thing, and of little purpoſe to your Ladyſhip, yet I own it is my duty. I never look upon your caſe but·I think it is in ſome things
ſingular. Your lot is caſt in a ſtrange land, ſe-
parated from your friends and acquaintances,
but communion and fellowſhip with God will
make your lot ſweet and pleaſant unto you,
and furniſh you with abundance of joy in every
outward

outward condition; and this, I hope, you are sometimes senfibly tafting: alfo, I doubt not but the company of your worthy brother, and fome dear foreigners, is not a little refrefhful unto you. Moreover, when I confider your circum-ftances, *Ruth*'s cleaving to *Naomi* is ftill brought before me; and without the leaft of flattery I fay it, I think what you have done for your dear fifter's family (coming from fincerity, of which, charity which is not blind, will not let me doubt) is as acceptable before God, and as much to be praifed amongft men. But knowing that this is a fubject, which, though I could not pafs, yet you, Madam, defire it not to be treated upon; therefore I fhall forbear it, and fhall fhew you fome of my thoughts (undiftinct and infignificant as they are) anent our poor *Scotland*.

1. I think we are not yet entered our *Jordan;* for though we have come through a miry and thorny wildernefs, yet our *Jordan* is before us, and it will be very deep, but it will not be very broad : when the ark of God enters it, it fhall be like to drown, but it fhall fuddenly and and admirably win to the other fide.

2. I think fafety fhall only be to thofe who have their hands neareft the ark. Oh then! many a woe to the minifters and profeffors whofe hands have been drawn back from the work, and thefe whofe malice is againft the burden-bearers; it fhall be as is faid, *Ifa*. xxvi. 11. *Lord, when thy hand is lifted up, they will not fee : but they fhall fee, and be afhamed for their envy at the people ; yea, the fire of thine enemies fhall devour them.*

3. I think that *Scotland* fhall be made a wafte and, ere God's controverfy againft it be ended;

he

he will fell the heritages of earls, lords, and others, yea, and their carcasses good cheap.

4. I think the Lord (until he raise his work again) will guide and manage it more by providences than by instruments; and this is, that his hand may be alone seen in it, and that he may get the glory; and what is most glorifying to him, should it not be most pleasant and rejoicing to us.

5. I think that when the Lord returns to us again, it will be with such a measure and outpouring of his Spirit, that the remnant that shall be left shall have a very heaven upon earth, and our land shall be made the joy of all lands.

But as to these, or such like, I shall say no more, knowing you are both really and distinctly exercised anent our case: And what is for us this day, but that we make Christ sure for ourselves, and spend our days here below in admiring the loveliness and condescendency of our Beloved, and our own happiness in enjoying such a portion. But this is a great work, time is not equal for it, therefore we shall get eternity for it. O let us study the increase of the beauty of holiness, for happiness is inferior unto it. It is by holiness we are made like unto God, and is not this true nobility? O! what is like unto it! If we knew more of this study and attainment, desertion would be less of our exercise, and we should enjoy more of the smilings of his sweet countenance, and breathings of his Spirit. Also, while in this our pilgrimage, let his will be ours in all things; whatever he may carve out for us, or any that we are concerned in, let us say *amen* to it; for if he will it, it is enough for us: Yea, let us lay our account with the

the worſt of it, that whatever come we may not be ſurprized.

Now, not to trouble your Ladyſhip further, praying that the all-ſufficiency which is in Chriſt may be forthcoming for you, that ſo you may finiſh your courſe with his honour, and your own true joy, with the teſtimony of a conſcience kept void of offence towards God, and towards all men; and that you may ſuck of the breaſts of his conſolations here, until you come to drink abundantly of the rivers of pleaſure at his right hand. I am,

Worthy Madam,

Your obliged and aſſured friend, and

ſympathizing ſervant in our ſweet Lord,

JAMES RENWICK.

LETTER XXXIX.

From the Rev. Mr. James Renwick, to the honourable Societies of Strangers at Lewarden in Friesland.

Feb. 18. 1686.

Hon. and dearly beloved in our ſweet Lord,

I Have had often bluſhes with myſelf, when I thought upon my omitting to write unto you; but I may ſay, it was neither voluntary nor wilful, but neceſſity: for a man under ſuch various exigences of providence as I am, cannot be maſter of his own purpoſes. And beſides that, I am daily looking out, either to be preſently killed,

K

ed, where I may be found, or elfe dragged into a prifon or fcaffold; various weighty and perplexing occurrences, day by day, come inevitably into my way, which take up my thoughts, filling my fpirit with care, and my hands with bufinefs. But if I had proven as forgetful of you, as I have been blocked up from faluting you with a line from my hand, I had been far out of my duty before the Lord, and grofly ungrateful toward you. Howbeit, right honourable and dearly beloved, I need not infift in apologizing for myfelf with you, for I know you have fuch a feeling of our burdens, that ye commiferate our cafe, and pity our perplexities: therefore I'll break off this, and go on in what the Lord giveth me to fay.

There is no rational creature which doth not fet fome one thing or other before its eyes, as its main end, and chief good; and according to the various predominants, in fenfual and madmen, are their various main ends. Hence it is, that there did refult fo many different opinions among Heathen philofophers about man's chief good. But here is the great miftake with foolifh vain men, that whatever they feek after, it is but few who bend toward the true chief good, which is God. There are indeed *gods many and lords many*; for whatever any fixeth his defires upon, and aimeth in all his actions at the obtaining and enjoying thereof, is his lord and his god, whether it be honour or riches, or fome object or other of vile concupifcence; yet there is but one God who is truly and only defire-worthy, love-worthy, and honour-worthy. This one hath not a match, or a parallel; for what can equal him? yea, what in any worth can come the length of the latchet of his shoes? He is that inestimable jewel, invaluable treasure, and incomparable pearl of price, that only worthy desire of all nations. O! take a look of him as he is the Being of beings, having being of himself independent of all other beings; and upon whom all other things depend in their being and operations: *In him we live, in him we move, and of him we have our being.* Doth not all the pieces of the creation, heaven, earth, and sea, sun, moon, and stars, the commonest and unworthiest creature that moveth upon the earth, bear large characters of his wisdom, power, and goodness? Doth not his mysterious common providence, making the sharpest sighted of his creatures hide their faces, and become silent before him, declare him to be God, and that he is *of one mind, and who can turn him?* Do not the various instruments that execute his will, signified by four chariots, *Zech.* vi. 1. bringing about various dispensations, signified by the different colours of the horses; whether calamities of war, signified by the red; or other doleful miseries, signified by the black; mixed dispensations, black and white, so to speak, of mercy and judgment, signified by the grizled and bay; or dispensations of mercy, signified by the white? I say, does not all these come forth from between the two mountains of brass? The one mountain signifieth his unalterable decree, and the other his effectual providence, which watcheth and waiteth that instruments bring nothing to the birth but what has been conceived in the womb of his eternal purpose. O take a look of him in his perfections; he is without measure and

limits,

limits, without beginning and ending: he is one and the same in his nature, in his counsels, and in his love; he perfectly knoweth himself, and all things that are possible; he can do all things that do not imply a contradiction, and argue imperfection: he is good and doeth good; he is righteous in himself, and equal in all his ways of dealing with his creatures; he is true without any dissimulation; he is holy and delighteth in his own holiness, and in every resemblance of it, in his angels, and in his saints. But O! who can think of him, and who can speak of him? He is infinite in all his attributes; and every perfection hath a perfect meeting in him: albeit some of his attributes be in some degree communicable to his creatures, yet they are in him in an altogether incommunicable manner and measure: and there is nothing in God, but what is God; for this is his name, *I am that I am.* And again I say, Who can think of him, and who can speak of him? who can comprehend him, or compass him about? Who by understanding can search out God? Humble and believing ignorance is better than curious and prying knowledge: for all, that we can know of him, is, to know that we cannot know him.

Let us yet come a little nearer, and take a look of him as he is our Saviour, in his condescendancy, love, power, faithfulness, and other properties. O! how condescending is he? tho' he be that high and lofty One, the Father's equal, yet he stooped so low as to take upon him the nature of man, and all the sinless infirmities that attend it; he became *flesh of our flesh, and bone of our bone,* and that in the lowly condition of a servant. He suits the creature's affection as if it were of some worth, and seeks men and women to match with him. O how loving is he! It is a strong love that he beareth to that seed of *Abraham*? Doth not this shine in all that he hath done? He emptied himself that they might become full; he made himself poor, though maker and possessor of heaven and earth, that they might become rich; he fulfilled the law for them, that he might purchase to them life and happiness; he made himself a sacrifice unto the death, that he might satisfy offended justice, and make reconciliation for them. O such a death! so cursed! so shameful! so painful! and so lingering! But above all, he had the full weight of the wrath of God to bear, which all the strength of angels and men could not have endured: but he being God, he could not fall under it. O what manner of love is this! In effect he did not care what he suffered; let justice charge home upon him with all its rigour and severity, seeing he was to gain his point, and purchase a part of mankind from Satan to himself, from sin to holiness, from misery to happiness: so that man, however unworthy, base, sinful, and miserable, yet is the centre of his love: O! how powerful is he? He is mighty to save, able to save to the uttermost; all the strong-holds of the soul cannot hold out against him; his power is irresistible, by this he can do what he will; and by his love he will do what we need: and again he is so faithful, that what he saith he doeth; he will not retract one promise that is gone out of his mouth; neither will he fail in fulfilling all his threatenings.

Much might be said of these things; but not the thousandth part of the truth can be told;

when

when we win to his houfe above, and fee him as he is, we will be afhamed of all our babblings about him. They that have been moft ravifhed with his love, and moft eloquent to fpeak forth the praife of his comelinefs and properties, will fee that they have been but, at beft, babes learn- ing to fpeak. O what fhall I fay! he is the won- derful, matchlefs, and glorious ineftimable jewel, and incomparable pearl of price: O who would not choice him! who would not give away them- felves to him! Let man look thro' heaven and earth, and feek a portion where he will, he fhall not find the like of Chrift. O then! let us be alto- gether his, and nothing our own; our time let it be his, our underftanding let it be his, our will let it be his, our affections let them be his, the travel of our fouls let it be his, our ftrength let it be his, our names, lives and enjoyments let them all be his; let us be fully furrendered and entirely confecrated unto him. This is a comprehenfive matter indeed. But what elfe fhould we be taken up with, but with the improvement of this refignation, always travelling through his properties, viewing them as our riches, delighting to improve our intereft in him, by receiving from his hand what we need; and that he improve his intereft in us, by doing with us, and taking from us, what he pleaf- eth. Let us fee him, and obferve, and fay, *What have we to do any more with our idols*. Oh! that vanity fhould get fo much as one look from me. I think, he never took more pains upon any that they might be emptied of all things befide him- felf, and not have a will of their own, nor affec- tion to any other thing; and yet, ah! the bad entertainment he gets off my hand. I can nei- ther efteem him myfelf, nor commend him to others;

others; though my work be to trumpet aloud his praise, and be an under suiter to gain the bride's consent to the lovely bridegroom, I can do nothing in it, and little can angels do in it to any purpose: Yet, I can tell this unto all, that my Master infinitely passeth my commendations; he is so excellent, that it would but be an obscuring his excellency, for me to babble about it.

O right honourable and dear friends, are ye not longing for the full enjoyment of him, looking out for the breaking of the day, and the flying away of the shadows, that ye may no more see him darkly as through a glass, but may behold him as he is, and enjoy him perfectly and constantly? This, O this! what a happiness is this? and what shall I say more? for ye know more of him than I can tell you; and all that I can say is but, as it were, to bring you to remembrance. I thank God on your behalf, that your zeal is heard of in many places: ye have become companions with us in our afflictions; your sympathy with this persecuted party is evident to us all, and we hear that we have a great room in your prayers. Man cannot repay your kindness to us, but I know ye look not to man in it, but do it out of love to the Lord, for ye have no outward encouragement to it. O that the Lord who hath joined together, a few in *Lewarden,* and a party in *Scotland,* in such oneness of mind and affection, may, when he returns to us again, join *Scotland* and *Friesland* in covenant together, to serve the Lord their God. And ye, O beloved, grow in grace, and endure to the end. I doubt not but ye have laid your all at Christ's feet. O take nothing back again: Be resolute in his cause, and

and valiant in his matters; when his kingdom is
so low, let him want none of your help that is
competent for you, and he shall help you; own
him, and he will own you; stand with him, and
he will stand with you, and make you victorious;
whoever shall fight against you, ye shall overcome: It is good fighting in Christ's camp, for
all his soldiers shall certainly prevail. O look to
your captain and his encouragements that ye faint
not; I apprehend that ye meet with sore blows
and bickerings; yea, I think, ye scarcely want
any conflict that we have, save only that ye are
not as yet in such hazard of your lives: But, as
nothing more than this doth endear you unto us;
so, no external condition will more draw out
God's heart towards you. But, this I will say, be
well resolved against whatever man can do unto
you.   I think, no Christian ought now to be secure, the man of sin is plotting and strengthening his force what he can, and he will not be
content with part of Christ's kingdom, his aim is
at all; he stirs himself now so fast in his saddle,
that, I think, it is not long to his fall: However, many lands may look for strange plagues;
though *Britain* and *Ireland* shall be made the
center of his judgments, yet his indignation shall
not be contained within their limits: O judgments! sudden and sore wasteing judgments are
coming on *Britain* and *Ireland;* Christ mounted
on the red horse of severity will ride through the
breadth and length of thir lands. The appearance of some parties did so fill me with temporal
expectations, but they did not make some change
their thoughts. As they knew little of God's
way, who looked for such good from such hands;
so I thought them fools who conjectured, that a
de-

delivery should come before a desolation. I say again, be well resolved against what man can do unto you; for, there are no moe Christians than there are martyrs in resolution and affection: *The kingdom of heaven must be taken by violence, and the violent take it by force;* and the moe and greater difficulties be in the way, a right sight of the kingdom makes the way the more pleasant. O fear not difficulties; for, many trials, that, when looked upon at a distance, seem big, and mounting, yet when they and you meet, ye shall find them nothing. If I could commend any thing beside Christ, it would be the cross of Christ: These things which make carnal onlookers think my condition hard and miserable, make me think it sweet and pleasant; I have found hazards, reproaches, contempt, weariness, cold, night-wanderings, stormy tempests, and desarts so desirable, that it is a greater difficulty to me, not to be ambitious of these things, than to submit unto them. O rejoice in the cross, for it is all paved with love; the fewer that will bear it, it is your greater honour to be friends to it. Follow Christ with the cross upon your backs, and set none else before you as your leader, for man is a poor fallible changeable creature; let it be your care not to fall upon the stumbling-blocks cast in your way. Wo to the world because of offences: Though ye have your own share of the revilings of this time, yet be not reproached with reproachers; though the sourness of others grieve you, yet let it not infect you; and let zeal be accompanied with meekness, that ye may be free from passion and prejudice; and let meekness be backed with zeal, that ye may be free of lukewarmess and indifferency;

ferency; let meeknefs be extended toward all perfons, and zeal againft all fin, and if ye would not lofe your ground, be pofitive againft fin in the firft propofal and motion thereof; ye will not get it fhifted by, and yourfelves kept free of it by huting yourfelves, and not appearing freely againft it, though there may an unwillingnefs unto it. I conceive, *Aaron* had no will to make the golden calf, and he thought to have put it out of the *Ifraelites* minds, by biding them break off their golden ear-rings, and bring them unto him; but this fimple fhift would not do it, the faint of God is pitifully enfnared; and if he was fimple in oppofing that abomination, he got as filly an excufe for himfelf; it would not have been thought that a child would have faid, *there came out this calf.*

Now, commit your caufe unto the Lord, for judgment and righteoufnefs fhall yet meet toge-ther again upon the earth: He is interefted in his own work, and therefore he can neither for-get it nor forfake it; and fuch as wait for him fhall never be put to fhame. But, O long and cry for his appearance, that he may right wrongs, and rule for himfelf and claim his own right of poffeffion; that the promifed day may come, that this fhall be voiced along the heavens, *The kingdoms of the earth are become the kingdoms of our Lord, and of his Chrift :* He is bufy in order to this; he is carrying on a difcovery of all forts of folk, enemies and others. I thought his dif-covery had been near through in *Scotland* before this, but he lets me fee myfelf a fool for fo judg-ing; he fees many things to be difcovered that man fees not : but happy are they who are fincere

cere and intire; they need not fear, for *when they are tried, they shall come forth as gold.*

Now, as to our present case, I wot not well what to say anent it, there are so many mercies and judgments in it to be spoken of. God hath taken this last year many from us, by banishment, and by death on scaffolds, especially on the fields, where none (for the most part) were to see them die, but the executioners; and yet God fills up their rooms again : neither are these things permitted to damp such as are left. Some have, which is more sad, fallen off from us; and yet God is filling up their places also, and making others more stedfast ; and notwithstanding both of persecutions and reproaches, the Lord hath opened doors for me in several places of *Scotland,* where there used to be no such access before, and hath multiplied my work so upon my hands, (I speak it to his praise) that I have observed my work, I say, to be now in some shires threefold, and, in some, fourfold more than it was. O that God would send forth labourers, there seems to be much ado in *Scotland* with them : Also, it is almost incredible, to tell what zeal, what tenderness, what painfulness in duty, what circumspectness of walk, in many young ones of ten, eleven, twelve and fourteen years of age, in many places of *Scotland*; which I look upon as one of the visible and greatest tokens for good that we have.

But, right honourable and dearly beloved, not to detain you further, I acknowledge myself your debtor while I live, for your many prayers put up for this poor distressed church, whereof I know I have had a share; for your sympathy and kindness otherways manifested to us; for
your

your care of that family with you, wherein we are all concerned; and particularly for your encouraging, ftrengthning of, and kindnefs to my dear and worthy friend, our right honourable delegate. I blefs the Lord who hath given you zeal for himfelf, and hath helped you to ftand with a poor defpifed party in making ftours for his intereft. I commend you to him, that he may make his rich grace abound in you; that he may perfect what concerns you, and make you perfevere unto the end, and himfelf be your exceeding rich reward. I hope I need not defire you to pray for me. I am,

Honourable and dearly beloved,

Your obliged friend, and

obedient fervant in the Lord,

JAMES RENWICK.

LETTER XL.

From the Rev. Mr. James Renwick, to the honourable Mr. Robert Hamilton.

Honourable and dear Sir,　　*May 3. 1686.*

I Have feen your letter to your dear and worthy fifters: as it fpeaks forth your fore bickerings and hot rencounters, it maketh me fad; but again I rejoice that your lot is fquared out fo like the cafe of the Lord's work this day. O though your travels be through many deeps, and the floods feem to be waxing upon you, yet

when

when your feet shall be established upon *Canaan's*
banks, you shall forget the same; though now
you be standing in the swellings of *Jordan*, yet
these shall away from you, and you shall be lifted up, and be set before the throne of the Lamb
of God cloathed with the robes of righteousness,
crowned with the crown of glory; with the palm
of victory and triumph in your hand; with the
song of *Moses* and of the Lamb in your mouth,
singing hallelujahs for ever and ever. O what
will you think of yourself then? O what will you
think of that posture? Let your eyes be still upon these, and glory in your present tribulation;
rejoice in your light affliction which is but for a
moment; count your antagonists your greatest
friends, for what are they doing by all the storms
they raise against you, but contributing to the
mass of your glory? O fear them not, but keep
your Captain-general upon your right hand, and
then cry to them to shoot their fill. I had written to your Honour far sooner, but as my work
keepeth me busy, so much of it lies in the re-
mote corners of the land, as *Galloway*, *Nithf-
dale*, *Anandale*, &c. I have not been near *E-
dinburgh* since the 16th of *October*, 1685, and I
have travelled since through *Clydefdale*, *Efkdale*,
some of the *Forreft*, *Annandale*, some of *Galloway*,
Kyle and *Cunningham;* and all these ways I examined the societies as I passed through, several
other persons coming to hear, and I found my
work greater this last journey than ever before;
also in lower *Cunningham*, where there had never been any field-preachings, I got kindly acceptance, and great multitudes came to hear;
and I have had several calls since from that coun-
try-side; such like have I found throgh *Ren-*

frew. Moreover, the Lord hath wrought a great change upon the barony of *Sanquhar,* the parish of *Kirkconnel,* and these dark corners ; generally they come to hear the gospel, and are quitting many of the defections of the time; yea, I may say (to the Lord's praise) that our meetings were never so numerous, and the work did never thrive more than since man opposed it so much. As for Mr. *Langlands* and my agreeing, there is little appearance of it ; for I am where I was, and he is rather further off than nearer hand. As for disowning the *Lanerk* Declaration, I think, you look upon it as so false, that I need say nothing ; and as for the ministers, they wot not what to do anent us, for, so far as I can know, they cannot two of them agree (for the most part) intent upon one thing. I heard of none of them coming forth to the country yet, but Mr. *Langlands* and Mr. *Alcorn,* and they travelled through some of *Kyle,* through *Carrick,* and some of the Shire of *Galloway,* and some of *Clydesdale,* and their preachings were kept, in a great measure, obscure. And as for such as are gone off from us, they are the most bitter against us. *Alexander Gordon* went into the *Bass* and *Blackness* with an information against us, containing many charges, wherewith, I hear, the ministers of *Edinburgh* are displeased, he having done it without their advice : Howbeit, we have written about six sheets of paper in answer to it, and we are to meet within two days about the concluding upon it ; however we will do nothing in it rashly, for every word in such a matter ought to be well weighed and considered. But there are none gone off from us, but these who at that party's appearance in Summer, went off: also, we have

had

had some conference with some of these, an account whereof I shall send you with some other papers. I have written a letter to the sweet societies at *Lewarden*, and will send it with the rest of the papers, and some other letters that I am to write: Moreover, I thought fit to acquaint you, that M. S. hath a purpose to go over again to *Groningen*; I desire you may be concerned with it, and lay it out before the Lord. O dear Sir, cry, cry for labourers to God's vineyard in *Scotland*, for I cannot express how much need there is of them, great is the work that is here for them. If an honest way of sending forth *T*. could be had, I would gladly have it embraced, for I do not dread the young man, he is not of a dangerous spirit; O lay it out before the Lord.

Now, go on resolutely in the strength of our God, and regard not your opposers. Hold fast what is right; but be not reviling unto a reviler, nor scoffing unto a scoffer; let zeal and meekness be your companions, the one in your one hand, and the other in your other hand, and wait on the Lord, and he shall give testimony for you.

Now, my love to the honourable sweet society, your dear sister, and all the sweet family. I am,

Honourable and dear Sir,

Yours, as formerly,

JAMES RENWICK.

L E T T E R XLI.

From the Rev. Mr. James Renwick, *to the ho-*
nourable Ladies Van. Heerm. *at* Lewarden.

May 8. 1686.

Right hon. Ladies, dearly beloved in the Lord.

MUltiplied confufions, and not forgetfulnefs
of you, have fo long hindered my writing
unto you; but being confident of your conftruct-
ing favourably of me as to this, I fhall add no
more for my own apology, and what elfe can I
fay which ye know not? Ye have learned both
from the Bible and experience, that the Chriftian's travel to the kingdom, is through much tribulation; and I hope, ye have laid your account,
for all that can come in your way: Our natures.
would have the way fo fquared as we might travel
without a rub, but it lieth thro'many a rencounter;
we would have it through a valley of rofes, but it
lieth through a valley of tears; we would have
it fo as to be travelled fleeping, but it muft be
travelled waking, and watching, and fighting;
we would have it to be travelled with laughing,
but it muft be travelled with weeping. But whatever folks do think, when great neceffity for,
and advantage by every difficulty is feen, the
more that they meet with, the way is the more
pleafant to the believers; and a fight of the recompence of reward maketh bold and refolute
to pafs through every oppofition: If they were
poffible, ten thoufand deaths, ten thoufand hells,
would feem nothing to a foul, who gets a fight
of Chrift at the other fide of all thefe. O Chrift
is

is precious, Chrift is your up-making. O what think ye of that noble exchange, to embrace Chrift entirely, and quit felf entirely? is not that receiving new wares for old? is not that a receiving of gold, yea, of gold more precious than the gold of *Sheba*, and a quitting of duft more vile than the duft of the earth? O lovely foul that hath embraced lovely Chrift, rich and happy that hath embraced precious Chrift! but wo unto them that would divide him, and not take him in all his offices; for they have not yet learned him: Wo unto them that think that they have no need of Chrift; for they know not themfelves: Wo to them that think they can clofe with him when they pleafe; for they are ignorant of grace: Wo to them that would have Chrift and their own fomething befide; for they have neither loved nor conceived rightly of him; Wo to them that make excufe for their not following of him; for they know not their folly; Wo to them that will not clofe with all the croffes and the inconveniences that they may meet with for Chrift; for they are rebellious fools that look only to the coft, and not to the advantages of religion; they fear at it, and give this anfwer to Chrift's call, His fayings are hard, and who can bear them? but none do account fo of His yoke, but they who have not taken it on; for it *is eafy, and his burden is light*. And thefe who will not believe his word for it, nor the experience of many faints and martyrs, let them take a trial of it themfelves, and if they get leave to weary, let them caft it off again: But, I am fure, there was never one that fully engaged with him that ever could find a heart to quit him again. O! that folks would not ftand at fuch a diftance, but come near and take a view of him, and they would fee that which would inevitably win their hearts. There are two things at which I cannot wonder enough; and thefe are, the invaluablenefs of Chrift, and the low value which the children of men put upon him; *Judas* fold him for thirty pieces of filver, but many now a-days fell him for lefs; and though they could get ten thoufand worlds for him, they but make a mad and foolifh bargain, who would quit him for thefe! Yea, fuppofe that it were poffible that one perfon could poffefs ten thoufand worlds, and that ever-laftingly, they could not have, in the ufe thereof, fo much contentment by far, as the fmalleft part of Chrift can give; yea, one half hour's enjoy-ment of him would far furpafs all the fatisfaction in the fuppofed cafe. O then! what muft the eternal and full enjoyment of him be!

Now, dearly beloved, ye who have made choice of Chrift, what think ye of your choice? O! ad-mire his excellency, and wonder at your own happinefs; and bend all your love towards him, who hath made you fo happy: feek to fhed a-broad the favour of his fweet ointments, by a holy and fpiritual walk; and improve difpenfa-tions to his glory, and your own good; and lean upon him in your travel through the wildernefs; and though there be fiery ferpents and drought in it, yet folace yourfelves with his company, who hath faid, that *he will never leave you, nor forfake you.* Regard not loffes, regard not re-proaches, for he is your exceeding rich reward. I doubt not but you meet with your own mea-fure of reproaches and contempt at the hands of this generation, for the great kindnefs you have fhown to a wounded and wronged wreftling

party in the furnace of affliction. But as this
doth endear our affections unto you so much the
more; so, I hope, you are better fixed than
that should prove a stumbling-block unto you.
The parties that we have to contend with, discover so much of a spirit of lying and prejudice,
for the most part of them, that none of tenderness, who know them, will be in great hazard
to be taken away with them. I am confident
God will stain their pride, and silence their boast-
ing, and that in a sudden: I may say, I am sorry for what I see coming upon them. But, O
worthy Ladies, keep ye near God, and go on
in your zeal, and persist in your stedfastness, and
in the close of the day ye shall be made to rejoice.

Now, I cannot express how much we are o-
bliged unto you, for your tender care of our family that is with you, and the great encouragement that ye are to our dear and honourable
delegate: the Lord be your reward, and keep
not back his hand from helping you in the time
of your need.

No more at the time, but, taking my leave
of you in the words of the Apostle. 1 *Cor.* xvi.
23, 24. *The grace of our Lord Jesus Christ be*
with you. My love be with you all in Christ Je-
sus. I am,

Right honourable Ladies,

Your assured and obliged friend

and servant in our sweet Lord,

JAMES RENWICK.

LETTER XLII.

From the Rev. Mr. James Renwick, *to the right honourable lady* E. B.

Right honourable Lady,   May 13. 1686.

DEarly beloved in the Lord, my insufficiency being in part known to me, doth make me stand in awe to write to you; but if I had the tongue of the learned, and the pen of a ready writer, I would imploy them both in speaking well of the name of Christ, and commending his way. O! his name is as ointment poured forth; and whoso gets a smell thereof cannot but love him; and his way is so lovely, that a poor soul that once gets his foot upon it, and the eye looking forward, cannot but chuse to trade in these paths, though rubs and crosses from enemies, both from within and without, should be never so multiplied: and no wonder, for when the children of God begin by grace to turn their backs upon their old lovers, and to shake off their weights, they get in hand the hundred-fold, ten thousand times told, and are made to say, as *Psal.* iv. 7. *Thou hast put gladness in my heart, more than in the time that their corn and their wine increased.* Many a time I think they can have no pleasant life who have not the Christian's life; whatever the world think, yet the believer gets that in time, which may sufficiently engage him to go through, if it were possible, a thousand deaths in obedience to the Lord. O then! since the imperfect and inconstant enjoyment of Christ is such a thing, what muſt the full and eternal enjoyment of him be! Of this it may be ſaid, *Eye hath not ſeen, nor ear heard, neither hath it entered into the heart of man to conceive, the things which God hath prepared for them that love him.* The believer cannot but have a happy life, when they have four things which the ſcripture calls precious, viz. The precious redemption of the ſoul, a precious faith, a precious Chriſt, and precious promiſes; and the redemption of the ſoul which is precious, is by a precious faith, laying hold on a precious Chriſt, held forth in precious promiſes. But when their happineſs ſhall be completed, than faith ſhall evaniſh into ſight, by the entire fulfilling of the promiſes, and the ſoul be drowned in the bottomleſs ocean of the love of precious Chriſt, and burſting up with love, continually flaming toward him again. O what a life muſt a life of love be? and what inconceivable joy will it yield? Chriſt will rejoice over his own ſpouſe when he hath taken her home to his own houſe, made with his own hand, and clothes her with robes of his own making, and entertains her with a banquet of his own dreſſing; and the invitation-word of the giver of that banquet will be this, *Song* v. 1. *Eat, O friends; drink, yea, drink abundantly, O beloved:* and that table will never be drawn, and the dainties will never wear taſteleſs; for, as our Lord ſaith, *Matth.* xxvi. 29. the *wine* there *is new,* and it never groweth old; and his ſpouſe's ſtomach will never ſuffocate, nor her appetite be ſatisfied; ſo, in heaven there is a continual eating and drinking, and a continual hungering and thirſting; a continual reſting, and yet a never reſting: Then ſhall the ſpouſe rejoice in her huſband:

husband : all her love shall be bended toward
him, and her joy shall arise from her enjoying
him ; her love shall be full and constant, not admitting of intermissions or variableness ; her joy
full and perpetual, not admitting of defect or
changeableness : and that which is a great part
of the Christian's exercise here, to wit, their
doubting of Christ's love, and their complaining
of coldrifeness of love to him again, shall then
be wholly removed ; and instead of grief, at least
mixtures of sorrow with their joy, they shall then
have inconceivable joy : And is not Christ fully
enjoyed, a match to love, and a prize to rejoice
in ? Now, long for this, and seek after the a-
biding assurance of Christ's love, and more and
more love-communications thereof in your heart,
until you arrive at this; and separate yourself
more and more from every unclean thing, that
cannot enter the gates of the city, where all this
is to be enjoyed : and seeing such rich upmaking
is to be had in Christ, especially seeing he is so
worthy, regard not what you may be called to
undergo in your owning of him. I hope ye have
studied to let yourself, your name, your enjoyments, and your all, ly at Christ's feet ; so as
ye can say of these, they are not your own ; and
the more ye do prove that they are his, by his
calling for them, and making use of them, the
more of his love he evidenceth towards you,
and the more honour he putteth upon you ; and
I think, men and women are for no use, but so
far as they are for Christ : and whatever errands
he calls you to run, fear not skaith nor hazard,
for it is he that rideth these ways upon you, and
so ye shall not stumble : for he hath promised,
Psal. cxxi. 3. *He shall not suffer thy foot to be
moved.*

oved. Let the low state of the church of *cotland,* and the dangerous cafe of the church *n* other lands, ly near your heart; for ah! we *nay* fay at this day, *The houfe of David is waxing weaker and weaker, and the houfe of aul waxing ftronger and ftronger.* I fear a fad *nd* general ftroke before it be better with the *hurches,* for few are valiant for the truth upon *he* earth; and nothing brings a church more *ow,* and a readier deftruction upon a land, than *egardleffnefs* of Chrift's matters, and filly and *nameful* flipping from them; and this is that *ihich* hath occafioned our breaches, and bred *ll* our divifions in this church : and becaufe fome *f our* worthies in our day, who have gone be-*ore* us, have been honoured and helped to hold *ihat* our worthy fathers did conquer with their *lood,* and bind over upon us by holy covenants, *nd* we are endeavouring to do the fame, they *nd* we have been reproached as followers of *new* ways; but *wifdom fhall be juftified of her hildren:* and feeing our way-marks in the fcrip-*ures,* and our never to be forgotten reformation, *nd* the cloud of witneffes walking in the fame *iaths,* we are not to regard much what men *ay;* but it were good for our reproachers to be *ober,* for a little time will filence their boaft-*ng,* and make them change their thoughts, *ihen* they fhall not get fpace to amend them.

Now, dear and worthy Lady, I cannot ex-*nrefs* my fenfe that I even have of the many *nbligations* which we all ftand under unto you, *or* your bowels have not been fhut up, nor your *iands* fhortened towards us; for your benefices *owards* us in this land, and thefe of us who are *imongft* you, have been large indeed; but we
are

are not so refreshed with what we enjoy thereby, as that these things are demonstrations of your love to God, and respect to his work. And what further shall I say, but go on in the way and strength of the Lord; be watchful, diligent, and spiritual; grow in grace, and persevere therein to the end. The God of all peace be with you. I am,

Right honourable Lady,

Your assured friend, and

obliged servant in the Lord,

JAMES RENWICK.

LETTER XLIII.

From the Rev. Mr. James Renwick, *to the ho-nourable Mr.* Robert Hamilton.

ı *Hon. and dear Sir,*   May 22. 1686.

I Have written to you a brief account of our af-fairs in another letter, but I know not if it be away yet; howbeit, I hope, it shall come to your hand; therefore, I shall now be the more short in what I have to say. As for news, they are not many amongst us: Only *York* hath writ-ten to his parliament for a liberty to the Papists, commending them, in his own way, very highly, as these who have been faithful to the crown upon all hazards; so the parliamentarians are consulting about rescinding the penal statutes a-gainst Papists, but are not like intirely to agree

about

about the fame; however, they have written back, that they will yield fo far to his defire in that, as their confciences will allow; and have offered a bond themfelves to oppofe all who may rife againft him upon any pretext whatfomever. But a great many folk are gaping for a diffention between the Popifh and Prelatic parties; which if it be, there will be an uncouth hotch-potch, for the moft part of old traders (to-wit *Argyle's* party) will ftrike in with the latter. *Kerfland* and Mr. *Boyd* were both of fome purpofe to go to *Holland* when I laft parted with them, but as to the time I am uncertain.

In my other letter I fpoke of fending you fome papers; but now, the fhortnefs of time will not allow me to get them tranfcribed, but I purpofe to do it afterwards. Alfo there is a rude draught of a vindication fix fheets long or thereabouts, drawn up chiefly by Mr. *B.* in anfwer to what charges are caft upon us; in which are many things very ufeful. However, as it is not likely to have paffage for the *Linning*, I durft not propofe it to friends that they fhould fend for it without being ftampt (*i. e.* Mr *Linning's* ordination) but this is my humble advice unto you, that if you can get it ftamped, and think that it will do good fervice, to effay it; and if you have any exceptions againft the ftamping of it, our merchants will not prefs for it; but if you have no exceptions, but only fears, which may fay fomething to yourfelf, but would not bear weight before men, then I would have thefe no more fpoken of than neceffity calls for, and not made mention of in the *Linning's* not being ftamped. Alfo, it will be fitter that you propofe to our merchants the fending for the *Linning*

M

than

than I, becaufe I am rather for wreftling under a
heavy burden, than to have an ill neighbour:
Some apprehend that I am for no help at all,
but it would be moft fit that the *Limming* fhould
fpeak, and fignify to our merchants the cafe, and
fo you and I both fhould come under the lefs
fufpicion, for we have a ftrange generation to
deal with. And as for *K*. his carriage here, fo
far as we can learn, he feems not to defign the
introducing of other parties, for he neither
fpeaks nor acts in their favours; as for your Honour, I can hear of nothing that he fpeaks againft
you, relative to the public caufe; but to fome he
hath faid, that ye have not carried right towards
their family : and as for Mr. *Flint* he is married
by *Tho. Ruffel* to one Mrs. *Moor*, who had been
one with *J. Gib*. Now, to be free with you about
your letter, it hath indeed gained the end of it,
in clearing you of what ye were charged with,
and fatisfied friends as to that; but many take it
very ill; fome faying, that it hath too much
bitternefs towards the antagonifts, and adduceth
perfonal failings. And fome, that it infinuates
too much of a commendation of yourfelf, holding forth that you are almoft alone in all your
actions; and fome, that it feemed to flatter this
party by too much commending of them; but,
for mine own part, I could take it all in good
part, and not mifconftruct your intentions; but
what you write to the whole, I would have you
fo to write as to men, fome of whom may be
your greateft reproachers the next day, and fo
may be feeking all imaginable advantages againft
you. But let the world fay what they will, I
muft fay this, and I fay it without vanity or flattery, that a little of *Robert Hamilton*'s fpirit in
fuch

ſuch a day as this, is very much worth. Alſo, I think fit to intimate unto you my purpoſe of reſcribing my teſtimony; not that I am refiling from any article thereof, but that I would have the ſame wiſelier, and yet as plainly and freely expreſſed, and more confirmed and corroborated; and alſo my mind anent ſome other exigences and controverſies inſerted: Moreover, I know not a man under whoſe name and patrociny I would commend it to following generations, but to deſpiſed, and yet much honoured *Robert Hamilton.*

Now, I ſhall ſay no more; Only, take ſuch a wiſe way with foreigners, as truth may get no loſs, and they kept as much upon your ſide as can be; for they come under another conſideration than theſe that are under the ſame bond of a covenant with ourſelves, and have the ſame word of teſtimony, and whoſe profeſſion imports not an oppoſite party, ſuch as Independents, Anabaptiſts, &c.

So, Worthy and dear Sir, go on in the name and ſtrength of your God, and quit not your confidence, though probability be againſt you, for it is a changeable rule; and theſe who win not to judge by another rule, I never look for ſtedfaſtneſs at their hand; and wait upon the Lord, who will guide all matters aright, and brings forth advantage to his work out of every oppoſition, and that, as univerſal as the oppoſition hath been made. Pray for him, who is,

Your Honour's moſt endeared friend,

and ſervant in the Lord,

JAMES RENWICK.

LETTER XLIV.

From the Rev. Mr. James Renwick, *to the hó-nourable Mr.* Robert Hamilton.

Hon. and dear Sir,   *Aug.* 13. 1686.

I Have not many news to write to you at this
time ; yet I thought it my duty to acquaint
you with some things. Our condition is in some
measure changed in this respect ; the enemies
for this year now have not been so hotly pursuing after us as they were ; whatever it may flow
from upon the enemies part, whether from the
Popish party being so busied in their contrivance,
and other grand persecutors discourted, or from
some other thing ; yet, we are to see the Lord's
restraining hand in it, and that he *stays his rough
wind in the day of his east wind :* We being so
taken up with other things, that, I think, it shall
be a plague to the generation in making them
carnal and secure. I have been for a season in
England, where, by the good hand of the Lord,
we kept our Sabbath meetings, all except one
day, in the fields, without any disturbance, but
upon our days of the week they were kept in the
night time. And in that land, I got some difcoveries of the Sectaries ; for at one preaching,
where there were many Anabaptists hearing, because that I asserted the divine right of infant-
baptism from Scripture, clearing the same from
the testimony of some ancient authors ; they who
before had seemed to have much love and affection, would not afterwards carry civil ; and told
us that they had been always willing to do, and
had

had done for *Scottish* sufferers, and that other
Scottish ministers had not fallen upon such heads.
Such an upcast was a little troublesome unto me;
but by it I perceived, as also I exprest, that their
hospitality to *Scottish* ministers and sufferers had
both done the ministers and themselves ill, for
it stopp'd the ministers mouths from declaring the
counsel of God, and made themselves lay weight
upon such deeds, and look upon *Scottish* ministers
as so much obliged to them, that they behoved to
tolerate them: But this I say, that they that deal
freely with them, will not get long their countenance. Howbeit, at my coming away, one of
them told me, that they were resolved to collect
for me, but they were informed that I would not
accept thereof; whereupon I told, that they
were my friends that informed so rightly, for I
went not thither for necessity, neither to seek
theirs, but them: also, at the desire of friends
in *Scotland*, some of us went to converse with a
Presbyterian minister, whom we heard to be well
affected toward this party, and found him, as we
thought, to be a very humble tender man, much
exercised with that church's case, and after information, did agree with us in the word of our
testimony, only he was not so streight as to some
matters of *England* as we would desire; but it is
not to be thought strange of, considering that he
hath none, either to go before him nor with him
in these things.

And now since we came to *Scotland*, I hear
that some of these ministers, particularly Mr.
Barclay, Mr. *Langlands*, and one Mr. *Bay* are
travelling in different places through the country. I hear not tell of much breaking among
friends: But some of the other party are going

through with as grofs flanders as can be invent-
ed; for one thing they are faying, that they
can prove that I was with the Chancellor at
Edinburgh; and they moſt partly profeſs, that in
their travels they are in a continual fear of us,
that we deliver them up to the enemy.

Now, What ſhall I ſay? Our caſe is fingular;
it is matter of great concernedneſs, the Lord hath
feen that our furnace by that inquiſition and torture of the common enemies, hath not been
fearching enough, therefore he muſt carve another kind of furnace to try us better: Bleſſed are
they who ſhall come forth as gold. God will
ariſe, and diſpell theſe preſent miſts and confu-
ſions, and let it be feen what great need there
hath been of all that comes to paſs. O faith is
a brave interpreter of diſpenſations, and never
carries bad tidings.

O dear Sir, you are called forth to fail thro'
a raging and rough-fea, but truſt to your pilot,
and he will bring you to your harbour. O fear
not, he will not let the waves overwhelm you,
and the rougher the fea be, the fweeter will
your harbour be. Think not ſtrange of that
ſtumbling diſpenſation fallen out with you, for
God hath a mind to let a generation ſtumble,
whom he thinks worthy of no other thing; it
ſpeaks out anger towards us, but more anger
to them that ſtumble at it: **God** is taking pains
to purify, refine, and purge us; and he ſays he
will have a pure people in *Scotland*, elfe he ſhall
have none at all: that diſpenſation feems to be
ſo immediately from Go 's hand, that we ſhould
ſay, *It is the Lord, let him do what ſeemeth him
good:* and our ſtudy ſhould be to make a right
uſe of it.

. As

As for the papers you received from *N. N.*
sent you them, and left them unclosed, that
n his paſſage he might let ſome friends ſee
hem, eſpecially that theſe at *Newcaſtle* might
ſee them. And I deſire to know your thoughts
of the reply to Mr. *Robert Langlands*'s letter,
which I wrote, moſtly for the behoof of ſome
that ſeem to be godly and exerciſed, whoſe
affections are towards us, but through various
informations are perplexed about ſome of our
matters: ſo I laboured to take that way in it
which I thought might be moſt convincing,
and for their advantage, without truths prejudice.
And as to the vindication we are about, it is
not yet perfected; neither in it will we do any
thing rashly; and friends have concluded, that
you and I ſhall ſee it before it go forth.
And concerning Mr. *Boyd*'s buſineſs, friends (except a very few) were againſt the giving him a
teſtificate for ordination, but yet did give it;
and the occaſion of a faſt day upon his account,
was to prevent diſagreement that was like to be
amongſt friends anent his buſineſs. And as for
that affair concerning you and *J. H.* I bleſs the
Lord that he hath helped you to lay it aſide. I
think it is according to his will; and I hope
you will have much peace in it. She was with
us few days, and was pretty free with us anent
ſeveral things, particularly the trials of their
family, and their being puzzled whether or not
to come home to *Scotland*, if ſo be their brother
would not ſtay abroad; but I would not adviſe
them to one thing nor another in that. As to
your own coming home or ſtaying abroad, I
apprehend that friends would eaſily conſent to
your ſtaying, or yet call you home, but I cannot

not well advise them to either of thefe, till I
know upon what grounds to do it from yourfelf
'Tis like that you and the family both will be
neceffitate through ftraitenednefs in living in
that land to come home; but if it come to that,
I would have you acquainting me, that you
might be called, which may be a mean to ftop
the infulting of many; or if it were better to
ftay there, and if a little fupply from our hand
could keep you there, we would be content to
give it. But man's malice is fo much againft
you, that I am afraid of you in ftaying, and I
am afraid of you in your voyage hither, and I
am afraid of you in your being here: but if the
Lord bring you home, I think you and I muft
not part, till the Lord by death, or fome fignal
way, do it.

Now, dear Sir, what fhall I fay? The Lord
hath carved out your lot after a ftrange fort: O
ftudy to get good by all his difpenfations toward
you, that you may bring forth the more fruit, for
*every branch that beareth fruit, he purgeth it that
it may bring forth more fruit.* Let your burdens
all ly upon the Lord, his back is ftrong enough.
Is not his all-fufficiency your portion? Are you
not then rich enough? and what can you want?
O rejoice in reproaches, rejoice in ignominy,
rejoice in wants, in perils, and in fufferings, for
his name; the more of that you are called to
endure, the more true honour is put upon you;
and feek you the more to honour and glorify him: Fight not againft the world with the
world's weapons of the flefh, *viz.* Pride, paffion,
prejudice, lies, and contempt; but let yours be
the weapons of the fpirit, *viz.* Zeal, meeknefs,
patience, and prayer to God, that he would ei-

ther

ther pity them and heal them, elfe draw them out of the way. And whatever you write unto friends, write as unto men, who are for you to-day, and may be againſt you to-morrow.

Now, I pray that the Lord may be with you, and that poor and ſweet family; that he may give you enlargement in your diſtreſſes; and when your ſorrows abound, he may make your conſolation to ſuperabound. My love to your dear and worthy ſiſter, the ſweet children *J.* and *R.* the worthy ladies *V. Heer.* and any other of your ſtrengtheners in the Lord. I am,

Honourable and dear Sir,

Even as formerly,

JAMES RENWICK.

LETTER XLV.

From the Rev. Mr. James Renwick, *to the honourable Mr.* Robert Hamilton.

Hon. and dear Sir, Ocꞇober 23. 1686.

I Received your letters, they were very re-freſhing unto me. Your rencounters are fierce, and you ſtand in the ſtour; but I hope you look upon your condition rather to be en-vied than pitied. O can you not ſay, that the fat feaſt of a peaceable conſcience, and the en-joyment of the light of the Lord's countenance, is the hundred fold, a thouſand times told? *Light is ſown for the righteous, and gladneſs for the up-right in heart,* Pſal. xcvii. 11. O read that pſalm, pfalm, and meditate upon it; and when you mind it, remember me, for it is a golden Scripture unto me. What would you and I have more than that, *The Lord reigneth, let us rejoice: Righteousness and judgment are the habitation of his throne.* But O who can take him up? who can behold his glory? Therefore he casteth *clouds round about him: let us be glad because of his judgments. A fire goeth before him, to burn up his enemies.*

As to what you write about my testimony, I am refreshed; yet when I look back upon the frame that I was then in, I have much peace in my ingenuity, and though weakly, yet I think, it hath the right state of the cause in it, and I hope never to refile from it: Also, it, having your name, doth the more commend it unto me; and when I shall write (which I have been hitherto diverted from) it will be but an enlargement upon, and confirmation of the foresaid testimony, with reasons, together with some additions as to what hath fallen out since; and for my changing my method in dealing with parents of children to be baptized, I declare them to be misinformers who have so said unto you; for, these persons that have complied with one thing or other, I do not admit them to present their children, unless they have evidenced a right sense and practical reformation, by standing out the temptation unto these things they have been chargeable with, and their engagement to give due satisfaction when lawfully called for; or else the attestation of some acquainted with their case, that in the judgment of charity, they appear to be convinced of, and humbled for their sin, and their engagement to forbear
their

their fin, and give fatisfaction in manner forefaid. But when compliers and perfons guilty of
defection come, who have not as yet defifted
from-their offenfive courfes, I do not let them
prefent their children; neither will or do I let
other perfons prefent their children, left the parents fhould be hardened in their fin thereby,
unlefs they engage to forbear, and give fatisfaction as faid is; and fome prove true and fome
prove falfe : Further, when the parents are
guilty of very grofs compliance, even though
they have given evidences of a right fenfe thereof, I do not admit them, but another to prefent
their children, for fear of reproach, albeit I
might do it lawfully.

But, dear Sir, my difficulty upon this head is
often times very great, the different cafes of perfons puts me fometimes to a nonplus. And this
I think ftrange of, that now when the minifters
are paffing through the country, many perfons e-
ven involved in the courfes of defection fcruple
to take their children unto them. But in anfwer
to what you write concerning *Kerfl.* I know him
to be nothing the better of the company of
fome, and I refolve that he fhall be dealt with,
both freely and tenderly at the next general
meeting. And as for Mr. *Boyd,* I ufed freedom
with him, in a line, before he went away; but
the reports that I have heard of him fince I faw
him, have been both troublefome and difpleafing
unto-me : I know not upon what grounds he can
exprefs his hope of union; for I fee no way as
yet how it fhall be obtained in the Lord : yea, as
matters now ftand, I hold myfelf obliged to re-
fent that information of his, for it puts fuch as
are coming foreward to ftand ftill; and for mine

own part, though I fhould be left alone, and
branded with fingularity, while they continue as
they are, I refolve not to unite, *dum fpiritus hos
regit artus ;* and there is little hope of their growing better : Neither will Mr. *Boyd* find that party amongft us, who are inclined to hear thefe, *&c.*
fo ftrong as he expects ; but after pains for information and admonition, we fhall then fhow
how we will carry towards them. And let me
be miftaken as men pleafe, this is my ftudy
not to partake in other men's fins, neither to
cover them ; but confidering the confufions of
this time, and the weaknefs of poor people, I hold
it my duty to be a help and a prop, as I can, to
thefe that are ftaggering, and to carry fo toward
fuch as will go off, as their ftumbling neither in
law, nor in my own confcience may be charged
upon me : And this is like unto my Mafter, who
hath promifed to *fave them that halt, and gather
them that are driven out.* As for the vindication
which Mr. *B.* did let you fee, I need not fpeak
any thing, for we have altered it, and fent unto
you a tranfcript of the prefent draught, which is
not yet condefcended upon, until you and our
focieties fee it. So let it not trouble you, neither the teftificate that was granted unto him ;
for though the moft part were diffatisfied with
fome things in him, and had their jealoufies a-
nent him ; yet confidering what he left behind
him written with his own hand, and that he was
not fully difcovered, they thought that they
could not deny fuch a teftificate unto him ; but
if he fhould make a bad ufe of it againft us, he
will be a man moft ungrate, and will contradict what he hath left under his own hand a-
mongft us ; and if fo, I wifh, it had never been
granted

granted unto him. Your coufin Mrs. *J. K.* was with us fome days, and we were pretty free with her ; but you know, fhe is ordinarily referved. As for what you wrote about the laying afide of that bufinefs, I blefs the Lord that he hath helped you unto it ; for many confiderations called for it.

Now, Right honourable and comfortable Sir, I remit you to the bearer for news amongft us ; he can give you an account of my progrefs in *England*; and alfo of *Colin*'s going to *Ireland*: But I think fit to fhew you, that at the laft correfpondence, friends judged it convenient to fend one to Mr. *Thomas Douglas* to converfe with him, and know where he ftands ; (which this bearer is refolved, according to their conclufion, to fet about) When they afked my concurrence and confent, I anfwered that I could not actively concur therewith, becaufe I knew not what to expect by it ; yet I fhould not oppofe their fending any of their number to confer with him ; for I thought the thing in itfelf could not well be denied to them: And alfo, I am (with many) under the fufpicion, that I defire no help, though the perfons were never fo right ; whereas, the Lord is my witnefs, it would be my greateft rejoicing this day, to have fome minifters to concur with me ; for it would be a great advantage to the work, and a great eafe to me ; for, notwithftanding of all breakings, my bufinefs multiplies ftill upon my hand, and people are more earneft now than ever I knew them after the gofpel: O that the Lord would fend forth labourers. As for this bearer, I am glad that he hath come unto you, for he hath his own diffatisfaction with you, whereupon he and I have had fome

hicker-

bickerings; but I do not know him to vent himfelf to your prejudice: Alfo he is very honeft toward the caufe, and fingularly ufeful; therefore
you may be free with, and tender of him, for I
expect he will be free with you.

Now, Dear and honourable Sir, being in hafte,
and alfo difturbed yefternight from writing, by
an alarm of the enemy, I fhall add no further;
but defires to know your mind anent a particular,
which is like to break us more than any thing
that the minifters can do; and it is, the joining
of children, fervants and others in the family-
exercife of their parents, mafters and others
who are compliers. Thus committing you, your
fifter and the fweet family unto the Lord. I am,

Honourable and dear Sir,

Ever as formerly,

JAMES RENWICK.

L E T T E R XLVI.

From the Rev. Mr. James Renwick, *to* ———

Hon. and dear Sir,   *Jan.* 10. 1687.

I Received yours, and am greatly refrefhed with
it, both in refpect of its coming from you,
and in refpect of the ftrain of it; for I perceive
in it a zeal for the right carrying of the ark of
God through this howling wildernefs: it would
be matter of my joy to obferve this fpirit in any
who beareth the ark, and in all who profefs to
follow it; for I am perfuaded, that the wrong way

of

of bearing and handling the ark, will keep it longer in the wildernefs, but will never carry it thro' *Jordan* and fettle it in the land of *Canaan*: And for mine own part, I fee it fo difficult a thing to move one ftep rightly forward with it, that I am in a continual fear anent what I do; and I wifh, I were more in the exercife of that fear, for it would put me to look more unto the Lord, whom I defire and aim to fet befcre mine eyes at all times; and if I fhall give the ark a wrong touch, I may fay (fo far as I can fee into mine own heart) it will be through blindnefs and not thro' byaffedneft. O to be framed for the work of the day; for there is none fit for it but fuch as have honeft hearts, ingenious fpirits, and the faces of lions; they will be ftrange fort of folk whom the Lord will make any fingular ufe of. As for the cafe of our focieties, am I in fome confternation of fpirit when I reflect upon it: There are a choice handful amongft them, whom I hope, the Lord will not forfake; but fome are not fo fixed and refolute as they ought to be, and others, I fear, have little principle, but follow example; and feverals little exercifed with their foul's cafes; and the Lord is hiding his face in fome meafure from the whole, which fome are fenfible of, and groaning under: Wherefore, I look for a mcre narrow fieve yet to go through us, and that the Lord will lay by many: O that fanning and winnowing that is coming! but the leaft good grain fhall not fall to the ground. Yea, I do not look that the Lord's work fhall be delivered till this generation of his wrath be hurled out of the way; and I think, they are blind who fee not a defolation coming upon the land: *In mine ears faid the Lord of hofts, Of a truth many houfes fhall be defolate,*

folate, even great and fair without inhabitant;
Iſa. v. 9. But *he that is left in Zion, and he that
remaineth in Jeruſalem, ſhall be called holy, even
every one that is written among the living in Jeruſalem;* Iſa. iv. 3. And for mine own part, I apprehend, that that dark hour is now very near
hand, which ſhall come upon the church before
the fall of Antichriſt, and the Lord's glorious appearing for his church, which ſhall be in the laſt
days. O bleſſed ſhall they be who wait for the
Lord *in the way of his judgments,* and who are of
the righteous nation which keep the truth, for the
gates ſhall be opened unto them, *Iſa.* xxvi. 2. 8.
I am,

Your honour's ſympathiſing friend

and ſervant in the Lord,

JAMES RENWICK.

LETTER XLVII.

From the Rev. Mr. James Renwick, *to the
honourable Mr.* Robert Hamilton.

Hon. and dear Sir,   *Jan.* 11. 1687.

I Conceive it is both to your loſs and our loſs,
yea, to the diſadvantage of the cauſe, that
you hear ſo ſeldom from us, and how matters are
amongſt us; but for my part, I cannot help it;
having always ſuch throng of weighty buſineſs,
continual travel through many a vaſt wilderneſs,
and ſometimes bad accommodation; ſo that it is
a rare thing for me to get a ſpare hour.

How-

However, confidering the importance of what was done at the laft general meeting, I judge it neceffary to give you a true account thereof. There came two minifters to the laft meeting *December* 22. 1686. *viz.* Mr. *David Houfton*, and Mr. *Alexander Shields*. But I fhall firft give you an account of our carrying toward the faid Mr. *David*, and toward the forefaid Mr *Alexander*. When I was in *England* the laft Summer, the general meeting of our focieties being in-formed that Mr. *David Houfton* refufed concurrence with, and fubjection to the minifters in *Ireland* becaufe of their defections, and that he preached faithfully againft all the fins of the times, did fend unto him *Colin Alifon* and *William Nairn* to know the verity thereof; who after full and free communing with the faid Mr. *David* anent all the heads of our prefent teftimony, received great fatisfaction; who alfo fignified unto them his refolution of coming unto us. But before we fent any unto him again, we did convocate all our friends who had been living any time in *Ireland*, and now come over to us, that we might inform ourfelves anent what they knew of the faid Mr. *David*, who could not relate any difference in his principles from us, but gave in fome accufation againft him which they had but by report, and were all *perfonalia*: All which accufations were drawn up and delivered to *James Boyle*, who was fent to *Ireland* to get the verity or falfehood of every one of thefe things inftructed, and finding them to be but calumnies, to conduct the forefaid Mr. *David* to us, according to his own refolution. So the faid *James* laying out fearch for information anent thefe reports, conferring with fome of Mr. *David's* ac-

cufers, bringing him and fome of them face to
face; likewife conferring with fome of his neighbours and ordinary hearers, and finding no
ground for the forefaid accufations, did conduct
Mr. *David* unto us, that we might fatisfy ourfelves anent him in a free communing with
himfelf.

Wherefore, Mr. *David* came to our laft general meeting, which was upon *December* 22. 1686.
being accompanied with one *James Kinloch*, who
was particularly fent by fome focieties in *Ireland*
to our correfpondence, and who alfo teftified before us all for Mr. *David's* honefty and innocency of the forefaid alledgances, after which,
we did read over in Mr. *David"s* hearing, the introduction to our vindication, wherein are fum-
marily comprehended fome fignal fteps of our
churches defection, and a brief declaration of
our prefent teftimony, both as to what we own
and difown, together with the fifth head of the
fame vindication, containing (among other things)
ten grounds, every one of which, we judge fufficient for withdrawing from minifters of this covenanted and reformed church, to whom they are
applicable in this broken and declining ftate:
and then we afked Mr. *David's* judgment of what
he had heard, and whether or no he was of one
mind with us as to every part of our prefent teftimony. To which he replied, that as to fome
matters of fact he was ignorant, but he agreed
with our judgment and principles in all that he
had heard, adding, that it was foretold by *Luther*, That before Chrift's glorious appearance
for his church in the laft days, the controverfy
fhould be ftated and rid about miniftry and magiftracy. So Mr. *David* being defired to remove,
we

we gave in our minds about his anſwer, and it was ſuſtained as ſatisfying in that point. After this, we conſulted among ourſelves what was further neceſſary to deſire for our further ſatisfaction anent him; and having heard from himſelf, that he had ſome papers with him which could tend to our information and clearing, concerning his carriage for many years; we called him to us again, and deſired to hear theſe papers. So, there was read in our hearing, firſt his licence, then his ordination, which was to the pariſh of *Straſtrie*, a little before the Reſtoration. Next (as I remember) a paper which he had drawn up himſelf, and given to the miniſters in *Ireland*, containing his reaſons wherefore he would not be ſſubordinate unto, nor concur with them, whereof their oppoſition to the ſuffering party in *Scotland* was one. Afterward were read ſome teſtificates, from the people in the reſpective places in *Ireland*, where he had exerciſed his miniſtry, ſome whereof being of a very late date, and one of them bearing, that they had been greatly refreſhed and edified with his preaching the goſpel amongſt them; but that he had denied them other privileges for reaſons ſatisfying to himſelf; by which he declared, they underſtood his refuſing to baptize their children, becauſe of their paying exactions to the enemy, and this we looked upon as the greater teſtimony. Further, we enquired how long he had kept a meeting-houſe in *Ireland*, and upon what terms; and declared the terms of his holding were not ſinful; for he was ſettled by the miniſters upon the call of the people; and whenſoever he knew of any tranſaction of the ſaid miniſters with the ſo called magiſtrate, that he forſook his meeting-houſe, and

and refused subordination to these ministers: which was a little after *Bothwel*. Moreover, he declared, and *James Kinloch* witnessed the same, that at the incoming of the associators, *Anno* 1685, he gave a plain and public testimony against that hotch-potch confederacy. Now, Mr. *David* being desired to remove again, we communed together anent what we had heard from his papers and from his own mouth, and found a great measure of satisfaction therefrom. Howbeit, to remove scruples yet further, we called him again to us, and dealt freely with him in telling him what was reported, by some, of him, desiring to hear what he would say to these things himself. All which alledgances he heard very patiently, and answered to them one by one, as they were given in, very pleasantly, and gave very demonstrating evidences of his innocency.

Now, from all the foresaids, we being in such a measure satisfied in our consciences, concerning the said Mr. *David*; our societies do both call him, and hear him preach for farther trial, whereunto I gave my consent, seeing no reason wherefore I could deny it. But he is not as yet settled amongst us as our minister by a formal and a solemn call for that effect. Howbeit, for the time, I know not of any ground that will be for excepting against it; for I hear that he preaches very zealously and faithfully whither he goes, and carries strictly in administering the sacrament of baptism. And for mine own part, from his expressing himself at our correspondence; I thought he seemed to have the right state of the cause, to have a right impression of the case of the church, to be tender-hearted and zealous in the frame of his spirit, particularly for the

royalties

royalties of Chrift, and againft the idol of the
Lord's Jealoufy, the ecclefiaftic fupremacy and
civil tyranny.

As for our carriage towards the forefaid Mr.
Alexander Shields, he having by the providence
of God made his efcape out of prifon, after a little fpace of time (without feeking after any party
of minifters againft whom we have exceptions)
came to the country, unto this contending and
fuffering party. And at length, upon the 5th of
December 1686, came to a meeting which we
had in *Galloway,* in the Wood of *Earlfton,* for
preaching; and fo going alongft with me from
thence, upon the day following, I told him, albeit I had fome fatisfaction concerning him from
what I had feen under his own hand, and albeit
I expected more by further converfe with him;
yet I thought it moft rational in itfelf, moft conducing to the prefervation of union amongft us,
and alfo according to the conclufion of our general meeting, *viz.* that nothing which concerns
the whole fhould be done without acquainting
them therewith; that the forefaid Mr. *Alexander* fhould not be employed in the public
work until he came to the general correfpondence, that all might be fatisfied anent him : which
he did take very well, and defired us to take that
method with him which we would do with any
backflidden minifter, if God fhould touch his
heart and bring him out from his defections unto the public work. Howbeit, we thought fit to
employ him fometimes to go about family exercife, not feeing any reafon why this fhould be
forborn, for thereby we might attain to more
clearnefs anent him. And indeed, in a certain
family, where fome neighbours (as is ordinary)
were

" longer contain, but I muſt confeſs unto the
" Lord before this people, I am aſhamed to of-
" fer my body a living ſacrifice to thee, yet I
" muſt do it; for I a priſoner and a preacher,
" might have been a martyr, and in glory with
" thee and thy glorified martyrs above; but
" I ſinfully and ſhamefully ſaved my life with
" diſowning thy friends and owning thy e-
" nemies; and it will be a wonder if ever thou
" put ſuch a honourable opportunity in my hand
" again." And very ſeldom did he go about exerciſe, but either in prayer, or in ſpeaking from
the ſcripture, he brake forth into heavy lamen-
tations, confeſſing particularly his defections. So,
the time of our general meeting coming, which
was *December* 22. as ſaid is, the foreſaid Mr.
Alexander came to the ſame; and we did read o-
ver in his hearing (he being preſent with Mr.
David) the introduction to our vindication,
wherein are comprehended ſome ſpecial ſteps of
our church's defection, and a brief declaration of
our preſent teſtimony, both as to what we own
and diſown; together with the fifth head of the
ſame vindication, containing, among other things,
ten grounds, every one of which we judge ſufficient for withdrawing from miniſters of this covenanted and reformed church to whom they are
applicable, in this broken and declining ſtate.
And then we aſked Mr. *Alexander*'s judgment
concerning what he had heard, and whether or
no he was of one mind with us as to every part
of our preſent teſtimony. To which he replied,

that he agreed cordially with us in all that he
had heard, and particularly in the forefaid ten
grounds, judging every one of them to bear a
folidity and fufficiency in point of withdrawing.
But, faid he, there are fome things there teftified againft, whereof I am guilty ; and I will take
a little time to unbofom myfelf unto you anent
the fame.   So he began his confeffion with fome
pre-occupying cautions; defiring that none might
think he was moved to what he was now about
to do, from the affectation of applaufe from any
man, or, that he might be in with a party (for
he knew he would not want alluring imployments
if he had freedom to embrace it) but only that
he might give God the glory, vindicate the
caufe, exonour his own confcience, and fatisfy
offended brethren : Intimating alfo, that he look
ed not upon the focieties as competent for
handling ecclefiaftic matters, and that he knew,
they did not affume the fame unto themfelves,
though they were falfely branded therewith : Yet
he held himfelf bound in duty, to declare with
forrow before them, wherein he had denied any
part of the teftimony which they did own.   Then
he proceeded to the particulars of his confeffion,
and acknowledged,

1. That he had involved himfelf in the guilt
of owning the (fo called) authority of *James* VII.
fhewing an exceeding finfulnefs in it, and taking
fhame unto himfelf.

2. He acknowledged himfelf guilty of taking
the oath of Abjuration, and of relapfing into the
fame iniquity ; the finfulnefs whereof he held
out at a great length, making it appear, that by
that oath many orthodox principles which concern us greatly to contend for, are abjured.   He
de-

declared the occasion of his being inveigled in these transgressions, was, the entering into an accommodation with the enemy; for he could propose nothing unto them but they still added and yielded to it, until they got him a silly fish catched in their angle. Howbeit, hereby (as he said) he did not extenuate or excuse his sin, for, albeit he had as much to say for himself as any man could have, who had declared in such a measure, yet he would neither stiffle his own conscience, nor blind the eyes of others; wherefore, he shewed both the sin and danger of entering upon any accommodation whatsoever with the enemy.

Now, he spoke largely to all these particulars, discovering such hainous and manifold sin therein, that, I think, none could have done it, unless they had known the terrors of the Lord: Shewing also the aggravations thereof, desiring every one to look upon their sin with the aggravating circumstances they can see in it: And he expressed so much sense and ingenuity, that none, I think, could require more of him, and I know not who would not have been satisfied as to the foresaids, who had heard him express himself so fully, so plainly, so freely, and with so much sense, grief, and self-condemning; and I thought it both singular and promising, to see a clergy-man come forth with such a confession of his own defections, when so few of that set are seen in our age to be honoured with the like.

So Mr. *Alexander* being desired to remove, we communed together about what we heard, and all declared, they found themselves satisfied as to the foresaids. After this, it was consulted amongst us, what was necessary to desire for our

further

further satisfaction anent him; and we judged it expedient to enquire how and by whom he was licensed to preach; whereupon, I having conferred with him before thereanent, gave a brief account thereof; and signified that a considerable while ago, I saw it under his own hand, that if the business of his licence were to be done yet, he would neither take it from such persons, neither would they give it him; and that of late he had said unto myself, that he knew not one of these who had granted it, that now he could concur with. However, we thought it convenient to call himself, that he might give an account thereof before us all; which he did, showing that he went to *London* with an intention to be an amanuensis to *Owen*, or some of their great doctors, who were writing books for the press, and had a letter of recommendation to one Mr. *Blackie*, a *Scottish* minister, who trysted him to speak with him a certain season, and had several ministers convened, unknown to Mr. *Alexander*, and did press and enjoin him to take licence; so, he being carried unto it in that sudden and surprising way, he accepted it from the hands of *Scottish* ministers then at *London*, but without any impositions or sinful restrictions. However, a little after, the oath of allegiance becoming the trial of that place, the foresaid Mr. *Alexander* studied, as he had occasion in preaching, plainly and satisfyingly to discover the sin of it; which was so ill taken by the ministers by whom he was licenced, that they threatened and sought to stop his mouth, but he refused to submit unto them.

Now, to this very purpose was the relation that Mr. *Alexander* himself gave. So, considering what is before related, the societies for
O
them-

themselves, and I, with the concurrence of some
elders then present, did call him to officiate in
preaching the word to the suffering remnant of
this church. Wherefore, upon the Sabbath following he and I did preach together, he having
his text 2 *Cor.* v. 11. in these words in the former part of the verse, *viz. Knowing therefore
the terror of the Lord, we persuade men.* In
which preaching, I may say, he particularly af-
serted every part of our present testimony, both
as to non-compliance with enemies, non-concur-
rence with defective parties, and disowning the
pretended authority of *James* VII.; and also doc-
trinally confessed his own particular defections;
and cryed out, that *knowing the terror of the
Lord* in these things, he *persuaded men.* And
having appointed a fast upon the *Thursday* following, I briefly drew up about the number of
forty four causes of humiliation, omitting no
piece of defection of old or of late, that I knew
or could remember, which causes he cordially
agreed with, and expressed the same publicly in
his preaching before the congregation, declaring
every one of them to be a great cause of humiliation; and confessed again his own defections, holding forth the sin thereof to be very hainous, with
much sorrow and regrete. So I find Mr. *Alexander*
to be one with us in our present testimony; I look
upon him as having the zeal of God in his spirit,
and the poor remnant have much of his heart;
and I think, the Lord is with him, and he cannot be challenged as deficient in the application
of his doctrine; and, for mine own part, I have
been refreshed with hearing of him, and have
been animated to zeal by his preaching and dif-
course.

,But

·· But there was a certain offence given by some, wherein Mr. *Alexander* was a partaker, and wherewith I was diſſatisfied, and that was their deſerting of the teſtimony which ſome eminent worthies at *Utrecht* keep up againſt Mr. *Fleming* miniſter to the *Scottiſh* congregation at *Rotterdam*, in withdrawing from him for his manifeſt ſcandal; which teſtimony I cordially (as heretofore) agree with, and look upon it (according as I know) as the firſt clear ſtating of our teſtimony in our latter times, againſt the daubers and plaiſterers of defection. Wherefore I did ſpeak with Mr. *Alexander* anent the ſame, who knows my mind well enough in that affair, and expreſſed my diſſatisfaction, and apprehended him to be ſenſible of the evils of that breach: And as we were occaſionally ſpeaking of it at another time, he called their withdrawing, their teſtimony againſt Mr. *Fleming*. Howbeit, conſidering Mr. *Alexander*'s partaking in the foreſaid offence being very little here known in *Scotland*, and ſo, they not being the perſons offended, conſidering his giving a practical teſtimony in that affair, by diſcountenancing the foreſaid congregation, ſuch time ſince that he hath been in *Holland*; conſidering his preſent ſtrictneſs, and cordial agreement with us in all our preſent controverſies, and not knowing how to manage that affair to the edification of the ſocieties; I ſay, upon theſe and ſuch conſiderations it was not brought before the general correſpondence.

Now, Right honourable and dear Sir, I have given you a true and full account of our carriage toward Mr. *Alexander Shields*; and if you were with him now, I think, you would ſay as much for him as I have ſaid, for he doth not carry a

mids-

mids-man betwixt us and other parties, or one
who endeavours to obfcure and caft dirt upon our
contendings, to juftle us off our feet and pervert
us from the right ways of the Lord, but hath tak-
en the defence of every part of our prefent teftimony. And when I was telling him in difcourfe
that the famous Mr. *Cameron* had faid in a fermon,
that the *Sanquhar* declaration would fhake the
throne of *Britain*; Mr. *Alexander* replied, Yea,
and the thrones of the kingdoms through the
world: And he hath a high efteem of the *Queens-*
ferry Papers, and expreffed his diffatisfaction that
they were not more valued. All which fpoke
forth his zeal and cordial agreement with the honeft ftate of the caufe; and in hearing whereof
I was not a little refrefhed. I think, the Lord
hath fuffered him to fall into the hands of enemies and fall before them, for laying him low in
humility, and raifing him up in zeal; fo, whatever come to pafs afterward, in the mean time,
I am made to look upon both Mr. *David* and his
coming forth in fuch a manner, as a mercy to
the poor church of *Scotland*, and it hath been a
mean to wipe away fome of our reproach from
among men, and to put fome dafh upon the confidence of our oppofers, who, for ought I can
hear, do look upon them both, as upon thefe
whom they judge moft obftinate among us. Howbeit, *(mi pater)* I fhall be glad to have your
thoughts anent what I have written, for I do reverence you and your judgment as much as ever.

Right honourable and comfortable Sir, I know
your bickerings are hot, and your rencounters
fierce, and thefe multiplied upon you: You are
hated and defpifed of men for your faithfulnefs
and jealoufy for your God. Yea, I am in great
fear

fear of your being in continual hazard of your life from *Scottish* men, or thro' their instigation; the consideration of all which fills my heart with sorrow, when it comes before me, and sometimes draws water from mine eyes. But again, when I remember what a fat feast you have of peace of conscience and joy in the Lord, together with what ye have in hope, I am made to rejoice in the midst of my sorrow, and to account you a blessed man. O go on in the strength of the Lord; fear not the antichristian enemies, nor all the men who are fallen in among the limbs of the whore. Grace is sufficient for you, victory is certain, and the prize waits for you.

Now, I leave the work upon him, upon whose shoulders the government is laid. I am apprehensive that the dark hour is now near hand, which will come upon the church before Christ's glorious appearance in the last days; but he will rise and make a discussion of his enemies, and who endureth to the end shall be saved. I am,

Right honourable,

Yours as formerly,

JAMES RENWICK.

P. S. I am sometimes very much exercised in my thoughts about your coming to *Scotland*; but, considering what strange things may come out of it, and what hazard you will run, I dare not be peremptor in desiring you, until I see a weighty and urgent call unto it; but if matters be so with you, as to determine positively, let me know, and a handful will call you,

O 3

who

who will be your brethren and servants in tribulation for Chrift.

JAMES RENWICK.

LETTER XLVIII.

From the Rev. Mr. James Renwick, *to the ho-*
nourable the Laird *of* Earlfton.

Hon. and dear Sir,   *Jan.* 27. 1687.

I Have not been forgetful of you, though I
have long delayed to write, and the real occafion of my fo long delay was, the throng of
bufinefs, (for having fo much to do, I being in
continual travel) together with a defigned forbearance, until I had this courfe finifhed in *Gal-*
loway, that I might give you an account of the
prefent cafe of this country. I had great accefs
in it to preach the gofpel, the Lord wonderfully
reftraining enemies, and drawing out very many
to hear, and moving them to give great outward
encouragement. We kept thirteen field-meetings, whereof four were in the day-light; and I
ftudied publickly to declare and affert in its own
place, every part of our prefent teftimony. We
had alfo nine meetings for examination of the focieties, cafting the moft adjacent together into
one meeting for that effect: And I hope, through
the Lord's blefling, that that fmall piece of labour fhall not want its fruit. But upon the other
hand, I meet with no fmall oppofition in *Gallo-*
way; I went to that fhire, and preached there;
a great many were vexed, and did their outmoft
to

to oppose it: and when I came to *Kirkmabreak*, there came two men and gave me a paper, subscribed by one in *Carrick*, in name of all therein between *Cree* and *Dee*, and also in name of the whole; which paper overturns many noble pieces of our reformation, calling hearing of curates, paying of cefs, and swearing the abjuration oath debateable principles, and above their capac:ty to determine, and bears a viperous protestation against my preaching, besides many other abfurdities in it: Which when I read, I gave my animadversions upon it before the two men: And upon the *Thursday* following, we keeping a public day meeting in the fields, between *Cree* and *Dee*, I thought fit after lecture, which was upon the xv. *Psalm*, and sermon, which was upon *Song* ii. 2. to read over the paper before the multitude, that I might let them know what was done in their names, giving my own animadversions upon the same, and exhorting them, if any such were there, who had given their countenance and concurrence to it, that they would speedily with sorrow draw back their hand from such an iniquity; and these who were free to take their protestation before the Lord that they were innocent, and did resent the doing of such a deed in their name: and withal warning them of the dangerousness of that course, and spirit of that party. Likewise, when I came to *Irongray*, *Cornlee* came unto me, and before some few, who were meeting for examination, and some others who accompanied me in my travels, took instruments against me, and against my entering into *Irongray*; whereupon I gave some weighty reasons, wherefore I could not look upon his deed as the deed of a faithful elder in that parish,

and

and cleared some controverted points of our testimony. But he was so drunk either with wine, or with the fury of the Lord, or with both, that he could hear nothing, and answer with nothing, but with clamour and crying, (the depths of Satan!) that I had destroyed the church, and that the ministers had a lible drawn up against me ; whereupon I, declaring that none of these things did terrify me, and that this was the work of the Lord, and that I was resolved, in his strength, to go on in it, while my breath governed my joints, and enjoined silence upon him. But, I think, by such an attempt that he hath done no skaith either to the work or to the owners of it.

Now, Right honourable Sir, you see some of my conflicts. I bless the Lord, none of these things terrify me : I think, they are very pusillanimous, who would not find such hot bickerings a mean to ding a spirit in them. O, that we might be such as we might say, *Isa.* viii. 9. 10. *Associate yourselves, O ye people; and ye shall be broken in pieces:—gird yourselves, and ye shall be broken in pieces. Take counsel together, and it shall come to nought ; speak the word, and it shall not stand ; for God is with us.* But further, as to the societies in *Galloway ;* there are some of them simple, whom we have much ado to keep right, do what we can: But there are some others, both in *Glenkers* and other places, whom I look upon as bows of steel in the Lord's hand ; and who, I hope, through his grace shall abide in strength.

Now, Right noble and dear Sir, I hope not to forget you, but to mind your case in my weak addresses to the Lord; I may say, you are very often brought before me ; and next to my own case

eafe, and the church's cafe, the cafe of you and
your family, they abroad, and they at home, do
ly upon my heart. Ly near the Lord and wait
upon him; who knoweth what the Lord may do
with you, and for you; he may be humbling and
polifhing you for fome great piece of work. As
to our way at our laft meeting with Mr. *David
Houfton* and Mr. *Alexander Shields*, you will fee
it in the letter directed to your worthy brother,
to whom I defire you may fend this, and the o-
ther directed for yourfelf, for his information, at
leaft fo much extracted out of this, as you think
fit, becaufe I cannot have time to write anent
the fame things unto him. I commend you to
your God, and am,

Your Honour's obliged friend,

and fervant in the Lord,

JAMES RENWICK.

LETTER XLIX.

From the Rev. Mr. James Renwick, *to the
right Reverend Mr.* Jacob Roolman, *minifter
of the gofpel in* Holland.

April 4. 1687.

Right Reverend and beloved brother,

I Received your letter in *Latin*, but knowing
that you are well verfed in the *Englifh*, I
need not write back to you in that fame language. I beg your excufe, for fo long delay of

an anſwer; for, as it was a conſiderable ſpace of time after the date of your letter, ere it came to my hand; ſo, ſince I received it, I have been in ſuch a meaſure buſied with weighty work and exceſſive travel, that ſcarcely could I borrow one hour from the one or from the other.

I thankfully accept of your miniſterial, friendly and brotherly advice unto union. So far as I can ſee into my heart (but a man cannot ſee far into a milſtone) I am as much for a right qualified union as any, and looks upon that as good and pleaſant, as *Pſal.* cxxxiii. 1.: But, the union which is had without truth and holineſs, I can call no other thing but a conſpiracy; ſuch as was found among the men of *Judah, Jer.* xi. 9. and the prophets of *Jeruſalem, Ezek.* xxii. 25. I cannot unite, where I muſt thereby harden the hearts and ſtrengthen the hands of ſuch as are engaged in, and carrying on a courſe of defection and backſliding from the Lord; and ſo partake of their ſins, and render myſelf obnoxious to their plagues. I cannot unite, where I cannot expect the propagating the words of Chriſt's patience, depoſited to us at this time to contend and ſuffer for. In reference to both caſes, in regulating my carriage toward miniſters of this organical church in this her broken and declining ſtate, I deſire to mind what is given in command to *Jeremiah, Chap.* xv. 19. *Let them return unto thee, but return not thou unto them.* I muſt not divide from the Head, to unite with any profeſſed members. But miniſters, even of this church, who are clothed with Chriſt's commiſſion, who are free of cenſurable perſonal ſcandal, who do own and maintain this church's teſtimony, and who either have kept free of the palpable and groſs
defections

ffections of the time, or elfe do relinquifh and
fent the fame; I fay, with all fuch I account
my joy, honour and duty to unite; and my
ractice proveth as much as I fay. As for my
rinciples, I am able to manifeft them to have
heir warrant both from the fupreme divine au-
hority in the word of God in the fcriptures, and
he fubordinate ecclefiaftic authority of our
hurch conftitutions: So this is no new way that
am following, but the good old way, wherein
fee the footfteps of our Lord, *cujus vita nos
mnia docere poteft*, and the print of the feet
f our worthy and refolute reformers, and thefe
ho in our day have valiantly and faithfully
maintained and fealed with their blood the re-
eived and fworn principles of our reformation.

I acknowledge, as you write, (Reverend and
eloved) that I may learn many things from my
rethren into which I have not enough penetrat-
d, for I am but of yefterday, and what know
? Though they were in a worfe courfe than
hey are, I would learn what is good from them;
or as famous *Luther* fays, *Fas eft ab hofte doceri*.
acknowledge many of them to be pious and
earned, and I will imitate them in what I find
o be right: But ah, I cannot fee, as they now
tand, how I can learn faithfulnefs and zeal from
hem; and as for their worldly prudentials, I
hope not to learn thefe; they have loft a good
pecial for the general; they have quit the Prefbyterian plea for the Proteftant, as is clear in
heir declaration, wherein malignants and fecta-
ies may compear for their intereft: But for my
part, I much rather agree with our venerable
Affembly, who, in a paper bearing the date of
July 25th, 1648, in anfwer to the offer of the
Com-

Committee of Estates, do shew, that they had represented to the high court of Parliament, that for securing of religion it was necessary that the Popish, Prelatical and malignant party be declared enemies to the cause, upon the one hand, as well as sectaries, upon the other; and that all associations, either in forces or counsels with the former, as well as the later, be avoided. I cannot see, that these means that have destroyed the work of the Lord shall ever be made use of by him, for raising up the same again. You say well, that this *irruita longe fortior est quam dispersa;* yet that must be taken with a grain of salt; for I must take heed *in quo et cum quibus vim irruitum;* I must unite my poor force both in a good cause, and with such persons as I may lawfully do it.

Now, I hope you will not take it in ill part that I desire you to beware of precipitency, in receiving and spreading informations against us. I know you are informed in many falsities, and you do credulously believe and sedulously spread the same; (this from the hand of famous, learned and godly *Roolman* is most wounding to me) but you will find in the end that they have not been your friends who have prompted you to such a work.

I cannot but admire the difference of your discourse with Mr. *Hamilton* at *Lewarden,* from the strain of your discreet letter unto me. We little need any to cast oil into our flames: for my part, it is my study not to be bitter against the bitterness of others; not to be reviled into a reviler, nor scoffed into a scoffer; so as to turn the same to others as they are to me; neither to throw back my brother's fire-balls into his

own

own face, left in cenfuring him I alfo be my own
judge; though the fournefs of others offend me,
yet it fhould not.   But I will quiet my fpirit in
waiting upon the Lord, until he bring forth the
righteoufnefs of his caufe, and the innocence of
his fervants.   I know fome can accufe or excufe
as they fee it makes for their purpofe : I can prove
it by many witneffes, that Mr. *George Barclay,*
and Mr. *Robert Langlands,* before a multitude,
accufed the church of *Holland* of Popery, in three
fprinklings in baptifm ; and of the groffeft of
Eraftianifm, faying, That the magiftrate would
fend the minifter a pair of fhoes, and difmifs
him when he pleafed.   This was exhibited as a
charge againft your whole church; but now I
am informed, that Mr. *Barclay* flatly denieth
fuch a thing : I defire to know whither or no you
judge the church of *Holland* wronged by this
means? And certain I am that a caufe maintained after fuch a manner fhall not fucceed.   Likewife I muft fay, that I think ftrange that any of
our minifters fhould feek to have an union procured betwixt them and us, while they do reprefent us to be as bad as heretics, and look upon
us as unworthy of a charitable conftruction.   I
like not to beg charity, but I would not defire
(if I may fay, demand) what is not right.   However, until he be melted, we can never be
moulded up into one.   If we had nothing a-do
but to pleafe one another ; and if we were
once fet right in our ends, an accommodation
about all the differences as to the means would
be the more facile and feafible ; *Prov.* xi. 3. 5.

Now, right Reverend, I fhall not detain you
further; I do thankfully accept your neceffary
and Chriftian advices, toward the clofe of your
letter;

Right reverend and beloved Brother,
Your affectionate friend,
and servant in the Lord,

JAMES RENWICK.

LETTER L.

from the Rev. Mr. James Renwick, *to* ————

Beloved Friends,   *April,* 1687.

AS my time will not allow me to write largely unto you; so ye must accept this short
and insignificant line, as a token of my consideration of your lot, and concernedness with
it. Your case is somewhat singular; for banishment will readily be looked upon as a great trial
for you, through the prospect of many snares,
fears, and distresses, whereunto ye may be subjected; howbeit, ye may have no small peace
and consolation from the consideration that ye
could not evite it, unless ye had denied truth:
and whatever sufferings ye may meet with from
your country-men, from the seas, and from foreigners, ye may reckon it all upon the honourable account of your duty. But, my friends,
O do not fear the difficulties and perplexities
that sense and reason may apprehend to be be
abiding you; for the Lord's children have often
                                        found

found it in experience, that their prefent fears have been greater than their future troubles; and that they have oftentimes been more frighted than hurt: He that made a paffage for his' chofen thro' the Red-fea and the fwellings of *Jordan*, can give you dry-foot paffage thro' all the waters and floods of your afflictions. Take your eyes off the vain things of this world; look not back to old lovers; but delight your fouls in Chrift alone, who is your exceeding rich reward, your fatisfying and everlafting portion. Take him with you; O he is fweet company! and he *will never leave you, nor forfake you*; yea, in the time of your greateft trouble he will be moft near you, and in your greateft diftreffes he will be moft kind. Be careful of nothing but how to pleafe him, and to honour him in all places whither ye may be fcattered.

Now, commending you to his grace, which I pray may be fufficient for you, I am,

Your fympathizing friend,

and fervant in the Lord,

JAMES RENWICK.

LETTER LI.

From the Rev. Mr. James Renwick, to the Honourable Mr. Robert Hamilton.

Honourable and dear Sir,   *July* 15. 1687.

YOU may readily be offended with my long delay in writing to you, but your know-

ing the cause thereof, I am hopeful, will remove
it; my business was never so weighty, so multiplied, and so ill to be guided, to my apprehension, as it hath been this year; and my body
was never so frail: Excessive travel, night wanderings, unseasonable sleep and diet, and frequent preaching in all seasons of weather, especially in the night, have so debilitate me, that
I am often incapable for any work; I find myself greatly weakened inwardly, so that I sometimes fall into fits of swooning and fainting.; I
take seldom any meat or drink, but it fights with
my stomach; and for strong drink, I can take
almost none of it. When I use means for my
recovery, I find it someways effectual; but my
desire to the work, and the necessity and importunity of people, prompts me to do more than my
natural strength will well allow; and to under-
take such toilsome business, as casts my body
presently down again. I mention not this
through any anxiety, quarrelling or discontent,
but to show you my condition in this respect. I
may say, that under all my frailties and distem-
pers, I find great peace and sweetness in reflect-
ing upon the occasion thereof: it is a part of
my glory and joy to bear such infirmities, con-
tracted through my poor and small labour, in
my Master's vineyard. But to leave this, I tell
you truly, that I have no more jealousy of you
than ever, for I know no ground for it; and I
hope you will not take up any suspicion of me:
Therefore though multitude of business, or bodily sickness, may divert me from so frequent
writing unto you, as need were, you would
have me excused, and construct rightly and favourably of me; I say not this, that I purpose

to neglect it, or that I will allow myself in that neglect, but to prevent my need of using any further apology of this kind.

Right honourable and comfortable Sir, if I had the tongue of the eloquent, and the pen of a ready writer, my desire would be to employ both in praise of the great King. O! *Who is like the Lord amongst the gods? Who is like him, glorious in holiness, fearful in praises, doing wonders!* We are rebels and out-laws, we are lost and undone for ever; but he hath made a covenant with us, and given himself a ransom: this covenant is everlasting, *well ordered in all things and sure:* It hath all fulness in it, for the matter; all wisdom, for the manner; all condescendence, in the terms: it is most engaging in its end, being made to bring about the peace and salvation of sinners; and it is most necessary, for there is no journeying to heaven without it. This then is the chariot that will carry us into the joy and rest of our Lord; this is the chariot wherein his glory, and our good, ride triumphantly together; for it is made for himself and the daughters of *Jerusalem:* this is the chariot that hath *the pillars of silver, the bottom of gold, the covering of purple, and the midst of it paved with love.* O what a pavement is there! what lining and stuffing is there! O happy are they who are taken up into this chariot! They stand upon love, they sit upon love, they ly upon love, and if they fall, they fall soft, for they fall upon love. These who are without, may see somewhat of its glistering and beauty, yet none can know the heart and the bowels of it, and the love that is there, but these that are within. O! Sir, can you not say, you are taken in with the

King

King into this glorious piece of his workman-
ſhip? Then why ſhould you fear? though Satan
and his inſtruments compaſs you about, and
ſhoot at you upon all hands, yet you are well
guarded; you are not only riding with the King in
his chariot, but lying with him in his bed, which
hath about threeſcore valiant men, of the valiant of *Iſrael*, ſtanding well appointed, and in
a ready poſture, for your defence; the angels
and the attributes of God are a good and ſure
defence: and however you are ſurrounded with
the world's malice and hatred, his love is ſtill
about you, and always next unto you. O advance with that princely diſpoſition and carriage
that becometh one of ſo royal a deſcent, being
a ſon of the great King, the Almighty Lord
God, by your adoption and regeneration. O
fear not what the worms of the earth can do
unto you, they are his poor, chained, weak
creatures; let them be counted as aſhes under the
ſoles of your feet; your cauſe is glorious, your
leader gracious, your victory certain, your reward ſure, and your triumph everlaſting. O let
all your care be to chuſe and do. in every thing,
what may pleaſe him; and encourage yourſelf
in him, for he will not fail you nor forſake you;
and you know not what great things he may do
for you, and by you, ere you paſs your ſojourn-
ing and pilgrimage in this earth. The more
dark and ſtormy that our night be, the nearer
is our morning. The hour of our great tribulation and temptation is coming, it is faſt ap-.
proaching, and it will haſte to its end, and
bleſſ'd ſhall every one be who keep the word of
Chriſt's patience.

I can inform you of little, as to the caſe of
this

this land, but what you know. The enemies
are reftrained from the execution of their rage in.
the former meafure, but they are confulting and
plotting the utter ruin and razing of the interefts
and followers of Chrift; for they neither follow
their nature nor defigns, whatever method they
follow: if this were believed, people would not
fo readily be hood-winked with their pretences
of favour; but after fo much fad experience,
none, who will not wilfully blindfold themfelves,
need to be beguiled.   There is a liberty now
iffued forth from the arrogated, abfolute, and
uncontroulable power of the intruder and ufurper,
upon the prerogative of the great God, bounded
with the reftriction that his government may not
be fpoken againft, and nothing faid that may
alienate the hearts of people from him; pre-
fcribing the place of preaching to be only in
houfes, inhibiting the worfhip of God in the
fields, commanding the fevere execution of all
the iniquitous laws againft all fuch meetings;
and requiring minifters to give up their names
to fome one or other of their civil powers; which
reftricted and ftrangely qualified liberties to Pref-
byterians, is conveyed through the caffing and
difenabling all our penal laws and ftatutes enacted againft Papifts, and toleration of all herefies
and fects.

The generality of this generation efteem peace
as their great good; and they covet and defi-
derate it upon any terms; but the Lord faith,
They fhall not have peace: they have left the
way of peace, and he will trouble them.   The
cloud is faft, faft gathering, which will fall down
as the irruption and inundation of a flood, and

over-

overflow the land : happy are they who are fled into their city of refuge.

Before the publication of this Indulgence, sundry Presbyterian ministers, who had been more lurking formerly, began to travel through the country, and officiate in houses; and that is somewhat of a public manner. But Mr. *Samuel Arnot* preaching upon a Sabbath, in the day-light, about a mile from *Glasgow*, a considerable company of people being within and without, doors, a party of soldiers went out of the town, and scattered the meeting, apprehending near to an hundred men and women, stripping them of their cloaths, and taking their money from them, and laying them in prison, who afterwards were sent to *Edinburgh*, and, as I am informed are all liberate, save one man, who would not call *Bothwell bridge* rebellion. But now the ministers are all generally preaching, and some who had been hearing the Curates are falling to again; but I hear of little freedom amongst them anent the sins of the time : some of them who had professed clearness against the paying the cess, begin now to tolerate it ; saying, that the narrative of the act falls, seeing the term is expired, though the cess be continued, and so it is not sinful : others say, there is no scandal in paying it, because they alledge it to be an epidemical fault, if they make it a fault, (O such horrid juggling with God.) I know none of them but who preach in houses ; and I see not but they must be interpreted to officiate under the cover and colour of this churlish 'berty; for, beside what compliance is with it; I hear not of a conscionable and practical testimony given against it. They do generally

shew

shew themselves more than formerly to be of the contrary part, and set against this poor witnessing and suffering handful; they fail not to cry out against us, they change us with false and gross transgressions; they press people every way to discourage and discountenance us; they carry as if their great design were to crush and ruin us; they spare no pains in preaching, converse, and writing, to effectuate this: and hereby they make many violent upon their way, but some are questioning, and likely to come freely off from them; the course they take is ready to let none halt between them and us: and none more brisk and headstrong than Mr. *Gab. Semple*, Mr. *W. Erskine*, Mr. *Robert Langlands*, particularly Mr. *Samuel Arnot*, who by sundry means discovers no small byassedness, credulity, and impertinence, to say no worse. I fear ere all be done, that it come to the putting forth of the hand with some of the parties; but if it were once at this, I hope our trial would not be much prolonged, whatever might be our extremity and perplexity for a time. Since I knew any thing of the corruptness of their way, I thought they were men of a strange spirit; but now I think more strange than ever. O to live near God that we may endure the storm. Mr. *Flint* and Mr. *Russel* are parted; the number of their followers is not increasing. I have been often informed of Mr. *Ross*'s preaching one time with a curate. But my great discouragement is from ourselves; though there be one part that is straight and stedfast in the matters of God, yet there is another part that is inclined to laxness and instability: they will not leave us, and we have not as yet sufficient enough ground to refuse

fufe their concurrence; but they are as weights upon our hands, and are always to be drawn, becaufe they will not follow. I think fome will yet fcour off, for, alas! we are not all right in heart with God.

As for Mr. *David Houflon* he carries very ftraight: I think him both learned and zealous; he feems to have much of the fpirit of our worthy profeffors; for he much oppofes the paffing from any part of our teftimony, yea, and fticks clofs to every form and order whereunto we have attained; afferting, pertinently, that if we follow not even the method wherein God hath countenanced us, and keep not by every orderly form, we cannot but be juftled out of the matter. He hath authority with him; which fome way dafhes thefe who oppofe themfelves; he difcovers the myftery of the working of the fpirit of Antichrift more fully and clearly than ever I have heard it.

As for Mr. *Kerfland,* I know nothing of his carriage here, but that it is both humble and ftraight. I am informed, by fome very zealous, that in conference both with minifters and profeffors of the contrary part, he hath fpoken pertinently; yea, I have been witnefs to fomewhat of it: I have heard him condemn the bufinefs of the affociation wherein we condemn it, but he much denies his being embodied with them: he takes upon him very much toil and travel to ferve the focieties in the corner where he wanders, and to further and attend the work of the gofpel amongft them: And to fpeak freely, according to my conceptions, I am afraid of him in nothing fo much as in the bufinefs of Mr. *Boyd.*

There

fundry focieties in *Ireland* come
defections of the time, who are
:fpondence with us; I. am defired
, and I purpofe, God willing, to
Mr. *David Houfton* was there in
he fpring, he was very free, and
numbers attended his preaching.
this time he hath admitted fome
lloway or *Nithifdale*, and I am to
he week following. But a part of
iis while hath been, to travel thro'
of the country where I had not
ore, and I hope not without fome
I was laft at *Edinburgh*, a confi-
ber of choice friends were banifhed
Mrs. *Binning* is gone to *Ireland*.
d of your travels through other
ur difficulties have been many, yet
n been with you. I am affrighted
d with the abounding of iniquity
n: The Lord hath a controverfy
, and he will plead it. Let us look
whole world, they are but very few
n fee or fay, that they are for him.
letters of information that are to
id, I fhall endeavour that it be done,
you fome fermons; but I have fo
ny hand, that I cannot get all done.
fome weeks that I will fcarcely get
eft, or be two days in one place; and
, there I am fo taken up, either
iing, examination, or conference,
ft can get no other thing done. I
hear if you have feen the Vindica-
hat are your thoughts of it; and if
:. *Alexander Shields* have met, and
how

how you have accorded : I am hopeful, if you did not miftake one another, there would be little or no diffention between you. As to your coming to *Scotland*, I can fay no other thing now, than I faid in my former.

Now, the Lord be with you; I forget you not, I feldom go to God but you go with me: and I have fome confidence that I need not defire you to remember him, who is,

Honourable and dear Sir,

Yours, as formerly,

JAMES RENWICK.

LETTER LII.

From the Rev. Mr. James Renwick, to the honourable Mr. Robert Hamilton.

Honourable Sir,

SInce my laft I have travelled through many damps and deeps, and feen many difcoveries of many things: the Lord by all difpenfations, faying, that he will have malice and miftakes, right and wrong, righteoufnefs and unrighteoufnefs, brought to light. O noble contrivance! O noble way! What fhall the upfhot of all the loffes, fufferings, and contendings, and difficulties of the remnant be, but the clearing the caufe to all beholders, fo that he who runs may read the righteoufnefs of it? Shall not truth be made thereby more precious and known? The Lord will have a people to reap

the

the sweet fruit of that we are put to this day.
Let us then be content to lay name, credit, enjoyments, life, and all, under his feet, that he
may stand thereupon, to advance the glory of
his own name, and to bring about the advancement of his kingdom.

As to what friends have written to you, I hope,
you will not be troubled thereat, but take it
in good part, for it hath flowed in real respect
to the cause, and love and tenderness towards
you in the most part; whatever you were prevailed to cede unto, through your own confusion, simplicity, and inadvertency, by the overpowering of a furious byassed party, at *Bothwel*;
I would advise your honour to this anent it; to
write to the remnant the way, and any reality
thereof, expressing your own sense thereof; together with your willingness to make acknowledgment thereof, according to the degree of
the offence, in the true church of *Scotland*. This,
I think, would be most for the glory of God, the
vindication of his cause, your own honour, and
the endearing of the remnant unto you. Also
you must write your innocency of what other
things are laid to your charge, with what probation there can be had, with this bearer; and if
we had these, we could stop the mouths of slanderers. Likewise, you must not be offended that
Robert is not sent unto you, for the meeting did
it not out of any dissatisfaction with him, or with
your desiring him, but as a mean to wipe away
that malice-like aspersion, that we are all lead by
you; and that by the mouth of more witnesses
words may be more confirmed. Also, I hope, you
will find the young man both distinct and honest
anent matters; and I doubt nothing, but you will

Q   be

be well pleafed with him. Moreover, friends are moft defirous to know how it is with *Thomas*; and if he be found, in fome meafure, qualified, as to zeal, piety and parts, they would gladly have all means ufed for the honefteft ordination; and I muft join my defire with theirs; for there is as much work to be had in *Scotland*, notwithftanding of all the perfecution, as would hold ten minifters bufy: (O bleffed be the name of the Lord) And if I had fome with me, to help to plenifh the country, and to act more judicially and authoritatively, through the Lord's affiftance, the cruelty of the enemy and the malice and underminings of other parties, would not be able to mar the work in our hands. And as to foreign churches, I would offer your honour my humble advice, that, confidering the bad information that they have got from thefe that have paft as fufferers, you would with patience wait on them, for a little time will give them a clearer infight of our matters: I think no wonder, though the various confufions of *Scotland* jumble them, anent the uptaking of *Scotland*'s caufe: and give not over to deal with fuch as are not poffeft with prejudice and malice; and for ordination for *Thomas*, if no other thing ftood in the way of it, I could be clear, that ye fought it from the pureft amongft the reformed; though they cannot win the length of approving all the circumftances of our caufe, providing they be faithful againft the fins of their own place, and not, with prejudice at us, fided with the backfliders in the church of *Scotland*: For there is a great difference between joining with minifters of foreign churches, and minifters of our own church; for the former, (as I have often told to thefe that

ob-

objected againſt my ordination) comes under a
general conſideration as Proteſtants, but the latter, under a far more ſpecial conſideration, as
may be clear from the ſuppoſed example; The
reformed miniſters abroad, who keep up a teſtimony againſt the ſins of their own place, and ſide
not themſelves againſt us, I could lawfully join
with them, though they cry not out againſt the
ſteps of our defection, becauſe that is not the
matter of their preſent teſtimony; yet if any of
them were coming to *Scotland*, and offering themſelves miniſters to us of one organical church, we
could not accept of them, unleſs they would keep
up our preſent teſtimony againſt all the ſins of
our place.

As for what paſt betwixt theſe miniſters and
us, I can inform your honour no more fully than
our friend's letter doth. And as to the preſent
ſtate of the country, *Clydeſdale* continueth firm
as it was; *Nithſdale* is as one man upon their former ground, together with *Anandale*; ſome in
Kyle are gone off, but many continue; many in
Carrick are jumbled, ſome, for the time, are
quite off, and ſome few continue; the few that
are in *Livingſton* and *Calor* are put all in a reel,
the Lord knoweth how they will ſettle. Since
our laſt meeting with theſe miniſters, I made a
progreſs through *Galloway*, and found never ſuch
an open door for preaching the goſpel, the people coming far better out than they did before;
and we got eight field-meetings kept there without any diſturbance, and ſix in *Nithſdale*, many
coming out who were not wont to come, and
none in any of theſe places ſtaying away that
came out formerly. Mr. *W. Boyd* hath made his
eſcape out of *Dunnotter*, and is clear in our con-

troverſies

troverfies againft thefe minifters; *Robert Goodwin* hath made his escape likewife, and continues alfo clear in our matters. *George Hill*'s family hath all been fick: And Mrs. *B.* hath been long fick in prifon; but this is but the ordinary calamity of the country; for I never heard of fuch a general ficknefs in *Scotland.*

As for choofing of elders, according to your defire, we have fome honeft old men, members of our focieties, who were elders in our fettled ftate; and we are refolving to fet about the chufing of moe, with fome deacons: But our various confufions and debates have much retarded this and other things hitherto.

In what I have here written, I intreat your honour that I may not be miftaken; for the Lord knoweth, I am the fame both anent the caufe and toward you that ever I was; all that hyaffed folk can fay, doth neither leffen my confidence in, nor eftimation of you: and what I have faid of *Thomas,* underftand me fo, that I would moft gladly have him for a help, but I would either want him ere he fhould be a hinderance; but becaufe I judge him not to be of a dangerous fpirit, I fufpect him lefs than many others, alfo I think it is more fimplicity of nature than want of honefty that is with him. Alfo, you would fpeak with this bearer anent fetting foreward to the work, for he hath paft his courfe at the college, and I think, hath the caufe honeftly ftated in his heart, tho' he hath but fmall means for enduing him with gifts; yet he wants not a fpirit for contending for the honeft fide. And as for ordination abroad, I would have all means effayed before we took another courfe; for we cannot defend our doing any thing of that nature, before all other

her lawful ways eſſayed do fail us, while we are.
a ſuch a caſe. I thought fit alſo to inform
you, that there is a general deſire among friends
that you ſhould come home a viſit, and return
again, through the apprehenſion that they have
of your doing a great good at this time; but ſince
our debates were brought to ſome cloſe, I cannot
be ſo anxious for it as I was.

Now, dear Sir, take heed to yourſelf, there
are many looking out for your halting, many
ſets are ſpread againſt you, both at home and a-
broad; but exerciſe yourſelf in this, to keep a
conſcience void of offence both toward God and
man, and the Lord ſhall bring forth your righte-
ouſneſs as the noon-tide of the day. Remember
me kindly to your worthy dear ſiſter, to *Thomas*,
and all the family. Pray for him who is,

Ever as formerly,

JAMES RENWICK.

LETTER. LIII.

From the Rev. Mr. James Renwick, *to the
honourable Ladies* ———

Much honoured Ladies,   *Aug.* 13. 1687.

THE zeal which I deſire to have for the advancement of Chriſt's kingdom, the love
which I bear to your ſouls, and my ſenſe of the
obligations which I ſtand under unto you in particular, have moved me to take upon me to ſa-
lute you with this line. There is not a rational

creature,

creature, that doth not propone unto
chief good, the obtaining and enjoyi
is the great intent and end of all its a(
will shew us any good? But, the w
mong men is, their setting up to then
naughty,. vain, and petty nothing, a
that wherein their real and chief ha
only ly, *rejecting the counsel of God (
selves*: this mistake is deplorable, f(
infinite lofer by it; it is desperate,
eth to be instructed. Hence is fo m;
prevailing natural inclinations anc
ing lusts as there are among the ch
dam; so many different chief goo(
gods many, and lords many. I am f
upon the folly and madness of the p(
that thus doth forsake its own mei
the world choose and follow what
to us there is but one Lord.

I am hopeful, much honoured
ye are turning your backs upon cre:
nal delights, and setting your faces t(
seeking after union and communion
is my foul's earnest defire, that it l
and if the comfortless and distractir
a present perishing world shall whe
witch you, that ye study not the wil
it shall bring great grief and sorrow
to me. I say, I am carried betwi
fear; I hope, the Lord will work
in you; I hope it will be, for I wor
be, and there are some appearances
I fear that the pleasant and easy y(
be looked upon as irkfome and v
you, when I consider your temptati
(seemingly) promising beginnings,

foms that I have feen in many, which have fallen away without bringing forth mature fruit.
Do not take my freedom in ill part, neither be
offended with it, for it cometh from affection, and
my ardent defire that ye fhould not neglect the
great falvation. Religion is a great myftery, and
a far other thing than even the profeffing world
taketh it to be. There are many hinderances in
the way of flying to Chrift, and clofing with him.
The natural blindnefs that is in man, whereby he
neither fees his fin and danger, nor his Saviour,
is a great hinderance, *Rev.* iii. 17, 18. His natural unwillingnefs and flat averfion to the way of
falvation laid down in the covenant, and held
forth in the gofpel, *John* v. 40. His hard hearted mifbelief, whereby he giveth no affent to the
righteoufnefs of Scripture precept and doctrine,
and juftice of fcripture threatening; nor confent
to fcripture promifes, making fiducial application
of them, *John* v. 38. *Heb.* xi. 6. His whorifh
addictednefs to his lufts, idols, and carnal en-
tanglements, whereby he doth not quit his profanity, nor leave the honour, applaufe, profit
and pleafure of this world, *Pfal.* xlv. 10, 11.
Song iii. 11. *Chap.* iv. 8. His miftaking the government of Chrift, counting it hard, melancho-
lic and unpleafant, *Matth.* xi. 28, 29, 30. His
judging religion but a fancy, and a politic in-
vention to amaze and amufe the minds of men,
Matth. xxii. 5. His conceiving a facility in religion, thinking there needeth not be fo much
ado about it, and that he can do all that is needful, when he pleafeth, *Matth.* viii. 19. ███ ██.
44. His poftponing the bufinefs of life ███ ███
from time to time, leaving that laft in doing,
which

which ought to be firft done, refolving to a-
mend cre he end; whereby his vain heart de-
ceives him, and Satan juftles him out of all
time, *Luke* ix. 61. His peevifh and foolifh
impatience, whereby he doth not forfake a
prefent imaginary good, for a future real happinefs. A man may think it a good thing to enjoy everlafting life; but becaufe that is an hereafter happinefs, and lieth now only in promife,
he cannot wait for it and take it as his portion,
but grafps at what is prefent, though it be neither contenting nor conftant, *Pfal.* iv. 6.
2 *Tim.* iv. 10. I fay, all thefe are great hinderances; fee that ye get over thefe, and all other
obftructions, and lay hold upon Chrift. O that
I could bewail the lamentable condition of man,
who is held in fo many chains, from this work
of great concern and eternal moment!

O, much honoured Ladies, confider the indifpenfible and abfolute need ye have of a Saviour;
confider the awful commands, full promifes, free
offers, hearty invitations, and ferious requefts
given forth in the word, all crying aloud with
one voice unto you, to match with the Lord of
glory: Confider the affurance that his own teftimony hath given you, of dwelling with him
throughout eternity, in his heavenly manfions,
where ye fhall fee him as he is, have a full fenfe
of his love, and a perfect love to him again, and
ever drink of the rivers of pleafure that flow at
his right hand, if ye fhall embrace him upon his
own terms. Confider the peremptory certification of everlafting deftruction, of dwelling with
continual burnings, and lying under the burden
of his wrath; a curfe running always out upon
you in the overflowing flood, if ye fhall neglect

to make your peace with him, and reject his salvation. I say, confider thofe things, *and give all diligence to make your calling and election fure;* and fee well that ye be not deceived; for there are many miftakes, and a great myftery in that bufinefs. Many think themfelves to be fomething when they are nothing, and fo deceive themfelves, and come fhort of the grace of God: inftead of founding upon the immoveable rock of ages, they build upon the fand of their own attainments. For folk may go a great length, and yet be void of true faving grace; they may have a great fpeculative knowledge of the matters of God and myftery of falvation, and ftrong gifts, 1 *Cor.* xiii. 2. They may abftain from many pollutions. and the grofs evils that others are given unto, *Luke* xviii. 11, 12, 13, 14. They may externally perform many duties, as reading, prayer, and be very much in thefe, *Luke* xviii. 11, 12, 13, 14. They may have a very great forrow for fin, not becaufe of the difhonour done to God, but the hurt to themfelves; not becaufe they are polluted, but becaufe they are deftroyed by it, *Matth.* xxvii. 3. *Heb.* xii. 17. They may have a defire after grace, which yet is not for grace's fake, but for heaven's fake, *Matth.* xxv. 8. They may have an hiftorical faith, and give an affent of the mind to all that is revealed in the word, yea, to the fpiritual meaning of the law, *Mark* xii. 32, 33, 34. They may have big hopes, and that in the mercy of God, which neverthelefs is but prefumption; for they forget that he is juft, and neglect to lay hold upon Chrift for fatisfaction of his juftice; whereas, he is merciful to none out of Chrift, *Job* viii. 13, 14. They may have the common ope-

operations of the Spirit, and a taste *of the hea*
venly gift, and the powers of the world to come
Heb. vi. 4, 5. 6. They may be convinced that
it is good to close with Christ, and comfort
themselves as if they had done it; whereas they
are still in their natural state, *Hos.* viii. 2, 3.
They may suffer many things materially for the
cause of God, and toil much in following ordinances, undergoing the same out of respect for
their own credit, 1 *Cor.* xiii. 3. I say, people
may, and many do arrive at all these and such
like attainments, and notwithstanding remain in
the gall of bitterness and bond of iniquity. It
may make us all tremble to think what a length
folk may go, and yet never have gone out of themselves, and passed through the steps of effectual
calling. Many will say to him in that day, *We*
have eaten and drunken in thy presence, and thou
hast taught in our streets; have we not prophesied
in thy name? and in thy name cast out devils, and
in thy name done many wonderful works? whom
he will chase away from his presence, with that
awful sentence, *DEPART YE;* professing unto them that he never knew them.

Let this alarm you to make sure work in this
great concern, and not deceive yourselves with a
counterfeit, instead of a reality, with a flash instead of conversion, and a delusion instead of
Christ. But get ye a sight of your sinful and miserable state, a sense and feeling thereof, putting
you in a perplexity, and discouraging you from
resting in it; a conviction of your inability to
help yourselves, and of your unworthiness that
God should help you out of it; and look unto
Christ, as your alone Saviour, receiving him
wholly in his threefold office, of King, Priest
and

d Prophet, welcoming him, and taking up his
ofs, againſt the world, the devil, and the fleſh,
d reſting upon him alone for ſalvation; and
en the buſineſs will be done, and all will be
e; and then you may defy devils and men,
plucking you out of his hand.

And if ye have thus cloſed the bargain with him,
en ye will find in you a war declared and main-
againſt all ſin, *Rom.* vii. 15. *Ezek.* xviii. 21.
John iii. 9.   A reſpect to all the command-
ents of the Lord, *Ezek.* xviii. 21. A liking of
e way of happineſs, as well as happineſs itſelf,
hn iii. 14, 15.   An high eſteem of juſtification
d ſanctification, *Pſal.* xxxii. 2.   A prizing of
riſt, and a longing to be with him, *Phil.* i.
. And an admirable change wrought in you;
ew judgment, new will, new conſcience, new
emory, new affections: In a word, all the fa-
lties of the ſoul will be new, in regard of their
alifications; and all the members of the body,
regard of their uſe, 2 *Cor.* v. 17.   Now, if
have attained to a ſaving intereſt in Chriſt, ye
ay find theſe, and the like marks and evi-
nces of it.

O halt not in this great matter, reſt not in un-
rtainty, and ſatisfy not yourſelves with a may-
: But *examine yourſelves, whether ye be in the*
ith; prove your own ſelves; know ye not your
vn ſelves, how that Jeſus Chriſt is in you, ex-
pt ye be reprobates? In ſetting your faces to-
ard *Zion*, ye may expect that Satan will raiſe
l his ſtorms againſt you; but fear him not, for
e grace of God is ſufficient for you.   Give
ourſelves wholly to the Lord, to ſerve him, and
love his name, to chooſe and follow the things
at pleaſe him; your greateſt honour lieth in
                                          this,

this, your greateſt duty, your greateſt profit, and your greateſt pleaſure. Count the coſt of religion; God is a liberal dealer, deal not niggardly with him, prig not with him about your eſtates; Who is in heaven like unto him? and who in the earth is to be deſired like him? Lay down to him your names, your enjoyments, your lives, and your all at his feet; for he is only worthy to have the diſpoſal of them; and the ſufferings of this preſent time are not worthy to be compared with the glory that ſhall be revealed. Think not much to quit the vain and carnal delights of the world; they cannot ſatisfy your ſenſes, and much leſs your ſouls: The earth is round, and the heart of man three-nooked; therefore this cannot be filled by that: And though ye could find content in them, yet how vain were it, becauſe unconſtant? and how unſolid, becauſe uncertain?

Regard not mens reproach, for ſo reproached they our Lord and the prophets; yea, there can be no contempt or calumny caſt upon you, for the goſpel's ſake, but what hath been caſt upon the faithful in all ages: Remember *Moſes*, who *eſteemed the reproach of Chriſt, greater riches than the treaſures of Egypt*: and *go ye forth without the camp bearing his reproach.* Chriſt's new name will more than enough compenſe the world's nick-name. Advance reſolutely in the way of godlineſs; your guide is faithful, your victory certain, your reward ſure, and your triumph everlaſting: Stumble not, becauſe religion is mocked at; for it is not the worſe that man thinketh ſo little of it: count it not a fancy, becauſe men deſert it; but *taſte and ſee that God is good.* Follow no man further
than

than he follows Christ; divide not from the head, to unite with any professed members: walk not with them who renounce their dependence upon Christ; or who are carrying on a course of defection, pressing a relinquishing of the present testimony, and casting reproaches upon the way of God. Keep yourselves from the pollutions of this time; and partake not with other men in their sins; but study to have a good conscience, and a good conscience will be a peaceable conscience, and a peaceable conscience will be a fat feast. Shun as much as ye can the company of carnal and vain persons: ye will not get this wholly evited, but ye may avoid unnecessary converse, frequency and familiarity with them: We are obliged to carry ourselves with courtesy, humanity and pity towards all, but not with friendliness and familiarity: ye know, evil company and communication corrupteth good manners. O! what shall I say? Watch always, be much in secret prayer, self-examination, spiritual meditation: Read the written word of God; seek to have your minds understanding it, your hearts affecting it, and your consciences and actions guided by it: Get his Spirit to dwell in you, by directing you into all truth, reproving you for sin, and bringing every thought in obedience to Christ, and leading you into supplication. Lay aside every weight, and run the race that is set before you with cheerfulness and alacrity; despise every opposition and obstruction in the way, and keep your eyes still upon the prize, having a respect to the recompence of reward.

Now, *The very God of peace sanctify you wholly, and, I pray God, your whole spirit, and soul*

R

and

and body, be preserved blameless, unto the coming
of our Lord Jesus Christ. I am,

Much honoured Ladies,

Your assured and obliged friend

and servant in the Lord,

JAMES RENWICK.

L E T T E R   LIV.

From the Rev. Mr. James Renwick, *to the
honourable Mr.* Robert Hamilton.

Hon. and dear Sir,   Nov. 5. 1687.

OUR troubles are growing, and enemies are
stretching forth their hands violently to
persecute; and they want not instigations from
our false brethren; so we are made the contempt
of the proud, and the scorn of them that are at
ease. Our sufferings were always rightly stated,
but never so cleanly as now; and why should
we not endure these trials? for they shall work
for truth's victory, and Christ's glory. O let
all the suffering remnant keep clean hands, for
therein shall be their strength; and wait with
patience, for he will not tarry, who cometh to
plead his own cause, to lay claim to his own in
terest, that is basely and deceitfully abandoned
and betrayed into the hands of man, to give a
fair decision. These whose souls are vexed with
the now abounding abominations, shall have
Zoar to fly unto, when the fire of God shall fall
                                                                  down

lown upon our *Sodom*: I am certain the Lord will have a fanctuary for his people. We muft once be brought to that extremity, wherein there can be no longer fubfiftence without prefent help; but God will not leave his people there. O this liberty hath let Satan loofe, and brought the truths of God, and the faithful, into great bondage: but God will loofe his judgments, and pour them out upon this woeful generation, that will not fee, till they be made to feel. There is now ftrange thirfting after my blood, but that moves me not; though they had it, they would not be fatisfied, for nothing will quench them till they get their own blood to drink.

As to Mr. *Boyd*, he came to our laft general correfpondence, and defired, that feeing he knew there was fomething wherefore we were diffatisfied with him, as alfo he was with us, we might commune freely with him upon the fame. So, firft, we fhewed our diffatisfaction with his taking licence without our knowledge, which was contrary to his own engagement, at leaft declared purpofe and refolution. Next, we took his paper, which he left in our hands when he went abroad, wherein, amongft other things, he afferted, his withdrawing out of the land, was no way to feparate or disjoin from us, and fignified his diflike of countenancing thefe minifters, againft whom we had valid exceptions. When we afked, How could his declaring, that he neither was joined, nor would join with us, nor any other party, confift with the former; and from the latter, we defired to know, if he judged the accepting of that liberty, as they call it, a fufficient ground of difcountenancing minifters? His anfwer to the firft of thefe, did no

way

way help him, nor satisfy us. His answer to the last was, If the question was concerning such ministers as might sit in assemblies with the addressers, and go out to places of the country at their direction and preach, he would not forbid people to hear them, whatever he would do himself. So, after some debating against his mind in this, I shewed the meeting, that I neither could nor would determine matters of such extent and importance without my brethren, who by providence were not present; yet, in the mean time, I would keep at a distance, and not concur with him in the public work. And they concluded that they would not call him, nor hear him elicitely; yet they would not discourage and discountenance him so far as not to hear him, in case of necessity, as if they should be providentially cast with him into one family, and he going about exercise, or the like. Moreover, he himself was not desirous to incorporate with us, what he may do after, I know not. There were also other particulars wherewith we were dissatisfied, but the foresaid were the most material, and also included sundry of the other, and much time was spent in reasoning about them.

I have seen the account which you gave to your sister Mrs. *J.* of *E. B. H.* her affair, you would not be too much pressed with it; the Lord is taking all pains to wean you more and more from the world, and win you more and more to himself: Remember *Joseph* in the dungeon; God hath vindicated, and will yet more vindicate you. Friends are very well, and desirous to have you at home; and I shall endeavour to manage that business sufficiently, and as

may

may be moſt for the advantage of the cauſe.

Now, the Lord be your guide, and heap the bleſſings of the everlaſting covenant upon your head. Pray that the Lord may ſpare his people, that he may purge his houſe, and pray for him, who is,

> *Honourable and dear Sir,*
>
> *Yours as formerly,*
>
> **JAMES RENWICK.**

LETTER LV.

From the Rev. Mr. James Renwick, to the honourable and well deſerving gentleman Mr. Robert Hamilton.

Hon. and dear Sir,   *Dec.* 29. 1687.

THO' I know not how this ſhall be tranſmitted to your hands, yet I judge it my duty to write a brief account of ſome things at preſent amongſt us. Mr. *Boyd* came to our laſt general correſpondence, profeſſing his agreement with our teſtimony, and his willingneſs to join with us: and when we came to ſpeak about the duty of teaching people the neceſſity of abſtracting themſelves from the accepters of the preſent toleration, he granted that it is lawful to teach it, but the expediency of it he did not ſee: however he had endeavoured to diſcover the ſin of the toleration's being accepted: thus he ſtood at this time. And when we were reaſoning with him, he ſaid, ere he were the inſtrument of a breach amongſt us, that he would

R 3   leave

leave *Scotland.* But it was no fmall perplexity
to us, to know how to carry anent him; it wa
thought that the refuling either to call or hear
him would caufe a very great animofity and
breach, and the ground of it was not valid e
nough. So, they came at length to conclude,
(with fome averfenefs in the moft part) that until the time of our next meeting, thefe who had
not clearnefs to call and hear him fhould not be
offended with thefe that might do it; and thefe
again, that might do it fhould not be offended
with thefe who had no clearnefs for it: Howbeit,
they were not for entirely incorporating with
him, and giving him a joint folemn call. And
as I declined to preach with him; fo I denied
my confent to the forefaid conclufion, and was
put in a perplexity, not knowing what to do,
feeing many fad inconveniences to follow, if I
had oppofed their determination; fo with a full
heart I forebore: but afterwards I opened my
heart to Mr. *Boyd* himfelf. I heard that *K.* was
of my judgment in this matter.

As for Mr. *David Houfton,* he went long ago
into *Ireland,* and is not yet returned, whereby
we have fuffered no fmall lofs. I am certain,
fome ftrange thing hath happened him: the report is, that he hath been fore fick: and I hear
there are many in *Ireland* turning Diffenters.
Kerfland hath taken from his factors about fixteen
hundred merks of his own rents. For what was
communed anent yourfelf and Mr. *Thomas Douglas,* your letter from the meeting will inform
you. We have written a teftimony of about five
or fix fheets of paper, witneffing againft this toleration, the accepting of it, addreffing for it,
and hearing of the acceptors: Teftifying alfo
for

for the obligation of our covenants; and shewing the necessary duty of field-preaching, in the present circumstances of this church.

I have been at *Peebles* this week, and thro' the Lord's providence wonderfully escaped; our intended meeting near to the town, about nine of the clock at night, in the time of our gathering, being by a strange providence discovered: it is a place I had not been in before, and we had no armed men; there are four taken and imprisoned. Sir, I hear, *Stansfield* is murdered by his own family, his eldest son had a chief hand in it.

Now, honourable and comfortable Sir, I have no more at the time to inform you of, but I have much to write if time would allow me. My fears were never greater anent the interest of Christ in thir lands, there is such an inclinableness in people to defection. But I believe, he will not want some to own his controverted truths. The next time I write to you, I purpose to write also to *Lewarden* friends. The Lord be with you. I am,

Right honourable and dear Sir,

Your sympathising friend

and servant in the Lord,

JAMES RENWICK.

LETTER

LETTER LVI.

From the Rev. Mr. James Renwick, *to some*
persons under sentence of banishment.

Beloved Friends;   1687.

IT is both my duty and desire to sympathize
with all who are suffering for the precious
name of Christ, especially with you who are call-
led to partake so deeply of the afflictions of the
children of *Zion.* Ye are now to be banished out
of your native land, but your enemies could not
have appointed that for you, unless the Lord had
from all eternity ordained it. His infinite love
and wisdom hath consulted and measured out your
lot; and as this should make you despise the instruments of your afflictions, so it may help you
to stoop, and chearfully submit unto the providence of God, who *is of one mind, and who can
turn him?* Yea, considering the preciousness of
the cause for which ye are persecuted, ye may
rejoice that you are are counted worthy to suffer
such things: for it is no less than the gospel of
Christ, and his great prerogatives, as he is King
of his own church, which he hath purchased with
his own blood; and as he is supreme Governor
and Sovereign of the whole world. O is not this a
precious cause? are not these great heads of suffering? If every one of you had a thousand worlds
of enjoyments, and a thousand lives, they would
be all too little to signify your love to Christ, and
your respect to so honourable a cause. You cannot glorify your Lord so much on earth, as by being faithful to the word of your testimony, and
                                                    suffering

suffering for him now, when men are declaredly topping with him about his supremacy both in his kingdom of grace and power. O my friends, regard not what you may meet with in this present world, but be careful to have matters standing right between God and you: see that ye attain to a saving interest in Christ, for if that be not secured, your duties will not be acceptable, your sufferings will not be acceptable; and whatever ye may endure here for a profession, ye may lay your account with lying under his curse and wrath, and the immediate strokes of his severe vengeance, to all eternity. O make Christ your own, and then ye may defy devils and men, to come between you and your happy state: give yourselves wholly to his disposal, for he is gracious and faithful, and will order every thing for his own glory and your good; study to maintain his cause whole, and wherever your lot may be, keep up the testimony of the church of *Scotland*; quite none of your sworn and received principles, whatever way these may insinuate upon you, who are engaged and persisting in a course of defection; make no tampering or bargaining with any, where it will infer a condemning of the cause of your sufferings, and justifying of the iniquitous sentence that men have past upon you: keep all stedfast and unite together in the truths of God; and beware of defection, which breedeth division; fall not away from any of the words of Christ's patience; but shun all unnecessary questions, needless strifes, and vain janglings; live at peace amongst yourselves, so far as holiness may sustain no prejudice by it, and this will be both pleasant and profitable for you. Now, O beloved, what shall I say unto you, I have no
time

time to enlarge. Do not say becaufe of your banifhment, Is there any forrow like unto your forrow? for I am perfuaded, that thefe whom ye
leave behind you have a greater forrow; I do
not fay, that any fhould flee out of *Scotland*, or
leave it without a neceffary and fufficient call:
yet that is coming upon the inhabitants, which
will make the ears of them that hear thereof to
tingle : The confumption determined fhall pafs
through, and the Lord will quiet his fpirit in our
deftruction; for his *foul fhall be avenged on fuch
a nation as this:* And who knoweth, but your
banifhment may be for the prefervation and hiding of (at leaft) fome of you, until the indignation overpafs. But when the time of gathering
cometh, the Lord will bring again his banifhed,
he *will bring them from all places whether they
have been driven; He will fay to the eaft, give up,
and to the weft, keep not back.* Fear not a long
fea voyage ; for *they that go down to the fea in
fhips, that do bufinefs in the great waters, thefe
fee the works of the Lord, and his wonders in
the deep:* Yea, though the deep fhould be your
grave, or though ye fhould die in a ftrange land,
yet your death of that kind fhall be a teftimony,
and cry for vengeance upon perfecutors; and
fhall be an outlet of all your mifery, and inlet of
your everlafting glory. But if the Lord fhall
meet you with providential mercies, whether ye
are carried, and give you any tolerable eafe,
fafety, or fuftenance; then, I fay, as ye would
not have your bleffings curfed, ye would not
lofe the badge of Chriftians and fufferers, fit not
down upon thefe things, content not yourfelves
with thefe things, and forget not the cafe of
the remnant whom ye leave behind you.

Now,

Now, I commend you all to the grace of God, hoping not to forget you in my weak addresses to the throne of him who is the hearer of prayers; and hoping to be remembered by you in like sort. I am,

Beloved friends,
Your sympathizing friend
and servant in the Lord,

JAMES RENWICK.

LETTER LVII.

From the Rev. Mr. James Renwick, to Mr. Alexander Shields, preacher of the gospel.

Dear Brother,   Jan. 12. 1688.

I Long to hear much how you are; the third night after I parted with you, I had a sore fit of sickness, but it lasted not, and through the goodness of God, I have been in ordinary health since; however, it occasioned a disappointment of a meeting for examination. And I came foreward to *Peebles*, where our meeting in the time of gathering was discovered by a wonderful providence, namely, as I am informed, the pursuing of some for theft, when people were observed to croud out of the town; which made the clerk to enquire what they were, and whither they were going; the report whereof coming unto me, being lodged in a most suspected house, I went forth, and passed on towards the place of meeting, until I came within speaking and hearing
ing

ing of the clerk and some with him, who were without all the town challenging people, and being in no capacity to resist, I turned again Into the town, where there was some little uproar, and went forth of it another way, where I waited a considerable space for my horse, which was at length got unto me, with some difficulty; and finding that the meeting could not be kept, I came away; but there were four persons taken. And since I came to this place, I have lodged with *Thomas* and *John*, and lest I should trouble mine own spirit, I have not desired any to keep silent anent my being here, nor reproved any for coming into my quarters, whatever the hazard might be; but left that to the providence of God, and people to their own discretion, and I find it not the worse way.

As for the books, they are come safe in boxes to *Wooler*. I have inserted in the papers which you left, what you desired to be transcribed out of *Durham* upon the *Revelation*; but I thought, I could not fitly add what concerneth *Kersland*, because I know not distinctly the manner of it, and to express it suitable to the matter of fact. But I have written to the Lady, desiring that she may give to Mr. *Had*. and Mr. *Lin*. a plain and full account of it; and I have written also to them, that they may insert it, and shown distinctly the place where it is to be added. And I thought this the fittest way, because people might possibly carp, if they were not acquainted with what concerneth them so near; and again, it will prevent any cavil about misrepresentation of that matter of fact. As for the testimony, the publishing of it is longer retarded than I expected, because *Michael* was not in health for writing;

but

but I shall be careful about it. I have added what was to be transcribed out of *Durham* upon scandal, and did oversee the writing of the most difficult places, and taken out some of the biggots, because the recurring too oft upon such epithets makes them unsavoury. I have not got any of the letters sent abroad, but I am using diligence. There are few news here: They are to proceed against Sir *James Stansfield*'s family for the murder. Mr. *Hardie* is still in prison, but it is thought, he will be liberate; he refuseth to tell the council what he had preached, but put them to prove what they could against him; whereupon they called some of his hearers, but they said, they were either sleeping, or at a great distance, and could not hear; so they were not the nearer their purpose. There are orders given forth for a day of thanksgiving, for the conception of the queen, and (as is reported) to pray that it may be a man-child. I am detained in this place some few days beyond my purpose, through the want of a guide; but I am now about to remove.

Now, being in great haste, I must desist. Your direction, encouragement, strengthening, comfort, health, and protection is prayed for by him, who is,

Your brother and servant,

JAMES RENWICK.

S   LETTER

LETTER LVIII.

From Mr. J. Renwick, *to the prisoners in the* Cannongate *Tolbooth.*

Dearly Beloved in our Lord, and much honoured sufferers for his name.

I Hear that men have passed sentence of banishment against you, but I hope, what man can do is no surprizal to you, ye having counted all cost that ye may be put to: Howbeit, as no created power can banish you from your God, or your God from you; so I hope, what men have now done against you, shall, by God's blessing, be a means to chase you nearer unto your rest. Yea, moreover ye do not know but that it is to hide you from the present calamity, which the Lord is immediately to bring on this land; I say, immediately, for he is hastening his work; ay, he is working fast, one step of his now, cannot stay upon another, for he is coming post unto us, and now he must come, for our mother is in her pangs, and now she must either get help and be delivered, or else she will die in travel; but die she will not, tho' she be in hard labour, for the greatness of her pain will only tend to make her delivery the more joyful. O joyful! a joyful delivery, and to make it joyful, our Lord must have a singular feast at it; he will give whole bouks good cheap; yea, he will have such a feast in *Scotland*, that proclamation shall go forth from the one end of heaven to the other, inviting all the fowls of the heavens, and the beasts of the earth to come unto the Lord's feast; a feast of the carcases of the inhabitants of *Scotland*, great and small. Neither

bitants

their wit nor their might will deliver them in that day. O happy is the man or the woman that is removed from hearing the very report of what is immediately coming on this land. Yea, the earth shall be made to tremble, ears to tingle, hearts to melt, bowels to found, and knees to smite one upon another, at the report of *Scot-land*'s judgments. They shall in that day be thought to have sped well, who have win away out of the gate of these things. Yet I cannot look upon this, but I must cast a view upon what is beyond it; Mercies, mercies, mercies are swimming toward the Lord's people; O they are strange mercies, and he will make them singular people who will be privileged with them.

Now, as for your parts, remember, *the earth is the Lord's and the fulness thereof;* wherever ye may be cast, study always to be in your duty, and let the Lord be *your portion in the land of the living.* And that he may make up all your wants in himself, shall be the prayer of him, who is

Your real and constant sympathizer,
in all your sufferings for Christ,
JAMES RENWICK.

L E T T E R LIX.

From the Rev. Mr. James Renwick, to all and sundry the prisoners for the name of Christ, in the tolbooths of Edinburgh, Glasgow, *and elsewhere in* Scotland.

Much respected and beloved in the Lord,

THE most holy and wise God hath seen it fit, to place his people, in this our day, in very strange circumstances; they having both

the

the fubtilty and cruelty of ftated enemies, and
alfo of pretended declining friends to graple
with; yea, I think, there was never a generation who had fuch fnares ftrawed in their way,
yea, fo many ftumbling-blocks laid before them
as we have. And is not this to be feen, that e-
nemies to God and his truths have much more
prevailed, by their hidden fnares, their fubtile
plots againft the work and people of God, vailed and mafked over with a pretence of favour,
than by their cruel outrages, virulent and violent
perfecutions, fcrewed up to the higheft pitch of
their bounded power? the confideration whereof, (together with a defire to refpect the advantage of the public work of God, and the welfare
of the fouls of people, and that we may be wife
at the laft, [*confidering] we have been made
to know by fad experiences the fin and danger
of [accepting] their pretended favours, and to be
mindful of the many bonds and obligations that
ly upon us from the Lord, and to difcharge my
duty and exonour my confcience as in his fight)
hath moved me to prefume to write to you, my
dear friends in bonds for Chrift, my poor advice
anent your duty under your prefent trials and fufferings, efpecially in reference to that late indemnity of the date of *February* 26th, 1685.
given out by the duke of *York*, under the name
of King *James* VII. I think, all pretended favours coming from the hands of fuch enemies,
may juftly be fufpected by us, confidering how
great ſkaith and damage that heretofore the work
and

* The words in this Letter put in the *Italic* cha-
racter, enclofed thus [ ] are fupplied by the Printer, as there was a blank in the manufcript where
they are placed.

and people of God have endured thereby; as witness by that indulgence before and after *Bothwel*. I hope, in the Lord's goodness, that this present snare shall not have such prevalency. Howbeit, that ye (whose soul's welfare I tender very much, and in whose trials and sufferings I desire to be a burden-bearer and co-partener) may be guarded the more against it, in all friendliness and humility, I call you to consider these few, among many other evils in the forefaid indemnity. As (1.) That these who accept of that indemnity do most directly homologate the pretended authority of *James* Duke of *York*, which is far contrary to our covenants, whereby we are sworn, in our stations, and to the utmost of our power to extirpate such; and do say, that it was lawful, just and legal, to proclaim him king of *Scotland*, &c. whereupon that indemnity is granted. (2.) These who accept of that indemnity do take with the name of wicked and seditious subjects and rebels, which the enemies in their proclamation put upon them; yea, they call themselves transgressors, for an indemnity or pardon is only extended toward such; and these who accept of it do palpably acknowledge a crime. (3.) These who accept of that indemnity do most grossly comply with the granters of it, who require that fugitives, in sign (mark it) of their acceptance of the same, do either take the Oath of Allegiance, or else find caution to transport themselves out of the three dominions of *Scotland*, *England*, and *Ireland*, and never to return again without licence, under pain of death. Now, seeing these enemies require such gross compliance, in sign and token of the acceptance of that indemnity, what must they hold the acceptance of itself to

be?

be? There are only two things, which they propone to the acceptors thereof to make choice of,
and thefe are, 1ft, The oath of allegiance; but
of this I fhall not fpeak, judging that none, who
have not furrendered altogether their confciences, and renounced their covenants, will fwear
allegiance to fuch enemies, efpecially to Papifts,
who are difcerned by acts of Parliament, to be
punifhed as idolaters, as enemies to the true religion, and all Chriftian government; and whom
we are, with uplifted hands to the moft high
God, many times fworn to extirpate; which is
inconfiftent with any allegiance. The 2d. is,
They muft find caution to transport themfelves
(as faid is) out of thefe three dominions, and not
to return without licence, under the pain of
death. This may-prove enfnaring to fome; but
it fhould not, neither will it, if they confider
what it impiies: For they cannot make that
choice, without acknowledging, and taking with
fuch grofs tranfgreffions and malverfations as
maketh them juftly to forfault all right of fub-
jects in thefe three kingdoms. O! I hope, no
true fons of the church of *Scotland* will fo renounce their intereft in *Scotland*'s caufe, covenants and contendings. Yea moreover, they
cannot make fuch a choice, unlefs they engage
to thefe enemies, for their peaceable behaviour;
which is to be underftood, as in their fenfe, a renouncing of duty, and a complying with their
impofitions, in that time, whatfomever, betwixt
the publication of the forefaid indemnity, and
the 20th of *May*, which is the time appointed
for their tranfportation. (4.) Thefe who accept
of that indemnity, do greatly tranfgrefs and fin
againft thefe who are excepted out of it, fucb as
minifters,

ministers, heritors, &c. For thereby they expose the foresaids, to be the butt of the adversary's malice and fury, and do deny to be any more sufferers with them for the interest of Christ. (5.) These who accept of this indemnity, do comply with the purposes of the enemies in general [and particular] which are to ruin the work and people of God, by breaking and [dividing them, and] cheating some of them out of their consciences; as we are to consider [them as following] the same purposes in their granting of pretended favours, and in [their grievous] persecutions and bloodshed; so we are to suspect and dread their favours [as the height of] cruelty, yea more, because vailed and masked over with [fair pretences;] like unto these who should make a bed to repose themselves in, and lay therein a naked knife or dagger with the point upward; As *Obad. v.* 7. *They that eat thy bread have laid a wound under thee;* whereupon, he is declared to *be of no understanding,* because he yielded himself to [them, and was brought] over by the subtilty of *his confederates,* and *these that were at peace with him.* (6.) Those who accept of that indemnity, do help foreward that purpose of enemies, in particular, in granting of it; which is, that they may get the better course taken with the more faithful, who trouble their kingdom most, and such as they are most mad against: For, as they say in their proclamation, they grant the said indemnity, before they determine their pleasure concerning such, which, say they, they hope to attain in a very short time. But as the hope of hypocrites, so the hope of enemies perisheth; for *Zion* is *a burdensome stone,* Zech. xii. 3. and their backs shall be broken with lifting at it. (7.)

These

These who accept of that indemnity do palpably break their covenant to the most high God; for there we are sworn not to be divided and broken off from our blessed union, either directly or indirectly by terror or persuasion. Now, that indemnity doth manifestly break off these who are excepted out of it; and these included, who do take it, from either acting in, or suffering for their duty together. (8.) These who accept of that indemnity do bind up their hands from acting any more for God, or against his enemies: for as in accepting of it, they take with a transgression; so, upon the matter, they engage not to transgress again; yea, do not the conditions of that pardon hold out very formally so much? And is not here a most direct breach of covenant, yea, a receding from the sum thereof? (9.) It would be considered that that indemnity is no indemnity, but (under that name) a subtile and masked traducing of people to a compliance; for it is granted upon such and such conditions, and that in sign and token of acceptance thereof. O then! is not that granter a liberal churl?

Now, dear friends, as to this purpose, I hope, I need say no more unto you, having spoken these things for your confirmation; judging that ye are clear of them already: Let enemies paint over their seeming favours as they will, yet considering the hand that reacheth them, we may justly dread them, and suspect them. *Do men gather grapes of thorns, or figs of thistles?* Can any drink clean water out of a corrupt fountain? Shall *Zion* ever expect any thing but a poisonable herb out of *Babylon's* garden? Or will ever an enemy do a favour? What hold shall we lay on Papists, whose principles lead them neither to give faith

to,

to, nor keep faith with hereticks, as they term
us? If ye would keep near God, keep far from
enemies both within and without, and make it
your work to be acquaint with the exercife of real religon: Ye have a noble opportunity for this
ftudy; for the Lord hath blocked you up from
many worldly cares and outward difturbances;
and why hath he done this? but that he may get
you taken up only with himfelf? I have heard it
of prifoners, that God made himfelf much more
known to them in bonds, than ever at liberty;
and I hope, that it is fo with not a few of you.
O the wifdom of God! who fhould make enemies inftruments of fo much good to his people.
O take him for you all, who is a non-fuch portion! In the fuppofed enjoyment of all created
things, there are ftill wants; but in the enjoyment of himfelf there is nothing wanting; yea,
more than a foul can defire, and than all created capacities are able to comprehend, is to be
found in him, for he is all in all. He is that
[treafure] of which enemies cannot rob you,
though they be permitted to come [and bereave
you of life,] and all created comforts; and is not
this a part of his excellency. [O then] make
him your choice, and according to his promife,
he will go through fire and water with you;
he will be with you in a prifon, in torture, in
bonds, in banifhment, and in death; and is
not his prefence enough; yea, all your trials
fhall work together for your good, (as he hath
faid) and therefore rejoice, not only in them,
but becaufe of them; and in all your feekings,
feek to have his image more and more renewed
in you. O employ the power and efficacy of his
grace for carrying on in you a progrefs in holinefs;

nefs; for the more of this ye attain to, the more of his fpecial manifeftations ye fhall enjoy, for it is his own image that the Lord delighteth to fmile and breath upon, and to converfe with. O holinefs! is it not many ways preferable to happinefs? albeit man's nature doth more affect happinefs than holinefs, becaufe he defires more that which is more pleafant, than that which is more excellent; yet without holinefs there can be no happinefs; for what is it that maketh heaven to be heaven, but becaufe there is there the full enjoyment of God, and perfect immunity and freedom from fin?

And as for the work and people of God, tho' I leave you to the Lord's free Spirit, for his exercifing you always fuitably anent their prefent cafe, yet there are thefe things, which I think ye fhould be much in wreftling for with God on their behalf; That he may give grace to his people to guide rightly their prefent cafe, for it is very hard to be guided, in refpect of the many mercies and judgments that are in their cup; alfo they are now, as it were, at fome pufh and extremity, the work being (if I may exprefs it fo) between the lofing and the winning; but it is in his hand, with whom nothing can mifcarry, let us leave it there, and be about our duty: That he may give direction to his people; for extreme difficulties put people to the greateft puzzle to know what to do; alfo a wrong ftep now will do very much fkaith; but his name is Counfellor: And that he may give them grace to perfevere and endure to the end; for I think we may expect the fharpeft of our trials to be yet to come; but his grace is fufficient: O! as they will be fharp, pray that they may be fhort, for the elect's fake, as the Lord hath faid.   And

And as to your own imprisonment, O my dear friends, wait upon the Lord for your outgate; ye know not what he may do: he can make prison-houses hiding-places. As I believe there is mercy in your lot, so there may be more than either ye or others can see: believe the best may be, and yet prepare for the worst; put ye a blank in the Lord's hand, and resolve upon the worst that men can do unto you, for that is the safest, and it shall not fare the worse with you, even as to the outward. And withall, I say, do not misbelieve, for God who hath hitherto restrained enemies, can bind them yet up from executing of their purposes against you.

Now, the multitude of business, and the shortness of time, forcing me to be but brief, which, I hope, your charity will cover with the mantle of a favourable construction: I shall detain you no further; but unto the Lord's grace I leave you, praying that ye may be kept faithful in this hour of temptation, that ye may be helped always to make a right choice in every condition; that ye may be so enabled to war against the world, the devil, and the flesh, as ye may not put a stain upon the honour of that holy name by which ye are called; and that ye may be still fed with the fatness of that land afar of, until ye come to the complete and full enjoyment [of him.] And, begging the help of your prayers, I am,

Dear Friends,

Your assured sympathising friend

in your tribulation, and

your servant in our Lord Christ,

JAMES RENWICK.

LETTER LX.

From the Rev. Mr. James Renwick, *to* ———.

Dear Friend in the Lord,   *Feb.* 6. 1688.

I Have no cause of complaining of my lot, there is a great necessity for it, and the Lord hath seen it for his glory, and he maketh me joyful in it. But there is one thing that doth a little trouble me, and yet when I look upon it again, I think there is not much cause of trouble. The matter is this: When I was apprehended and searched, there was found upon me a little memorandum, containing the names of some persons, to whom I had lent, and from whom I had borrowed some books: as also, a direction of letters to some doctors of divinity, or ministers, abroad. Upon this I was interrogate in the tolbooth, by a committee, who said, they had orders to torture me if I was not ingenuous. So as to the direction to the doctors, or ministers, abroad, which were full in the memorandum, I told, that there was a purpose of writing letters to them, but none were written: and being asked about the scope and design of the letters, I told that it was to represent our sufferings, and to procure their sympathy. It was asked, with whom I kept correspondence abroad? I told, with Mr. *Robert Hamilton*, which, I thought, could do no injury. And as to the names of other persons, which were written short, I judged there was no hazard in explaining their names, who were in the same hazard already: so I told,
that

ıs *Alexander Shields.* And being
was in *Scotland?* I thinking that
aching would not let him be hid,
fed he was; but told no definite
M. S. was *Michael Shields;* but
of abode: That *Ja. Wil.* and *Ar.*
es and *Archibald Wilson's;* and being
ne place of their abode, I anfwered,
'dale: That *C. A.* was *Colin Alifon;*
no place of abode: That *Peter R.*
ining; for I thought he was with-
ch: and being afked about his oc-
abode, I told, he trafficked within
England. *Peter Aird's* name was
and being afked particularly about
he was a man of the country of
'alfton, or *Evandale,* I knew not
mes *Coftoun's* name was thus full,
ced of his abode, I told, he lived
oun of *Galloway,* or thereabout:
: man, and this was true of him,
e is now: That *M.* was my mother,
no place of abode. I was moſt
who *M. M.* at *Gl.* was, with whom
; and I anfwered, that I was not
g any other perfon into trouble,
y might do with me. They faid
efs could not bring any into trou-
did not now proceed againſt folk
ters; and that their defign was on-
from torture, which thy could not
at I would be ingenuous about that
wered, that I would in no ways ex-
me, unlefs they would not trouble
They faid, they would endeavour
l trouble of that kind. Therefore,

T   l

I thinking that the perſon's name was already among enemies in the place, and ſuppoſing there were ſome others of that name ; and alſo conceiving, that trouble upon that account could hardly be expected ; they gueſſing that *Gl.* was *Glaſgow,* I told the advocate alone, that *M. M.* was Mrs. *Millar.* Her name was not ſet down in write by their clerk as the reſt were, and he hath no witneſſes upon it ; ſo I think it not probable that ſhe can incur any injury, for I was not more particular.

Now, I ſhall ſay no more as to this, but only adviſe perſons in my circumſtances, either not to write ſuch memorandums, or not to keep them upon them, which I did inadvertently and inconſiderately. You may communicate this to whom you think fit, eſpecially to the perſons concerned ; but ſee that you take along with you all the circumſtances. I ſtudied to ſave myſelf from lying, to preſerve them from trouble, and to evite the threatened torture. I was preſſed much to tell my haunts and abodes theſe ſeveral years by-paſt ; and I told them I ſometimes reſorted to *John Lookup*'s houſe, where the officers came upon me, but further I would give them no notice : ſo I paſſed.

Now, if there be any thing in this that may be offenſive to friends, I ſeek their forgiveneſs for it ; for if I had apprehended any ſin in all this, or that any perſon would thereby incur injury, I would then, and now alſo, rather undergo all the threatened torture.

The keepers of the tolbooth have frequently told me of marrying the herd in the *Leeps,* and ſome perſons in *Pentland.* And *Alexander Weir,* who is with the provoſt, told me of baptiſing a
child

child to one —— *Scot's* husband, but I endeavoured to boast them out of it. . As for my pocket-book, which contained only the sum of my two last sermons at *Braid's Craigs*, with the time and place: I owned such doctrine.

I have no further to write at the time, for I resolve to write some after this, which I would have more public than this. I desire that none may be troubled upon my behalf, but rather rejoice with him, who, with hope and joy, is waiting for his marriage, and coronation hour. I am,

Your friend and servant in the Lord,

JAMES RENWICK.

. LETTER LXI.

The Rev. Mr. James Renwick's *last Letter to the right honourable Mr.* Robert Hamilton.

Right hon. and dear Sir,   *Feb.* 17. 1688.

THis being my last day upon earth, I thought it my duty to send you this my last salutation. The Lord hath been wonderfully gracious to me since I came to prison, he hath assured me of his salvation, helped me to give a testimony for him, and own before his enemies all that I have taught, and strengthened me to resist and repell many temptations and assaults, O! praise to his name.

Now, as to my testimony, which I left in your hands, when I entered into the work of the

mini-

miniftry, I do ftill adhere unto the matter o
it; but I think the manner of expreffion is ii
fome things too tart, and it containeth fundr'
mens names, fome whereof are now in eternity
alfo it is not fo pertinent to our prefent affairs
for the ftate of our controverfies is altered
therefore I judge it may be deftroyed, for I have
teftimony fufficient left behind me in my writtei
fermons, and in my letters. But if this trouble
you, and if you defire to keep it for yourfelf
and your own ufe, you would keep this lettei
with it, and not publifh it further abroad: ye
you may make ufe of any part of the matter o
it, that may conduce to the clearing of any controverfy. And as for the direction of it untc
you, if I had lived, and been qualified for writing a book, and if it had been dedicated to any
man, you would have been the man : For I have
loved you, and I have peace before God in that.
and I blefs his name that I have been acquainted
with you.

Remember me to all that are friends to you,
particularly to the Ladies at *Lewarden,* to whom
I would have written, if I had not been kept
clofe in prifon, and pen, ink, and paper kept
from me. But I muft break off. I go to your
God and my God. Death to me is as a bed to
the weary. Now, be not anxious, the Lord
will maintain his caufe, and own his people;
he will fhew his glory yet in *Scotland.* Farewel
beloved and comfortable Sir,

   Sic fubfcribitur,

    JAMES RENWICK.

            The

The following LETTERS *were written by different Perſons, during the perſecuting Period; ſeveral of which are printed from the original Manuſcripts.*

LETTER LXII.

Mr. *John Livingſton*'s letter to his pariſh of *Ancrum*, being his farewell before his baniſhment from *Britain* and *Ireland*, upon his refuſing the oath of ſupremacy.

To the flock of Jeſus Chriſt at Ancrum, *light, life, and love, and the conſolations of the Holy Ghoſt be multiplied...*

Leith, April 13. 1663.

Wellbeloved in the Lord,

THat which your ſins, even your ſins and mine, hath been a long time procuring, and which has been often threatened, is now come, even a ſeparation; how long it may continue is in the Lord's hand, but it will be our part to ſearch out and mourn for theſe ſins, that have drawn down ſuch a ſtroke. It is not needful to look much to inſtruments, I have from my heart forgiven them all, and wiſh you to do the like, and to pray for them, that it be not laid to their charge. But let us look to him without

T 3. *whoſe*

whose doings there is no evil in the city; for, *he hath torn, and he will heal; he hath smitten, and he will bind us up: Let us neither despise his chastening, nor faint when we are rebuked of him.* It may be we shall not suddenly find out every controversy he has against us; but if there be upright dealing in such things as are obvious, and an impartial endeavour of discovering what is hid, he will reveal even that unto us: neither is there a greater hinderer of repentance, than a secure desperate questioning whether he will accept or not. Jesus Christ has been and will be in all ages, *a stone of stumbling, and a rock of offence,* to those that stumble at the word, and refuse to receive his rich offers; but to others a *foundation and corner stone, elect and precious, and he that believeth in him shall not be confounded.* We have reason to believe, that whatever he does is only best: God saw all that he had made, and behold it was very good; that word will hold good to the end of world. For my part, I have reason to bless his name, I have great peace in the matter of my suffering: I need not repent. Ye know my testimony of the things in controversy: Jesus Christ is a King, and he alone hath power to appoint the officers and government of his church, 'Tis a fearful thing to violate God's oath, and to fall into the living God's hand. It could not well be expected, there having been so fair and general professions through the land, but that the Lord would put men to it; and it is like the trial will come to every man's private door, that when every one have, according to their inclination, acted their part, and he seems to stand by, he may come at the last and act his part, and vindicate his glory and truth.

I have often shewed you that it is the greatest difficulty under heaven to believe there is a God, and a life after this; and for my own part, I have often told you, I could never make it a chief part of my work to insist upon the particular debates of the time, as being assured, that if one do drink in the knowledge and love of the main foundations of the Christian religion, and have the work of God's Spirit upon his heart, to make him walk with God, and make conscience of his ways, such a one, except he be giddy with self-conceit, shall not readily mistake God's quarrel to join either with an atheistical profane party, or with an atheistical phanatic party; but *the secret of the Lord* will be *with them that fear him, he will shew them his covenant.* And I have thought it not far from a sure argument, that what course is not approven of God, generally all the godly, and all the profane turning penitent, scunner at it, and it may be cannot well tell why; and generally all the profane, at the first sight, and all that had a profession of piety, when they turn loose, embrace it, and it may be cannot tell why. There may be both diversity of judgments, and sometimes sharp debates among them that are going to heaven; but certainly one spirit guides the seed of the woman, and another spirit guides the seed of the serpent; and blessed are they that know their Master's will and doth it; *blessed are they that endure to the end.* And both you and I have reason to bless the Lord, that however I be the unworthiest of all that ever spake in his name, yet my labour among

mongſt you hath not been in vain altc
ſome have given evidence of a real
Spirit of God upon their heart and li
ſome are already in glory, and othe
thro' an ill world : and, I truſt, ſome
given great evidence yet, may have
God in their heart, which may in d
orth, at leaſt at their death. But
may be ſaid of them in whom the
ſpirit of drunkenneſs, of greed and f
ſpirit of licentiouſneſs and wilful ign
no zeal of prayer, for all the means
that have been ſtirring amongſt us, v
will be glad now that they get looſe
to all wickedneſs ; they may be car
open apoſtacy and perſecution. Th
of you, I requeſt, in the bowels of J
yea, I obteſt and charge you, in th
authority of him that ſhall judge th
the dead, that ye turn ſpeedily to
and make conſcience of praying m
evening, and read, or cauſe to be re
ſome of his word, where you will fin
neceſſary for faith and converſation.
ſnares and temptations are many and f
Satan, from the world, from the
heart within ; but faith in God, a
ſeeking of him ſhall overcome them a
not the care of your immortal ſouls
the love of this life, or any thing in t
O that ye would taſte and ſee the g
the Lord, and take an eſſay of the fi
ing of God for a while, and prove
not open the windows of heaven,
out a bleſſing. Let me obtain this o
recompence of all the labour I have h

you, and as an allaying of my sufferings I am put to, that, after you read this, you will set some time apart, alone, or in your families, as you have convenience, to think on these directions, that have been formerly given you from the word of God; and deal you earnestly with him, that ye may remember them, and look them over, and engage your hearts to him, that in his strength ye will walk in his ways. And if any shall stubbornly neglect such a wholesome counsel, that comes from an earnest desire of your salvation, I will be forced to bear witness against you in the day of the Lord, that light was holden forth to you; but I desire to hope better things of you. If the Lord see it good we may see the day wherein we may meet again, and bless his name solemnly, that although he was angry, yet *his anger is turned away;* but, if not, the good-will of the Lord be done. I think, I may say, I could have been well content, although it had been with many discouragements, to have gone and served you all, as I could, in the gospel of Jesus Christ; but the prerogative royal of Jesus Christ, and the peace of a man's conscience, are not to be violated upon any consideration; neither could there be a blessing expected when ought is done against these.

I was desirous, and have used means, that I might have come and seen you, and, at least in a private way, bidden you farewell ere I had left the country; but wife providence has otherwise ordered it: However, I carry your names alongst in my book, yea, I shall carry them on my heart whithersoever I go, and begs your mutual prayers for me, that I may be keeped
fruitful,

fruitful, and faithful, and blameless, even to the end; and that, if it he his will, I may be restored to you. Mean time, love and help one another; have a care to breed your children to know the Lord, and to keep themselves from the pollutions of an ill world. I commend to you above all books (except the blessed Bible, the word of God) the Confession of Faith, and Larger Catechism: Be grounding yourselves and one another against the abomination of Popery, in case it should prove the trial of the time. Let a care be had of the poor and sick; there is as much left as will suffice for meat and money a year and more. I cannot insist in the several particulars possibly wherein ye would take advice: the word is a lamp, and the Spirit of Christ will guide you in all truth. The light that comes after unfeigned humiliation, self-denial, earnest prayer, and searching of the Scriptures, is a sure light.

I know that my word and write are of small value, yet I could not forbear, but in few words salute you ere I went. And now, farewell, dearly beloved and longed for: *The Lord of all grace, who hath called us into his eternal glory by Jesus Christ, after ye have suffered a while, make you perfect, stablish and strengthen you: To him be glory and dominion for ever and ever.* Amen.

By your loving servant and pastor,

JOHN LIVINGSTON.

LETTER

LETTER LXIII.

From the Rev. Mr. John Brown, *to the much re-spected and worthy Mrs.* Jean Ker, *daughter to the Laird of* Kersland, *now a prisoner for* Christ *within the castle of* Dumbarton.

Utrecht, Sept. 24. 1670.

Worthy and dear Mistress,

HAving this occasion to salute your dear father, now a prisoner for Christ, and not knowing when I should have occasion to write again, I thought I was called of God to write this line to you, and therein to exhort you in the Lord to rejoice in your lot; which love, free love, and everlasting free love, hath measured out to you. All your tossings, and the time when your tossings should begin, and the manner of your tossings, and the occasion of your tossings, all was wisely decreed from everlasting; yea, all was covenanted from eternity betwixt the Father and the Son. (O blessed bargain! the solid and comfortable stay to all poor tossed souls.) Means and ends were both covenanted and determined; for, *whom he did foreknow, he also did predestinate to be conformed to the image of his Son, that he might be the first-born among many brethren,* Rom. viii. 29. Now then, it was a decreed thing, that as the Captain of our salvation was made perfect through sufferings, so, through much tribulation should we also enter into the kingdom of heaven. Head and members must wear one livery; and this is our crown, and our glory, that we are put to follow his foot-

steps,

steps, and to be conformed to his image. May not this satisfy us, that *neither tribulation, nor distress, nor persecution, nor famine, nor nakedness, nor peril, nor sword, nor death, nor life, nor angels, nor principalities, nor powers, nor things present, nor things to come, nor height, nor depth, nor any other creature, shall be able to separate us from the love of God which is in Christ Jesus our Lord!*

Dear Mistress, the Lord hath seen it meet to tryst you with tossings in your young days, that you may learn betimes to be acquainted with Christ's school; and to know that *we have no continuing city here,* and that *you may seek one to come,* and look out for that *city which hath foundations, whose builder and maker is God.* And now, the solitary walls of that rocky hill is as near to this city above, to this new *Jerusalem,* which cometh down from heaven, as any place in the world; as was the soil of your nativity. And those barren walls cry, O Mistress Jean, Look up above where is your Father's house, that pleasant soil; your elder Brother is there, your husband is before you: There, there, is your rest; there shall you have satisfaction; and the consolation which we cannot yield; nay, nor the most pleasant, fertile, and desirable spot in all the world. 'Dear Mistress, it shall be no grief of heart to you one day, that you was forced for Christ's sake, to dwell on that barren and dry rock of *Dumbarton:* No, it shall increase your joy so much the more. O Mistress, mind your love, your only husband, to whom you have given yourself; forget him not, for he doth not, he will not forget you: you are engraven upon the palms of his hands. You are

are written up with your mother *Zion* there; you are sharing with her, therefore rejoice in your lot. Though you mourn now, you shall rejoice when God shall put a song in her mouth. We should wait and believe; and though the fig-tree blossom not, we should rejoice. Oh! if we would sing on luck's head; and indeed we have good ground, for all was well concluded in the parliament of heaven; and all the powers and parliaments on earth cannot change or alter one article of this grand parliament. Mistress, hold fast your grip of him, or rather put your poor weak hand in his, that he may hold your grips of him fast and sure. The time is coming, when time shall be no more; no more tossings, and no more temptations; no more mourning, but an everlasting song of praise to God, and to him who sitteth upon the throne, even the Lamb, world without end. Since we can do no more now, let us join our *Amen* to all the songs of praises, which the blessed choir of angels, and the spirits of just men made perfect, are singing this day, and will never give it over. You have reason to bless God, who hitherto hath letten you see your own nakedness and misery, and hath hidden pride from your eyes. O be humble still, and walk under the sense of a body of death; for the puffing up of some (of whom I had expected better things) makes me fear what the issue shall be. Some of these persons are already Ana-baptists and Antinomians, and are fast drink-ing in the notions of the Familists, and other phantastic persons, whose carriage, in a great part, became at length scandalous. My soul is feared for them: The Lord prevent them with his mercy. Dear Mistress, keep humble and

U

keep

keep near Chrift, then you fhall be happy. Good words, and fair fpeeches will not be enough. Let our hearts be right with him; and not think that all is gold which gliftcrs. His grace be with you.

Dear Miſtreſs,

> *Yours in the Lord Jeſus Chriſt,*

> > J O H N B R O W N.

L E T T E R LXIV.

From the **Rev. Mr.** John Brown *to Mrs.* Jean Ker, *daughter to the Laird of* Kerſland.

Worthy and dear Miſtreſs, *Aug.* 9. 1677.

MY long filence as to writing, hath not been through forgetfulnefs. I may confidently fay, I neither do, nor can forget you; and, which is to you infinitely more, the Father of mercies neither doth, nor will forget you: O how happy is it to be interefted in him, to have a fhare of his crofs, to be following him through adverfi-ty, and to be owning him and his defpifed caufe. It may be, it is fomewhat bitter at prefent; but afterward, O what joy and confolation will it yield to a foul going into eternity, to remember, and reflect upon the toffings and hardfhips he hath endured, and been put to fuffer for the fake of Jefus, and his glorious truth and inter-eft, and there fee the fpecial love of God, call-ing him or her out to ferve him, and to endure the difpleafure of men for his fake. I hope,

you

you find, Dear Mistress, the unseen incomes of
joy, refreshing your soul, in the midst of all your
other hardships, that make you say, you would
not change lots with the best: the four cross is
made sweeter than all the honied rest, wealth,
pleasure and ease would be, that others delight
themselves with, and sit down upon as their portion. Up your heart, my dearly beloved, the
Lord is coming. He hath seen all that young
Jean Ker hath been made to suffer for his sake;
all is fresh in his rememberance; and all *Jean
Ker*'s tears, tossings, groans, sighs, and sore
hearts, &c. are written up in his book of remembrance. You will think all little enough
one day: and when you see, with a full sight, his
glorious face, you will say, O is this he for
whom I suffered disgrace, harrassings, disaccom-
modations and other evils? had I known what
an one he was and is, I would have been willing,
and accounted it my glory, to have suffered ten
thousand times more than I did. O mistress,
how joyful will your heart be, when he shall
come to the door of heaven; and welcome you
into glory, and with his soft hand wipe all your
tears away, and put on *beauty for ashes, the oil
of joy for mourning, the garments of praise for the
spirit of heaviness;* and put the new song, the
song of *Moses,* and of the redeemed, in your
mouth? Can you now imagine, how your heart
will leap then for joy! Take courage then, believe and hope. He is true, and will not deny
himself; his word is tried; his promises are sure.
Let us give him glory by faith, and in patience
possess our souls; for not one word that ever he
spoke shall fail. Let all your work be to get
your heart wrought up more and more to love
him,

him, and to wonder at his difpenfations of love
toward you. Give him glory that ever he put
that honour upon your father's family, to ftand
by the banner of Chrift, when many that feemed fomething of old, have forfaken him, and
have embraced this prefent world. Fear not, a
delivery will come; but I am afraid, the dawn-
ing of that day fhall be terrible: The righteous
God muft be avenged on an adulterous generation. But, in the mean time, he will be an hiding place to his own. His grace be with you
now and evermore. I remain,

Yours in the Lord,

JOHN BROWN.

LETTER LXV.

From the Rev. Mr. John King, *unto the prifoners in the back of the* Gray-friars *church-
yard.* 1679.

*My dearly beloved in the Lord, and highly ho-
noured prifoners for Chrift,*

I Have my love chearfully remembered to you
all, who am alfo your fellow-fufferer and
companion in tribulation, for the fame honourable caufe. Dear friends, I would not have you
think it ftrange concerning the fiery trial, as
though fome ftrange thing happened unto you,
and to the remnant in *Scotland,* by this prefent
difpenfation; for the like has fallen out, when
the people of God has got a call from the Lord,
and

and yet have fallen before the enemy, as ye may find in *Judges* xx. *chap.* and ye may read at length what follows; therefore I am sure, it is the sins of the people of the Lord, which has provoked the Lord to let his people fall before his enemies, and yet have no respect to the enemy; for, no doubt, they are a people devoted to destruction, except they repent. Ye see in *Jer.* xii. 4, 7. he has been provoked to do this to his people, even *to give the dearly beloved of his soul into the hand of their enemies,* and with no respect to these whom they are given up to, ye will find it in the 14. verse, *Thus saith the Lord against all mine evil neighbours, that touch the inheritance, which I caused my people Israel to inherit, Behold, I will pluck them out of their land, and pluck out the house of Judah from among them.* This is the thing, we may see the Lord's anger not turned away from the remnant in Scotland, but his hand is stretched out still, that has caused him *deliver up his strength into captivity, and his glory into the enemies hands.* And I am sure, my dear friends, you are Christ's glory in *Scotland,* so many young men jeoparding their lives in the high places of the fields for Christ, whom he has given into the hands of the enemy; and I hope that the Lord will arise yet, as a strong man after wine refreshed, and smite his enemies upon their hinder parts; and therefore, my dear friends, seeing ye are Christ's glory, it is your glory to suffer for his name's sake, and it should be your rejoicing that ye are counted worthy to suffer for the sake of Christ; and therefore be of good chear, my dear friends, for Christ is greatly concerned with you, for he has a fellow feeling with you in all your troubles,

and

and Chrift is fuffering more in his glory than all
your fufferings; and therefore be encouraged,
dear friends, feeing Chrift is fuffering with you,
Heb. iv. 15. who cannot but *be touched with your
infirmities.* John xv. 20. *If they have perfecuted
me, they will perfecute you: if they have kept my
fayings, they will keep yours alfo.* Zech. ii. 8.
He that toucheth you, toucheth the apple of his eye.
But that may be your complaint, which was the
church's, *Ifa.* xlix. 14. *But Zion faid, The Lord
hath forfaken me, and my Lord hath forgotten me:*
but yet the Lord anfwers in the 15 ver. *Can a
woman forget her fucking child, that fhe fhould
not have compaffion on the fon of her womb; yea,
fhe may forget, yet will I not forget thee. Behold
I have graven thee upon the palms of my hands,
thy walls are continually before me.* Therefore
it is your part to act faith upon the promifes, although your cafe and the church of *Scotland's*
feem very difmal like; for if ye prefently look
through the cloud unto Chrift, and take a look
of Chrift's fufferings, what he fuffered for your
fakes, and for the fake of the elect, and that
the faints before now have fuffered; for Chrift
has told his people, that *through many tribulations they muft enter the kingdom; and all that
will live godly in Chrift Jefus, fhall fuffer perfecution,* 2 Tim. iii. 12. Thefe that will be Chrift's
difciples muft *deny themfelves,* and *take up their
crofs, and follow him,* Mark viii. 34. Indeed,
dear friends, it is fad to you, to endure what
you are put to, fo many of you together, what
by the fcorching heat of the fun, and what by
rain, there is no doubt your vifage is marred;
but yet, I would have you taking this for your
encouragement, in *Ifa.* lii. 14. *As many were
                                        aftonied*

astonied at him, his *visage was so marred more
than any man, and his form more than the sons of
men;* and therefore, dear friends, be encouraged, 2 *Tim.* ii. 12. *If ye suffer with him, ye
shall also reign with him.* Luke xxii. 28. 29. *If
ye continue with him in his tentations,* he has promised to you *the kingdom* and honour, and your
*momentary affliction is not worthy to be compared
to the glory that is to be revealed;* and so do not
fret nor repine under your troubles, 1 *Pet.* iv.
14. *For the spirit of glory, and of God shall rest
upon you,* if ye suffer chearfully; and bless God
that ever he choosed the like of you to be witness for him; and ye may all cry out with *David,
What am I, and what is my father's house, that
thou hast brought me hither* to suffer for him, for
had it not been free love that prevented you, ye
might have been among these that have been
lifting up a banner against the Son of God;
which some, alas! whom we would not have
expected, have joined in this combination a-
gainst Christ, for which I wish them repentance,
or else they shall smart for it. The Lord has
honoured you before many of the professors of
Scotland, that were as much concerned, and
personally sworn and engaged to stand to the defence of that interest. But alas! I think, this is
one of the greatest controversies the Lord hath
with *Scotland,* that is, not adhering to our Covenants; the League and Covenant, and National
Covenant are cast behind the back of the generation; not only by the malignant party who
have perjured themselves, but also by a great
part of the ministers and professors of *Scotland,*
in not adhering to the ends of these covenants,
but have connived and complied with adversaries,

ries, and ſtrengthened their hands againſt their
poor brethen, that are now bearing the burden,
and in the heat of the day, and they are ſtanding aloof at their ſcorn, counting it their wiſdom
to ſtand at a diſtance: and the Lord has been
witneſſing, dear friends, by your eſſay to ſet
Chriſt upon his throne again in *Scotland*, and re-
ſtoring the ancient liberties of our church from
under the bondage of tyrannizing Prelacy, that
the land has been groaning under theſe eighteen
years by-gone; a yoke that neither we nor our
fathers were able to bear, and which has been
contended againſt at the hazard of lives, yea,
many lives have gone in that quarrel; and this
appearance of yours doth not only witneſs againſt
the open and avowed enemies, but alſo againſt
all thoſe that have not joined with you that were
in a capacity, that is, profeſſed friends; and he
has taken you, O poor things in the world, to
confound the rich; and fooliſh things to confound the wiſe; and young things to confound
the old; and things that ſeemed not to be, to
counfound the things that were. Although the
Lord hath not favoured you with victory, yet
it tends to the praiſe of the Lord's rich grace
in you, and ye are the Lord's witneſſes this day
in *Scotland*, witneſſing againſt the defection of
your brethren, and againſt all the avowed enemies of Chriſt's crown and kingdom in theſe nations. And as to you that are old men, highly
honoured of the Lord, your gray hairs are a
crown of glory; like *Zabulon* and *Naphtali* ye
have *jeoparded your lives upon the high places of
the field*, for your maſter's honourable cauſe;
and although, *Joſeph* like, the archers are ſhoot-
ing ſore at you, yet your bow ſhall abide in

ftrength, and ere it be long ye fhall be promoted to a greater kingdom than *Pharaoh's*, ye fhall reign with the Lord Chrift through all the ages of eternity; and no doubt the Lord will be forth-coming to your pofterity: but I wifh from my heart fpeedy repentance to thefe your brethren, that it may be, counted it their wifdom, that they have not joined with you in the defence of fo honourable a caufe. I am fure, that their wifdom is foolifhnefs with God, and I cannot tell how they cannot tell how they can be free of that curfe that is mentioned in *Judges* v. 23. *Curfe ye Meroz, faid the angel of the Lord, curfe ye bitterly the inhabitants thereof, becaufe they came not out to the help of the Lord, to the help of the Lord againft the mighty.* They may think to enjoy their liberty and their eftates, but it is like, if it be fo, it fhall be at a dear rate. But as for you, my dear friends, that have jeoparded your all for Chrift, lives and liberties, relations and poffeffions, you have Chrift's promife, you fhall have a hundred fold in this life, and life everlafting in that which is to come. Ye have the word of a king for this who cannot err, who is the true and faithful witnefs; and therefore it is is your part to act faith upon the promifes. Whatfoever prefent ftraits you and your families may be reduced to, the Lord will be forth-coming to you and yours. Therefore, dear friends, beware of any finful way to relieve you or yours. Although you may have temptations by your friends, for that may be fome of your trials, as it was *Job's*, by his own friends and his own wife; yet refift the temptation come from what airth it will, and tell them that they fpeak foolifhly: for we doubt will

feek

seek to winnow you as wheat in a sieve, for he likes to fish in drumley waters; and ye know, what blasphemies and reproaches it will occasion against God, and against his ways, as it is already, and how wounding it is to you that are godly, to hear enemies mouths opened; and ye may judge what sorrow it will be to the godly in *Scotland* if ye miscarry, and how more and more it will open the mouths of the adversaries: and therefore, dear friends, seeing it is like to be the lot of the people of God either to sin or suffer; it is your part rather to suffer, and to choose with *Moses, rather to suffer affliction with the people of God, than to enjoy the pleasures of sin for a season;* for ye see what the cloud of witnesses suffered, *Heb.* xi. *Tortured, not accepting deliverance, that they might obtain a better resurrection.* Some have *had* trials, as yours, *of cruel mockings, some, of bonds and imprisonments; some were stoned, some were sawn asunder, were tempted, were slain with the sword; they wandered about in sheep-skins and goat-skins, being destitute, afflicted, tormented; of whom the world was not worthy:* Yea, *they wandered in deserts, and in mountains, and in dens and caves of the earth.* Chap. xii. 2. *Looking unto Jesus the author and finisher of their faith; who for the joy that was set before him, endured the cross, despising the shame, and is set down at the right hand of the majesty on high; Considering him that endured such contradiction of sinners against himself, lest ye be weary and faint in your minds.* Look into all the scriptures, and there ye will see what has been the lot of the saints that are all singing hallelujah at the Father's right hand this day: and if ye follow them with faith and patience,

ence, it shall be your lot ere long, as it is the lot of some of your honourable and renowned brethren; therefore I would not have you to be discouraged, for the Lord can make the day's breaking and scattering of his people tend to the furthering of the gospel, and the Lord has said it, *Rom.* viii. 28. that *all things shall work together for good to them that love him, and to these that are called according to his purpose.* Although this seems very improbable to sense and reason, yet the Lord's word cannot lie; and it has been an old saying among the worthies, that the blood of the saints is the seed of the church, which has been made out in all days; also we have the experience of it in our own day, for since the break of *Pentland,* since the honourable worthies suffered, some in the fields, and some on scaffolds, that was the beginning of a great rise of the gospel in *Scotland,* which many of you are the seals of, and all of you that are young men, which are witnesses to that same cause: Therefore be of good chear, for the Lord can make you conquerors by your sufferings; therefore although it hath given a dash to the faith of the people of God in *Scotland,* yet there is hope, seeing the Lord hath taken a sacrifice off some of your hands. But I would that ye and all the professors in *Scotland* were searching and trying our ways, and turning again unto the Lord. Doubtless there is an *Achan* in the camp of our *Israel,* so that we could not stand before our enemies; but *Ephraim* like when the day of battle came, they were faint-hearted, and turned back, *Psal.* lxxviii. because they were not faithful, nor stedfast in God's covenant. And we shall say no more but commit you to the great

Shep-

Shepherd of the flock, that brought again our Lord from the dead, that he may watch over you, and judge his people, and repent him for his fervants, when he fees their power is gone, and there is none fhut up or left. *Rejoice, O ye nations, with his people, for he will avenge the blood of his fervants, and will render vengeance to his adverfaries, and will be merciful to his land, and to his people.*

Yours, to power,

Sic fubfcribitur,

JOHN KING.

LETTER LXVI.

From the Rev. Mr. Donald Cargil, *to the Lady* Earlfton, *younger.*

Madam,   *Feb.* 22. 1680.

I Shall not pafs the expreffions of your affection to me:—I am truely forry, that there is nothing in me that can either requit the kindnefs, or anfwer the expectations of any. And I am truely refrefhed to hear of your frame, and your courage and ftedfaftnefs in that way, which is God's. And I am perfuaded, the further you ftand off from them, and the more zealoufly you deteft their doings, it is ftill the better. Fear not, your forfeiture fhall not be long, and your *de novo damus* fhall be from heaven, more fure, and more bleffed, if you take it not from earth; and your rent of one year lifted by another,

(which

(which to me yet is doubted) shall not enrich the receiver, and shall bear interest unto you. He is not only putting me on petitions for higher and greater things than these private, but also himself is making me to crave of himself, in behalf of these that are afflicted, the hundredfold in this life, and it shall be sure to them, or to their heirs. However, for the present, make sure, and bring your comfort not only mainly, but only from the other; for, as this is your season to seek, so you shall find it his season graciously to give; for, I think, he would never have suffered you to come to this strait for him, if he had not purposed to gratify you with his exceeding great reward: and I am persuaded if it be sought by all, nothing will hinder the performance; no, not our own personal sins, if they be rightly acknowledged.————

As for Mr. *Richard Cameron*, I never heard any thing from him, in the Lord's truth, but I am both ready and willing to confirm it. But woes me that I have not more worth and authority for that cause: but truth itself, if it be rightly pleaded, will have authority upon consciences. My re'pects being remembered to your nearest friends, and all other friends that are right in his cause,

Madam,

> *Your servant in our Lord,*

DONALD CARGIL.

X   LETTER

LETTER LXVII.

From the Rev. Mr. Donald Cargil, *to his well-beloved friends* Alexander Gordon *of* Earlfton, *Mr.* Ardoch, *and Mr.* M'Millan *in* Arrendar-roch.

Dearly Beloved,   *Gilkie, April* 14. 1680.

I Have purpofed, according to your defire, to vifit you, but have been hitherto hindered. The caufe of my prefent return, after I was come mid-way, our brother will fhew you, and, I hope, will fatisfy you; and if the Lord give opportunity, I fhall yet fulfil my purpofe. What I purpofed to have imparted to ———, who was gone before I came, I have imparted it to him, who will communicate it to you; fo that I need not write of them further. Only leave your own things for a little, till ye receive them from God in a better way; for not only is the feeking but the receiving of favours from men, ftated in fuch oppofition to God, as not without a fnare to the foul: and if it begets a juft jealoufy in God, to have any converfation with thofe with whom he hath fuch enmity, and feeing providence hath clofed the door of doing for yourfelves in thefe things, lay ye them afide alfo; and what comfort ye have within yourfelves, what work ye fhall give yourfelves too; and what intereft ye fhall efpoufe: but let all things be little to you in refpect of this, to have the land brought about to be the Lord's, and to have the Lord reigning in it. Be frequent in prayer and humiliation, for I will affure you, ye

will

will find those duties to be more easy and sweet
in performance, more hopeful in their expectation, and more prevalent as to their effects,
than before they have been. But never think
yourselves right till ye have repented of what
is past, and have intended to reformation in all
things. And let the desires and designs of your
hearts be such, that, in a manner, he cannot
but both avouch you, and prosper them; and
severe yourselves from the sins, interests, and
courses of this present generation; otherways
these who have been chastised by themselves,
may be again chastised with them in their judgments, which shall be both dreadful and near.
But haste you out of the city, for that hinders,
and seek to be united to God, and to one another in truth and love; and this cannot be without the pouring out of the Spirit, which must be
obtained by prayer; and beware of patching up
with men, for they have their own cards to play,
and their own way to go, which are not only
diverse from, but directly opposite to God's; and
if I mistake not, God's intention this time is
clearly to sever us, that he may shew us kindness
by ourselves (and till that be, we shall never have
him as we would) and employ us as we desire to
be employed: and fear not, for the fewer, we
shall not be the less strong; and forget not to
shut yourselves up in a covenant with him, that if
we must die in the common lot, we may die
with repentance, and such purposes in our heart,
and leave a model to them that come after, of
the temple we minded to build to him, that these
may go on according to that pattern, and do
well.

As for our brother, ye both ought, and I

know.

know ye will receive him gladly, and encourage him in all things, for he doth the work of the Lord; and ye shall find the Lord hath provided better for you than if I had come. The Lord establish you in every good work. *Amen.*

Yours, in true affection,

DONALD CARGIL.

P. S. There is one thing I have forgotten; Seek not to them that have been joined with us in some things, if they have owned that interest, or sided with these courses of defection: nor though they seek to you, accept of them not, till they seriously resent, and utterly renounce these things.

LETTER LXVIII.

From the Rev. Mr. Richard Cameron, *to Mr.* Alexander Gordon *of* Earlston.

Right Honourable,   *March* 22. 1680.

I Was this day within five miles of *Nith*, in order to meet with your Honour; but one is come to me from other friends, who has made me turn my head to another airth: the business is of moment, of which you may after this (if the Lord will) be informed. But if you be to write to *Holland* (as I doubt not but both you and your lady will) I am to send a brother of mine thither; his voyage is not to be delayed, and therefore you will not delay to have one in once
this

this week to *Edinburgh*: I mean I will be content, if bufinefs will permit, and counfel fought from the Lord, that yourfelf were there; for we are to have confiderable things in hand; but if you cannot win, I'll make all the hafte I can to fee you and friends with you. I intreat you to fignify this to our friends in *Dalray, Kels*, and *Glencairn*: I hope the Lord has fome work for them yet, though I were gone, which will not be while my Mafter has work for me. O to be ready to be bound, yea, and to die. I dare not fit this call, whatever be the hazard. The Lord will carry on his work maugre all oppofition: *The daughter of Zion fhall yet arife and threfh*, &c. *Micah* iv. 13.

I have feveral encouraging things to impart to you when there is an opportunity of once meeting afforded. I hope to meet in heaven with not a few out of the houfe of *Earlfton* and *Aird's* one family. O how refrefhing will it be to fee in that day feverals who lived in the *Glenkens*, together with fome from *Balmagie* and *Corfemichal*.

The Lord be with you all. I doubt not but you mind me in your prayers. My refpect to both your ladies, fifters, &c. not forgetting the young laird, as fure as any I know, and my own Mrs. *Ann*. Referring other things till meeting, Sir, I bid you farewell.

RICHARD CAMERON.

LETTER

LETTER LXIX.

From the Rev Mr Richard Cameron, *to Mr.*
Alexander Gordon *of* Earlston.

Right Honourable,   *May* 22. 1680.

I Hope you'll have me excufed for not writing
to you on *Thurfday* laft, for I was then perplexed for Mr. *Donald*'s not coming, and had no
time, but I met with him fince : he is not to come
to this country at this time. However, if you
know nothing to obftruct our appointment on
Friday next, I am willing, in the Lord's ftrength,
to keep it, and before that, if health and other
things will permit you. I defire to meet with
your Honour upon *Wednefday*'s night, or *Thurfday*'s night at fartheft. You may appoint the
place, and I fhall endeavour to wait upon you.
If you be not able, you will write to me with
the bearer, that he may be again at me once
upon *Wednefday.*

We muft go on in the ftrength of the Lord,
whatever be the difficulties and difcouragements
in our way: Our Lord's ends are well worth
the purfuing, he is coming, *his reward is with
him, and his work,* to wit, of judgment, *is before
him.* Eye hath not feen, nor ear heard, what
he hath prepared for them that wait for him :
yea, bleffed are the eyes who fhall fee what he
will do for the remnant that are in this land,
and for his church throughout the earth. Happy are they whom he is now chaftening, that
he may hid them from the day of evil : A large
fhare of prefent fufferings is well worth the having ;

ing; for the consolations of such shall much more abound: the Lord will make our hearts glad, according to the days wherein he afflicted us, and makes us to see evil. It is the better we cannot easily win out of our afflictions.

The blessing of the Lord be upon your lady and children, whom I salute in the Lord ; as also your sister, and other friends, both young and old, particularly *David Gordon*, whom I look upon to be flourishing and full of sap in old age, which is rare in this day. Referring other things till meeting. Farewell.

If you can let us meet on *Wednesday's* night, I would be content to be at your house if convenient; but the Lord will do all well.

RICHARD CAMERON.

LETTER LXX.

From the Rev. Mr. Richard Cameron, *to the Lady* Earlston, *younger.*

Madam,

I Once intended to have been at *Earlston* the last week, but was detained by the unseasonableness of the weather, and the present discomposure of the country, with the alarm of the soldiers being come to *Dumfries*, because the country will be unsettled, until they see what course is taken by the adversaries; and also because Mr. *Donald* has not come. I have now resolved to go to a place in *Clydesdale*, if the Lord will, from which I may conveniently ride into

Edinburgh, in order to meeting with friends, and after that to return with all the speed I can to *Galloway*, that I may see your Ladyship, or at least tryst with the Laird. My Master laid ties on me to the *Glenkens*, and some other two parishes in *Galloway*, that I was not looking for. I am bound, while I live, to remember with thanksgiving the Lord's condescendence · and kindness to me in *Earlston*, where I am sure we had some good days, not to be forgotten. I am more and more refreshed with my thoughts of the Laird, and of what God hath done and is doing to him. I am hopeful that the Lord shall carry him and you through your tribulations, which may be great for a little time. And now you may be sure that your steps shall be more observed than any forfeited family in *Galloway*: therefore I hope you will not be high-minded, but fear; happy is the man that feareth the Lord always: You should also *trust in him at all times, for in the Lord Jehovah there is everlasting strength:* There is enough in him for bearing your charges. You have now a notable opportunity of giving proof of your love to our sweetest Lord Jesus, who hath done so much for us. Praise, praise, to him that hath pitched upon you to witness for him, and that he is still keeping possession of that family of which you are now a mother,—and that the honour thereof is screwed up to so high a pitch in your time; and that this laird, who seems to be far inferior to the three that have gone before him, should in some respects be honoured even above his uncle and grandfather, whose names are, and will be savoury to the generations to come: This is the Lord's doing; his ways and thoughts

are

are not as our ways and thoughts. I defire to remember your fon and daughter, &c. I intreat that your Ladyfhip and fifter may remember me: ye know what need there is for praying for one another.——The Lord be with you all.

Madam, Farewell;.

RICHARD CAMERON.

LETTER LXXI.

From the Rev. Mr. Alexander Pedan, *to fome Friends.*

Dear Friends,.

I Long to hear how you fpend your time, and how the grace of God groweth in your hearts. I know you and fome other of the people of God, by reafon of the prefent trial, have got up a fafhion of complaining on Chrift; but I defy you all to fay any ill of him, except you wrong him: fpeak as ye can, and fpare not; only I requeft you, let your expreffions of Chrift be fuitable to your experiences of him; and if ye think Chrift's houfe to be bare and ill provided, and harder than ye looked for, I affure you Chrift's mind is only to diet you, and not to hunger you: Our Steward knows well when to fpare, and when to fpend: Chrift knows whether heaping or ftraiking agrees beft with our narrow veffels, for both are alike to him; fparing will never enrich

rich him, and spending will never impoverish him: he thinks it ill won which is holden off his people. Grace and glory come out of Christ's lucky hand: our gifts are but feckless gifts; his fulness is most straitened when it wants a vent: 'tis sweet and easy to Christ when he is holden busy in dividing the fulness of his Father's house to his poor friends: he desires not to keep mercy over night; every new day brings new mercies to the people of God. Christ is the best mercy that ever the people of God yoked with: if ye please the wares, and what of his grace makes for you, he and you will sort about the price; he will sell good cheap that ye may speer for his shop again, and draw all the sale to himself. I counsel to go no further than Christ: and now when it seems to be come to your door, either to sin or suffer, I counsel you to lay your account for suffering; for an outgate coming from any other airth will be prejudicial to your souls interest. For your encouragement, remember he sends none a warfare upon their own expences: and blessed be the man who gives Christ all his money; for ye will be forced to block with him at last, when ye have no hand-money, and thou hast no heart to suffer; and so it is best for you to keep in with your old acquaintance, for new acquaintance with strange lords is a ready way to make a wound in grace's side, that will not heal in haste; yea, your eyes may close before your wounds dry up; for grace is a tender piece, and is very easily distempered in the backslidings of our times; and if the wheels of it be once broken with sin, all the moyen in the world will not make them go about again, until they be once through Christ's Lands.

L

'I hope I have faid more upon the fubject than needed; for I have feen the marks of tenderness drawn upon your carriages: but the temper of our declining and backfliding times invites you to double your diligence in feeking God; for I think God has a mind to fearch *Jerufalem* with lighted candles, and to go thro' the whole houfe to vifit all your chambers, and there fhall not be one pin within all your gates, but God fhall know whether it be crooked or even. He will never reft till he be at the bottom of mens hearts: he has turned out fome folks hearts already, and flitted others; it feems he has a mind to make the infide the outfide. There was but a weak wind in former trials, and therefore much chaff was fheltered and hid amongft corn; but God now has raifed a ftrong wind, and yet Chrift's own cannot be driven away; he will not lofe one hair of his peoples heads, he knows them all by head-mark. O! if our hearts and love were blazing after him, we would rather choofe to die believing, than to fin by compliance.

I defy the world to fteal a lamb out of Chrift's fold unmiffed. What is wanting on the laft day of judgment. Chrift muft make them all up. That ftorm will not ly long, when the people of God have the worft of it; when the wind is both on their face and on their back, a great fire in God's furnace will foon divide the gold from the drofs. God's mill hath been grinding faft, and it will not ftand for want of water. If the people of God would but hold out of the gate, and give enemies a redd field, that God may be full of his enemies flefh: why, may he not give enemies a ftroke over his peoples heads?

God

God is giving his faints a little trial, somewhat
sharper than ordinary, that they may come out
of the furnace like a refined lump, that they
may run and be ready at tuck of drum. It is
honourable to serve and be a footman in Christ's
company. The weakest of God's people to run
at Christ's foot from morn to even, he will not
tyre, to gang and ride time about; he will take
his friends on behind him, when they begin to
weary, and dow not hold foot, Christ will wait
on. O how sweet will it be to see Christ marching up in a full body, and all the trumpets sound-
ing the triumph of the Lamb's victory, when the
sword shall be red with the blood of enemies;
when all the Heathen shall be rounding amongst
themselves, that he hath done great things for
them. Verily I fear the followers of the Lamb
shall be forced to tread upon the dead bodies
of the wicked ere all be done: the whole land
shall have enough to do to shool them in the
earth, ere all the play be play'd. Christ will kill
faster with his own hand, than all the hands of
the kingdom shall be able to bury. Many shall
be buried unstreight; and moals shall be the
winding-sheet of many that look life-like the day.
The blood of God's foes shall preach strange
things to his people, and we shall rejoice with
trembling. They that will not serve God, to
themselves be it faid. The day is near, when
BLOOD shall be the sign of Christ's soldiers;
and, *NO QUARTERS* shall be their word;
DEATH and *DESTRUCTION* shall be
written with broad letters on our Lord's standard. A look of him shall be a dead stroke
to any that runs in his gate. It is best for you
to keep within the shadow of God's wings, to
cast

cast Christ's cloak over your heads, until you hear him say, *The brunt of the battle is over, and the shower is slacked.* And I am confident the fairest way to cheap the way, is to speal out of God's gate, and keep within the doors until the violence of the storm be gone, and begin to ebb, which is not full tide as yet. Christ deals tenderly with young plants, and waters them oft, least they go back. Be painful, and lose not life for the seeking.

I recommend this to you, to be read as an extract of God's love, that in crosses, and out of crosses, ye may rejoice.

ALEXANDER PEDAN.

L E T T E R LXXII.

From Messrs. James Renwick, William Boyd, *and* John Flint, *to their friends in* Scotland.

Groningen, February 24. 1683.

Dearly Beloved in our Lord Jesus Christ,

IT is a great part of our duty to be mindful of you, to be keeping up a sympathizing frame of spirit with you, and to be wrestling with the Lord upon the behalf of his broken down work, and precious truths, which are set at nought and trampled upon: But, O! we fail in all duties, and come short in this also. Yet we may be persuaded, if we shall forget you, the Lord will forget us; and if we take ease to ourselves in this day of *Jacob's* trouble, the Lord will lead us forth with the workers of iniquity, when he shall cause peace to rest upon his *Israel.* O! our dear

Y   friends,

friends, let us join all hand in hand together, and wreftle with the Lord; who knows but he may come and leave a bleffing behind ▮▮; let us cry unto him, and refuse to be comforted, until he come and comfort our mother that is caft out in the wildernefs. Are not all the Lord's difpenfations calling for this at all our hands, to return unto the Lord our God, for we have fallen by our iniquity: *For Afhur fhall not fave us, we will not ride upon horfes;* for in the Lord the fatherlefs findeth mercy. If it were fo with us, would not the Lord heal our backflidings, he would love us freely, and his anger would be turned away. O! may not our fouls rejoice to think upon the many, the noble, the ftrange ways, that the Lord hath taken to purge away our drofs, and to make us a people zealous of good works; and upon the other hand, fhould we not be afhamed at ourfelves, becaufe the Lord's dealing with us hath had fo little effect, for we have not yet learned the language of the rod and him who hath appointed it. O! he is taking all ways with us, to caufe us take himfelf, and himfelf only for our all. Why hath he brought us fo low, but that we may be made high, to fee our ftrength only to be in himfelf, and that his hand may be only feen in raifing us up? Why doth he fuffer us to be brought into fo many difficulties, but that he may manifeft and magnify himfelf in taking us out of them, and carrying us through them? and alfo to try our patience, whether we will bear his indignation becaufe we have finned againft him. And we think, there is nothing will help us fo well to patience, as a full fight of the wrongs that we have done to the work of a holy God; we would then be

made to fay, we are *afflicted lefs than our iniqui-*
ties deferve. We would be then put to defire no
deliverance from the yoke of our oppreffion,
without a deliverance from the yoke of our tranfgreffions. And why hath the Lord brought us to
fuch a pafs both as to our fpiritual and natural
food, being deprived of the one as to the public ordinances, and brought to great ftraits as
to the other; but that he, for both, may be only
depended upon: he will have his people's eyes,
this day, to be upon nothing but himfelf for
all that they need. O noble contrivance! O
noble mean that the Lord makes ufe of to get
himfelf made great to his people. Is it not e-
nough to us that he lives and reigns? Are we
not rich enough, who have him to go unto? O!
let us remember that the Lord hath faid, *When*
the poor and needy feek water, and there is none,
and their tongue faileth for thirft; I the Lord will
hear them, I the God of Ifrael will not forfake
them. I will make the wildernefs a pool of water,
and the dry land fprings of water. That they
may fee, and know, and confider, and underftand
together, that the hand of the Lord hath done
this, and the holy One of Ifrael hath created it.
This is the thing the Lord will do unto you,
and he will have himfelf only to be feen in it.
Your children fhall have this to fay unto their
children, The Lord brought our fathers into the
wildernefs, that he might fhew them his wondrous and mighty works there: He made them
to wander from mountain to mountain, in the
peril of their lives, that he might teach them
to feek reft only in himfelf, who is that true
reft, who is the mighty rock in a weary land;
and that they might betake themfelves only to

him, who is life itfelf. He made them to travel
in the wildernefs without leaders and teachers,
that he who teacheth as never man taught,
might teach them, yea, be their only teacher,
who *is the true Shepherd*, who makes his own
fheep to hear his voice: He difcovered unto
them the treachery of hirelings, that thereby
his care of his own fheep might be made manifeft: He led them through a valley of falt pits,
that his fkill in leading them might appear:
Yea, he fuffered rocks to be upon all hands, that
his own might have himfelf only to glory in for
guiding him by thefe: He brought them into all
extremities, that he might have opportunity to
do them good, and that they might be made to
fee himfelf only therein. O dear friends, as the
children of *Ifrael* had many of the Lord's wonders to tell, in leading their fathers out of
Egypt through the wildernefs; fo fhall your
children have many of his wonders to tell in
leading you through fuch wildernefes; but the
carcafes of the murmurers muft firft fall and
dung the land.

O therefore truft in God; it muft be by faith
that ye muft overcome; through faith ye fhall
quench the violence of fire; out of weaknefs ye
fhall be made ftrong; ye are compaffed about
with a great cloud of witnefles, who have all obtained a good report through faith; they *had
trial of cruel mockings, they were ftoned, fawn a-
funder, tempted, and flain with the edge of the
fword; they wandered in defarts, and in mountains, and in dens and caves of the earth:* Yea,
*they were tortured, not accepting deliverance, that
they might obtain a better refurrection.* Therefore, *lay afide every weight, and run with pati-*
ence

ence the race that is set before you, looking unto
Jesus the author and finisher of your faith, which is
touched with the feeling of all your infirmities.
Therefore go boldly unto the throne of his grace,
that ye may find grace to help in the time of need.
And seeing ye have a great high-priest, that is
passed into the heavens, Jesus the son of God, hold
fast your profession. O be zealous for him, who
for the joy that was set before him, endured the
cross, and despised the shame. And he says unto
you, I will never leave you nor forsake you; so
that ye may boldly say, The Lord is our helper,
and we will not fear what man can do unto us. As
trouble from the world abounds, let your love
to God and your zeal for him increase; that will
be a good mark of true zeal. O be zealous, be
zealous; there is a generation rising up, who will
wish to have been living in our days, that they
might have given a proof of their zeal for God.
And for ourselves, we wot not well what to say;
but we must be otherwise framed and disposed,
ere the Lord make any use of us: The case of
this day is extraordinary, and whom the Lord
will make use of in any piece of work, he will
also give more than an ordinary frame; he will
have them humbled, he will have them self denied, he will have them filled with zeal, he will
have them to be lions in his cause. O pray, O
pray, that the Lord would work his own work,
make use of whom he will to be instruments; and
dear friends, pray for us, who desire to be

Your companions in tribulation,
and servants in the Lord,

JAMES RENWICK,
WILL. BOYD, JO. FLINT.

LETTER LXXIII.

From the Rev. Mr. William Brackel, *minister of the gospel in* Holland, *To the strict persecuted party of the Presbyterians in the Church of* Scotland. 1682. *

To our Fathers and Brethren that are under the persecution, in the Church of Scotland.

ALthough I do not esteem my gifts so great as to write to you who are so eminently taught of the Holy Spirit; yet I cannot keep silent from shewing you, that my soul is knit to yours, which sometimes uses to be a comfort to the afflicted, to wit, to have some to bear burdens with them.

Whether I shall weep for sadness, or rejoice for gladness, is to me a great doubt. If I gave way to affection, grief would prevail; but when I consult with reason, joy abounds; because I heartily embrace the cause of this, although joined with the cause of the other; and I would not wish the cause of that taken away, with any disadvantage to this.

My heart is not a little wounded with sympathy, when I call to mind the sad things you are meeting with; when I consider how you are deprived of all the good things and means of life, that you are put to lodge day and night in the open air, without any shelter from the sun's heat, rain or cold, (how do you live? surely God feeds
you

* This Letter was written originally in *Latin,* and faithfully translated by one who desires to be a friend, *Feb.* 19. 1683.

you from heaven) when you embrace the bare
rock for a bed, having the heavens, or it may
be the cold snow for a covering; when I consider what it is to see the little ones (it may be)
weeping for hunger and cold, and cannot get
wherewith to warm them; when I consider what
it is to be always surrounded with deadly foes,
and to hear sometimes of the husband, sometimes of the father or mother, wife, son or
daughter to be taken to execution, and all
the day to be as lambs alloted to the slaughter;
what brother? what Christian? yea, what unby-
assed man can think on these things but with
excess of grief?

But, upon the other hand, when I consider the
heavenly abounding blessings, the great abundance
of the Spirit, and spiritual joy, the deniedness to
all worldly things, the ardent love to God and
your neighbour, the chearful martyrdom for the
name of Jesus, the holiness of life, &c. which
God your father has in a more abundant manner
bestowed on you than any church in the world
in these times. When I call to mind that God
is preserving you as a remnant of anciently a-
most flourishing church, and calling you as the
first fruits, yea, I say, the first fruits of a church
shortly; yea, I say, shortly to be raised up:
When I see our Lord and Master Jesus Christ,
the only head of his church, glorified in your
miraculous preservation, and encompassing you
as with a wall of fire round about, calling you
either living or dying, and setting you forth,
and preferring you to all, either godly or ungod-
ly, who are lurking in quiet here and there,
for to give a testimony for himself. I say, when
I seriously ponder these things, how can I be sad?
what

what shall I say, but glory be to the L
shall I do, but most willingly approve
holy and wise government of his hous
follows you with a greater and more
eternal love and good-will than I c
should I seem to repine by wishing
and so disapproving of his dispensati
the most holy and merciful God doe
well.

But what shall I say unto you, m
thren? I approve of your careful a
correspondence with one another, a
churches; I approve of your strict
both as to the private life of every me
also as to your separation from these
pride Bishops and their adherents. A
I approve of your separation from
have accepted the indulgence from th
gistrate, and so have acknowledged a
extraneous power in the church, and
it into the church against the sole p
of our only King Jesus Christ, which
the destruction of the church, and t
hinderance to its restoration. I appr
your separation from the frighted a
though otherwise pious men, and the
inclining to the indulged side, loving
dily ease, though with a check of
who deprive themselves of all that op
they ought to have, and entrap them
extricable snares, not considering how
they do to the church. O how muc
it to be choiced to die a noble and (
fying death, and to obtain the crown
dom, or to endure all sorts of injuri
pressions in the deserts and mountai

enjoy the pleasures of sin for a season, for what fellowship hath righteousness with unrighteousness.

Go on therefore, dear brethren, as ye have begun; *Come out from among them, saith the Lord, and touch not the unclean thing; Then shall I receive you, and be to you a father, and ye shall be unto me as sons and daughters, faith the Lord of hosts.* Let not the devil and his instruments and followers fright you, who is come unto you full of great wrath, because he knows his time is but short, for the God of peace shall bruise him under your feet.

Let not the cruelty nor subtilty of enemies, nor hunger, nor cold, nor the prison, nor a gallows, nor the sword, fear you: *none of these things can separate you from the love of God. Yea, your light affliction, which is but for a moment, worketh for you a far more exceeding and eternal weight of glory.* Let always that saying of our Saviour's be in your mind, *He that takes not up his cross and follows me, is not worthy of me. He that finds his life shall lose it, but he that loseth his life for my sake shall find it.* Neither let your peace entice you to comply with those, who, altho' they be godly men, yet they live only for themselves, and not for the good of the church; nay rather for its hurt. O how pleasant and noble a thing is it to lay the foundation of a more pure church, to make a a way by which King Jesus shall enter to restore his church in *Scotland.* O! how profitable will it be to after generations to have you for a good example to follow? and that they can say of you, so and so did our forefathers, such and such things suffered they in such and such a case; they behaved themselves so and so. O what excess of joy shall they have, who (after the persecu-

tions

tions are over) shall see the people of God in peace glorifying him. How shall they then be confounded who are sitting silent, frighted, and deserting the cause and people of God? How shall they then come trembling and confessing their faults to you? and these who are now persecuting you, how shall they blush and be ashamed? Let me speak to you in the words of *Isaiah*, *Hear ye the word of the Lord, ye that tremble at his word, your brethren that hated you, that cast you out for my name's sake, said, Let the Lord be glorified; but he shall appear to your joy, and they shall be ashamed.* Then says the Psalmist, *The righteous shall rejoice when he seeth vengeance: he shall wash his feet in the blood of the wicked.* So that a *man shall say, verily there is a reward for the righteous, verily there is a God to judge in the earth. Seeing it is a righteous thing with God to recompence tribulation to them that trouble you; but to you who are troubled rest.*

Therefore, my brethren, watch, stand fast in the faith, quit yourselves like men, be strong, and God will strengthen your soul. All ye that hope in him, be ye stable, unmoved, always abounding in the work of the Lord. *Hold fast that you have, let no man take your crown. Be ye faithful unto the death, and God shall give you a crown of life. For the rod of the wicked shall not rest always upon the lot of the righteous.*

Farewel, Reverend Fathers, dear brothers and sisters; the Lord enlighten you with the light of his countenance, and grant you to taste of his all-sufficiency, and strengthen you in the faith that ye may always behold these things that are invisible, and live by them; and that he may fill you with the spirit of joy and gladness, and that he may cherish you in the hope of the life to come, and sanctify you more and more, that ye may do all things in his sight, in faith, as the sons of God through Christ Jesus, in love, in fear, in obedience, with chearfulness, wisdom, patience and constancy.

The Lord be your sun and shield, and rock of habitation, yea, all in all to you, both in time and throughout all eternity. —— —— shall shew you our mind in the rest. Be mindful of me in your prayers, that the Almighty may give me a greater measure of his Spirit, for comfort, holiness and faithfulness in my work, and fitness to go about it. The Lord be with you. I greet you with the right hand of fellowship.

WILLIAM BRACKEL.

LETTER LXXIV.

From the Rev. Mr. William Brackel, *to the fathers and brethren who are in* Scotland *under the persecution.*

February 9th 1683.

Most loving fathers and brethren in Christ Jesus our glorious King,

IT is not only come to my ears that ye wrote and sent to me a letter of answer, but also a copy of it is come to my hand; but where itself sticks, or by whom intercepted I know not.

It rejoiced my soul greatly to know your affairs both by the foresaid copy, and also by your
letters

letters fent to us; efpecially the miraculous divine protection of you makes me both greatly to admire and rejoice; who being courageous and bufied in your convention, by taking a care of your church affairs, did fee the cruel enemies even threatening death, feeking you, even compaffing about the houfe, ftricken with a certain *Sodomitifh* blindnefs that they could not enter.

How admirable are the works of God! how unfearchable is his deep goodnefs! truely we find that he hath favour and mercy towards his faints, and perpetual care towards the elect; truely he is a firey wall about *Jerufalem*, and his angels compafs about thofe that fear him, and delivers them. He that fits under the covert of the Moft High fhall lodge under the fhadow of him that is omnipotent. Let praife and glory be fung to our Lord, by all who hear thefe things, both angels and men. It is needful that this experience of the moft efficacious prefence of God fhould ftrengthen your confidence; that he who delivered you out of the mouth of the bear and lion, fhall alfo in the time to come deliver you from all dangers that fhall fall in your lot, to the glory of his waited-for divine defence. But if God fhould fuffer this or that man, or even many, to fall into the hands of enemies, or rather, that he himfelf fhould give them; by this ye fhall be taught experience, that that has not fallen out, becaufe of the defect of divine protection; but that God has called them out, name by name for a teftimony of himfelf; yea, although they fhould feem to die in the eyes of enemies, and their end to be an ignominious affliction, yet they, I fay, go away in peace, and are crowned with a joyful crown and immortality. Neither
are

are the martyrs of the church of *Scotland* killed,
that it may be extirpate, but that it may be
builded; for the blood of the martyrs is the feed
of the church: the church was founded by blood,
and it grew by blood: the more cruelly *Pharaoh*
oppressed the people of God, the more fertilely
they were multiplied. We are very defirous of
the coming of the Lord; faying, we wish *that
falvation may come out of Zion; when the Lord
shall turn again the captivity of his people, Jacob
shall be glad, and Israel shall rejoice.* But let no
man cast down his heart, becaufe God is only
trying your patience; he is alfo making our
way plain, and a way to himfelf, to his greater
glory in all lands. Would *Israel* have been
more happy if he had been delivered out of lefs
oppreffion in *Egypt?* Was not his deliverance
the more glorious the heavier the perfecution
was? Wait therefore for the falvation of the
Lord: how great shall his goodnefs be, which
he hath laid up for them that fear him, which he
hath prepared for thofe that betake themfelves
to him, before the fons of men. Shew yourfelves
men in the time of diftrefs. Let him that is
weak in ftrength, leaning upon his Head, fay,
I am a man of excellent valour. He that hath
God near unto him (as is made known to you
by many, both public and private experiences)
from no man would fear either threatenings,
fwords, or ropes. Learned men, great men,
albeit godly, of great name, err in this matter, but God hath chofen thefe that were fools
in the world, as wife; thofe that were weak, as
ftrong; the ignoble, and thofe of no efteem,
that he might bring to difgrace thofe who are in
honour. In the mean time, let unanimity,

love, fervency of mind, gladnefs in juftifica-tion, remain among you; and out of thefe, holinefs, and a perpetual intercourfe of the foul with God. This one thing I exhort you, that every one may teach another; the fathers, mo-thers, aged and more learned, may teach the little ones, and others who are more ignorant of the way of the Lord, the fundamentals of reli-gion; leaft the church fhould perifh through lack of knowledge, or leaft any fhould waver in the true faith.

The three ftudents chofen by you to the pafto-ral office are bufy at their ftudies; the fourth we are waiting for: By God's grace we hope you fhall fee them the next year, and hear them preaching.

Since the time that I have known your eftate, I have judged it neceffary that certain men, en-dued with the Holy Ghoft, piety, authority, and years, fhould be chofen to the paftoral office, and fhould be fent unto us, for the fpace of one or two months, that they might be inftructed in the method of forming of preachings, and fome other things. Next that they fhould be examin-ed in a lawful way by fome paftor in an ecclefiaf-tic convention, (let not little knowledge deter any man) and in the name of the Lord fent unto his vineyard, and be confirmed in that office by the impofition of hands; and fo return to you in fuch a ftate of the church. I care not much for the knowledge of tongues, and literal in-ftruction, although in itfelf and other circum-ftances, I think much of it; for not by the de-fect of learning, but of the Spirit and piety, is the church of *Scotland* brought into fo miferable a condition; and I think it is not to be reftored

by

bȳ learning, but by the Spirit and piety. I propofe thir things to you, that you may ferioufly
confider that thing of fo great moment; and
that ye may either do or reject that, as ye fhall
think fit. The Lord be a fun and fhield unto
you. And, I am,

Your lover, and promoted minifter,

WILLIAM BRACKEL.

LETTER LXXV.

*From the Rev. Mr. Alexander Shields, to the
Prifoners for Chrift in Dunnottar Caftle; concerning the Boundaries of Chriftian Fellowfhip;
efpecially with whom it is lawful to join in divine Worfhip, and from whom it is duty to
withdraw.*

Edin. June 1685.

Wellbeloved and honoured in the Lord,

GOD is love, and he that dwelleth in God,
dwelleth in love; and he that dwelleth in
love delighteth in union, the native fruit and
effect of it: That union that hath moft of
God and love in it, and hath a tendency to
lead to, and keep near God; that union, that
hath love for its cement, and Chrift for its centre, and truth for its foundation: Therefore it
follows, that the clofer a people cleave to Chrift
and his truths, the more inclinable they will be
to union, the fooner they will obtain it, and the
furer they keep it; that is both the beft means

Z 2 and

and the trueft meafures I can con
for attaining or entertaining union
ed and declining day, as this our da
my, trouble, and rebuke is It hath
found, that departing from God ha
the father, the fofterer, and the
divifion; as our wretched defection
the unhappy caufe of all our wofu
among profeffors in this age: There
the caufe be removed by fome joint
ing unto the Lord, and an unanin
ledging and difowning of thefe, th
never ceafe. All other healing mei
getting or forgiving, or forbearin
things difhonourable to Chrift, or c
his caufe, are but ill-tempered pli
ing the wound flightly; not curir
to take away the malignity of the
is always defirable, as abfolutely i
the well-being of a church, efpecia
the furnace of affliction; then, if c
be expected; then, if ever, it o
ftudied. The union of enemies ou
upftirring motive to it, and the f
own preffures fhould make us lea
uneffayed to accomplifh it; efpecia
nothing more fuitable than for prif
hort and ftir up one another to thi
example of the Apoftle, *Eph.* iv.
one way of walking worthy of tl
wherewith we are called, to endeav
the unity of the Spirit in the bond of
as this is an unity of the Spirit's worl
fluencing, fo it muft be of the Spiri
and directing; and not according to
of man's reafon or prudence, to tl

of truth. O if the Spirit of God, in mercy to us, would exert his power and gracious conduct, in discovering and determining all of us to submit to the means and measure thereof, laid down in his word! O if there were a joining in praying for, and pursuing after this! then all our disjoinings would be soon jointed together.

Now, the greatest matter of our divisions is about joining in worship; for our defections have been so diforderly, that the most tender have thought they fall under that command of withdrawing from *disorderly walkers*: and this is the question we would enquire a little into.

I would not have you to expect a decision of it from me, with any tolerable accuracy; for the question itself is so *difficult*, the stating of it so *intricate*, the cases so *various*, and my unacquaintedness with circumstances, and insufficiency for solving doubts so *palpable*; that, were it not that I would do all things to testify my respect to you, and contribute my poor mite for your help and instruction, I should not have dared to meddle with it: And all that I can do is, to propose some generals to your consideration, and offer some distinctions to clear the state of the question, not imposing upon you, but only telling you my judgment.

I think then there may be considered several sorts of JOINING in worship.

First, There is a *joining* which we call *Catholic*, amongst Christians, considered as such; and there is a *joining* which, for distinctions sake, we call *ecclesiastic*, among the members of the organical church, considered as church members. The *first* is founded upon the *communion of saints*, obliging all the members of the same mystical body,

body, to join in all things that may evidence
that union: And this is capable of several *sub-
distinctions*; as,

1. There may be a joining more *general* with
all Christians, holding the same fundamentals,
being of the same one body, under the conduct
of the same one spirit, maintaining the same
one hope of their calling, confessing the same
one Lord, professing the same one faith, and
partaking of the same one baptism, *Eph* iv. 3—6.
Holy devout men out of every nation under
heaven, may be capable of joint acts of worship
with edification; whether they be *Parthians*, or
Medes, or *Elamites*, Acts ii. 5. 9. &c. Of *a truth*
it is, *that God is no respecter of persons;—he that
feareth God, and worketh righteousness, is accepted with him*, Acts x. 34, 35. And forasmuch as
God is pleased to give any, of whatsoever nation, the like gift as he has given to us; we must
not withstand God, by accounting of any unclean,
or separating from them, as unclean; as *Peter*
expounds his vision, *Acts* xi. 9. 17. And so,
wherever providence casts our lot, we may join
even in worship with all, in whom we find the
same spirit of faith, though their cause and the
word of their testimony be not the same way
stated as ours is: and so we might join in worship with any that we find serious among the *A-
byssines*, if we were in *Ethiopia*, whose testimony
is stated against *Gentilism*; or, if we were in
Armenia, and some other places, as the *Lesser
Asia*, we might join in worship with Christians
there, whose testimony is stated against *Turkism*,
and that abomination of *Mahomet*, suppose they
were qualified, as is above mentioned.

2 There may be a joining more *special* with
all

all Protestants, conceited in one common opposition to all the enemies of truth, and owning
and designing the advancement of reformation;
though their respective oppositions, contendings,
and wrestlings be not the same way stated, nor
against the same enemies, and the testimonies be
not the same, for one and the same truth that
ours is; and even though their sentiments about
other things, extraneous to their testimony, be
not the same: Providing always they hold by
the truth, and nothing but the truth, and nothing contrary to any of the reformed churches
testimonies. Hence, as we may pray for, so
we may pray with, *all that are sanctified in Christ
Jesus,* and *all that in every place call upon his
name,* who is *our Lord and theirs both,* 1 Cor. i. 2.
With all that hold the same head Christ, and
own the same allegiance to him, and dependence upon him; and are *not carried about with
every wind of doctrine;* but *speaking the truth
in love, do grow up into him in all things; from
whom the whole body fitly joined together, and
compacted by that which every joint supplieth, according to the effectual working in the measure of
every part, maketh increase of the body, to the edifying of itself in love,* Eph. iv. 14, 15, 16. With
all who seek and maintain the pure doctrine of
the common *salvation,* and do *earnestly contend
for the faith once delivered to the saints;* though
their contentions be not about the same particulars with us, *Jude,* ver. 3. With all that *hold
fast the form of sound words, in faith and love,*
which is in Christ Jesus; tho' the form in every
part and respect be not the same, 2 *Tim.* i. 13.
supposing it is not contradictory; for that rule
must be observed, in 1 *Tim.* vi. 3. *If any man
teach*

teach otherways, and consent not to
words, even the words of our Lord
and to the doctrine that is according
ye must carry towards him, as he
scribed by *withdrawing from him :*
we find Protestants found in the main
ful to their own peculiar testimony,
they differ in some things from us (as
in such things as were not so tolerable
our own church, owning the same
with ourselves) yet that is not suffic
disjoining from them upon: For,
postle, *If in any thing ye be otheru*
God shall even reveal that unto you ;
whereunto we have already attained,
by the same rule, Phil. iii. 15, 16.
very church and party hath their pe
of Christ's patience to suffer and wre
we may join in worship with any of
lified as above said; without furthe
inquiry, if they hold not some cor
consistent with their own testimony
were in *France,* we might join with
there, contending against Popery, t
do not contend with us against Prel
were in *Holland,* we might join w
formed there, witnessing against S
Arminian errors, though they do
with us against *Erastianism:* If in H
Germany, we might join with *Calvi*
wrestling against the *Lutheran* divisio
they do not wrestle against those defe
are amongst us: If in *England,* we
with *Dissenters* there, testifying agai
mity with *liturgical* worship, and the i
snares and sins they have among the

they do not teſtify againſt our *compliances*, or *indulgences*, or *teſt*, &c. or our other *oaths* and *bonds*; and even with *Independents* we might join occaſionally, for that difference is not the matter of our preſent teſtimony. And this leads me to another ſub-diſtinction, *viz.*

3. There may be a joining more *particularly* with all our covenanted brethren, all our fellow-confederates in the ſame Solemn League, owning the ſame Covenant, and proſecuting the ſame ends thereof, though there be difference of judgment about the circumſtantiate duties of it; and inequality as to the attainment of the ends of it; and a diſconformity in ſome points of practice, that are extraneous to them, and not the matter of our preſent teſtimony; yet if there be an unanimous concurrence for the eſtabliſhment of the things covenanted, and for the extirpation of the things abjured, we may join in worſhip with them upon occaſion, and in every thing that may ſtrengthen and ſtabliſh them in that covenant; ſee *Iſa.* ii. 3. *Jer.* l. 4, 5. Eſpecially I ſpeak of fellow covenanters of ſeveral churches and nations in league together, and not of the members of one church, I am not come to that yet: As if we were in *England*, or *Ireland*, many things might be allowed among our brethren, both miniſters and profeſſors there, which cannot be ſo amongſt ourſelves in our own land, without ſcandal: for the conſtitution of the nations governments is different, and the duties that the ſame covenant obliges to, with a reference to theſe reſpective governments are different, and they never attained to that pitch of reformation that we arrived at; and therefore there may be many things

in their practice not consentaneous
and yet we may join with them. T
the same reason for our joining with
mong ourselves; they may take an
for freedom to their meetings, on far
than we can do; for it is not deriv
same supremacy, nor pretended to
virtue of the same; though I think t
right neither; yet there was not th
ciency of a foundation to withdraw
there was from ours: and theirs di
to our testimony. They might ackr
plead for the freedom of their pai
were scandalous to do so for ours,
corrupted, that they require *perjurj*
cessary qualification of their men
may own and acknowledge a magist
these terms, that the constitution o
ment, and the obligation of our c
us make indispensible; and so they
veral transactions with their rulers,
not admit of with ours: they may
of allegiance in *England*, as it is th
ed, and yet I think we may admit
joining in acts of worship with thei
I think these things are not faults;
they are not such things as may oblig
off from this that I call catholic C
ing with them in worship.

Secondly, There is a joining whi
clesiastical, among the members of
or formed society of professing b
only concerted together in the sam
may be, engaged in the some c
promoving and prosecuting the sam
reformation; but also owning ar

ubjection to the fame reformed doctrine, worhip, difcipline and government, enjoying the ame pure ordinances of Chrift, difpenfed according to his own inftitution, by his own appointed officers and minifters, approven and chofen, or fubmitted unto, by all the fellowmembers of that fociety or church : and this is a nearer joining, and requires more ftrict conditions, and more certain qualifications than the other. Yet this alfo may be confidered in feveral cafes : As,

1ft. There may be an ecclefiaftical joining in a church conftituted, and in a beautiful order, and in a fettled condition, with all the fellowmembers of that church, of a found faith, and blamelefs profeffion; and holding forth the word of life, with all that own the common principles, follow the common duties, profecute the common intereft, feek the common peace, oppofe the common enemies of that church, even though there be fome corruptions in it that we cannot help, fome infirmities that we muft bemoan, and yet bear with what we cannot help; we cannot have fo pure a church, but it will have a fpot in it : It is only the completement of the love of Chrift, when he fhall prefent it a glorious church, that can make it without fpot or wrinkle, or any fuch thing. All the churches that *Paul* wrote to, had faults, errors and corruptions taxed in them ; and yet he enjoins the receiving one another, bearing with infirmities, bearing one another's burdens, forbearing one another, and calls for love, peace and concord. The churches of *Afia* had feveral corruptions in them, and fteps of defection charged upon them, in our Lord's epiftles to them ; as entertaining them that held

the

the doctrine of *Balaam*, and the *Nicolaitans*, and suffering *Jezebel* to seduce; lukewarmness, indifferency, &c. and yet there was no disjoining amongst them upon these accounts, no *schism* fixed thereon. There was, no doubt, among the faithful, a conscientious withdrawing from them that held these doctrines, and maintained such practices; for no pretence of prudence, or peace and concord, can ever dispense with the obligation of that: this shall be at all times, and in all cases. But there was not a disjointing from that church, that was deficient in their discipline against, and correction of these doctrines and practices, for that would have been *schism*: For I take the true notion of schism to be not every debate, dissention, or contention about truths, that's *division*, not *schism*; nor every falling away into error, that's *apostacy*, not *schism*; nor every withdrawing from the communion of the church, upon grounds true or false, that may be *separation*, not *schism*: but I take *schism* to be a factious and disorderly disjoining and breaking off from a constitute church, into which persons were formerly joined; and taking separate courses at their own hand, without any respect to the peace, or order of the church; or the methods laid down by Christ, to take away that which scandalized; or to their own sphere or capacity in which they are, that is *schism*. I cannot find it but once exprest in our translation, that is, 1 *Cor.* xii. 25. where the way to cure and prevent it, gives us some understanding of the nature of it, to wit, *That the members should have the same care one for another;* and where, without any regard to this, we *turn aside by the flocks of Christ's companions*, and leave the shepherds and the

flocks,

flocks, and will feed by ourselves, *Cant.* i. 7, 8. we commit schism, a great sin; but it is many times charged on practices which will not bear it, and in seasons when it cannot readily be committed; for, in the broken state of a church, keeping ourselves free of defections, though in a separate way, withdrawing from persons which we were never joined with, in a time when the church hath no order to rectify or remove offences, and Christ's method cannot be obtained, that can be no schism; but when the church is rightly constitute, as the causes of disjoining and withdrawing from congregations, or persons, may be orderly removed; so the cases wherein it may be allowed, and the methods of it, may be more easily stated; Christ's common rule doth sufficiently order all things in that case, *Matth.* xviii. 15—20. I stay the longer upon this, to obviate the cavils of some, against conscientious withdrawers from, and witnessers against defections, whom they call, upon that account, *Schismatics* and *Separatists*, because they break off from them at their own hand, and will not join with persons guilty of defection or scandals; and yet the case is not determined by a church judicatory. I grant indeed, from what is said, it will follow, that if our church were *constitute as formerly,* if we should disjoin from worship with the Indulged, or Countenancers of Prelacy, or Banders, or Testers, or Alledgers, *&c.* we might incur a censure somewhat like that; but it cannot be so now, when that method cannot be followed; yet we are obliged to follow it as much as we can, and that is by doing the equivalent. Such as, it is manifest, would incur the sentence of excommuni-

A a   cation,

cation, after admonition rejected, we may withdraw our communion from them; such as would be liable to a suspension, we may withhold our hearing and joining with them; such as would be severely rebuked, we may show some discountenance, to testify our dislike of their ways; not taking upon us to inflict these things as censures, for we have no power, but only signifying our sense of the moral obligation and equity of these censures, whether they be inflicted or not. But before I leave this I would add a subordinate distinction of this joining, in a twofold case.

1. When a constitute church is advancing, and growing up gradually unto a reformation, there may be a joining with many things, that otherwise we ought not to countenance: we may then wave and forbear some debates about things not so material, nor the matter of the present testimony; contending about which might retard and hinder the intended reformation. Hereupon we find that the apostles and elders, in the first general assembly at *Jerusalem*, condescended to some things, to please the *Jews*, laying upon the *Gentiles* some things (only ceremonial burdens) as *abstaining from meats offered to idols, and from blood, and from things strangled*, Acts xv. 19. 29. which decrees were afterward retracted, and were of no force: In this case the Apostle's rule is to be observed. 1 *Cor.* ix. 19—24. and all things are to be done by way of condescendency, consistent with duty and edification, to avoid offence to the church of God, 1 *Cor.* x. 32, 33. Then special regard is to be had to these excellent gospel-commands, of *having peace with one another*, Mark ix. 50. 1 Thess. v. 13.

v. 13. *By love serving one another*, without biting and devouring one another, *Gal.* v. 13. 15. *With all lowliness, and meekness, and long-suffering, forbearing one another in love*, Eph. iv. 2. *Bearing one another's burdens*, Gal. vi. 2. and many others. And so we find that our fathers suffered many things, that are not so tolerable, as hearing of Episcopal men; bearing long with lay-patronages; voluntary submitting to the magistrates unjust sentence of confinement, &c. all which are exploded and expelled out of the societies of the faithful.

2. When the same constitute church is declining and falling backward from a degree of reformation attained, tho' there may be joining with the same church (as was formerly proved from the instance of some of the *Asian* churches) yet there must not be a joining in these defections, nor with those that promove them; but an earnest contending, and a zealous witnessing and wrestling against the first motions of them; and a contending for the faith once delivered to the saints, *Jude* 3. Then we must with all diligence and faithfulness, *hold fast what we have attained*, Rev. ii. 25. chap. iii. 11. Then we must *strengthen the things that remain and are ready to die*, v. 2. *and stand fast in the liberty wherewith Christ hath made us free*, and not to be entangled with any yoke of bondage, *Gal.* v. 1. These same decrees of the apostles, of abstaining from meats offered to idols, were afterwards declared indifferent, 1 *Cor.* viii. and x. chap. and afterward both that, and other indifferent observances, were condemned, as in the case of *Peter's* doing the same, *Gal.* ii. 11. It was allowable that *Timothy* should be circumcised; but

this

this would have been finful to do it to *Titus.*
No, *Paul* would not fubject to that for an hour,
nor condefcend to the quitting the leaft hair-
breadth of truth, or Chriftian liberty, to pleafure
them, whom yet he had pleafured before, *Gal.*
ii. 3. 5. no, the cafe was now altered.

2*dly.* There may be a joining in a church brok-
en and born down, and perfecuted; then union
is moft defirable and neceffary. The fheep fhould
run together when the wolves are ravening a-
mongft them : Chrift's doves fhould flock together to their rocks, when the ftorm is moft boifterous; then a gathering together, though as
a nation not defired with one confent *before the*
decree bring forth, and the day pafs as the chaff ;
and a feeking the Lord, and a feeking with *one*
confent; and a feeking *meeknefs* as well as *righ-*
teoufnefs, that *it may be* they be hid together :
And it is very fuitable, that the furnace fhould
make the gold run together in a lump, even
though fome drofs be infeparable from it. Then
an union in the Lord, and a joining, as far as
it can confift with truth and duty, is a thing
earneftly to be endeavoured, and, I hope, in-
tenfly defired by all, who are fenfible of the prefent *breach* and woful *defection,* and wretched *di-*
vifion of the church of *Scotland* But in this cafe,
as this joining is moft defirable, fo it is moft
difficult ; and the due meafures thereof hardeft
to be determined, and the true methods thereof moft warily to be fixed ; for certain it is that
it muft not be unlimited and unreftricted, nor
promifcuoufly to be fought and kept with all, with
whom formerly in the church's conftitute and
fettled condition we joined, and with whom we
took fweet counfel together, and went into the
houfe .

houfe of God in company. We would indeed join with all that will declare themfelves for our Lord, in this day of the heathen's raging, and the people's tumultuating againft him; and his interefts; with all the faithful friends of Chrift, in a joint oppofition againft all his enemies; with all the lovers of *Zion,* that *take pleafure in the ftones, and favour the duft thereof;* with all that own and efpoufe our Lord's quarrel, and every part of it, which the enemy oppofeth : In a word, with all that keep their ground and go forward, but will not go back one ftep from the attained-unto reformation. But we muft not join with all, nor fay, *A confederacy* with all that fay it, out of fear, or a prepofterous defire of peace, with prejudice to truth and duty; even though we fhould be *for figns and wonders in Ifrael,* Ifa. viii. 12. 18. For that were a combination a-gainft the Lord, rather than an union in the Lord : Nay, we muft rather prefer to embark our lot with the little flock, that follows Chrift, and refufes to hear the voice of ftrangers, and the few names that have kept cleaneft garments, than the multitude of thofe, who leave the right way; even though reputed wifer and more pru-dent, and continuing ftill eminent in piety : We would love peace, but we muft love the truth firft, and beft, *Zech.* viii. 19. As I faid, in a declining time, even while the church continues conftitute, we muft not give fuch a latitude to our joining with perfons and things, as formerly we might, when reformation was upon the a-fcendant; fo much more in a broken ftate ought it to be reftricted yet more; for neither are we to join with all whom, for the prefervation of the church's order, we might join with them :

for now that is not, nor can that fame method
and order of fufpending our withdrawing from
perfons or things, until the church's jurifdiction
decide it, be obferved; for then it would follow, that nothing, or no perfon, fhould be withdrawn from at all; for the church now hath no
juridical power. In this cafe, then the queftion
may be twofold:

(1.) What minifters we may join with?
(2.) What profeffors we may join with?

(1.) For the firft, we need not infift on it;
for neither do ye ftand in need to be informed
of that, nor is it the prefent queftion that ye
are inquifitive about; nor, alas! are ye in a capacity to hear any, nor (which requires a more
weighty *alas!*) are there many to be heard by
any that long after Chrift's pure ordinances:
but yet, by the way, becaufe it falls in here, I
fhall hint a fhort word of my thoughts on that too.

I judge then they may come under a twofold
confideration. Either as they are minifters of
a national church, devoted to the fervice of that
confociation of churches in one nation, united
under one kind of government, and fubject to
the conftitutions of that collective church; for
fo, next to this their relation to the church univerfal vifible, they are to be confidered, as having a primary relation unto, and a dependence
upon, and incorporation with that church, as
the object of their miniftry: Or, they may be
confidered, as the particular paftors of a congregational church, ordained for and chofen by the
members of that particular congregation. This
laft, as to the exercife of it, may be hindered
by mens violence, though the relation itfelf can
never be taken away, but by them that gave it,

and confented unto it; fo that we ought to have
a particular tendernefs of refpect to them, who
were our paftors by and according to Chrift's appointment; when we cannot enjoy their fixed
miniftry; and we fhould be loather to difcountenance them than any: and if we could do it either in confcience or fafety, if he will abide
with us, we ought to adhere to him; but fo, as
not to confine him, or monopolize the gofpel to
ourfelves, with prejudice of the public good of
the national church. Yet I think every parifh,
as it is called, that had a faithful minifter, who
continues fo ftill, fhould maintain and entertain
him, as much as they can, without wronging
others. But fuppofe a minifter could have a
fixed ftation amongft a people, even in this difturbed ftate of the church, and turned either in-
fufficient or fcandalous, or unfaithful, and fo de-
ferved a fufpenfion, I conceive the people have
power from Chrift, when a prefbytery cannot be
had, to do the equivalent of it. But now, when
this is not practicable, we muft look upon all
our minifters under the firft confideration, and
carry towards them, by joining with them, or
withdrawing from them, as the faithful, or elfe
as the unfaithful minifters of the church of
Scotland, according as they carry towards the
common caufe for which they are confecrated,
and the common teftimony for the word of
Chrift's patience, which they are called to bear,
And hence, becaufe they are our own minifters
by the neareft ties, that we can have in this difordered time; therefore, being faithful, we owe to
them all the duties that we can difcharge to them in
this national capacity, which we could owe to them
in a congregational, if we were in that capacity;

as to *know them that labour* amongst us, and *admo-nish* us, and to *esteem them very highly for their work's sake,* 1 Thess. v. 12. 13. and to *obey them that have rule over us,* and submit ourselves; *seeing they watch for our souls, as they that must give an account; that they may do it with joy, and not with grief; for that is unprofitable for us,* Heb. xiii. 17. And it follows also, because they are our own, therefore, being unfaithful, we should take the greater faithful freedom to tell them when they offend us, and discountenance them, when they deserve it, more than is incumbent upon us, or pertinent for us to do with others; we would not take upon us to judge them, but we would have a judgment of our own duty, how to carry towards them: and this cannot be offensive to conscientious ministers, who, as they should be, are more tender of their Master's honour, than of their own personal credit: and I judge, there are none such in *Scotland* this day, whom the zeal of their God, and of his house is eating up, and on whom the reproaches of them that reproached him are fallen, and who are conscientiously tender also of the church's peace, consistent with truth; but they are so conscious of their own short-comings, faintings and failings, in the duty of this day, that they will be content. the best of them to be reproved, by the poorest plowman in the nation, that hath the cause of God rightly stated in his heart; and will take it as oil to his head. And I am sure, if more of this gospel spirit were amongst us, our difficulties and divisions might soon be overcome: but alas! it is not so; and therefore many poor mourners are in the mist what to do, and with whom to join.

J.

I would only propose in the general, who I
think we should have a care of joining with: It
is difficult to determine particulars, and I think
it a great defect, that hitherto (notwithstanding
of the heat of this debate, and the hurt of our
darkness about it; yet) this question hath not
been determined about *hearing* and *not hearing*:
we would be tender of ministers, and think it
dangerous, upon light grounds, to break or deny
a minister's commission; it cannot be every difference of judgment, or personal failing of infirmity, or some discovered hypocrisy, self-seeking,
or emulation, that may be a sufficient ground of
our withdrawing from a minister; some may
*preach Christ out of envy and strife, of contention,
not sincerely: notwithstanding every way, whether
in pretence or in truth, Christ is preached,* and
herein we ought to rejoice; if he be preached
by them that have a call to it, *Phil.* i. 15,—18.
Yet upon several grounds we may warrantably
withdraw, and refuse to join with many.

1. As *first*, we cannot join with such as Christ's
ambassadors, who never had a commission from
him in his orderly appointed way, but either
took it up at their own hand, or else from them
that have none themselves to give; as the Prelatic curates, ordained by the bishops; these are
such as run, and are not sent, *Jer.* xxiii 21, 22.
and *how shall they preach, except they be sent?*
Rom. x. 15. these are strangers, that the sheep
should not hear, *John* x. 15, &c.

2. We cannot join with such, as it may be,
had a commission, but they have wholly subjected it to the disposal of strange lords; either to
lay it aside, or to take a new one from them: as
such old Presbyterians as conformed to Prelacy;
and

and such as submitted by the act of *Glasgow*, to their deposition, and never avouched publicly their ministerial exercise since; but privately would preach now and then: and such likewise who have consented to the giving a bond not to exercise their ministry for such a time, upon the council's order; these are light and treacherous persons, polluting the sanctuary, who have done, and suffered violence to be done to the law of their master, *Zeph.* iii. 4.

3. We cannot join with such, who pretend to keep their old commission, but they have changed the holding of it, and taken a new grant of it from the usurper of their Master's prerogatives, with such instructions as are dishonourable to him, and destructive to his kingdom's liberties; which, though they did not keep, nor possibly did not mind to keep them, yet they did not disown and reject them with a testimony: these have become servants of men, and have not kept their Master's command *without spot, unrebukable, until his appearing;* such are the indulged, and their brethren, the connived at clergy, who tacitely, though not so expresly did officiate by virtue of the same new grant. I could never find a solid argument against hearing of the curates, which did not as forcibly militate against the indulged.

4. We cannot join with such as have perverted their commission, or corruped it, either by preaching false doctrine, or making false application of true doctrine; condemning the generation of the righteous, perverting people from the right ways of the Lord, condemning duty, and approving sin, and leading into snares, and defending and pleading for defection. We must
cease

ceafe to hear the inftruction that caufeth to err from the words of knowledge, Prov. xix. 27. And *fuch leaders caufe the people to err, and they that are led of them are deftroyed,* Ifa. ix. 16. Such are many of 'our time-ferving *daubers with untempered mortar,* Ezek xxii. 28.

5. We cannot join with fuch as thereupon *caufe divifions and offences, contrary to the doctrine which we have learned;* either by maintaining the caufes of thefe divifions, or cafting fewel on that fire, by reproaching the faithful; or by good words and fair fpeeches deceiving the hearts of the fimple, *Rom.* xvi. 17, 18.

6. We cannot join with fuch as have forfeited their commiffion, either by grofs fcandals and diforderly walking, either in their perfonal or minifterial capacity; or by lying by, and doing nothing in fuch a day, wherein there is fo much to do, not lifting up their voice like a trumpet, *&c.* but are finfully filent, as to the fins and fnares of the time; *have not difcovered our iniquities, but have feen for us falfe burdens, and caufes of banifhment,* Lam. ii. 14. We fee the fentence and cenfure of fuch *Levites* from the Lord, *Ezek.* xliv. 9,—15. Thefe would deferve the cenfure of the church, if ever they recovered their orderly jurifdiction; but all that Chriftians can do in recognition of that, is to withdraw from them; there is no other remedy without approving of their fin: but I do not think this fhould be done haftily at firft, but in the gofpel method, after admonition, and telling them to take heed to their miniftry, again and again repeated, and rejected; and then it muft needs follow, ay and while the offence be taken away by fome acknowledgment or amendment.

The

The *second* inquiry is more of your concern ment, What profeſſors may be joined with in ſuch a day? And alas, that there ſhould be ſuch occaſion given for that queſtion by the ſcandal ous ſtumblings of many, and jumblings of others but it is a day wherein the joining that is deſire cannot be in and upon the ſame centre Chriſt and ſo cannot be ſtedfaſt; a day wherein he that is for a ſanctuary to ſome, is a ſtone of ſtumbling and rock of offence to others ; and ſo there can not be a good agreement among ſuch, and *many, e* ven the greateſt part, *have ſtumbled, and are fallen and broken, and ſnared, and taken,* Iſa. viii. 14 15. and this makes it a day of trouble, and o treading down, and perplexity in the valley o viſion, *Iſa.* xxii..5. This makes it difficult to determine ; and this difficulty is ſo much the greater miſery, that there are ſo few that re tain any profeſſion ; and yet among theſe few there cannot be a joining in the Lord, withou jars and janglings : this is ſad, and ought to be mourned over, and all endeavours ought to be uſed to have it removed: we would deſire to ſtudy tenderneſs, to ſtrengthen that much decay ed brotherly love, ſo much commended, and ſtrictly commanded in the goſpel; it is the new commandment of our Lord, in the New Teſta ment, whereby we ſhall be known to be his diſciples, *John* xiii. 34, 35. *The followers of God, as dear children,* ſhould *walk in love, as Chriſt alſo loved* them, *Eph.* v. 1, 2. It is the deſire of my ſoul to be at that *conflict,* that the apoſtle had, for all the profeſſors in *Scotland,* *that their hearts might be comforted, being knit together in love, and unto all riches of the full aſ- ſurance of underſtanding,* Col. ii. 1, 2. But as for

hren, *as touching brotherly love*, I
d not *that I should write unto you;*
are taught of God to love one ano-
. iv. 9. Division is always a great
t never so miserable, as in a declin-
g time, and a desolating day as this
much the holy apostle is concern-
and what account the Spirit of God
1 *Cor.* i. 10. iii. 3. xi. 18, 33. And
be less division, if love to Christ
ren were in vigour; and I am con-
where it is sincere, differences in
l not alienate mutual affection, nor
practice. or fault which the mantle
over, will be a sufficient ground of
iongst friends to the cause of Christ.
in join with all that are faithful to
f Christ, as in their understanding
hat are foreward in expressing their
, that are faithful in a gospel conver-
vill join with us in a free and full
irfaking and mourning over the ini-
time; even though they and we
e same thing in every respect; yet
ree in the matter of the present
id word of Christ's patience, in this
tation, we desire to join with them,
be. But it is undeniable, that we
ith all that have a profession, or a
me do walk, of whom we may say,
th weeping, that they are enemies to
Christ, both to the doctrine, and
reproaches, and bearing of the cross
iny so disorderly in their walk, that
honour of the gospel, for our own
ir their edification and conviction
B. b   we

we muſt withdraw both from their way and f[...]
their worſhip; many ſo whoriſh in their g[...]
ing from the Lord, and ſo treacherous in t[...]
departings from his right way to the com[...]
ances of the time, that we muſt not join w[...]
them in their ſacrifices, becauſe diſpleaſing[...]
the Lord, *their offerings are as the bread of mou[...]*
ers; all that eat thereof ſhall be polluted, for t[...]
bread for their ſoul ſhall not come into the ho[...]
of the Lord; and ſhould not, by our conſe[...]
Hoſ. ix. 4. And ſo much the rather we ſho[...]
note them, and be cautious in our joining w[...]
them, becauſe they are brethren; if they were lo[...]
ed upon only as Chriſtians in a common relatic[...]
we could allow many of them a catholic joinin[...]
if they were only reſpected under the notion[...]
Proteſtants, we could allow many of them a g[...]
neral joining; if only as our covenanted conf[...]
derates or Preſbyterians, we could allow them[...]
more particular joining: but being brethren[...]
the ſame national church, we muſt take a mo[...]
narrow and particular cognizance of their carr[...]
age to us, and of ours to them. We grant,[...]
the church were in its eſtabliſhed ſtrength c[...]
order, we needed not be ſo pinched, nor ſo pre[...]
ciſe in our withdrawings in Chriſtian fellowſhip[...]
for then congregational, or preſbyterial, or pro[...]
vincial diſcipline, would, by their cenſures, pre[...]
clude all ſuch ſcruplings, by putting a note upo[...]
ſuch, in an orderly way: but now, all that i[...]
left us to do in the caſe, is to teſtify our diſap[...]
proving their enormities, by our withdrawin[...]
from, and non-communion with them. But her[...]
alſo, ſeveral caſes are to be diſtinguiſhed.

Firſt, There may be an occaſional joining wit[...]
profeſſors, whom providence may caſt in ou[...]

mpany, or us into theirs; and in this, I think
need not be fo critic, but we may very cor-
ally join with fuch, who in their difcourfes and
riage favour the things of God, and the con-
ns of his kingdom; with all who feem to have
e image of Chrift ftamped on them, with all
to feem to be fellow-heirs of the grace of life,
th all who in the judgment of charity cannot
charged or fufpected to be fcandalous, or di-
ers, or patrons of defection: For, as on the
he hand, Chriftians (though unknown to one
other) yet have a fecret fenfe and feeling of o-
rs their fellow-partakers of the like precious
th, and the fame divine nature; as they that
ve the mafon-word are faid to know brethren
f the trade by their common figns; fo they
ve a common inclination of love one to ano-
her, and a conftant liking of that meffage we
eard from the beginning, that we fhould love
ne another, 1 *John* iii. 11. And this is the
property of love, that it is not fufpicious, love
behaveth not itfelf unfeemly, thinketh no evil,
it beareth all things, believeth all things, hop-
eth all things, endureth all things, 1 *Cor.* xiii.
5. 7. Therefore we ought not to withdraw from
our brethren, whom we difcover to be fuch, before
we difcover them alfo to be falfe brethren, or
fuch as we cannot join with; except in difcourf-
ing of the courfes of the times, they evidence
themfelves to be guilty of fuch things, as we
cannot join with.

Secondly, There may a fixed, ftated joining
with profeffing brethren in focieties and fellowfhips, formed and appointed for prayer and conference, which is the beft model we can have
now, inftead of, and in imitation of our old

broken

broken congregations; and moſt neceſſary to
kept up, as being often bleſſed ſeminaries of
ligion, nurſeries of zeal, and of the life of go
lineſs; bleſſed often with the preſence and cou
tenance of God, and not wanting his inſtitutio
as well as approbation. It was the approve
practice of the fearers of the Lord under the O
Teſtament, to *ſpeak often one to another, and*
Lord hearkened and heard it: and a book of r
membrance was written before him for them; *th*
ſhall be mine, ſaith he, *in the day that I make u*
my jewels: If any be ſpar'd in a day of deſ
tion it ſhall be they, *Mal.* iii. 16. 17. This
in their private ſocieties. So we find in the Ne
Teſtament, both the places where they were
and their work they were employed about; th
was one of them at *Philippi,* where *Paul* wen
out by the *river ſide, where prayer was wont t*
be made, where ſome women reſorted, *Acts* xvi.
13. And ſome alſo that were not baptiz'd, a
mong whom was *Lydia;* and therefore I think,
ſome ignorant creatures that deſire to be inſtruc
ed, ſhould be admitted to your Chriſtian fellow
ſhips to hear, where conveniency will allow,
though not to be employed. So I think, ſuch
private ſocieties as theſe are intimated, when
we read of a church in ſuch a family or houſe
hold, as in *Rom.* xvi. The church in *Priſcilla*
and *Aquila*'s houſe; them which are of *Ariſtobu-
lus*'s houſehold; theſe of the houſehold of *Nar-
ciſſus,* and the like; they were only families;
theſe cannot be called churches, nor were they
congregations, having their own elected elders
and miniſters; there could not be ſo many of
them in the church of *Rome* at that time; therefore they muſt have been only Chriſtian fellowſhips.

Their

Their work was, to comfort themselves together, and edify one another, and warn the unruly, confirm the feeble-minded, and support
the weak; to consider one another, and to provoke one another to love, and to good works,
and exhort one another. For this cause, they
were *not to forsake the assembling themselves together, as the manner of some was*, Heb. x. 25.
And it is-to be remarked, that it is reckoned a
wilful sinning, the danger of which is there held
forth, to forsake such meetings. But there is not
such question made about their institution as
their constitution, or who they are that may be
admitted members of such societies? and who
ought not to be admitted? It is difficult to pre-
scribe particular rules in this matter; only in the
general, I think it undeniable, that there must not
be a promiscuous admission of all that may desire
it, nor of all that might be continued members
of a particular congregation; for persons may
be admitted to that who are ignorant, or children;
here that were very unsuitable, for there is a
great difference betwixt the two. They differ in
the terms of the entry, as we may perceive; for
either if they be children of church members, or
persons of a blameless walk, they may be admit-
ed there: this requires more qualifications: they
differ in the order of exclusion; there they have
the advantage of an authoritative decision, and
potestative sentence; here only can be a brotherly and charitative discountenancing, and
note of non-communion: they differ in the nature and ends of their constitutions; the one is
for gathering and converting of souls to the
grace of the gospel by the ordinances, dispensed
by officers, as well as for edifying; the other,

only for confirming, comforting, admonishing,
exhorting professing believers, and praying together for their mutual help in the duties of
Christianity; so that it is supposed, that they are
qualified Christians, at least visibly called and
professing saints, that are to join together in
such a society; and therefore, as they ought to
be persons of unstained profession, and unrebukable integrity, and some experience in the
way of God, who are by turns to be employed as the mouth of the rest in prayer or conference; though it be not requisite that they give
a distinct account of their being in a state of
grace, or evidence much knowledge, yet the
more of that the better, and the more comfortable, at least they ought to give discoveries of
their seriousness, in minding religion as their business; so there must be some kind of trial and
knowledge of the persons prerequisite: and albeit it be not necessary, and is not attainable,
that the persons be all of one mind in every
thing, yet there must be an agreement in the
chief controversies of the time, and the matters
of the present testimony, and in the things that
that community have stated their witnessing and
suffering upon; otherwise they cannot avoid debates in their conference, and jars and justlings
in their prayers, and so can have no comfortable
communion together, which is very inconveni-
ent; and therefore, there may be somewhat like
articles condescended upon; but these should
be as few and general as may be, to avoid the
censure and scandal of singularity or separation.
I shall therefore give a hint what I think ought
not to debar persons from our societies, and
what

that ought, and may be fufficient grounds of on-admiffion, or exclufion.

1. I conceive, that ignorance in matters of act, or of duty in fome things, through want of information, fhould not debar a man; or that which follows upon the former, a fcrupling or doubting to approve or condemn fome things, that they had no opportunity to be inftructed in before, need not hinder a joining; for fo we find *Aquila* and *Prifcilla* took unto them *Apollos*, knowing only the baptifm of *John*, and expound-ed to him the way of God more perfectly, *Acts* xviii. 26.

2. Difference of judgment ought not to hin-der joining, if it be either in things indifferent or not material, nor not the prefent word of pa-tience and matter of teftimony; for in thefe things; if we account ourfelves ftronger and more knowing, we ought to *receive him that is weak, but not to doubtful difputations,* Rom. xiv. 1. Nor, that which follows upon the former, every dif-ference in practice according to light and the judgment of confcience; in things that are not formally diforderly, though we could not allow it in ourfelves, ought not to demur us in our joining with the man, that did it with regard to the Lord, *Rom.* xiv. 6. &c. *Judge nothing before the time, until the Lord come, who will bring to light the hidden things of darknefs, and manifeft the counfels of the hearts; and then fhall every man have praife of God,* 1 Cor. iv. 5. See alfo *Phil.* iii. 15, 16. a paffage much to be pondered.

3. *Weaknefs* or *infirmities* ought not to hinder our joining: *We then that are ftrong ought to bear with the infirmities of the weak, and not to pleafe ourfelves,* Rom. xv. 1. This weak-nefs

ness may be considered as threefold : (1.) *Natural weakness*, as infirmity of parts, of knowledge, or courage, &c. These are infirmities and very disadvantageous to those that labour under them : but we must *bear one another's burdens, and so fulfil the law of Christ*, Gal. vi. 2 (2.) *Spiritual weakness*, as of the grace of faith or love, zeal or patience ; when we perceive some evidences of hypocrisy, or unbelief, or security, or coldness, or some risings of passion &c. we must not cast at them for such things ; but bear with them, and forbear, with all lowliness and meekness, *Eph.* iv. 2.   (3.) *Moral weakness*, that is, sins of infirmity : I call sins of infirmity either sins of ignorance, or personal escapes allowed, or such as the person hath been hurried into by a surprising temptation, out of fear, or in desertion, &c. which we durst not do, nor would he have done, if he had been himself, though we ought to reprove our brother for these things, and not suffer sin upon him ; yet we must not disjoin from him, but receive him for all that ; *Receive ye one another, as Christ also received us to the glory of God,* Rom. xv. 7. Now, ye know Christ received us with many faults ; so likewise *if a man be overtaken in a fault, we which are spiritual should restore such a one in the spirit of meekness, considering ourselves, left we also be tempted,* Gal. vi. 1. These, and the like, are not sufficient grounds of demurring, or refusing to join with our professing brethren. But, .

Secondly, I think these following are sufficient.

1. *Heresy*, or *dangerous errors*, ought to debar men from our fellowship, and us from theirs, *Titus* iii. 10. *A man that is an heretic, after the first and second admonition, reject :* which command

and muft have place, even when ordinary jurifdiction, and orderly procedure of church difcipline cannot be had; for the reafon fubjoined
cleareth it, *Knowing that he that is fuch, is fubverted, and finneth, being condemned of himfelf:*
And therefore, where the error is fuch, that the
perfon owning it is fubverted, and it is of a fub-
verting nature, and others like to be in danger
of the leaven of it, he is condemned of himfelf, there is no need of our fufpending, of our
withdrawing from him, till he be legally condemned. I do not think that this is to be reftricted to thefe errors that are called *fundamen-
tal*, overturning the doctrine of falvation; but
to be extended even to thofe that are contradictory to our common Confeffion of all orthodox truths, as received by all of our communion; either by maintaining errors condemned
thereby, or condemning truths maintained thereby: We mean, if fuch errors be owned by fuch
as were, or are, looked upon as our brethren;
for otherwife we may allow them a catholic or
occafional communion.

2. *Apoftacy*, or falling from the truth formerly profeffed by our brother, and now ftated by
us as the matter of our witnefs and teftimony;
that as *John* defines it, and prefcribes our carriage in that cafe, *Whofoever tranfgreffeth, and
abideth not in the doctrine of Chrift, and whofoever
fuch fhall come unto you, and brings not this doctrine, receive him not into your houfes, neither
bid him God fpeed: for he that bidd th him God
fpeed, is partaker of his evil deeds*, 2 John 9, 10,
11. This is no breach of brotherly love; for
*this is love, that we walk after his commandments;
and this is the commandment, that as ye heard from
the*

the beginning, ye should walk in it, verses 5th and 6th of that epistle.

3. Such as do not, in their own judgment and practice, fall from the truth, yet *maintain, defend,* and *patronize defection,* and strengthen it, and harden them that are engaged in it ; so that none doth return from his wickedness ; such must not be joined with : which was the *horrible thing* the Lord saw in the prophets of *Jerusalem,* Jer. xxiii. 14. It is also horrible in professors. Some will not actually join in building the wall themselves, but they will *daub it with untempered mortar,* and by their countenance and concurrence strengthen the .builders, Ezek. xiii. 10. &c. A *WO* is there pronounced against such as *sew pillows under arm-holes,* and *make kerchiefs upon the head of every stature ;* and upon such as *make the heart of the righteous sad, whom the Lord hath not made sad ;* and *strengthen the hands of the wicked,* v. 18—22. We should have a care to avoid that *wo,* which we cannot do, if we be partakers with them, *Eph.* v. 7. We make ourselves partakers with them, when we countenance them : we must have a care of such leaven in our societies ; for *a little leaven leaveneth the whole lump :* so we must not be unequally yoked in our joinings in fellowship *What fellowship hath righteousness with unrighteousness ?--light with darkness ?--Christ with Belial ? Wherefore come ye out from among them, and be ye separate, and touch not the unclean thing, &c.* Cor. vi. 14. to the end. The place is not only meant of affinity in marriage, but of Christian church-fellowship ; and is spoken of such as did not make conscience of separating from idolatry and uncleanness altogether, but thought that they

might

might join with both. The Apostle calls that an *unequal yoking*. If then we must separate from all these things that are unsuitable to Christian communion, then we must leave these that will not separate, but will maintain their own, or others way of lax compliances, which do provoke God to separate from them. I do not say, that we must separate from all, that have not the same clearness of separating from every thing that we separate from; for that may proceed, either from ignorance, or want of information, or difference of judgment, or weakness; which, I was shewing before, could not be sufficient to found a withdrawing upon: but I speak now of obstinate defenders of palpable defections; I judge these are not to be joined with.

4. More especially and undeniably, such as are *guilty of defections* in their *practice*, unruly and disorderly in their way, walking contrary to the received rule, and in a way inconsistent with the present testimony of the godly, are not to be joined with; especially if they have the sense, and come under the notion of brethren: for so much may the Apostle's dissuasive bear in the general, when he wrote unto the *Corinthians*, in an epistle, *Not to keep company with fornicators, covetous, extortioners;* not so much with others in the world (for, if common converse must be denied with these, then must we go out of the world) as especially, if any that is called a brother be such, with such an one, no not to eat, nor communicate with him in any Christian fellowship, 1 *Cor.* v. 9. 10, 11. Much more must we avoid them, if they be deniers, or deserters of the cause and truths of Christ: if compliers with wicked courses and snares of the time; if

conformers with the gayfe of this world, in oppofing our teftimony, the argument will hold
good *a fortiori:* You have the Apoftle's indifpenfible command, *in the name of our Lord Jefus
Chrift, that ye withdraw yourfelves from every
brother that walketh diforderly, and not after the
tradition he hath received of us:* And, *if any man
obey not the word,* (efpecially if it be the word
of Chrift's patience) *note that man, and have no
company with him, that he may be afhamed; yet
to account him, not as an enemy, but to admonifh
him as a brother,* 2 Theff. iii. 6, 14, 15.

5. I think alfo, fomewhat of that enjoined
order of Chrift's muft not be baulked, and
wholly laid afide, even when the church cannot
have its exercife of jurifdiction and legal cenfure,
in the cafe of a brother's perfonal trefpafs, or
offence, or fcandal, even in leffer matters, if he
be obftinate and contumacious, after many repeated admonitions; then, when we cannot get
a church to tell it to, we may put a note upon
him (at leaft when we cannot pafs a fentence)
that he may be afhamed; that is, by withdrawing from him, and not to admit him to join, as
before, in our fellowfhips. I doubt not but our
Lord did leave fomething of this order to be obferved in all times, even when in his wifdom he
did forefee, that his people might be in fuch a
condition, as that they could not have a church-
judicatory; and this he feems to infinuate, when
he allows fomething of this power and promife
alfo, to two or three met together in his name,
Matth. iii. 15—20. There is certainly much need
of caution here, to beware of prejudice or prefumption, or precipitancy: but as far as can
confift with our own peace of confcience, or

our

edification, all place would be given
⟨w⟩ith, and forbearing, and forgiving
against ourselves; as *Peter's* quef-
ften he muft forgive his brother,
⟨⟩l's parable in explaining the anfwer
⟨⟩ion, makes apparent, *Matth.* xviii.
⟨⟩ofe. But this fhould not hinder that
⟨oth⟩er fcandalous offences, though not
⟨⟩ hainous in themfelves, attended
⟨b⟩y, fhould be thus noted, as I have

⟨a⟩nd the Apoftle gives direction, and
⟨ea⟩rneft intreaty, to *mark them that*
⟨⟩s *and offences, contrary to the doc-*
⟨⟩ *have learned, and avoid them,* Rom.
⟨⟩ therefore, any of our brethren will
⟨d⟩ividing courfes from, and contrary
⟨whic⟩h we have learned to be truth and
⟨wh⟩ich we have ftated as the matter of
⟨⟩vitneffing and fuffering, and will op-
⟨⟩, and will maintain and propagate
⟨⟩l go to profelyte us into his way,
⟨⟩ us into debates, not for informa-
⟨fo⟩r divifion; I can fee no other way,
⟨⟩ to join with him, as the mark we
⟨u⟩pon him.
⟨fo⟩me other grounds of warrantable
⟨⟩ you may think upon; but none o-
⟨cur to⟩ me at prefent: thefe in the gene-
⟨ral ar⟩e clear, and may be to many more
⟨⟩bfcribe to particulars, when conde-
⟨⟩n, as the grounds of our difowning
⟨⟩ving from our profeffing brethren in
⟨⟩t to give my thoughts of thefe alfo,
⟨⟩nguifh betwixt a *voluntary* and a
⟨⟩g.

First, There may be a *voluntary* joining in and with fixed focieties, in admitting others, and accepting of admittance of ourfelves into the fellowfhip of all that love and adhere to the Lord' righteous caufe, as it is ftated this day againft his enemies; with all that own, and wreftle and witnefs and fuffer for the covenanted work of reformation from Popery, Prelacy, and Eraftianifm in *Scotland;* with all that are ferious in mourning over all the evidences and effects of the Lord's anger againft us, and are impartial in fearching into all the procuring caufes of it; though perhaps, we may find out moe fteps and degrees of both, than they find. Finally, With all that are willing to concur with us, and imbark their lot with the perfecuted remnant, in the profecution of the duties of the day: and from others we muft withdraw. But who thefe are, and how to rank them, you, who are more experimentally acquainted with cafes incident, know better than I; fo that I need not infift to fpecify particulars. Only I think, that, upon the former general grounds,

1. All that conform and fubmit to Prelacy, by hearing curates, &c. are to be noted, and fellowfhip to be refufed with them: that being an error long fince exploded and abjured by the church of *Scotland,* and engaged againft by Covenant; all who decline, or difown that Covenant, ought to be withdrawn from.

2. All Sectarians, who do not own our covenanted reformation, nor the government of our church, by prefbyteries, fynods, and general affemblies, ought not to be owned, nor adjoined with in our focieties.

3. Such as do actually countenance, or con-

.cur

r to the upholding of the wretched Indul-
ence, the bane of our church, by hearing the
indulged, or pleading for, or taking the patrociny of their woeful, Chrift-difhonouring, and
church-rending defections; for which they deferve to be noted, as the *betrayers of the rights
of the church of* Scotland, by all who do concert with that caufe, and teftimony thereof:
thefe are not to be joined with.

4. Such as practically and intentionally contradict and condemn the prefent ftated teftimony of the fuffering and witneffing remnant,
owned of God, fealed by their blood, and for
which others fuffer great afflictions; either by
virulent and viperous reproaching, flandering
and calumniating them; or by renouncing and
abjuring (efpecially before the enemy) their declarations, apologies and vindications of themfelves, and the truths they adhere to: Such as
difown their avowed oppofition to the tyranny
of the times, and their rejecting the prefent
tyrant's ufurpations, and their neceffitate endeavours to defend themfelves from, or to avenge
themfelves on their murderers, or to bring them
to condign punifhment, as the Lord fhall give
them a call, opportunity, and capacity; fuch,
I fay, are to be withdrawn from, as being not
only offenders but condemners of the generation
of the righteous; and confenters to, and jufti-
fiers of the effufion of their blood. Therefore,
I think, that the takers of the late Oath of Abjuration, do deferve this kind of *note:* I fay,
thefe that did it practically before the enemies;
for, I do not think, that all that cannot own
that Declaration, there abjured, are forthwith
for that to be feparated from; for they may have

scruples out of ignorance, or misconstruction
against some things in the *form*, or some *expressions* of it; yet will not condemn the matter of
it *absolutely*, nor any part of it practically-before
the enemy. Some again may quarrel at the
unseasonableness of it; others, through misin-
formation, may have condemned it practically
but not intentionally; conceiving that that *A-
pologetical Declaration* did assert the lawfulness of
murder, and assassination. These are not to be
withdrawn from, meerly because they have done
so; if so be, after better information and admonition, they do not obstinately defend their
own deed, and condemn the said *Declaration*
intentionally.

5. All such compliers, as do not only own
the authority of the present party now in power,
but transact and bargain with them, by subscribing their oaths, tenders, bonds, and impositions
whatsoever: As, for instance, the takers of that
detestable *Test*, the *Bond of Peace*, *Regulation*,
Conformity, &c. the subscribers of their *oaths* of
Allegiance and *Supremacy;* such as engaged never to rise in arms against the present government upon no pretence whatsoever; and all
strengtheners of the present opposition of Christ's
kingdom, by paying cess or the like, are to be
withdrawn from.

6. All such as are deprehended in any scandal,
or offensive practice, dishonourable to the profession, such as drunkenness, or lyeing, &c. are
to be separated from.

Secondly, There is a *forced joining*, in a forced society; that is in your case, that are by the
unjust violence of men shut up in a prison, in one
room with locked doors, wherein ye cannot,

omit public worſhip; in which caſe,
enlarged ſo much in the general, I
iſt; your own diſcretion will direct
particulars; for it will not admit
r of doubt, or queſtion, but that ye
h all from whom ye would not with
voluntary ſtated ſocieties; and if it
rith truth and duty, or your preſent
d ſtate of your ſuffering, you would
in more, for your own peace and
converſe, for holding up the worſhip
ut diſcord, for avoiding the odious
malicious obſervations of your com-
s, who are glad and greedy to ſee
ar breaches. But you muſt prefer
th to all conveniences and advan-
ver, and hold faſt your teſtimony,
u have learned of Chriſt, let who
ded. Only there would be ſome
owed in your carriage to theſe who
admitted, and thoſe who deſire to
a their communion. The firſt re-
enderneſs and condeſcendency; the
caution and peremptorineſs. I
you are the greater number in a
you are to give propoſals to theſe
in with you, and if they will not
t, I think, ye cannot hinder them
vilege of public worſhip amongſt
convenient turns, if they demand
were altogether unbrotherly, and
much of ſupremacy. But if you
number there, and cannot join with
think, you ſhould plead for your pri-
ping up public worſhip among your-
s ye would hear theirs without join-

ing, yet in an inoffensive posture, and a place separate by yourselves: so they cannot deny, and you cannot well refuse, to take either one day and they another, or rather one time of the day of your own choosing, and let them take the rest for going about their duty; for this is not joining with them by turns, but a separate fellowship of your own, taking your own turns, and pleading your own privilege, whereby you may have the advantage of letting them hear your public regrete, and bemoanings of their offensive courses and disorders, for which ye cannot join with them; whereby also much contention and irritation may be prevented, and mutual affection convincingly entertained, notwithstanding of differences; which, that it may obtain with the blessing of the Lord, shall be the prayer of

Your wellwisher,
and companion in tribulation,

ALEX. SHIELD

N. B. Mr. *Alexander Shields,* wrote this Letter during the time he was prisoner in *Edinburgh.*

LETTER LXXVI.

From Mr. Alexander Shields, *Preacher of the Gospel, to the Ladies* Van. Her. *and* E. T. V. in Lewarden *in* Friesland. *October* 1687.

Much honoured and dearly beloved in our Lord Jesus Christ,

GRace, mercy, and peace be with you, from God our Father, and from our Lord Jesus

us Chrift, in whom, and through whofe grace, you have been called to a participation of his heavenly bleffing and unfearchable riches; fo out of his abundance, you have been helped to give fach experiments of love to him, in compaffion to his afflicted members, that ye have won the bleffings of them that are ready to perifh, and have canfed the widow's heart to fing for joy, in laying many obligations on the poor wounded and wafted remnant of Chrift's perfecuted witneffes in *Scotland*, to make joyful and thankful remembrance of you in their prayers and praifes on your behalf; with whom, and in whofe name, I take the boldnefs, though I cannot have the happinefs to fee you at this time, which is my regrete, to confort and concur in returning bleffings to our God, and congratulations to you, for the graces beftowed on you, and fruits thereof brought forth by you.

1. That the Lord hath been pleafed to enlighten you with the knowledge of his truth as it is in Jefus; and given you to underftand by experience, the excellency of the knowledge of Chrift, infinitely preferable to all time's things and fancied excellencies, which are but lofs and dung befides it; though the world's worms, whofe eyes the god of this world hath blinded, and bewitched with the charms of evanifhing vanities, cannot and will not behold the vanity thereof, yet to believers, Chrift is the only pearl of price; and to lofe all to win him, is thought the greateft gain. It is matter of joy, to the fufferers of *Scotland* chiefly, that their beloved matchlefs One is in fuch efteem with you, and his great falvation meets with

welcome

welcome entertainment among you, which is little regarded by the moſt part of men.

2. That not only you lay religion to heart, and make it your choice and exerciſe, which is the main buſineſs; but the cauſe of Chriſt, which is ſo univerſally ſtumbled at and forſaken, is to you the great intereſt, for whom ye would have a throne ſet up in the church, that there his royal ſcepter may bear ſway, as well as in your hearts; and a reformation may be advanced from remaining corruptions, according to the kingly ſtandard of his law and revealed will; the defect whereof is to you a burden, as it is to all the faithful ſubjects of our exalted Prince, who will not be content to have his favour and fellowſhip for themſelves only (though that be their heaven here to have it, and their hell to want it) but they muſt have this for their deſign, to deſire to bring him to *their mo-ther's houſe, and to the chambers of her that conceived them.*

3. It is the joy of all the lovers of Chriſt, to hear, that not only the cauſe is ſeated in your hearts, but avowed and defended in your profeſſion; being not aſhamed even of the re-proaches of Chriſt, whom not only you love with ſuch fervency of zeal, that you will not ſeek him by night on your bed only, but riſe and profeſs it, in going about the city, in the ſtreets and in the broad ways, and make ſerious enquiry for him, whom your ſoul loveth, even though the watchmen ſhould ſmite you, and the keepers of the wall ſhould take away your veil, becauſe you cannot, you muſt not want him: for whoſe indignities, done to him, and the injuries done to his church, you are

not

not only secretly difcontented, but openly declare your diffatisfaction, in a profeffed difcountenancing of them.

4. It is their rejoicing, that your name is
not only favoury among the serious profeffors
of Chrift, but enrolled among the faithful confeffors and witneffes of Jefus Chrift, contending
for the truths, and efpoufing his fide of the
controverfy in their teftimony for reformation,
againft the relicks of mens inventions, againft
the *Cocceian* novations, and againft the *Eraftian*
encroachments and ufurpations, under which the
Netherlands are labouring as a woman in her
pains. Wherein, though you have few to concert it with you, or to affift you in it, yet, becaufe the caufe is Chrift's, it fhall overcome,
and you in it and by it.

5. All your Lord's weeping friends rejoice to
hear, that though ye have yet been preferved
from the firey trial, yet you are not at eafe in
Zion, but are ambitious to be marked among
the mourners, *that figh and cry for the abominations done in Jerufalem.* Ye lament after
the Lord, and for the difhonour done to his
Majefty, both by his declared enemies and profeffing people; and all the caufes and effects
of his holy indignation, gone forth againft
them this day through the churches; and that
for this end to ftir up and encourage one another to this work, you keep fellowfhip together,
as becomes the fearers of the Lord in fuch a
day, to fpeak often one to another, which the
Lord will hearken to, and note it up in his
book of remembrance, for your behalf, in the
day when he maketh up his jewels.

6. The poor afflicted remnant in *Scotland* are
much

much encouraged to know that ye fympathiz
with their cafe, and are concerned in the
caufe, when they ftand fo much in need of i
and can find fo little either at home or abroad
But, *their foul is exceedingly filled with the fcor*
of them that are at eafe, and with the contemp
of the proud : And were it not that they hav
fome feelings of your High-prieft's fympath
fupporting them under all their burdens, the
would fink under the fame, in the fight, an
without the pity of all fpectators.

7. It is in a fpecial manner refrefhing to them
that all the calumnies and reproaches wherewit
they are induftrioufly and invidioufly laden, bo
by enemies and profeffed friends, to make the
and their caufe odious, get not fuch credulo
entertainment with you, as to make you ftand
far off from their fore, for the mifinformatio
of traducers, from which, we have confidence
our Lord, that at length he will bring forth th
righteoufnefs as the light, and their judgment
the noon-day, when he will arife and plead t
caufe that is his own.

8. They are bound to return all thankful a
knowledgment of obliged gratitude; and I defi
for myfelf, and have their allowance, and defi
in their name (which is all the recompence the
can make) to give unfeigned thanks for yo
tender fympathy, affectionate kindnefs, Chrif
an charity, and loving liberality, fo long con
nued, fo largely extended, and fo frequently r
newed towards Chrift's perfecuted little flock
confeffors and witneffes in *Scotland,* and partic
larly towards their dear and much refpect
friends. who are the more endeared to the
that for their fakes they have fuffered fo mu

and rage; namely Mr. *Robert Hamil-*
,thers, with that poor afflicted family,
ye have taken such courteous care and
; for which, as I hope, so long as there
of that suffering remnant in *Scotland* to
the teftimony, your kindnefs fhall ne-
orgotten ; fo he, for whofe fake, and
fe account ye fhow it, fhall remember
labour of love, in the day when he fhall
uiry what good or hurt hath been done
e ones, to repay it as done to himfelf;
I am confident ye fhall not have caufe
of your kindnefs to them, to whom all
e been fo cruel; and I perfuade myfelf,
tinuance in giving them your counte-
d the encouragement of your favour,
anding all reproaches and attempts to
you againft them, will yield you fweet
the end, and that you fhall never have
be afhamed of it. That poor handful
d are indeed a very fuitable object of
, and not unworthy your patrociny,
nce and protection, their cafe being now
y circumftantiate, by reafon of the op-
hey meet with from all hands; the rage
es, incenfed by their contempt of their
favours, and the envy of them that are
becaufe they continue ftill in their con-
againft the antichriftian party; from
e other are laid by, and lulled afleep
bewitching toleration, and laden with
ach of both. Yet they are encouraged
odnefs of their Captain, and juftnefs of
fe, to fuftain all conflicts, feeing their
y is honourably ftated for the covenant-
nation of the church of *Scotland,* where-
-of

of what is left unruined, is now defigned to be totally razed, by this gap opened by this liberty to introduce Popery and eftablifh tyranny: particularly it hath been their honour to witnefs and fuffer for the prerogatives of Chrift's kingly glory, both as he is a king in the church, and hath the fole fovereignty over his own myftical body, to' appoint his ordinances, inftitute his officers, make laws binding the confcience, and eftablifh the doctrine, worfhip, difcipline and government that he, as only law giver, will have obferved in his church, without either addition, diminution, or alteration, which prerogative hath been encroached upon and ufurped by Prelacy, by the Eraftian fupremacy, and now by the open attempts to bring in Popery; againft all which they have wreftled and witneffed, by following their pure gofpel ordinances, by their declarations, by their fuffering of great oppofitions, bonds, banifhments and blood, and for which they have been killed all day long, and counted as fheep for the flaughter. And they have been called likewife to contend for the prerogatives of his kingly glory, as he is a king of the world, whofe incommunicable property it is to be abfolute, in fubordination to which he hath ordained and reftricted magiftracy for his glory and the good of mankind, which prerogative hath been invaded by tyranny and abfolute power, arrogated over all law, confcience, reafon, religion, and liberty of the people, againft which they have been called to witnefs; maintaining their teftimony againft the leviathan of illimited and abfolute tyranny, and declining and refufing to own it as the authority of God's appointment, when, upon pain of death this was impofed upon

their

their consciences; for which they have been tra-
duced by enemies, and reproached by many
professors, as seditious despisers of government,
or at least sufferers for phantastic points, wherein
religion is little or nothing concerned. But,
though this be the great device of the dragon,
this day, to destroy religion and the single sincere professors thereof, covertly under another
notion; yet, as wisdom is, and will be justified
of her children, so it is their peace and confidence before God and man, that they suffer for
the cause of Christ, the concern of all churches,
and the interest of all mankind, and for nothing
which is not consonant to, founded upon, and
confirmed by the testimonies of the church of
Scotland in all her periods, and have been aiming at a witness and testimony against all defections and declinings from the attained reformation
of that church, without being silent at any; as
now they find themselves obliged to testify a-
gainst this abominable toleration, and the acceptance thereof, and addressing for the same; and
keeping up their meetings in the fields, though
interdicted and discharged, under pain of death
both to preachers and hearers, looking upon it
as a case of confession to witness against that present confederacy with *Babylon*'s cruel mercies, to
enjoy her ordinances there, where her favours
extend not, and where they are interdicted or
discharged by the same wicked acts that allow a
toleration to all that will not oppose her; wherein, though they are exposed to all the rage and
reproach that men can invent against them, yet
they expect the Lord's countenance and concurrence, and that he will be the more kind that
men are so cruel; and do hope for the continu-

D d ation

ation of your sympathy, and are confident th
their long intermissions of their correspondin
in returning due acknowledgment for all yo
favours, will not interrupt either your kindn
or their gratitude.

And now, much honoured and dear friends,
must conclude with a regrete and confession, i
stead of an apology for my omission, in not se
ing you, and writing to you before this tim
I have nothing to say for myself, but that I a
grieved for my unhappiness, that I have n
been in capacity to discharge the business I ha
been called to here, nor to have liberty to enj
myself, nor time to obtain the comfort of yo
communion, and chiefly, that I have been so lo
detained from the public work of my functio
to which I have impatient longing to be restore
and therefore having this opportunity, I am n
cessitated to return homeward, and leave th
work I have been waiting upon, and taken
with incessantly, night and day, since I came
this country, unperfected and not absolved, b
left to be printed and lying at the press, not b
ing able to defray the charges: But what is dor
already, I thought it my duty to communica
unto you, and therefore have sent you some vi
dications of the poor persecuted remnant, repr
senting their contests with, and clearing them
the reproaches cast upon them by their professin
antagonists; there is another larger treatise re
presenting all the succession of testimonies of ou
church, and stating the present testimony with
deduction of heads of sufferings sustained there
upon, and vindication of all the heads thereo
which is now interrupted at the press, but when
ever it can be set foreward and finished, car
sha

all be taken to convey it to your hands. Now,
:gging your excuse, and entreating your pray-
:s, I rest

Your real, though unworthy and

unacquainted friend and servant,

in the Lord Jefus,

ALEX. SHIELDS.

L E T T E R LXXVII.

From the honourable Mr. Robert Hamilton[*], *to*
fome Friends in Scotland.

Lewarden, May 24. 1683.

Right honourable and dear Brethren,

THough, as the Lord knows, I have been
often made to defire and refolve upon a
:ottage in the wildernefs, yet it has feemed good
:n his eyes, to have me otherways employed,
ind kept up, not only at home, but in all
places of my pilgrimage, as a beacon on the top
of a mountain, and a witnefs for his precious
and honourable caufe, interest and people, a-
gainft all his and their enemies, whether country-men or ftrangers: and, however, my real
infufficiency and great emptinefs did often terri-

D d 2   fy

---

[*] It was thought proper to infert this letter of
Mr. *Hamilton*'s in this collection, as it is not amongft
thofe of his, publifhed fome time ago, in a pamphlet
called *The Chriftian's Conduct*, &c.

fy and affright me, at firſt fight, to venture up
on ſo great and ſo hot encounters, as I have
been tryſted with; yet he, in his great love
and infinite condeſcendency, ſpared no pains
(as forſooth, I had been ſomewhat, and could
have done ſomething for him) once to allure me,
and next, as it were, to get my conſent to the
ſervice. And when he did let me find (O!
wonder of wonders!) in ſome meaſure what he
would do for his own name's ſake, in abundantly furniſhing, wonderfully leading on, and honourably bringing me off; that, O praiſe to his
glorious name! he made it often, not only a-
ſtoniſhing to myſelf, but admirable to onlookers,
and the greateſt of my enemies: for once having entered and got me to a cheerful ſubmiſſion,
and rejoicing in his will and way, I may ſay,
I had often no more ado, but to *ſtand ſtill, and
ſee his ſalvation :* and though he uſed his own
way in correcting my untowardneſs and miſbelief, yet, O my friends! in ſuch a way, that
the world could never diſcern it. O what am
I, ſuch a lump of ſin, that ever was counted
worthy to be ſo dealt with, and chaſtiſed with
ſuch ſweet, ſugared, and honourable rods; no
leſs than the golden rod wherewith our lovely
Lord, heir of the inheritance, was ſtriken with.
Courage, my honourable brethren, your chaſings,
wanderings, fightings, and contendings for matchleſs, O matchleſs Him! cannot but be infinitely
more glorious than all the painted, crowned
vanities of the world: O they bear their reward
with them, that the world knows not of; and
no wonder, when dealt out by ſuch a lovely
hand, and in the fight of ſuch a noble General,
who deals out to every man his poſt, and his
blows,

furnifhes accordingly; and is moft
imfelf in the battle, and in the car-
own, that they may be all honour-
ceive the crown, and the noble
of eternal glory with himfelf thro'
ich he has laid up and purchafed
n blood. O continue, continue to
he and you fhall once judge the ty-
ie furious bulls of *Bafhan* here be-
y him, and ye fhall get the victory,
more than conquerors.

Chriftian friends, having this fo
on; I could not but give you fome
t, as to the Lord's leading, in and
great and laft piece of fervice, not
it may be the laft edition of fervice
ie land that ever I fhall be honour-
i; as alfo, hoping it might be for
ging and ftrengthening, and a mean
on to the bearer. And, I hope,
grace of God, the great Mafter of
s, his embaffage and mafter-like
ill be more than able to commend
i all. And I have been made to
might be the firft ftone of our
, and indeed to fome in this place,
on was to them, as the laying the
the fecond temple, *weeping and*
it however it be, I hope the Lord
at glory by it, and yet more and
e, as he hath hitherto done in a
y. But,
Lord's preparing and leading me
rk, it was thus: He hath been pleaf-
(praife, O praife to his name!)
d to me a poor worm, to let me

fee

fee fomething of his ftately goings and manage-
ments in this day, as his working out of his
moft noble and moft intricate pieces of fervice,
through poor defpifed means and fecklefs inftruments, and that both of the minifters and
others; as alfo, his moft glorious victories obtained of the enemies, when feemingly they were
moft conquering; as alfo, making many as prophets in and for his houfe, giving warning of
the trials that were to come, and partly as come,
and of the defections, with great bleffings on them
that fhould faithfully ftand out; indeed, *Balaam*-
like, the moft of them, and now, all of them in
the enemies camp, are ftating themfelves as head
of the rebels, and chief in the rebellion againft
thefe, who through the bleffing of the Lord,
took with the warning, and are to this day
ftanding faithfully to their poft; as alfo, his
making the greateft of our enemies (even when
our *Eliafes* were taken away) on their death-beds,
confirming to the remnant, in being their own
heralds, denouncing the righteous judgments
of God againft themfelves and their pofterity;
and in all, vindicating the poor wreftling remnant, whom they in their health delighted to
butcher, and breathing out their laft, foretelling
the glorious days that fhould be yet in *Scotland*,
with the raifing that buried-like caufe again; as
alfo, his righteous judgment, and holy juftice,
in taking the difcipline of his own houfe out of
the hands of the perfidious fhepherds, who, at
their beft, in a terrible manner mifemployed it.
O what ftately goings, doing more as to the
difcovery of jugglers, mockers, and hypocrites,
than the wit of man could have done in a genc-
ration; and it is obfervable, that in a fpecial

way

ies thefe who looked upon them-
ould have others to do fo, as above
and cenfures; fo that if any poor
a holy zeal and tendernefs, had
to reprove a minifter, it was as
and no more peace for them. O
teoufnefs of God! let us fall in love
iis infinite love in managing of that
grievoufly mifmanaged; and in fo
our rods, that he that runs may
i our judgment; for how has he ftir-
thin ourfelves, blafphemoufly cloath-
with that fupremacy, to drive out
.nd he fhall yet punifh in another
:r) for that horrid fupremacy that
our beft times amongft profeffors,
ly minifters, and this day doth as
i them and the generation as ever.
O ftately goings! who notwith-
t he hides himfelf, yet abundant-
he is God and King of *Jacob*, tho'
an afs, and upon a colt the fole of an
; of *Zion*, and mafter of rejoicing to
,hters thereof. O noble ground of
hen he gives out the order, and
trument for that effect, when it nei-
will mifgive. And O! unfpeakable
ndernefs! in keeping up hitherto a
tneffing and contending as nobly and
s day as ever; having it to declare
orld, that they have hitherto lacked
d no wonder, I cannot but think, that
way the credit of our Lord, fo to
igaged for that land, and for you,
eminently ventured foul and body

Now,

Now, thus as to his preparing of me; next as to his leading of me.

When our worthy friend Mr. *Renwick* came laſt over, I was very inquiſitive (being for a long time greatly weighted with that buſineſs) to know of two things from him. 1ſt. How it was betwixt him and the Lord, as to his ſtate and intereſt. 2dly. As to his inward encouragement and call from the Lord as to his undertaking in that great work of the miniſtry. To both which I had very great ſatisfaction from him: as alſo, of his lively uptakings of the Lord's way with his church and people in this day, all which were engaging to me. After his parting with me, and going to *Groningen,* I was made to hear, as it were continually in my ears, *By whom ſhall Jacob ariſe, for he is very ſmall?* Wherewith I was for a time greatly weighted, till it pleaſed the Lord, after the ſame manner, to give me that other word, as I thought, an anſwer of the former; *Not by might, nor by power, but by my Spirit, ſaith the Lord.* And by this the Lord, as it were, anew again, let me ſee his glorious and ſtately dealings, after the ſame manner as formerly, *viz.* his going by that which the world calls *great parts,* learning, policy, and worldly wiſdom, and the idols of this generation; and not only ſo, but has had them, and to this day has them, all muſtered againſt him; and O the noble foils they have gotten already, and that by the world's fools, from babes and ſucklings trained up in Chriſt's ſchool. While I lay again wonderfully led in, and wondering in theſe things, I received a line from our friend Mr. *Renwick,* with a ſhort account of a notable piece of ſoul exerciſe he was in at that preſent, which

was

after this manner. " (To the praise of his
ree grace I muſt ſpeak it) when he helps me
ither to pray or meditate he is not want-
ng; but in other things I do not find him.
However, I think this may be the cauſe of it,
 cannot win to uſe and keep them in their
wn places: but there are ſome things good
 themſelves, and good when made right uſe
f; but to me they are as *Saul*'s armour to
David, I can put them on, but I cannot walk
ith them; and I cannot ſay but I could put
em on, unleſs I ſhould lie of the Lord, who,
bleſſed be his name) hath given me in ſome
eaſure, a diſpoſition * ."
fter the reading over of his letter, I found
 heart greatly tyed to him, and was brought
 a pleaſant frame and calmneſs of ſpirit. But
n, in two or three days, I was brought into
t perplexities for the caſe of the church in
ral, and more eſpecially for my mother-
ch; but I thought I found always my former
ion ſounding within me, and that with great
er, yet not ſo as perfectly to calm me; till
 days after Mr. *Renwick* wrote another letter
y ſiſter concerning his ſoul's caſe, which I
 as the Lord helped me, returned my
ghts of. And the evening after, going out
alk, I was ſtrongly overpowered with the
eſſion that Mr. *Renwick* was preſently to be
ined, and that I muſt lay out myſelf there-
and as I thought, won to great certainty,
whatever difficulties ſhould be in the way,
ſhould be removed; for he himſelf ſhould
ern himſelf in it. While thus, I went to our
worthy

* See Letter XI. page 31..

worthy friend Mr. *Brackle*, and laid out the whole cafe to him; who no fooner heard of it, but was as one out of himfelf, with the great fatisfaction and joy he had in it, which helped to my ftrengthening. Whereupon we refolved to write prefently to Mr. *Renwick* anent it, and that without the leaft thoughts or relation to the other two; and having but fmall time, we wrote but in fhort to him; which letter you may fee from himfelf, as it came to his hands: he fhewed it to the other two; who, on what grounds, I know not, refolved to concern themfelves alike in the affair as if the letter had been written to all of them. And after fome days, Mr. *Renwick* fent us a very fatisfying and refrefhing letter, for our encouragement to move further in it; as alfo, the other two pretending the fame clearnefs, wrote to me thereanent, which indeed was both furprizing and weighty to me, on many accounts; for the Lord, from my very firft hearing of them named, led me in a quite contrary way as to them than to the other; and I think I am not, and alas for it, difappointed of any of them, turn as they will.

Now, as to the difficulties I had to wreftle with, and our Lord's noble managing of his own caufe, and poor worms concerned in it, it was thus; *1ft.* Our friend Mr. *Brackel* had not only a great inclination, but told me, after the receiving of the letters, that he was fully determined, that they fhould all of them be ordained at *Embden*; which I durft not confent to; for the main man intended to have the management of it was *Cocccian* in his judgment, though he feemingly pretended otherwife, however I could not get him off that. A *fecond* reafon, as I told him, of my

being

being againſt it, was that ſince the Lord had
moved *Groningen* to own us, and to ſhew kindneſs to us in our low eſtate, we could not paſs
by them, without firſt giving them the offer.
However, nothing could prevail, and we were
like to loſe our friend in it; as alſo, others of
my friends at *Lewarden*, who would not condeſcend to let me go from them. Yet I durſt not
yield, neither durſt I ſtay, but as I had done
formerly, venture myſelf on my ſweet, rich, and
lovely, and O kind Lord's hand, who never fail-
ed me; yea, was ay better than his promiſe; when
they ſaw I was coming away, Mr. *Brackel* promiſed
to follow me within ſome days, and gave me a
letter to one of the miniſters, (which was all the
recommendation I had from men) deſiring me to
deliver it to one of the miniſters at *Groningen*,
providing he was any thing acquainted by friends
at *Groningen* of my deſign of coming there; and
finding them all ſtrangers to it, I reſolved as to
my recommendation, to caſt myſelf on the Lord,
and not to deliver my letter until Mr. *Brackel* came
himſelf, thinking it might be a mean to engage
him the more for us. When he came, I told him
my reſolutions as to *Embden* were the ſame as
formerly, and that I was rather confirmed than
altered, having got further notice from one of
the profeſſors in the place, that *Embden* was not
ſo pure in ſome things, eſpecially as to the magiſtrate's uſurpation, as *Groningen*; and withal
begging he might propoſe it to the miniſters in
Groningen, which he did; who told him, that it
might be done well, and with great ſecrecy by
the profeſſors of the college, which ſatisfied our
friend greatly; who alone laid down the whole
way of it with them, who, after his acquainting

me

me of it, departed out of the town, leaving me
to manage what he had proposed and concluded.
· But, before I go farther, I shall give a short
account of Mr. *Flint* and Mr. *Boyd*: So soon as I
came to the town, I examined all of them seve-
rally, but really I could find no satisfaction in a-
ny of them, save in our friend. Mr. *Flint*, I
found him floating and unstable: as for Mr. *Boyd*,
Mr *Flint* informed me and the rest very sadly of
him, both of his untenderness in his walk, and
unacquaintedness in our case; that he was not
only ignorant of much of it, but taken up, for
the most part, with the arguments of the adversaries, a defending against his brethren; though
indeed I did meet with no great disappointment,
yet on many accounts it was trying, and many
were our fears, as to acquainting him with our
resolutions, in not letting him pass at the time.
However, when we wan to be positive in it, and
stated upon such noble grounds, as not daring
to lay his house with such stones, &c. the Lord
removed that difficulty wonderfully, and made
Mr. *Boyd* not only seemingly willing to omit,
but also, confirmed others as to their duty in
what they had done. Now, I say, this being
done, and our worthy friend Mr. *Brackel* out of
town, I went to the chief professor, and confer-
ing of our business with him, I found it could not
be done without the concurrence of another bro-
ther-professor of his, who was professed *Coccei-*
an; and using freedom with him, to tell him
my scruples; he answered me, that the other
was but to examine, and not to lay on hands:
I asked, if it could be done without him; who
said, no: then I told him positively, that we
could not admit of it in such a way; his being

prefent, *viz.* a *Cocceian*, was effential to the
ordination. So parting with them, with this refolution, to write to Mr. *Brackel* what was next
to be done, and acquaint him with the cafe; fo.
writing to him; he could fee no hazard in that
way: However, if I could not grant it, there
was a neceffity yet to refolve upon *Embden*: and
there was a ftrange providence in his letter; for
in the end of it, to make me come over my former fcruple, he tells me, that he could affure
me, unlefs I had a full teftimony from the whole
profeffors of *Groningen* to the minifters of *Embden* for the ftudents, they could not be owned
there. This was a mean to clear me the more, that
Embden was not the place that the Lord feemed
to be then calling us unto, fince we could no
more accept of the *Cocceian*'s recommendation
than ordination, as it was then circumftantiate.
So that matters again feemed worfe than ever,
being likely to have both *Embden* and the whole
profeffors, and others our friends, againft us.
But our kind Lord was then at hand, who had
determined otherwife; that when I went again
to Mr. *Johannes a Mark*, the honeft profeffor,
and to one of the minifters, and told them our
cafe, and the weightinefs of it, and that there
was no other thing before our eyes in it, but the
glory of God, and durft do no other way than
what we had told. So begging they would lay
it to heart, and take it upon them to prevail
with the claffis, that they would take it in hand,
which, to the great admiration of fome of us, they
undertook moft willingly. However the profeffor called for their teftimonies, (for they were
to have his alfo to the claffis) and which was obfervable, all was miffing fave Mr. *Renwick's*,

E e

which

which was to the fore by a fpecial providence
having got it in my hand but fome few days be
fore. When the profeffor did fee it, he wa
willing to take it off our hand, but one of th
minifters being then prefent, told, it would ne
ver pafs before the claffis; fo I told them, tha
it could not be expected, confidering the toffe
cafe of our church, that it could be in fuch
drefs and order as otherwife were to be defired
and the profeffor owned me, and backed me in it
So that both faid, fince it was fo, they though
my teftimony, with Mr. *Brackel*'s, to the claffis
ay until another was procured, were fufficient
which I could not refufe, and it was of the Lor
in a fpecial way. However, there lay a trial t
me in it, which was very great, *viz.* to have
fpecial hand in Mr. *Flint*'s paffing, the teftimon
being laid fo to my door; and confidering ho
the Lord had led me, and I thought, by all dif
penfations, was even leading me by him; as al
fo, from what I was difcovering in him, it wa
to me a fore ftrait; for he, on the other hand
was preffing it violently. Whereupon, I wen
to him, and fpake in private to him, anen
the bufinefs, with great tendernefs, fignifying
the weightinefs thereof; as alfo, how the
Lord feemed every way to difcountenance hi
paffing; for, as to myfelf, I told him, I coul
give him no encouragement to it; but on the
contrary, from the firft time that I had feen him
and Mr. *Boyd*, I was made to tremble at thei
coming over upon fuch a defign. As alfo, tha
the letter that Mr. *Brackel* and I wrote to Mr
Renwick was no ways defigned for him: and alfo
of the miffing of his teftimonial. However,
told him, if he had the Lord's call to it, as be
wrote

rote to me, thefe all might be but as trials and
ours in his way. However I again begged him,
s he loved his own foul, that he would not ven-
are on fuch a weighty work rafhly. Notwith-
;anding of all, he faid he would go foreward;
io I, not without great heavinefs of mind, was
orced to countenance him; and fo going firft to
ne profeffor for his teftimony, I wrote next for
ur worthy Mr. *Brackel's*, which he prefently,
ad moft chearfully fent me; after thefe were
ad, and the day of the claffis come, being de-
vered to them, they were fuftained valid; and
fter Mr. *Flint* had a little harangue before
hem, they were fent out a little, and the claffis
aking our caufe into confideration, after, firft
ne of the minifters rifing up, and laying it
penly out, and then another, all of them, with
ears, cried out, It is the Lord's caufe, and coft
that it would, if all the kings of the earth were
gainft it, they would go on in it. And, which
; obfervable, one of them afking, How it came
re paffed by the profeffors, and took not ordi-
ation from them? another of themfelves rofe
p, and from that took occafion to lay out the
overnment and difcipline of our church; and
hat it was inconfiftent with our noble order to
ake fuch a courfe, and that we were much to
e encouraged for it. Another that was a de-
ute of the general fynod, defired to be excufed,
or he feared he could not attend, it being at
uch a diftance where he lived from the place;
he reft of his brethren, with tears in their eyes,
tood up, and requefted that no coft, pains nor
harges might be looked unto in fuch a noble
aufe; whereupon he confeffed that it was fo. It
eing alfo the cuftom of that place, that every

one

one that paſſed muſt pay twenty *guilders* for the
public uſe of the church; the brethren jointly
declared that they would be at all the charge
themſelves. O dear friends, praiſe him! praiſe
him! who has been ſo mindful of us in our low
eſtate. And after all this, calling them in a
gain, they received them in a moſt friendly way
as never hitherto had been; their injunction
our friend himſelf will ſhow you. But, which is
alſo remarkable, that Mr. *Flint* in his harangue
gave an open teſtimony againſt all the forms and
enormities in their church. O wonderful guiding
and leading of the Lord!

Now, after all theſe wondrous ways of the Lord
with us, it might have been expected that we ſhould
have been more knit to one another, more ſerious
tender, and zealous than ever. However, on the
contrary, Mr. *Flint* ſtrikes in with his old antago
niſt, he had informed ſo againſt, and ſtates himſelf
moſt bitterly againſt our friend Mr. *Renwick*, to the
great grief of friends, and ſtumbling of ſtrangers
who were witneſſes to it. When it came to my
ears, however heavy his carriage was to me, e
ſpecially conſidering the circumſtances, yet I
thought it was not without the ſingular provi
dence of God, who had permitted him to kythe
and diſcover himſelf before he came a greater
length: as alſo I thought I had now fair grounds
to ſtop his going on any further in that ſo great
a work; ſo I ſent for our worthy friend *G. H.*
(who has been greatly encouraging to me ſince
he came over, and a great help to me) and for
Mr. *Flint*, and in all tenderneſs to lay it to him
what an extraordinary work he was about, and
how extraordinary his call to the land was, and
the way of his now deſigning to return; and
that

that in all, I thought it required more than an ordinary cafe, frame and walk, of which I could fee no evidences in him. While I was to go on on my difcomfe, he interrupted me, falling out in great bitternefs, declaring he would no more meddle in it; and that he was pofitive, that upon no account he would go on in the work, nor go home with our friend Mr. *Renwick;* giving thefe for his three unreasonable reafons; 1. He faid, he was fure he would never agree with him. 2. Becaufe, he faid, He (*viz.* Mr. *Renwick*) did read too little. 3. Becaufe of his fpirit of fupremacy he fhewed in *Scotland.* I afked him, why he could not agree with him? He could give no reafon. As to the fecond, I afked him, if he did not read, I defired to know how he fpent his time? If in prayer, or meditating, or any other way? He anfwered, he durft not but think he was much in that exercife. To which I anfwered, thefe were the ftudies in this day moft accomplifhing for every work, and efpecially the work in hand. And for his laft, he could alfo give no ground for it. After I had got this from his own mouth, I thought we were fairly loofed from doing any more with him, and then we fent for Mr. *Renwick,* who came; and we gave him, before Mr. *Flint,* a relation of what had paffed; who would have paffed from fome things that he afferted, yet adhering to his non-paffing at that time, but to ftay a longer time, and another occafion: fo having prayed, I again begged him to lay things to heart; how the Lord was provoked; and preffed, that whether he ftaid or went, they might be as one heart. However, when he went home, he fignified to all, his refolutions to ftay, and bought books at a ftrange rate, and fet himfelf.

self to learn the *Dutch*, and went, without ad
vertifing any of us, to the *Dutch* kirk on the
Lord's day, and was prefent at all their form
without the leaft refentment; and had tokens
And as before he had joined hand in hand with
Mr. *Boyd* againft Mr. *Renwick*, now again his
paffion turned into its old channel againft Mr.
Boyd, which is wrath-like.

Now, dear Brethren, I ftand aftonifhed, and
wonder how we are now again put to it, for he
had received the profeffor's teftimony, with Mr.
Brackel's; as alfo his being before, and harangu-
ing before the claffis: fo that it threatened no
lefs than a fad blow to all the beginnings and after expectations in that place; as alfo to the
caufe and whole remnant at home; as alfo to
put a ftop to our friend's paffing. This coft fore
fighting and wreftling, though indeed Mr. *Flint*
and Mr. *Boyd* were no more concerned in it than
no fuch thing had been; but on the contrary,
evidenced tokens of their fatisfaction with all; as
alfo, in their expecting a ftop as to our friend's
paffing. At laft I wrote to Mr. *Brackel*, adver-
tifing him that we thought Mr. *Flint* could not
pafs: and with his anfwer I was yet more difcouraged than ever, preffing me by all arguments,
that he fhould pafs; and if he did not, how prejudicial it would be to the caufe, and fuch like.
Now, (which made our cafe heavier) we durft
not vent ourfelves fo freely to ftrangers as we
would, fearing the confequences that might follow. However, travelling in thir difficulties until time would fuffer of no more delay, the time
of ordination being at hand, we refolved to go
to the prefes of the claffis, and give him notice
that Mr. *Flint* could not pafs. When he firft
heard

heard of it he was greatly difcouraged, and had
this word which was obfervab'e; " Sir, he faid,
" if ye had told me of it but a day fooner, I
" could have ftopped it, and gotten a delay un-
" til Mr. *Flint* was ready, and fully recovered."
(for he himfelf pretended a diftemper of body)
I told him, I hoped, he would let it be no hinderance to our friend's paffing: He objected a-
gain, If that Mr. *Flint* was but able to fit on a
chair before the claffis, it would be fufficient,
and he might ftay after in the land until he were
recovered.   At laft, I did let fomewhat fall of
his other diftempers that we feared were raging.
in him; which, when he perceived, he feemed
prefently fatisfied, and undertook moft Chriftian-
lv the management of the bufinefs, and that Mr.
Renwick fhould be ordained.   O wonderful love
and condefcendency and noble Governor, who
can ply, and doth ply the hearts of all as he
will! Then I went to another of the minifters,
who had all along been a great agent in the bufinefs, and told him Mr. *Flint* was refolved not
to pafs. He enquired a reafon; I told him, he
pretended his ficknefs; he told me, that could
be none, for he and all the minifters and profeffors of the town faw him daily on the ftreets,
and but one day before in the public college.
(Now the ordination was to be the next day)
Seeing it was fo, I told him the whole account
of him, which when he heard, he was fo far
from being offended, that he adhered to all, and
approved of our tendernefs; yet he faid, it
would greatly reflect upon us, our caufe, and the
whole remnant at home; and preffed, that if it
were poffible, he might offer himfelf to the ordination, and then we needed not let him go home

until we found him accomplished. This again began to work new ftirs upon us; yet after fome time laying it before the Lord, he was pleafed to let us fee that it was but a temptation, and that upon no account were we to offer him a facrifice of that we could not take to ourfelves. After this, all our fears and fcruples were removed, and we fully determined to lay it all on the Lord, and the management of events and confequents on himfelf. So immediately going to Mr. *Flint*, I defired to know his mind; which, he. faid, was the fame, not to pafs, or go home. After fome fpeaking to him, I defired he might go to the prefes himfelf, and make his own excufe, but not to pretend that which was not, *viz.* his ficknefs; which he did, and the prefes accepted of it well. O my friends, who is to mean, that has fuch a God for their God! fo condefcending, fo loving, fo mighty, and fo powerful, that he can do in heaven and. earth what he will. There is yet one remarkable trial, and honourable outgate that we had, *viz.* before the ordination; the minifter had told me that it was impoffible, and could not pafs, without fubfcribing three things; the one was, their catechifms; the other two our friend will give you an account of: I defired to fee their confeffion, and we find that there is in it mention of the forms, and enormities of their church, which we plainly told them we difowned, and were engaged in our folemn vows to the contrary. This was again like to ftop all. However, I went to others of them, and gave them an account of our Confeffion and Catechifms, and that we could fubfcribe none but thefe, which, at laft, they condefcended unto; a practice never

ver.

ter before heard of in thefe lands. O praife and wonder! and wonder and praife! for his yet minding of us in our low eftate, and concerning himfelf in us before ftrangers. I alfo defired of them to have liberty, with our friend *G. H.* and my brother Mr. *Gordon*, to have accefs, to be witneffes to the on-laying of the hands of the claffis, or prefbytery, which likewife they granted, though not ufed in that place.

Now the day of ordination being come, Mr. *Renwick*, with my brother Mr. *Gordon*, and *G. H.* came into my chamber, but none of the reft; after prayer we went out to the church, where the claffis was to hold; and walking together in an outer room there, as we had been defired, until our friend was called in, which they did in a moft honourable way, not only by the ordinary fervant, but by one of the brethren minifters. After he was in, we returned, and fpending fome time together in prayer, we again returned, and about two in the afternoon, (the examination lafting from ten to two) one of the oldeft of the minifters was fent out (as they had promifed) to call us in, to be witneffes to the onlaying of the hands: when we came in, the whole of the minifters faluted us moft kindly, affectionately and friendly; after fome exhortations, they propofed to him the fubfcription, which they jointly declared to be nothing elfe than the fubfcribing of our own confeffion. After their reading it over again and again, Mr. *James* ftarted a fcruple in it, which, through the Lord's bleffing, was both feafonable, and made acceptable to all, and then he fubfcribed it. Then with prayer they went about the laying on of the hands, in a moft folemn, and a moft tender way;

and

and the whole time our friend was upon his
knees, the moſt of the whole meeting were
joining with the tears in their eyes. After, he
was deſired by the preſes to take the brethren by
the hand, which they all gave him in a moſt affectionate way; and after he had done, he (our
friend I mean) had a moſt ſerious, grave and
taking diſcourſe to the whole claſſis, and ſo was
diſmiſſed. When going out of the room, the
preſes called me, and deſired that Mr. *Renwick*
and I might dine with the claſſis; which we promiſed; and coming in amongſt them, they were
as brethren at a ſtrait, every one of them how
to expreſs their kindneſs to us. The preſes deſired me to ſit on his right hand at the head of
the table; and after a little ſitting, he declared
to me the great ſatisfaction the whole brethren
had had in Mr. *Renwick*, that they thought, the
whole time he was before them he was ſo filled
with the Spirit, that his face did ſhine; and that
he had never ſeen ſuch evident tokens of the
Lord's being with them, as in this affair all a-
longſt, and ſo bleſſed and praiſed the Lord for
what he had ſeen. Then he deſired a relation
might be given to the brethren of our cauſe;
which I did, both of our ſufferings and wreſtlings;
who were all ſo affected, that ye would have thought,
they were both weeping and rejoicing; grieving
for our caſe, as they ſaid; and rejoicing that the
Lord had honoured us in ſuch a noble piece of
ſervice; promiſing to mind us both in public and
private; and alſo offered themſelves anew again
for the ſame ſervice, whatever might be the hazard. Then the preſes told them, that the magiſtrate was uſurping as much upon them, and
there was as great yielding amongſt them as in

our

our hand; and if they followed not our practice,
the church would be ruined, and they and their
posterity rooted out. There was also another
minister who declared, he had been twenty
years a minister in that place, but had never seen
nor found so much of the Lord's Spirit, accom-
panying a work, as that; and declared, he would
die and live with us. O tune up your harps, and
sing praises unto him, whose mercy endureth for
ever, and has had yet compassion on us in our
low estate

Now, my honourable Brethren, here ye have
a short account, yet not the hundred-fold of
what the Lord hath done for us in this affair;
the bearer, with our dear and honoured friend
in the Lord, will give you a fuller account of
matters than I was able in the time to do, (viz.
G. H. But now, when we thought the battle was
fought, and the storm over, it begun afresh again
upon us from another airth, representing itself
as terrible as any of the former; though, blessed
be his name, through his rich blessing, we were
never once suffered to be cast down at the
thoughts of it! and O again admire and wonder!
The morning after the ordination, as I was lying
in my bed, I received a letter from Mr. *Brackel*,
wherein he gives me an account of a letter from
Holland to stop the ordination, for he was to receive a lybel against us all, subscribed by the
church of *Rotterdam*, Mr. *Br.* Mr. *Hog* younger,
and Mr. *Thomas Langlands*, accusing us of many
terrible things, and sent me three or four of the
prime of them, which I have sent with our friend;
and withal desiring me, so soon as it came to
my hands, to show his letters to me to the
classis, and either to vindicate ourselves before
them

them, or otherways to ſtop Mr. *Renwick* and
Mr. *Flint*'s ordination; (for then he had not
known Mr. *Flint*'s determination and ours) and
upon that pretence of Mr. *Flint*'s ſickneſs, the
letter was ſent by an expreſs to me for its
greater haſte, and might have come three days
ſooner to my hand than it did, but the Lord in
a wonderful way ſtopped it, but what way we
could never yet learn. O wonderful Counſellor!
for if it had come but a day ſooner, by all probability it had ſtopped our friend's paſſing, for
there had been a neceſſity for my ſhewing it to
the claſſis; and they could have done no other
at leaſt, than to have taken it to conſideration,
and to have delayed the diet for that time: but
O his wiſdom! infinite wiſdom and power! After
I got it, I went to the profeſſors, and miniſters,
and others of the godly, and gave them a full
account of all, and of all my letters, who were
nothing troubled, but juſtified us in all our dealings againſt theſe miniſters, and promiſed to own
us in all, and give us an account of any informations that ſhould come againſt us; for Mr.
Brackel's letters told us, they were preſently to
write to *Groningen* againſt us, and cauſe print
their accuſations againſt us. So the Lord was
ſtill gracious unto us, in keeping us in continual
exerciſe, that our dependance might be the more
on himſelf: for when he had wrought for us and
broken the ſnare, we were made to fear Mr.
Brackel and friends in *Frieſland;* for in his letters, they had promiſed to have their libel ready
againſt us at *Amſterdam*, againſt ſuch a day as
they named; and Mr. *Brackel*, without acquainting any but one or two, caſts himſelf to be at
Amſterdam the ſame day, but when he came, the
libel

libel was not ready, but they would have been
at telling it by word of mouth to him, but he
refufed to hear them unlefs in write; and indeed
he was wonderfully help'ed to own the Lord's
caufe, and poor *Scotland*'s caufe. When he left
them, they promifed to have the information
and libel againft us at him within four or five
days: But now the time is long over, and there
is no word of it! And fo he returned to us all,
to the wonder of all, and the joy of many, more
our friend, and *Scotland*'s friend than ever.
And he told me a ftrange paffage, That the day
before he went to their meeting, he was walking
in his own yard, and there he faw a little fmall
bird hotly purfued by a great hawk, and, after
many toffings and turnings, the bird, at laft, flies
to him for fhelter, and he relieved it, which
was born in upon him at the time, as a lively
emblem of ours and the church's cafe. O
praife to him! when we had win to good hopes
of that ftorm's being broken, we muft yet a-
gain enter into another, threatening as terrible
as the other. That fame day, in the evening,
that I received Mr. *Brackel*'s letter with the a-
poftate minifters libel, arrives *James Ruffel,
Patrick Grant,* and *David Robertfon,* with full
affurance to ftop the ordination; but, through
the Lord's goodnefs, they came alfo a day too
late, and were difappointed, I think, every way;
as to that affair I refer you wholly to the bearer.
They are ftill ftaying here, I fear their defign
be not good; and I think, in that place they
fhall have none of our two, Mr. *Flint* and Mr.
Boyd, much againft them. O Lord, give wifdom, and come yet and be feen. O honourable

F f

friends, hath he not been glorioufly feen in the
bufinefs!——

Now, what can I fay unto you, our engage
ments are great, let our thankfulnefs be anfwer
able; get you the gofpel, O the precious gofpe
again amongft you; hold it up by prayer among
you; be more in tendernefs, humility, watch
fulnefs, crying, and wreftling than ever; for h
is a holy and jealous God. O be much for him
downright and upright for him, coft what it will
he is more than able to bear your charges, o
whofe fhoulders the government is laid. And
my poor advice would be, That with all hafte
you would write to *London*, difcharging Mr. *Nif
bet* to come here, for his bafe fitting of time
and fuch fpecial calls. As alfo to fend for the
two that are here; for now we are keeping fire
in our own bofoms, and, if the Lord prevent it
not, putting weapons in mad-mens hands. As
alfo, to feek the Lord's mind in ordaining o
moe minifters, and that among yourfelves. My
own judgment has been, that providing you can
find fuch qualified with holinefs, tendernefs, ex
amples, as *Paul* fays of the believers, in word,
in converfation, in fpirit, in faith and purity;
and fuch as *Acts* i. 21. which accompanied you in
your tribulations, and have been witneffes to your
contendings and wreftlings, and given proof of
their conftancy and faithfulnefs. And indeed
that is the way, I think, that would bring in
moft glory to our Lord, and which would be
much like our cafe, and my foul would moft ply
with every way; for I am far from the mind that
the Lord will make much ufe of learning for the
building of his houfe again. It is, and has been
fo much boafted of amongft us, fo trufted to,
and

and improven againſt our Lord, that, I think,
for a time, he will put a mark of ignominy upon
it, and train up at his own ſchool. O my bre-
hren, it is *Scotland* that muſt make fit for mini-
ters, elſe here it will never be.———— I think,
ye ſhould ſend over three of the moſt eminent
among you, with the firſt occaſion, in room of
theſe ye are to call home, that our cauſe may
be keeped up in that college, and ſome to witneſs againſt *James Ruſſel*, and the others, who
have ſeated there, or any that may oppoſe us.
As alſo, letters of thanks ſhould be written to
that college, and to the claſſis; as alſo, an approbation of what they have done. As alſo, a
joint declaration againſt the church of *Rotterdam*,
firſt, for their ſetting down to the Lord's table a
promiſcuous multitude, men of blood, that have
been at *Pentland* and *Bothwel* againſt the Lord;
men banded, ceſſed, and what not: as alſo, de-
baring from it ſuch as were faithful, as worthy
Rathillet, &c. *Item*, for receiving in amongſt
them Mr. *Fleming*, who is rather *Charles Stuart*'s
miniſter than Chriſt's. As alſo, their cruel dealing and handling of their countrymen that came
there, who are faithful in their day, threatening
to ſtarve them out of their conſciences, notwithſtanding of the large ſupply, they have from the
magiſtrates of that place, for the effect of the
poor. *Item*, Their taking into their ſeſſions, as
members thereof, men void of both principles
and tenderneſs, and their not exerciſing the diſcipline of our church, nor preaching faithfully
againſt the ſins of our time. As alſo, their li-
cenſing all to preach amongſt them, however
notour for their open defection, and avowed rebellion againſt Chriſt; ſuch as have devoured the

flock at home, and feek to purfue thofe in a ftrange land who have efcaped out of their claws. As alfo, their open and practically dif covering themfelves this day againft our mother church, &c.

My advice would be alfo, that your teftimo ny would relate of a declaration, that you would fet out alfo, laying out the rebellion of minifters all alongft it, and how they have now forfaken Chrift and the poor remnant; fo that if ye had the occafion, ye durft not further own them; and lay it out to the churches, that pro viding any of them come by them, that they or none others be owned without they have a tefti mony and approbation from the fuffering church of *Scotland*. As alfo, letters of thanks would be fent to Mr. *Brackel*, for his kindnefs and faith fulnefs in the caufe of God, and to the fufferers here.

I can fay no more, my dear and honourable Brethren, but what I omit, I hope the bearers will fupply it.——Let me hear more frequent ly from you all, for your letters are very re frefhing to me; though many times I be, but little in care to write unto you, yet I defire that you may find my practical kindnefs, and not miftake my filence.

Now, *The bleffing of him that dwelt in the bufh be with you all.*

Your fympathizing brother,

and real fervant,

ROBERT HAMILTON.

wing Letters by Mr. *Mi-*
nields were moſtly wrote
direction of the General.
g.

Michael Shields, *to ſome Friends.*

ids,   *July* 5. 1683.

ie occaſion of the bearer, I thought
 not omit, but write a line to you;
s it is, counting myſelf obliged to
ore many ways. It is our duty to
ng with, bearing burden, and mind-
er ; but as I am ſhort in all duties,
. Diſtance of place, or ſeparation
ꝛm another, or being in diverſe na-
not be a cauſe of our forgetting
eſpecially in this day when ſo ma-
ꝛtten God their Maker, their vows
his people, with whom they were
d. O let us not do ſo, but be minding with and for one another, and
d ſtirring up one another to love,
works. And now when I have put
, what can I ſay? I am unfit for
itle I can ſay either for counſel or
it : but this I ſay, Look unto and
him who is all ſufficient for both;
ings ye want or can want. He is
n and well ſpring of grace, glory,

F f 3   and

and happiness. Delight yourselves in him, and
ye shall have the desire of your souls.

Dear Friends, since it hath pleased the Lord
to determine your hearts to fall in love with
him, and in token thereof to meet together in
Christian fellowship for prayer, and other duties
incumbent for you in your station : and not only
so, but to join with, and cast in your lot among
the poor suffering, tossed, reproached, condemned, and dispersed remnant of the church of
Scotland, who is this day like a lily among
thorns, and a silly chased bird among vultures
and ravens. As you have begun, so hold on :
endurers to the end only get the crown. O
labour (if such an one as I may desire) to keep up
your meetings ; forget not the assembling of
yourselves together ; let not that stately tower
that we have yet left in our *Zion* (of the many
strong bulwarks, comely ramparts, and high
hedges that once we had in and about her) fall
down ; left it prove crushing and piercing. Seek
him where he hath promised to be found ; rest
not till ye find him ; refuse to be comforted till
he return and be gracious, and be pacified towards the remnant of his heritage. *Let your light
so shine* (ye dwell in a dark place) *before men,
that they seeing your good works may glorify God ;*
and that they may have no ground to blame your
good conversation in Christ. Labour to be living witnesses for Christ and his precious truths,
and against the enemies and their abominations in the place you live in : and your sympathy with your afflicted brethren in *Scotland*,
let it continue. It is a duty much commanded and commended by God in his word ; and
fellow-feeling with the suffering members of
Christ,

Chrift, is a mark that we are members of that
fame body whereof he is the head. Let us not
be lying at eafe in a day of *Jacob's* trouble,
eating, drinking, and making merry, left we
be guilty of the woe pronounced againft fuch,
and be led forth with the workers of iniquity,
when peace fhall be upon his *Ifrael*. When
trouble from the world abounds, let our love to
him, and zeal for him, increafe; and the more
our Lord Jefus is perfecuted by the wicked of
this generation, and his image in his members
hated, let us love him the more, and be known
to the world that we do fo, although perfecution
never fo great follow; and labour to get his
image more renewed in your fouls. This is a
day wherein we have a fair opportunity to give
a proof of our love and loyalty to King Chrift,
who is wronged, wounded, flighted, defpifed
and contemned, and fpitted upon by the wicked
of this generation; yea, and many of the
wounds and wrongs he gets is in the houfe of
his friends. O let us lay hold upon fuch oppor-
tunities; for many have longed for the like,
and have not obtained. It fets us well, and is
well our common, to fear, love and obey him,
who loved us when we could not love ourfelves,
nor no eye pity us. O wonderful condefcendency O let us labour to get our eyes and
ears to affect our hearts, that we may be fuitably
affected, and deeply wounded and concerned
with the many wounds precious Chrift hath gotten, his glory, truths, caufe, covenant and people
have gotten and are getting this day. Let us re-
fent and teftify againft thefe wrongs, left we be
found guilty. We ought to contend and fuffer
for hairs, hoofs, and pins of precious truth.

O

O noble privilege, and high dignity to be honoured to suffer for the least of them, if any of them may be so called.

Dear Friends, let us rejoice in tribulation and persecution for his sake ; let us rejoice in being robbed, spoiled, and nothing left us; let us rejoice in being put to wander, though it were in mountains, dens, and caves of the earth ; (we have a cloud of witnesses that have gone before us) let us rejoice in cruel mockings, reproaches from enemies and pretended friends ; yea, in being put to cruel tortures and deaths ; none of all these things shall harm us, if we be followers of that which is good; yea, in all these things we shall be more than conquerors, *through him that loved us, and washed us in his blood.* Here is enough though we be under persecution all our days, it sets us to be silent, and not to quarrel with his doings, for he is the governor of heaven and earth, he can do us no wrong. O for submissive spirits, Let us *bear his indignation patiently, because we have sinned against him*: and to be learning the language of the rod, and him who hath appointed it. The dispensations that fall out in our day are very strange, deep, and mysterious: he is bringing to pass *his act, his strange act.* He is by them making himself to be known to be God, whose ways are equal, although many a time to us they seem crooked, when we measure them by the crooked rule of our own making. He is taking many ways to make himself great and high in his peoples eyes and estimation, by taking instruments (and these great ones) and means out of the way. I think this is one language that their dispen-

faitions

fations have, *Be ftill, and know that I am God,* &c.
It fets us better to be fitting filent, and wondering and adoring at infinite fovereignty in. his
way of working, than to quarrel and cry out,
Why is it thus? And another language is, *Look.
unto me all ye ends of the earth, and be ye faved*;
let us look to him only for falvation, both from
inward and outward enemies, and no longer to
hills and mountains. Let us *ftand ftill and fee
the falvation of the Lord,* who hath a holy hand
in fuffering us to be brought into fo great diffi-.
'culties, as it were the Red-fea before us, rocks
on every hand, and the *Egyptians* behind, that
he alone may be feen exalted and glorified in
delivering us out of them. A look from himfelf can divide the Red-fea, and make his people
to walk on dry land, and make the chariot-
wheels of our enemies to drive heavily.

Dear Friends, there is one thing I am fomewhat preffed in confcience to tell you of, and
that is, fince you have joined with the fuffering
remnant in *Scotland,* and adhered to the controverted truths our dying martyrs have laid down
their lives for, and our living witneffes are contending for, and in particular, that in protefting
againft the unfaithfulnefs and finful filence in
minifters, by their withdrawing from them, it
were your wifdom to be even-down in this, and
to take good heed whom ye hear, leaft, if rafh
in this, ye be found to contradict what they
have done; efpecially now when we have given
them a call, which if they embrace, it is well, if
not we, muft ftand ftill and not go to them, leaft
we lofe our ground, but they muft return to
us. Do not miftake me, as if I were defiring
to caft at the gofpel, or minifters: No; Lord
for-

forbid; the Lord is my witnefs, that is not my defire: it is only to have you to ceafe to hear the inftruction that caufeth to err from the words of knowledge, and to wait till we get the gofpel, which we have finned away, back again, faithfully preached by faithful minifters, that I defign. It is my foul's defire, if my heart deceive me not, to long to hear the gofpel, and to fee faithful minifters; (O what is more defireable than to hear Chrift fpeaking to us in the calm voice of the gofpel again, who hath been long fpeaking to us in the loud voice of his judgments and threatenings) and to long to fee that day when the reproach of being againft miniftry and magiftracy fhall be rolled away from his people; and when both fhall be duely and rightly adminiftred according to his word. Dear Friends, let us mourn and weep for our former flighting of the fweet gofpel, and wreftle with him night and day, that he would return and vifit us with the offers of his gofpel, and let yet *the voice of the turtle be heard in our land, the time of the finging of the birds,* and the fpring time come. O let us long and thirft for fuch fweet and defirable days.

I draw to a clofe with this: Thefe three of you whom the Lord hath honoured with a prifon, and to bear his crofs, have the foreftart of the reft. I wifh heartily grace, mercy, and peace, be their allowance, and the confolations of his Spirit make their prifons fweet to them; and that he may keep them in the hour of temptation, and help them to endure to the end: and it is the duty of all the reft of you to be preparing for fuffering.

. I earneſtly deſire ye would do me the favour
as to write to me.   I remain,

Your ſervant at command in the Lord,

MICHAEL SHIELDS.

L E T T E R LXXIX.

From Mr. Michael Shields, to ————.

Rev. and worthy Sir,   Auguſt 1. 1683.

WE deſire to bleſs the Lord on your behalf,
that he hath made choice of you to be
an inſtrument to appear for your Maſter's wronged cauſe in this perſecuted church, which, thro'
the good hand of God, hath proven an effectual mean for the raiſing up of Chriſt's fallen
banner in this backſlidden land, wherein there is
none to appear valiantly for him, according to
the command of God, and our ſolemn vows and
engagements; but, upon the other hand, are
homologating with the enemy, and have turned
violent reproachers and perſecutors of the poor
afflicted, perſecuted, ſuffering remnant, and that
both of the living and the dead, to the ſtumbling,
weakening, and turning back of many who were
beginning to look after the Lord, and had put
their hand to the plough, in witneſſing and teſ-
tifying againſt the abominations of our day and
time, which clearly doth appear from theſe their
moſt odious and ridiculous calumnies, which the
letter ſent to us by our faithful delegate, is a
new certification of.

                                          Sir,

Sir, we shall, as in the sight of an holy God declare the truth in every point of these accusations ye received from these ministers of *Rotterdam* against us.

1. As for our casting off and rejecting of *Charles Stewart*, and all them they call magistrates ruling under him, we own it; and desire to mourn for our being so long in doing of it: the reasons of our doing thereof, we hope, ye are sufficiently informed by our worthy and faithful delegate sent to you. But as to setting up of magistrates among ourselves, there is no truth in it. And as to that of our killing all that will not adhere to us, and are not of our opinion, we declare to be false and calumnious, and a thing detested by us.

2. As to the second accusation, that we are not pure in religion: Alas! we are not as we ought to be in that. But as to the putting any questions to these whom we admit to fellowships, we declare we put none but such as we have from divine precept, and former engagements to God, and to one another.

3. As for the third accusation, we think not strange that they calumniate us as a faction, and not as a church; for these ministers and people whom they hold to be the church, did reproach our most noble suffering ministers and martyrs as erroneous, and of a Jesuitical principle; as witness, Mr. *Kid*, Mr. *King*, Mr. *Cameron*, and Mr. *Cargil*, who, in our declining age, were the only witnesses, as ministers, for the true church of our Lord Jesus Christ, and against the incroachments made thereupon

As to the second part of the third accusation, that the silent ministers say, that they are the

most

most pure church, and that they have paftors and prefbyteries: It is true they fit in prefby-tery and condemn the innocent, by juftifying the lawfulnefs of taking the Bond and the late Indulgence, upon which head, amongft many others, our worthies have fuffered, teftifying a-gainft it; and feveral of them hear the tefted cu-rates tlremfelves, and advife others to do fo; and the generality of them refufe either to preach or adminifter the facraments: as witnefs, when any comes to them, with a teftificate, for the benefit of baptifm, they refufe, and defire and advife them to go to the tefted curates. And this is a part of the parity of their church.

4. As to the fourth accufation, that the ftu-dents are not of unblameable life. In anfwer to that, thefe three who are fent to you, to be edu-cated in order to the miniftry, as to their life and converfation while they were with us they walked blamelefly, fo far as could be difcerned by us.

Worthy Sir, to conclude, not defiring to be tedious, we, the poor fuffering remnant in the church of *Scotland*, give you hearty thanks for your faithful pains and diligence anent the or-dination of Mr. *James Renwick;* and are glad and rejoice to hear of your, and your worthy bro-ther's fatisfaction with him; and take it for a token for good, that the Lord will vifit and gather to-gether again his poor fcattered fheep in our land. And alfo, that our and your God fhall recom-pence your labour of love and pains, and dili-gence, fevenfold in your bofom.

Sic fubfcribitur,

MICHAEL SHIELDS.

G g

LETTER LXXX.

From the Anti-popish, Anti-prelatic, Anti-eraſtian true Preſbyterian church of Scotland, *To theſe that deſire to join with the cauſe of God, at* Dublin *in* Ireland.

October 3. 1683.

Dear Friends and covenanted Brethren,

THE Lord brought us to a high pitch of a glorious and bleſſed reformation, in the ſeveral ſteps thereof, from Popery, Prelacy, and Eraſtian ſupremacy; and took us into covenant with himſelf, to ſerve him after the due order, and to maintain his intereſt with our lives and li-berties, as we ſhould anſwer to him at the great day. Whereby our land was made the glory of the nations, and our church terrible to her ene-mies, *as an army with banners, holineſs to the Lord* being the badge; ſo that we may ſay, our *vine which the Lord brought out of Egypt, did fill the land, and the hills were covered with the ſha-dow of it, and the boughs thereof were like the goodly cedars.* But alas! there are crept in a-mongſt us little foxes to ſpoil the tender grapes.; malignant men diſaffected to the cauſe and peo-ple of God, who got footing in judicatories and armies, who ought to have been purged out, that their places might be filled up with men of known integrity, according to the word of God, *Exod.* xviii. 21. 2 *Sam.* xxiii. 3. Yet that duty was not only hindered and condemned by a prevailing company of carnal hearts; but alſo, public reſolutions were fallen upon to bring in
known

...own malignants, enemies to God and godliness, into places of power and trust: and commissioners authorized to close a treaty with this
man *Charles Stuart*, king of malignants, and to
give him the crown, upon his subscribing such
demands as were sent to him, after so many discoveries of his malice against God, and of his
still persisting in the same, and notwithstanding
they knew him not to be hearty, but juggling in
what he condescended to; who no sooner got
footing, but used all means to ruin the work of
God. And in their first parliament took, as it
were, the royal diadem off King Christ's head,
(O horrid blasphemy!) and set it upon their
king, whereby they made him an idol in his person; who, by virtue of that sacrilegious robbing
of the Son of God, commanded our ministers to
leave their flocks, over which the principal and
good Shepherd had set them, which they almost
all did, as if they had been hirelings, and suffered the wolf to catch and scatter the sheep; so
that we may say, Our pleasant things were not
taken from us, but we gave them away with our
own hands. We betrayed the interest of Christ,
and gave enemies all their asking, and made the
Lord's pleasant portion a desolate wilderness. Yet
the Lord, because he had compassion on his people,
and on his dwelling place, stirred up some to go
to the high places of the fields, and jeopard their
lives unto the death, in proclaiming the truths
of God; whereby there were great inroads made
upon Satan's territories, who finding himself at a
loss and disadvantage, spewed out sinful snares
amongst us, to ruin the work of God, and to
break us, *viz.* indulgences and indemnities,
whereby Christ's crown was established upon a

man's

man's head, which some men, loving worldly
ease more than truth, embracing, they betrayed
the cause of God, and yielded the day to the
dragon and his angels; others who had not the
offer, yet gaping after it, struck in with them,
to strengthen the devil's side; and many who
professed to be against such courses themselves,
yet tendered more the credit of discreditable
men than the honour of God; and instead of using means for their reclaiming, strengthned their
hands in their perverse ways, and sided with them
against those whom the Lord raised up to be
faithful and free, and (weakly, though not. de-
signedly I hope, for we desire to be charitable
to them) wrought together to gain the end of
the common adversary; who, as they gained
ground, increased the persecution; which now
hath discovered the thoughts and hidden hypocrisy of many hearts. Yet in all this, (blessed be
the holy and wise Lord) he had still a remnant
who keeped their ground, and through his assistance, wrestled for him, by faithful preaching of
his will, appearances, testimonies, declarations,
and sufferings; so that there is not one step of
all our public defection, but that he hath honoured and helped a party to witness against, and to
seal their testimonies with their blood, both ministers and people of divers qualities.

And now, we desire nothing but, the Lord
assisting, to follow the good old way, and to
stand upon the ground whereunto the Lord, by
our worthy reformers, brought us, and for which
we have been wrestling and contending: we say,
we are seeking nothing but to take the Lord's
part against his enemies, to stand under *Michael's*
banner to fight against the dragon, and to have

our

our banished King Christ brought back again; and in order to this, studying to shake our hands clean of the causes of his displeasure at us, which keeps him so long away, and to set about the duties of Christianity with mourning, humiliation, fasting, and prayer.

Therefore, being all engaged in one common cause, and bound in covenant together, and having some knowledge of your case, and also of your desire to know and follow duty; we thought it expedient to write unto you, ye having been, to the grief of our souls, led aside by the cruel and subtile dealing of adversaries, and the treachery and unfaithfulness of these who gave themselves out for your leaders; desiring, as brethren, that ye would lay to heart the sad case our church is reducted unto by reason of our sin against the Lord: and consider what is called for at your hands, if either you desire to see his return again to *Britain* and *Ireland*, or to transmit his truths to the succeeding generation, as to the shaking yourselves clean of the abominations of the times, and also withdrawing yourselves from these backslidden ministers altogether unfaithful to our wronged Lord and Master: for as to your meeting-houses, not knowing what underhand dealing hath been with the wicked powers of the time, neither thinking the case to be formally the same with our hell-hatched indulgences in *Scotland*; yet the effects are much one. For,

1. The embracing of these meeting houses was a dividing of themselves from their more righteous brethren and their sufferings, exposing them to be the only butt of the adversaries malice, and to shift for themselves contrary to our

en-

engagements, whereby we were to take one common lot with the common cause.

2. It was an embracing of a snare, whereby they were drawn into, not only, a supine and loathsome formality and neutrality in the Lord's cause, but into unfaithfulness in the highest degree, paliating the sins, and covering the abominations of the tyrannical powers, least they, having the arm of flesh upon their side, should cast down their meeting-houses, and cast out themselves; and in no measure discovering the duty of the day to people, so that they are ignorant of what these cruel adversaries have done against our blessed Lord, and of their own sin in strengthening their hands in their working wickedness, and upholding that fabric of rebellion against the heavens. Oh! what shall we say, sin and duty hath been both hid, and the souls of the people not cared for, neither the standing of the interest of Jesus Christ which they have palpably betrayed; and have most actively given their consent to the enemies taking and keeping the houses of God in possession. And,

3. They have quit their meeting houses at the command and threatning of men; for albeit their entry was hurtsome to the cause, and the exercise of their ministry nothing but a selling of truth, and a buying of sinful liberty to themselves; yet that does not warrant another step of declining duty, in explicitly and more fully delivering up the privileges of Jesus Christ; yea, one pendule of his crown should not be yielded, though it should cost us all our lives: and we may cry out, *Let it not be heard in Gath, nor published in the streets of Askelon,* that the Covenanters in *Britain* and *Ireland*

should be standing with their heads upon their necks in that day when King Christ's crown was taken from him.

O beloved Friends and covenanted Brethren, go on in your duty, and follow no men, but them who will follow the Lord Jesus Christ; consider, truth as naked, abstracting from all persons, and resolve firmly in Jehovah's strength to stand to it alone, albeit none should stand with you; and never take carnal reasons and arguments to plead yourselves out of your duty, but consider ay the case, whether it be duty or not, in all its circumstances; and if found to be so, then up and do it upon the greatest of hazards; and think not to walk so as the abused laws of man shall not reach you, for if they do not, the law of God will; for they are now confronted one against another, and the cry is gone forth from the Lord to all that will side themselves with him, to take his part against a cruel and a treacherous generation. *Say not a confederacy unto them, neither fear ye their fear, nor be afraid. But sanctify the Lord of hosts himself, and let him be your fear, and let him be your dread; and he shall be for a sanctuary unto you,* Isa. viii. 12, 13, 14. *Wherefore come out from them, and be ye separate, saith the Lord, and touch not the unclean thing; and I will receive you, and be a father unto you, and ye shall be my sons and daughters, saith the Lord Almighty,* 2 Cor. vi. 17, 18. O come out from among them, *that ye be not partakers of their sins, and that ye receive not of their plagues: for their sins hath reached unto heaven, and God hath remembered their iniquities,* Rev. xviii. 4, 5. O make haste, and get in under the shadow of the Lord's wings, and give up with every false and wicked

wicked way, that now ye may be hid from the fire-ry indignation; for he *is coming to shake terribly the earth, and to punish the inhabitants thereof for their iniquities.* There is *a sword bathed in heaven to come down upon Idumea, and upon the people of his curse;* and spare whom he will, he will not spare ministers, yea Presbyterian ministers, for they have betrayed the interest of Jesus Christ; yea, not only consented unto, but concurred with enemies spoiling him of his princely robes, and of the power he hath in his own house: They have made sad the hearts of the righteous, whom the Lord hath not made sad, and strengthened the hands of the wicked, that he should not return from his wicked way, by promising him life, and have seduced the people, by seeing visions of peace for them in their sinful backsliding courses, when there was no peace from the Lord.

O dearly Beloved in our blessed Lord, follow none further than they follow Christ; and cease to hear the instruction which causeth to err from the words of knowledge; and *mark and avoid them who cause divisions and offences contrary to the doctrine which ye have learned, for they that are such, serve not our Lord Jesus Christ, but their own bellies, and by good words and fair speeches, deceive the hearts of the simple.*

We shall trouble you no further at the time, but heartily and fully approving of the carriage of your hearty friend and wellwisher in the Lord, Mr. *James Renwick,* among you, (who is for us a faithful minister of Jesus Christ) in not joining with these men-ministers with you, and in declining them as to the seeking and accepting their call to preach, or giving them satisfaction

as

as to his ordination; yet, as often he said unto yourselves, we hold ourselves obliged in duty to satisfy you who have been his hearers; therefore we have sent unto you a true transcript of the testificate of his ordination in *Latin*, and the *English* version thereof, with some other papers for your clearing and information in the Lord's cause; thanking you heartily for the great kindness, he reports, that ye shewed unto him, taking it as if it had been done to all of us: And desiring that ye, shaking yourselves clean of the abominations of the time, may embody yourselves in Christian fellowships and societies, with all tenderness and brokenness of heart, crying mightily to the Lord, that he would return and be reconciled unto the remnant of his heritage, and reclaim his captivate declarative glory out of the hands of the proud enemy; and we shall keep a correspondence with you, and help you with any whom the Lord sends forth unto us, cloathed with his commission, to proclaim the glad tidings of salvation. The Lord, the Lord God, the covenanted God of *Britain* and *Ireland*, be with you.

LETTER

LETTER LXXXI.

From the Anti-popish, Anti-prelatick, Anti-era-stian, true Presbyterian, but poor and persecuted Church of Scotland, *to the right honourable, truely gracious, and really sympathizing Brethren and Sisters in* Friesland, *and more especially in the city of* Lewarden.*

October 28. 1683.

THE Lord did vouchsafe such gracious and glorious privileges upon us, that he brought us unto a high pitch of reformation, and many engagements to be for him, beyond many (yea, we may say to the praise of his free grace, and with reflection upon our heinous ingratitude, beyond any) lands: but he hath been many ways provoked by us to lay us low as at this day, which indeed we must confess we have deserved, yea, and more at his hand; but we desire to take all in love from him, who chasteneth and loves, and loves in chastisement; and in seeking by this hot and fiery furnace to get a remnant purified for himself, amongst whom he may take delight to dwell. And now when the furnace is still growing hotter and hotter, should not we look beyond the outside of dispensations, into the Lords glorious purposes and intentions; who, the more hot he makes the furnace, minds to produce the more pure metal thereby? Also when we think upon (of which we are sure ye are not without the apprehensions) the sad and deplorable case of all national and other churches,

by

by reason of unfaithfulnefs to the Lord, little efteem of his precious truths, want of zeal for his glory, and not following him fully as he ought to be; we are indeed perfuaded, that where he hath thoughts of love, and purpofes of kindnefs, thither he will come, and fit as a refiner's fire to purge and refine. But, O! ever blefled be his holy and exalted name, he who is able to raife children unto *Abraham* out of the ftones, will not want a teftimony for himfelf, and a company of living witneffes : and we may fay, to the praife of his glorious free grace, and gracious condefcendency to our once glorious, but now bleeding and wounded, yet wreftling and contending mother church, that in our land he hath had this; we fay, a company, a party whom he ftill honoured, and is yet honouring and helping to burft out with decla-rations, proteftations, teftimonies, refiftances, and that unto blood, againft all the heinous in-dignities done to him, whom he hath not left helplefs nor comfortlefs. And among our other refrefhings from himfelf, this is one, and not a fmall one, that he hath ftirred you, our right honourable and dearly beloved brethren and mi-fters, to wreftle fo diligently, and to contend fo faithfully, zealoufly, and valiantly for our church; and to bear burden, and really to fympathize with us in our afflictions, trials and tribula-tions, evidenced by your fincere love, and great kindnefs unto, and fingular fympathy with our right honourable friend Mr. *Robert Hamiltou*, who hath been much dignified and owned of the Lord, in his many engagements, appear-ances, contendings, and fufferings at home, for the Lord's caufe, and our caufe ; and in his ma-

ny wreftlings abroad, which ye are not ignorant
of, having given many evidences of his care,
diligence, faithfulnefs, and zeal for the Lord:
And alfo evidenced by your great love and fympathy with our right honourable friend *Earlfton*,
and his perfecuted and caft-out family, who is
the branch of an old ftanding houfe for the
Lord; he himfelf honoured to be greatly active for his caufe, and now called to be immediately under the enemies lafh upon that account
And, moreover, evidenced by the great charges
ye have been at in helping our diftreffed and
caft-out families, in collecting fo liberally for the
fame; for which we defire to blefs the Lord
and to thank you, praying earneftly that he
himfelf may reward you, who will not forget
your labour of love and compaffion of us in
our bonds. O! what fhall we fay, we are all
members of one body, fubject to one glorious
head, our Lord Jefus Chrift, who hath purchafed
us to himfelf: and this is manifefted by you in
deed. Therefore let us go on in evidencing
the ftrict conjunction of us his members, that
when one fuffers, all fuffer with it; and when
one rejoiceth, all rejoice with it. And alfo
making to appear our love to our lovely and
bleffed Lord, by following him fully; labouring not to be put off our ground by the violent
and boifterous winds of perfecution which we are
toffed with, and which ye may expect to be liable
unto. O! have we not a noble and glorious
Captain to follow, who hath fuffered more for
us than we can do for him, *delivering himfelf
for our offences, and rifing again for our juftifica-
tion.* O! it is highly defirable to be like him
yea, fuch a high defire, that loft worm may
dur-

durſt not have attempted it, if the Lord himſelf had not, out of his infinite and free love, con- deſcended both to provide the means, and call us unto it: and as it is highly deſirable to be like him in every thing, ſo alſo in his ſuffering, *(who was made perfect through ſuffering)* not be- ing divided from him in his patience. O! ſhall we not look beyond what is in time, and in this howling but ſhort wilderneſs, unto what he hath provided for, and promiſed unto thoſe who over- come? who hath ſaid, *They ſhall walk with him in white.*

Now, right honourable Friends, we cannot expreſs the love we owe unto you; but we may ſay, we have our hearts unite unto you, as we do not doubt but yours are alſo unto us, though we be not in the capacity to manifeſt the ſame, as you have done many ways: but we deſire to be often and much at a throne of grace for you, begging that ye will be ſo for us, in our con- tendings and extreme ſufferings. So remains,

Your hearty wellwiſhing, really endeared, and very much obliged brethren, ſiſters and ſervants in our ever bleſſed Lord,

Subſcribed in our name, and by our direction, by the clerk of our general meeting,

MIC. SHIELDS.

H 1   LETTER

LETTER LXXXII.

Ecclesia Scoticana Classi Groninganæ salutem.

Nov. 28. 1683.

Reverendissimi Domini vigilantissimi Pastores,

THE Lord having now, to our great joy
and encouragement, restored unto us our
beloved friend and minister Mr. *James Renwick,*
and brought him through many imminent dangers; (for which we desire to rejoice in him, praising his holy name) who hath given us such an
ample and savory account of your real concernedness with our Master's cause, and affection to
and sympathy with us in *Scotland,* that we must
burst out in expressing our sensibleness of, and joy
in the same, by writing unto you: again and
again blessing the Lord, and thanking you for
the singular mercy which we enjoy, by your confirming of our foresaid beloved friend Mr. *James
Renwick* in the work of the ministry (for which
he was sent over unto you by us) whereof the
Lord gives special evidences of his own approbation, being singularly with him in that great
and weighty work, to our great refreshing and
encouragement: and also testifying and confirming the truth of that faithful Mr. *William Brackel* minister at *Lewarden,* witnessed in his friendly testimony of our students before your presbytery, *viz.* That the testificates and calls subscribed by us unto them, particularly to the
foresaid Mr. *James Renwick,* were delivered into the hand of the right honourable the laird of
Earlston.

Edinston. We acknowledge ourselves many ways your debtors, both in spirituals and temporals, and are very sensible of your care of the church of God, evidenced so many ways unto us in our low case and condition, now when the enemies of our Lord in this land have casten down the Lord's house to the ground, and laid his pleasant portion desolate, and casten many of us out of our houses, being violently persecute, and that unto death, with all the subtilty and cruelty which the powers of hell and earth can devise. O! the fury and wickedness of enemies is come to a great height, and the malice of backsliders is swelled to a great measure, not only Christianity but humanity being altogether given up by the most part of the nation; so that all things speak forth the cup of the *Amorite* and *Edomite* to be near full, and that the Lord is even at the doors with a great deluge of his wrath, to be let loose upon the generation. But in the midst of all our distresses and difficulties (O! blessed be the name of the Lord) we have no reason to complain, for he speaks comfortably to us in this wilderness; he is a present help to us in the time of our need, and puts songs in our mouths in the midst of this hot fire; and is wonderfully seen in hiding, preserving and encouraging us; it being no small refreshment unto us, that he hath put into your hearts to stand still and to hear our complaints, and to become companions with us in our tribulations; for which we desire to praise the Lord, and to pray unto him, that he who is not unrighteous to forget your labour of love may reward you, for putting to your hands to strengthen and help a wrestling and bleeding church; and that he may make you ever faithful in his vineyard, following your labours with his rich bleſſing, to the glory of his great name, and the advancement of his kingdom in the earth, and in the ſouls of his people. O! mind the diſtreſſed and afflicted, bleeding caſe of the once glorious church of *Scotland*, as we deſire to mind you, both in public and in private. We remain,

Your aſſured friends and obliged ſervants to our full power in the Lord,

Subſcribed in our name by the clerk of our general meeting, MIC. SHIELDS.

LETTER LXXXIII.

To all and ſundry true Proteſtant Churches to whom thir preſents may come.

Nov. 28. 1683.

WE do not in the leaſt doubt, but in ſome meaſure it is known unto you, how that our antient and reformed church of *Scotland* did ſometime gloriouſly flouriſh with the great and bright ſplendour of the true religion, ſo that her light was viſible to all adjacent churches: but now, deſervedly for our ſinning againſt the Lord, we have occaſioned his vineyard in our land to be overſpread and trodden down with foxes, and devoured with the wild beaſts of the field; we being under various and ſad exigences, great perſecutions and reproaches, which alſo we may be perſuaded are come unto your ears. The
weighty

weighty confideration whereof (together with
the great hope we have of your concernednefs
with us in our low and defolate cafe, whereunto,
as to the external face of our church, we are
redacted; yet dignified and helped, though
weakly, but willingly to *contend for the faith
once delivered to the faints*, and for the privileges
of the church of God) moved us to fend and
commiffionate the right honourable Mr. *Robert
Hamilton*, unto all you who are wellwifhers unto
the commonwealth of *Ifrael*, and that upon
many deliberate and weighty grounds; knowing
that our caufe and cafe is fadly mifreprefented
unto you by the fubtile dealings of our adverfaries and backflidders, who are finfully active,
but moft vigilant in giving mifinformation, and
falfe relations of what we act and do; as if our
principles and proceedings were contrary to the
written word of God, the fupreme judge of all
controverfies, and true Proteftantifm. Whereas,
we jointly and unanimoufly declare, that we
neither maintain nor hold any thing contrary to
the fcriptures of truth, our ancient laws ecclefiaftic and civil, and our noble work of reformation; but defire (yea, and have been helped through the Lord's grace) to fquare our actions and proceedings according thereunto, for
which we this day, and for more than the fpace
of twenty years, are, and have been fuffering afflictions, perfecutions, outcaftings, banifhments,
imprifonments, and reproaches, yea, and death
itfelf.

We therefore, the true Proteftant, Anti-po-
pifh, Anti-prelatick, Anti-eraftian, and perfecuted Prefbyterian church of *Scotland*, do con-
credit this our commiffioner, giving him our

full

full power, consent and assent, faithfully and truly to inform all true Protestant and reformed churches, kingdoms and commonwealths, unto which he shall or may come, of our present case, principles, former and later proceedings: and that we are only, through God's grace, labouring to keep ourselves still clean in the way of the Lord, as it hath been walked in by our predecessors, (of truly worthy memory) in their carrying on of our noble and glorious work of reformation, in the several steps thereof, from Popery, Prelacy, and Erastian supremacy; and it is upon these heads that our sufferings have been and are stated. And for the more clear and full knowledge thereof, we recommend you to the information of this our right honourable and faithful commissioner, as being seen in all our affairs, and of one judgment, and under the same sufferings with us; and also, while he was in our own land, highly dignified and countenanced of the Lord in his many contendings and wrestlings, engagements, rencounters and appearances against the common adversary, contendings and wrestlings against defection and backsliding courses, and great and many sufferings for truth.

So we humbly intreat and desire that whatever information ye have gotten, or may get, from any hand whatever, either enemies or backsliders, particularly ministers who have forsaken the Lord, and deserted us, of us, our principles and proceedings, contrary to the word of God, our Covenants and engagements unto him, may not be credited nor believed by you, they being only false aspersions and calumnies, through malice, cast upon us, yea, nor contrary to the information of this

our

)ur right honourable truftee, and faithful commiffioner, whom and whofe information we
)umbly, but earneftly, defire and requeft all
:hurches, kingdoms, and commonwealths, whi-
:her he may come, to receive and entertain him,
ıs ye would not rejeĉt the fuits and petitions of
:he once glorious, but now afflicted, toffed,
wounded, and bleeding, yet wreftling church of
Scotland; and in receiving of him, it fhall be
ıs done to all of us. Therefore all ye·lovers
)f Zion, do not flight, but ponder deeply, the
fad cafe, we, as a fhare of ˙the proteftant intereft, are redacted unto, holding up the fame in
your prayers to the Lord: for God calls all to
fympathize together, and to confider, that the
plottings, confultations, malchievments, and
acftings of adverfaries, are intended againft the
whole; and when one member fuffers, all ought
to fuffer with it. And we, for our parts, (which
is all the remuneration that, at the time, we can
give) fhall not ceafe to pray for your flourifhing
in fpirituals and temporals.

Subfcribed in our name, and by our direction,
by the clerk of our general meeting,

MIC. SHIELDS.

LETTER LXXXIV.

The contending and wreftling fuffering and diftreffed reformed church of Scotland, to the true reformed church at Embden.

July 31. 1684.

Right Revd. and dearly Beloved in the Lord,

OUR long delaying to teftify our acknowledgment of your kindly fympathy and friendly commiferation of us in our diftreffed, bleeding and perplexed cafe, may make you apprehend that we are forgetful of the great benefits which we received from your hands, and ungrateful towards yourfelves: but we earneftly intreat, that no fuch thoughts may be entertained; for though our tranfmiffions of letters to you hath hitherto, by reafon of fome providential exigences, been obftructed, yet the fenfe of the duty of thankfulnefs, which we owe unto you is, and we hope will be, always upon our fpirits. Albeit we be in fuch a poor cafe, as we are not able, though moft willing, to manifeft the fame by remunerating you any manner of way, according to your kindnefs fhown, and liberality extended towards us; but we know in what ye did, therein ye had your eye upon duty, and not upon reward. And your charitable frame of fpirit which was evidenced to us by your bounty, and declared by our right honourable commiffioner, was more encouraging and refrefhing to us than all wordly things could be: for we look upon the founding of bowels among Chriftians as a great token of good to the univerfal church,

which

which (as we a poor part thereof are in a deplorable cafe) is in a very dangerous condition;
the rage of enemies being infatiable, not bended
againſt us as men, but as Chriſtians, yea as Proteſtants; and the more they prevail againſt us,
the more courage they take to enter into univerfal plots and conſpiracies againſt the whole reformed churches. Therefore let us account the
ſuffering of one member as intended againſt all;
and ſo let us take heed to ourſelves and to our
common goſpel intereſt; for the plots of Satan
and his inſtruments are no more deep than univerſal. Let it be our ſtudy to be led in the way
of truth and holineſs, which is always the way
of pleaſantneſs, and to ſtand up as one man a-
gainſt Antichriſt, and whatever men of antichriſtian and malignant ſpirits would intrude upon the kingdom of our Lord. Let us beware of
affronting our noble Captain by yielding to his
enemies one foot of ground, for the cauſe is his,
and therefore it is worth the contending for. It
is ſo honourable and precious as nothing is too
coſtly to beſtow upon it. And if the Lord were
not letting us ſee that this cauſe, which we a
poor broken and diſtreſſed church are contending
and ſuffering for, were his own cauſe, and that
the heads of our ſufferings are his crown, and the
pendicles thereof, were it not ſo, we would ſoon
yield and give it over; for theſe men who are
the rod of the Lord's anger againſt us have their
ſpirits ſet on edge by the fire of hell; their fury
is ſo firey, their rage ſo cruel, and their ſnares
ſo ſubtile, that our caſe hath none ſo like it, as was
the condition of the godly in the *Netherlands*, in
the time of the *Spaniſh* inquiſition. But we cannot
get time to look upon our miſeries and dangers,

being

being forced to turn our contemplation another way, to wit, to behold the wonderful works of the Lord in his doing for us in this our low condition, by stirring up the spirits of you, and of some, to sympathize with us, by bearing up our spirits under this firey trial, you drawing out his breasts of confolation in such meafure amongft us that are the burden-bearers in the heat of this our day that many are made to cry out, Their work is eafy, their lines are fallen to them in pleafant places; and by wonderful delivering us out of the claws of this roaring adverfary, and plucking us a prey out of their teeth, when fenfe reafon, and probability faid the contrary; fo that from his power and faithfulnefs, meeting with many inexpreffible proofs of the fame, we défire to believe, that becaufe of the glory of his great name, he will do great things for us, yea work wonders; for indeed no lefs can raife up his born-down, yea ruined work in *Scotland*. But though the church's difeafe at this time be defperate, yet we dare not look upon it as incurable, feeing Jéfus Chrift the faithful phyfician (who meddles only with defperate difeafes, that his fkilfulnefs may the more appear) is engaged to look upon it, and to help it. He *will heal* her *backflidings*, and *will love* her *freely;* and will *turn away* his *anger from* her, yea, *and will be as the dew unto* her, fo that fhe *fhall grow as the lily, and caft forth* her *roots as Lebanon.* Her *branches fhall fpread,* her *beauty fhall be as the olive tree, and* her *fmell as Lebanon.* We defire to wait for that longed-for day, and for the time when judgment fhall return again to righteoufnefs, and when men fhall difcern between the righteous and the wicked.

So,

So, Right Reverend, much Honoured, and
early Beloved, make many errands to the
throne of grace for us, praying earnestly and
frequently that the Lord, who is the great ma-
ster-builder of his own work, may work, and ac-
complish his work amongst us, and perfect the
same over the belly of all opposition; and that
ye may be strengthened with patience to endure
to the end, standing out resolutely against our
outward and inward enemies, and no ways stain-
ing the honour of the glorious Captain of our
salvation.

Now, the Lord God of hosts be with you, and
fortify your spirits against all the machinations of
satan, making you all good soldiers, cloathed
with his armour of proof, that ye may endure
to the end, and enjoy the crown which he hath
laid up for all that fear him. We shall detain
you no further at the time, humbly desiring (if
possible) to be dignified with a line from your
hands, which shall be most refreshing and reviving unto

Your most obliged and endeared friends, and
 obedient servants in all Christian duty,

Subscribed in our name, and by our direction,
 by the clerk of the general meeting.

MIC. SHIELDS.

LETTER

LETTER LXXXV.

From the contending and suffering reformed church of Scotland, *to their Right Honourable and trusty Delegate Mr.* Robert Hamilton.

July 31. 1684.

Right Hon. and dearly Beloved in the Lord,

IT is like our correspondence together, by reason of the distance of place, your intended travels, and the difficulty of transmitting letters, may be for a season interrupted. However, as we are bound in duty, we shall endeavour, through the Lord's gracious assistance, to keep up a mindfulness of you, and that work wherein the Lord hath employed you for us, always praying the Lord may direct you wisely to manage his cause against all his opposites; (as in a great measure he hath done heretofore) may make you a brazen wall and an iron pillar in his house; may bless your labours and travels; and that, when his holy will is, he (preserving you in your work) may restore you unto us, loaded with the spoils of Antichrist, tropies of the kirk of Christ, and the longed for fruits of your painful labours.

O right honourable and trusty Commissioner, go on in your work, fear not man, the cause is the Lord's, and he will gloriously own it. What shall we say to his praise and to your encouragement, but we are meeting with many proofs of his power and faithfulness even when our furnace is hottest; we may say, he is still delivering us, either by preventing trials, or

sup-

support under trials; he, as it were, lays the
bridle upon the mane of adversaries, and yet
lets it be seen that in some measure they cannot
get us reached. O how glorious is he in wisdom,
power, holiness, justice, goodness, and truth;
he is laying pledges into our hands that he will
do great things for us, whereof we shall be glad,
and which he shall proclaim among the heathen.
We are persuaded he is posting upon his way to
appear for his broken and buried work; he will
come at an unexpected time, and in an unexpected manner, and happy shall they be whom he
will find at their work, and who are not sleeping
with the generality of this generation: But sure
we are, there are sad days abiding such as are
dealing with a slack hand this day, and who refuse to answer his call now, when he is many
ways presenting himself to his people, and testifying his willingness to return again to them. O
we do not doubt but he will return, and that
suddenly; and he hath great mercies abiding
these that are waiting for him; but judgments,
judgments, judgments we are sure shall usher them
in. Let us prepare to wade through judgment
towards his mercies; and O noble way that he
takes, for we cannot be otherwise prepared for
mercies.

'How shall we open up our hearts, or unfold
our thoughts unto you? the Lord he is God and
the captain of our salvation, a cleared sight whereof would obscurate all the difficulties that are in
the way, and carry the eye over both the long,
weary, slimy, and thorny wilderness, and the
proud swellings of Jordan, beholding and contemplating the good and promised land. We
hope, the Lord hath taught you better than to

regard oppofition in your way of ferving and following him, for the more fad your ways be, the
more glorious fhall be your victory; you will mif-
ken yourfelf when, inftead of a crown of thorns,
you get an immortal crown of glory put upon
your heads, and a cloathing of white raiment, always beholding him who is the wonder and praife
of the family of that higher houfe.

But now, we commit you to the Lord for directing, comforting and fupporting grace, praying that he may be with you in your intended
travels, and make your pains tend to the up-raifing
of his work; and for what he hath done by you,
we defire to blefs him, putting a prize upon all
his mercies, efpecially upon that ineftimable benefit of his gofpel, which is as reviving from the
dead. Let us, if poffible, hear from you ere you
depart from the place where you now are, and
let us know wherein it lies in our power to be
encouraging and ftrengthening unto you. So a-
gain we leave you upon the good hand of your
God and our God, hoping that we need not
defire you in prayer to be mindful of us, who
are,

Your Honour's obliged and endeared friends,
brethren, and fervants in the Lord,

Subfcribed in our name and by our direction,
by the clerk of our general meeting,

MICHAEL SHIELDS.

LETTE

LETTER LXXXVI.

From the contending, wreftling, fuffering and dif-
treffed reformed church of Scotland, *to the true*
Proteftant and reformed church at Groningen,
particularly the minifters thereof.

July 31. 1684.

Right Reverend and dearly Beloved,

THE fweet experience which we have had
of your receiving, and faithfulnefs in
weighing, our former addreffes, with the circum-
ftances wherein we ftand, hath given us abundant
encouragement to catch hold of this prefent opportunity of the unfolding fomewhat of our for-
rows, which your love and our neceffity invites
and calls, yea commands us, to reprefent to your
fympathy and compaffion ; however, we are confident we may commit much to the faithfulnefs
of our right honourable Delegate, to lay open
unto you our fad and deplorable condition. And
we are affured that the love ye bear to the common caufe of all Chriftians will not fuffer you to
fhut your eyes from the bleeding and lamentable
condition of the poor diftreffed church of *Scot-*
land. Should we not therefore feek to eafe our
burdened hearts, by pouring them out into your
bofoms? for if we fhould neglect this, we would
feem ungrateful towards you, who have given fo
large and ample evidences of your readinefs to
to do for us and fuffer with us.

Affuredly, if ever a poor church was battered
at by Satan and his inftruments, we are that
church; if ever a poor people were befet round with

right and left hand oppofites, we are that people! if ever a poor remnant were the objects of
Antichrift's cruelty, and apoftatical malice, we
are that remnant; for the Lord hath called forth
and ftrengthened an enemy againft us, *the rod
of his anger, and the ftaff of his indignation,* a generation of men whofe fpirits are fet on edge by
the fury of hell, under whofe exafperate, cruel-
ties we figh and mourn, they drawing their fur-
rows upon your backs: many of us are daily led
as lambs to the flaughter; yea, and at the hour
of our death not permitted to commend the
free grace of God in Chrift, to fpeak to the love-
linefs and defirablenefs of the crofs, to exhort
others to ftedfaftnefs in the caufe, nor to proclaim that the lines are fallen to us in pleafant
places: fome are fhut up in prifon houfes, laid
in irons, and fo barbaroufly kept that thefe who
they are moft ftrictly tied unto, either by the bonds
of nature or Chriftianity, can have no accefs unto
them: others are fent away to foreign Plantati-
ons to be fold as flaves: and all of us, we may
fay, put to wander with our lives in our hands,
and to eat our bread in the peril of our lives,
many of our refidences being in the wild mountains, dens and caves of the earth, the enraged
adverfary ftill fearching and purfuing after us,
and many ftill permitted to fall into their hands.
But O! we need not exprefs unto you the in-
veterate and deadly malice of this malignant,
prophane, and antichriftian faction; for what
true Proteftants know it not, that the rage of
ftated enemies againft the church of Chrift is infatiable. However, the Lord is our witnefs, that
our grief and trouble is not fo much becaufe of
the dangers we are in, and of the mifery which
we

we are ... ...; but that which mostly affects
our hearts, is the danger which we behold the
whole Proteſtant reformed churches are in at
this juncture, through the univerſal conſpiracies
and combinations amongſt avowed enemies to
religion, their ſtrength, by appearance, ſtill increaſing. If our God will lay our bodies as
the ſtreet under our feet, and pour out our blood
as duſt before their fury, his holy and wiſe will
be done; for if our blood would be a mean to
recover or preſerve the reſt of the true churches
of Chriſt from antichriſtian tyranny, we are willing to offer it up for the ſervice; but we know
their fury is inſatiable, and will not die with us,
they being armed againſt us, not as men, but as
Chriſtians; yet what ſhall we ſay, we dare not
quarrel nor repine at our low caſe, but we ought
rather to rejoice in it, ſeeing that it makes for
the manifeſtation of the Lord's attributes towards
us; for we may ſay, he gets new occaſion to
make his power manifeſt, taking hold of our
extremity as his opportunity; ſo that we may
ſay, we are troubled on every ſide, yet not deſtroyed; we are perplexed but not in deſpair; perſecuted, but not forſaken; caſt down, but not
deſtroyed. For we are not made ſo much to
mourn becauſe of the length that enemies are
permitted to proceed againſt us, as we are made
to wonder, that they get not more of their purpoſes accompliſhed, for day and night they weary
themſelves in purſuing after the guiltleſs; many
times we are delivered out of their hands as a
prey plucked out of their teeth, and this we e-
ſteem much, not as it is our deliverance, but as
it manifeſts the Lord's power and faithfulneſs towards us, and encourages us to believe that he

shall do great things for us: Wherefore, our mouths shall be filled with laughter, our tongue with singing, and we shall be made to proclaim among the heathen, *The Lord hath done great things for us, whereof we are glad;* Yea, we are always delivered, for we account it a blessed and happy deliverance, that (though some faint, yet) many are kept faithful unto the death, choosing rather to quite with their heads than any of the precious truths of Christ, they singing in the hot furnace, and crying out that their lines are fallen to them in pleasant places.

Now, Right Reverend and dearly Beloved in our Lord, we have the more encouragment to lay out our case every way unto you, that your brotherly sympathy and labours of love hath been manifest to us all, and throughout the world, by your kindly acceptance of our right honourable and faithful Delegate's informations, your respecting and crediting him whom we owe so much respect and credit unto: By your affectionate kindness unto, and ordaining of Mr. *James Renwick,* who is for us a faithful minister of Jesus Christ, which hath furnished us no small encouragement and refreshment in this day of our distress; the Lord giving evidences that he is his messenger. And also, by your hitherto friendly entertaining of such as have been sent from us, unto your colleges. Withal, earnestly, though humbly, begging and intreating, that (if there be any possibility of it) ye would condescend upon some way, for the future maintaining of some of our youths at your colleges; for we may say, as we are not able to maintain them abroad, so our schools and colleges at home are so corrupt and ensnaring, that none who will not run with them

them into the same exceſs of error and riot, can or dare meddle with the ſame. However, we ſeriouſly deſire that none from this land be owned or acknowledged by you, who have not our teſtificate, or the recommendation of our Delegate. And as to theſe, who, without our knowledge or counſel, have already crept in among with their errors and calumnies, tending to the weakening of the Proteſtant intereſt; we hope we need not again warn you, judging that ſo to be already broken. So, in a deeper ſenſe of our caſe, and with greater confidence of your ſympathy (having had many proofs of the ſame) than we can expreſs, we make this humble addreſs unto you, in the bowels of Chriſt, earneſtly imploring your moſt fervent prayers for us to the Lord, who is the hearer of prayer, that he who hides his face from us, may yet return again and lift up the light of his countenance upon us, may reclaim his captivate declarative glory, and ſubdue and ſcatter the enemies thereof.

Now, the Lord proſper you, and preſerve us, that we may all as one man, ſtand up againſt Antichriſt and all his limbs, and whatever is contrary to ſound doctrine and the power of godlineſs, that ſo the work of theſe latter ages may be carried on, to the honour of God and the church's joy, through Jeſus Chriſt. So, we remain,

Your obliged friends, and

humble ſervants in the Lord,

Subſcribed in our name, and by our direction, by the clerk of our general meeting,

LETTER LXXXVII.

To some Friends in Newcastle.

Jan. 8. 1685.

Drly *beloved Brethren in the Lord,*

WE have heard from *John Scot,* whom we conceive to have had commission from you for that same effect, the difficulty and trials in your present case, which are in no small measure affecting to us. But, O! be not discouraged, but rather rejoice, that the Lord will not give unto you ease, which is very undesirable now when *Zion* is in trouble; neither think your firey trials strange, for it is but the same in measure with what happens unto your brethren: And though no affliction for the present be joyous but grievous to flesh and blood; yet we cannot but look upon the greatest tribulation, when the work of God is so low, to-be the greater testimony of his love.

However, as to our mind and advice anent your present strait, we judge it,

1*st*, Matter of great concernedness, both to you and us, that some of you should be redacted to that intricate extremity, that your sin and suffering is upon the one hand, and the suffering of our nearest and dearest relations upon the other, which we know assuredly, will be more bitter to you than any thing that can be brought upon yourselves in following your duty. But,

2*dly*, Ye, as we hope, not having consented actively or passively, by silence or concurrence, to your relations their purchasing your liberty,

by

by a bond to present you again before the ses-
sions. We judge it cannot be your duty to be
either active or passive in presenting yourselves,
but that ye ought to make out of the way, seeing ye know assuredly that ye will be apprehended. (1.) It would infer your consenting to what
your relations have done, in tampering with
the adversary. (2.) It would infer your having
a hand in your latter sufferings, which surely
is both a sin in the sight of God, and very dis-
quieting to the conscience; for though we ought
cheartully to imbrace suffering when the Lord
sends it in our way, yet we ought first to have
no hand in it ourselves, no not by omitting our
duty in using what lawful means may prevent
the same: When we are *persecuted in one city,
we are commanded to fly to another.* Let all of
you that are at liberty use all lawful means to
keep yourselves so; for if you shall cast yourselves into the trial, ye know not what snares
the Lord may subject you unto. as your punishment, whereof ye may be made to repent out
of time.

But, dear Brethren, let not your present trials
damp or confuse you, for if the Lord had not
seen such a case for his glory and your good, he
had not brought you unto it. Seek not the
carving out of your own lot, but put it in the
Lord's hand, and subscribe your consent unto
what he sees meet to do unto you; study to walk
before him in the way of duty, in paths approven by him and wellpleasing to him; and there,
and there only, ye shall enjoy the comfortable
light of his pleasant countenance, wherewith
he beholdeth the upright: seek the upmaking
of all your wants in himself, who hath promised

to take you up, *though father and mother should* both *forsake you.*

Now, if ye incline thereunto, and see it fit to come into *Scotland*, and take part and lot with us, know affuredly, that ye shall be moſt acceptable; and though we can promiſe you nothing but perſecution, yet ye shall have our countenance, and all the encouragement that we can beſtow upon you: and we hope that ye shall not think your lot hard. So, leaving you upon the Lord, for the light of direction and conſolation, we remain,

Your affectionate brethren, ſympathizing friends, and ſervants in the Lord,

Subſcribed in our name, and by our direction, by the clerk of our general meeting,

MIC. SHIELDS.

LETTER LXXXVIII.

From the ſuffering and wreſtling remnant of the church of Scotland, *to the right honourable the laird of* Earlſton, *priſoner for the cauſe of Chriſt.*

Much honoured Sir,   *Jan.* 8. 1685.

YOur letter, directed to the right reverend Mr. *James Renwick*, was very refreſhing and encouraging to us all; yea, we may ſay, a little reviving to our ſpirits in our bondage, having not heard from yourſelf, nor particularly of your caſe, for a conſiderable time before,

together with the many troubles
ɔ and are tryſted with, hath occa-
ɔt writing unto you : and although
t heard from us after this manner,
e not been forgotten by us.   But
d are deſirous to   know   your
keep up that due ſympathy and
; with you, in your bonds for pre-
which we ought.   However, we
; the Lord upon your account, who
you, for the manifeſting the riches
race, through ſo many and ſo vari-
d temptations,   from   within and
n malicious enemies and flattering
ends ; yea, hath brought you again
:s of death, and ſides of the grave,
' to devour you, thereby diſapoint-
of his people, and expectations of
which you ought to look upon as
ɔf his love and fatherly chaſtiſe-
before you be unpurged and turn
furnace, he will take great pains
:d take you from one fire to an-
: be a veſſel fitted for his ſervice;
emies think to add ſorrow to your
making you like an owl in the de-
lican in the wilderneſs, by ſhutting
oſe priſon, far from the converſe
ɔds and relations ; that then and·
uld viſit you with his loving kind-
your ſoul with a ſenſe of his love,
ɐ ſing in the midſt of theſe hot
ɔderful love, and matchleſs conde-
and to ſay that heart-raviſhing and
ng word, mentioned in your letter,
d not only ſo, but to give you ſuch a
lively

lively and favoury impreffion upon your fpir
of his public work, and noble caufe in thi
day, when it is worn off the fpirits of many
who feemingly had it once; and, alas! too
much off many of our own, All which, we fay
as it is ground of encouragement, and matter of
praife to us before the Lord; fo you ought,
in a fpecial manner, to praife and magnify him
for the fame, and to make the experiences of
his former loving kindnefs to your foul, as mo-
tives to believe, and helps to confide in him for
the future; that he, who hath brought you thro'
the depths before, remains faithful and cannot
change, can and will bring you through the like
again; yea, though he fhould fee it fit in his
holy wifdom to make you wade through waters
deep and broad, and to make you go through
fires more large and hot; yet, O faint not, truft
in him who hath done fo great things to you
and for you: Remember Chrift, your Head and
Captain, is above the waters; he waded thro'
deeper waters, and ran through hotter fires,
(and all for the redemption of poor loft finners)
than you or any of his people can do: Remember him, *who endured fuch contradiction of
finners*, and for finners; *who being tempted, knows
how to fuccour thefe that are fo.* Labour to put
a blank in his hand, that you may not quarrel
with him, whatever lot he may tryft you with.
O his prefence will make any lot defirable, for
it fupplies all wants, and makes the creature to
rejoice, when robbed and fpoiled of all other
things; it makes afflictions light, and trials eafy;
it makes a prifon a palace, and the threatenings of men to be defpifed; yea, it will make
the

he foul fing and rejoice, when *going thro' the valley and shadow of death*.

Much honoured Sir, what shall we say more or your encouragement, but this, Go on, go on, in your suffering for precious Christ; the cause you are suffering for is Christ's own cause, and he will own it in his own due time, and own all who own it sincerely: He lives and reigns, and will reign; *The crown shall flourish on his head, and all his enemies be cloathed with shame.* And although enemies in this land will not have Christ to reign over them, having robbed him of his crown and royal preroga-tives; and sense and reason would say, he would never reign in this land, yet faith, which sees clearly in the darkest night, will see him sitting on his throne, reigning and ruling in and a-mongst his people, and over his enemies; coming cloathed with the garments of ven-geance, and cloak of zeal against them, and with the garments of salvation and mercy to his people. O happy soul that will be found in his way, and about their work when he comes, to whom his coming will only be sweet. What shall we say more to his commendation? He is good and does good, his cross is easy, and his bur-den is light. He hath done and is doing great things for us and to us; he hath been and is at great pains with us to purge us from our dross, and make us a holy and cleanly people for himself. He hath given us the gospel, and it seems he is countenancing the same, and en-creasing the followers thereof. And O he seems to be about to do some great work in this land, to bring to pass his act, his strange act.

Much honoured Sir, you make mention in

K k   your

your letter of your refolution to write at m——
length to us, when the opportunity ferve
That opportunity is longed for by us; for you
laft was fo refrefhful, that we earneftly defire t
hear from you again.——So, leaving you u
on the God of *Jacob*, for his direction, affiftanc
and confolation in time, and the enjoyment o
himfelf throughout eternity; begging that while
in the body, you will not be unmindful of us,
who are not forgetful of you. We are,

Your Honour's affured and fympathizing friends,
   brethren and fervants in the Lord,

Subfcribed in our name, and by our direction,
   by the clerk of our general meeting,

                           MIC. SHIELDS.

LETTER LXXXIX.

To Mr. David Houfton *minifter of the gofpel in*
   Ireland.

At.——— *the* 23d. *of Sept.* 1686.

Right reverend Sir,

W Hen we confider the neceffity of a ftanding gofpel miniftry, for the converfion
of fouls, the confirmation of the converted,
and the difcovery of the fins and duties of the
time, and the great lofs that his poor afflicted
and wreftling church hath fuffered, in being deprived in a great meafure, for fome years, of
the faithful and free preaching of the gofpel;
we look upon it as a great duty incumbent up-
                                                   on

iy out ourſelves, in our places and ſta-
he utmoſt of our power, to recover
and lamentable loſs, and that our
njoy the ineſtimable benefit of a pure,
od plentiful goſpel: Wherefore, we
your zealous inclinations and affecti-
poor ſuffering church, did ſend over
nfer with you, whoſe information a-
ath been ſatisfying to us; whereupon
intly reſolved to ſend over the bearer
confer further with you, and to con-
nto us, according to your reſolution;
may meet together, which we deſire
y, through the Lord's goodneſs, tend
ur and our ſatisfaction.

:verend Sir, we hope that you will
to your conſideration, and not look
in the caſe of our land; for though
, and ſo our need of help the greater,
ay ſay, that through many places of
here is now among people more long-
earneſt deſire after the faithful and
:hing of the goſpel than formerly we
ved. But we ſhall not inſiſt upon this.
r reports anent yourſelf, (which we
ot fit to inſert here, and whereof you
well to clear yourſelf of) we refer
: information of the bearer, until that
e meet together, if the Lord pleaſe
ſo in his holy providence. Thus, de-
ntreat the Lord, that he may conduct
unto us; and that our meeting to-
y be bleſſed with a right and full un-
g of one another, and joint concur-
her, for the advancement of his pub-
,and earneſtly begging the help of

K k 2   your

your prayers, we commend you to the grace
that is in Chrift-Jefus, your mafter, and we are,

Reverend Sir,

Your endeared friends and

fervants in the Lord,

Subfcribed in our name, and by our direction,
by the clerk of our general meeting,

　MIC. SHIELDS.

LETTER XC.

To Friends in Ireland.

March 2. 1687.

Loving Friends, and dearly beloved in our Lord
Jefus Chrift,

WE received your kind and chriftian letter,
very refrefhful and acceptable to us;
not only becaufe coming from fuch who *have*
obtained like precious faith with us, through the
righteoufnefs of God, and our Saviour Jefus
Chrift, and whom we refpect as our brethren,
under the fame indiffolvable bond of our holy.
Covenants, engaged to concert the fame common caufe, and teftimony for the precious
interefts of our princely Mafter ; with whom
we have defired a more clofe and intimate correfpondence than hitherto we have obtained ;
and coming from fuch, at fuch a time, when we
were groaning under that bitter grievance, a-
mong many others, of being deprived of, and
　　　　　　　　　　　　　　　　　　fe-

questered from that desirable and much desired
comfort of communion with our brethren in o-
ther churches, which we could not enjoy as we
desired, because of the universal decay of love,
zeal and sympathy, every where too visibly de-
creasing, and because of the many odious and
invidious obloquies we and our cause have been
spersed with, which yet we find hath not got
so credulous entertainment with you, as to block
up your hearts, and bind up your hands from
shewing such tender affection toward us as ye discover in your letter: but also, because of the
manner of its conveyance, by a hand very welcome to us, wherein you demonstrate no small
care and concern to be informed of our case
and cause, in that you spare no pains to purchase
the understanding of it. And chiefly your letter
was very grateful to us, because of the matter
of it; relishing so much of a gospel spirit of
sympathy with us, in our conflicts of sufferings
and contendings for truth and duty, and of a
savoury sense of our worthies witnessings for the
regalities of our royal Master, which they sealed
with their bonds and blood; and of heart affecting grief, condoling the misery of our unhappy
divisions, and of love to us, prompting you to
such a serious solicitousness to be informed of
our integrity to the sworn truths, and of our
way in the Lord, the better to stop the calumnies of adversaries; and of zeal for the common
cause in expressing your desire, to keep up har-
mony with us in pursuance of the ends of the
Covenants, and acts of venerable assemblies, and
that the mouths of liars may be stopped. The
fragrancy of which graces that your letter did
savour of, did very much endear it to us, and

K k 3   in-

incites us to some earnest diligence (as our uncertain wanderings would allow) to endeavour a speedy return. But, in confidence of your kind construction, we must apologize with regrete, that neither our condition for the time will admit, nor our capacity furnish us with so speedy and satisfactory an answer to send you as we desire ; and therefore must entreat your favour, both for our shortness in the abrupt abridgment of our answer, and for our longsomness in sending .

It would be tedious both for you and for us, to give a full deduction of the manifold tracts and steps, travels and traversings, turnings and windings, ups and downs we have had in our conflicts and contendings, with open enemies and professed friends, with cruelty and craft, with rage and reproach, with censures and calumnies, with persecutors of hand and persecutors of tongue, with defection and division, with the extremes of left hand declensions and right hand extravagancies, in our continued (and yet, through mercy, uninterrupted) course of our weak wrestlings against the corruptions of the times, and the indignities done to our Lord Jesus Christ, and his crown prerogatives. We must refer the more ample account of these, to our *Informatory Vindication* we propose to emit ; and also to send to you, assoon as the times difficulties will permit us : only at the time to answer your desire in some measure, that you may be informed about these reports of our animosities fallen out among ourselves; and how it comes, and why it is, that now in our land, *Judah* should fight against *Judah*, even at *Jerusalem*, which causes your spirits to faint to hear the various
rious

rious reports of it; we would, in some short
hints, and open hearted ingenuity, give you to
understand something of the causes and effects,
rise and result of these animosities, and what
our carriage hath been under these dissentions,
and of our present abstraction, amidst these dis-
tractions, whence it sprang, and where it stands
with us.

Though we be most unworthy of the honour,
and very uncapable and insufficient for the work
of prosecuting a testimony for the covenanted
reformation of this once renowned church; yet
it hath ever been, and still is our ambition and
endeavour to aim at it; and insist in the footsteps
of the most zealous and faithful promoters of it
that have gone before us, and to advance in it
as they left it, without any abandoning or foregoing any part of it, or altering, (further than
that progress, or rather application to our present case, the times have called us to make) so
that however we be reproached with new principles or practices, which we have forged and
fostered to maintain our new way, as many even of
our backsliding brethren do call our present testimony, yet we can truly say, we know of none
that we have espoused, either contrary to the
venerable church constitutions, in our best and
purest times, or contradictory to what our ministers preached before these divisions began, or to
what we ourselves professed when united with
them, who now brand us with the odious characters of changlings and schismatics, which we
will not now stand to refute by recriminations,
but can easily vindicate ourselves from it, by a
naked deduction of the controversy, as managed
by us since the first rise of it.

Our

Our teftimony hath been in fome meafure continued and propagated ever fince the fatal cataftrophe of overturning the work of reformation, by the reintroduction of tyranny, fupremacy, and Prelacy, fince which time, we have always defigned and defired to adhere to, and imbark with fuch minifters and profeffors, as did from time to time zealoufly withftand and witnefs againft all the feveral fucceffive gradations of this national revolt from the Lord, and were incorporate with the body of them that did bear and follow the Lord's ftandard, in the work of field-preaching before *Bothwel;* with whom we had fweet and foul-fatisfying communion; while their *feet were beautiful upon the mountains, bringing glad tidings, publifhing falvation,* and proclaiming, as heralds, that *Zion's King reigned;* while they jeoparded their lives in the high-places of the fields with us, in the work of the Lord, in negotiating a treaty of reconciliation between the Lord and us; fhewing forth all the counfel of God to us, and all the caufes of his contendings with us, and preffing us to all the duties of the day, neceffary for keeping up the teftimony, and bringing our King back again to the land, whom our provocations had banifhed: for which end they inculcated upon us, our covenant engagements, to keep and contend for the word of the church of *Scotland's* patience, to wreftle againft all the encroachments made upon our *Mafter's kingdom,* and to weep over all the indignities done unto his name, by this apoftate and malignant party, revolted from, and rebelling againft him, and to ftand at the fartheft from all countenancing of, or complying with them, or ftrengthening their hands by
bearing

hearing of the curates, or anſwering their courts,
or tranſacting with them any manner of way,
in taking their enſnaring bonds or oaths, (whereof we had many then impoſed, of the ſame nature with theſe forged ſince, though now more
univerſally accepted) or in paying their iniquitous exactions, for maintaining them in their
wickedneſs, profeſſedly impoſed and required.
for that end; yea, when many of our much honoured watchmen ſpared not to ſet their trumpet to their mouth, and cry againſt all the defections of their brethren impartially, particularly againſt all that church-rending and ruin-
ing detection of the acceptance of that indulgence, the baſtard brat of the blaſphemous ſupremacy, then our ſouls were refreſhed in going alongſt with them; but when ſelf-credit
and intereſt did ingage ſome to take the patrociny of that ſtep of defection, and prepo-
ſterous prudence and reſpect to peace, with prejudice of truth, did prompt others to palliate and.
daub it, we adhered to theſe that faithfully continued to contend againſt it; who, for their ſo
doing, were much contemned and condemned;
and ſome of them in ſundry preſbyteries were
cenſured and rebuked; yet did we not break off
communion with theſe who then were labouring
to quench our zeal, and cool our fervour againſt
that Chriſt-diſhonouring ſin, though at that time
we were much diſcountenanced by them, but
endeavoured to go on with the teſtimony, both
againſt the detection, and the tyrant's uſurpation upon Chriſt's crown, thereby explicitely
exauctorated, from which it had its riſe; and.
accordingly the teſtimony at *Rutherglen* was e-
mitted *May* 29. 1679. againſt the declaration
con-

condemning our Covenants, the act for keeping
that anniversary day for the setting up the U-
surper, and against other wicked acts made a-
gainst the interest of Christ in the land, which
were then publickly burnt, which is now condemned by many that then approved and ap-
plauded it. After which, when, in prosecution
of the same testimony, the Lord favoured us
with a notable victory at *Drumclog*, that expedition of *Bothwel* following thereupon was
broken, by a holy provoked God, for our sins,
by occasion of our divisions and confusions, fo-
mented by the opposers of our testimony,
wherein we were unite, before some ministers
and others favouring the Indulgence, did contend for inserting the interest of the usurping
indulger in the state of the quarrel, and opposed
the inserting of the indulgence, as it was ob-
truded and accepted, among the causes of humiliation, that we then pleaded for as a necessary
duty that appearance called for : whereupon
followed that lamentable overthrow, wherein
much precious blood was shed, and many of
our dear brethren were led in triumph captives
by the insulting enemy ; some of them sealed
that testimony we then contended for with
their blood ; others of them refusing the insnar-
ing indemnity (condemning that and all other
appearances as sin) and the Bond of Peace then
tendered, as the test of that compliance, were
banished : and in their voyage murdered, by being shut up under hatchets, when the ship was
lost. Many came off by taking that bond, being tempted by the persuasions of some ministers, and the silence of others, who refused to
give their advice. At which time a number of
our

our ministers formed themselves into an assembly, wherein they voted for a new indulgence, with the Cautionary Bond, in some respects more derogatory to Christ's prerogative, and the gospel's liberty, than the former: and from that time, such as had not the benefit of the indulgence, in homologation of that imposition, did confine their preaching within doors, or near houses, that that shadow of obedience, might be a sconce for their protection. Then did our perplexities begin, that did much astonish us, and brought us to our wits end; yet did not our hunger after the ordinances abate, but we adhered to the few ministers we had, that would concur and venture in the work of the gospel. And when Mr. *Richard Cameron* used all diligence and patience in inviting and inciting others of his brethren, then lurking, to a concurrence, he could not obtain it; yet with the concurrence he had, and our adherence, he went on with the testimony, both against enemies usurpations, and the shameful and sinful yieldings of his brethren thereunto. And accordingly, considering the wickedness, usurpations, and tyranny of the late tyrant, then raging as a roaring lion, and ranging bear over the poor people, imposing upon their consciences, robbing, spoiling, and pillaging their possessions, hunting and cruelly handling, imprisoning, torturing, butchering, and murdering, their bodies, for conscience of duty; affronting and defying the most high God, in heaven-daring wickedness; inverting, perverting, and diverting, the ordinance of magistracy; and destroying all laws and liberties, all securities of mankind, and overturning the whole work of reformation,

breaking

breaking and burning the covenant with God,
and compact with the people, and arrogating to
himself a blasphemous supremacy over the
church of Christ: he did, with the concurrence and adherence aforesaid, publish a Declaration at *Sanqubar*, *June* 22. 1680. difowning and disclaiming the tyrant; and in some expectation of a further capacity, did declare a
war against him, and all that took his part. But,
instead of that obliged concurrence which ministers ought to have given to this testimony so
stated, this action and the owners thereof were
generally condemned by them: and being so
deserted and abandoned of them, in the holy
providence of God, we lost that worthy standard-
bearer, and many other worthies, at *Airsmoss*;
where many died valiantly fighting for that testimony, others were taken and barbarously
butchered, hanged, and quartered, sealing the
same with heroick courage, and the countenance
of the Lord signally shining upon them, who yet,
by the opposers of our testimony, though professed friends to the cause, were condemned as
dying foolishly, upon insufficient grounds. Then
had we none to concur with us but worthy Mr.
Donald Cargil, of whom the land and we were
not worthy; and therefore shortly after this,
the Lord deprived us of him likewise, and gave
him the crown of martyrdom, in owning the
same testimony. That was a day of our perplexity and treading down in our valley of vision.
Then the word of the Lord was precious, and
there was no open vision; the standard was fallen, and there was none to take it up, of all the
ministers that were then in the land; tho' they
had many reiterated calls from several corners,
yet

yet none would come forth to preach publickly,
but fitting and flighting or fhifting our calls, did
either lurk in the land, or went abroad and deferted their work. Whence, being left in that darknefs, many went aftray to the right and left hand.
On the one hand *John Gib* and his accomplices
difcovered their wild extravagances, to the reproach of the way of God. On the other hand,
many deferted our teftimony, and made defection unto the time's compliances: and generally
all were jumbled into fuch confufions, that fcarcely could one underftand the language of another,
or know who concurred in the teftimony: But
in that extremity, the Lord made fome inftru-
mental to gather us together in a general correfpondence; where this method was fallen upon,
which we have hitherto kept up, of meeting together from all the focieties of our embodied
community, to underftand one another's minds
about the duties or fins of the times, and to encourage one another, and to do all things jointly, by mutual advice and common confent, in
profecution of the common teftimony, which we
call our General Meeting; which proved in fome
meafure encouraging to us. For immediately,
upon the firft commencement hereof, though
when we were few in number and deftitute of
paftors, another declaration was publifhed at
Lanerk, *January* 12. 1682. confirming the former, and further teftifying againft the reception
of the duke of *York*, and admitting him to pre-
fide in parliament, and againft the teft, &c.
which declaration did fet us more alone, and
made us more the butt of enemies malice, and
of our brethren's contempt than any thing formerly; for from thenceforth, many did more

declaredly oppofe us, and informed againft us both at home and abroad; laying heavy things, which we knew not, to our charge, without either trying the truth of them, or taking pains to admonifh us of them. Wherefore, in the next general meeting, we fell to deliberate how our cafe might be reprefented, and our caufe vindicated to ftrangers; and we refolved to fend fome abroad to make it known, that we adhered to all the principles of the true Prefbyterian church of Scotland, in its doctrine, worfhip, difcipline and government; after which, by fpecial providence, a door being opened for the inftruction of fome ftudents at a college in the Netherlands, we fent fome young men thither to ftudy; and in procefs of time received back Mr. James Renwick an ordained minifter, who hath hitherto laboured among us in the work of the gofpel, not without a feal of his miniftry through the Lord's blefling; however it be oppofed and defpifed of men. After which, the fury and violence of enemies was let loofe upon us, as well as the fcourge of tongues, to the effufion of much of the precious blood of our brethren, and the bondage and banifhment of others; and wicked acts were given out for all to apprehend us wherever we could be found, and to raife the hue and cry after us, inhibiting all to refet or correfpond any manner of way with us, under the fevereft penalties; which brought us to great ftraits, and even to defperate extremity, without any probable hope of relief, by reafon of the enemy's vigilancy the country's readinefs to obey, (being already much wafted with oppreffion, and fearing greater devaftations) and the wicked malice of many intelligencers and informers, whence we were neceffitated

seffitated to put forth another declaration, affixed
on feveral market croffes and church doors,
November — 1684. confirming and explaining
the former, and vindicating us and our teftimony from fome odious afperfions, to the intent to
deter and fcar the country from giving intelli-
gence of us: which, though it did fcrew up
our trial to a greater height than ever, (the
enemies bloody cut-throats having a commiffion
to murder us where ever they met with us) and
though it proved a fnare to many, while an oath
abjuring the fame was generally preffed through
the country, in very fmooth and fubtile terms,
which coozened many; yet it deterred many
from their former diligence in informing againft
us, and alfo drew out fome to join with us, even
fome who had taken that oath of abjuration;
when they had difcovered the guilt of it in their
wounded confciences. However, we cannot re-
count the number of our dear brethren that we loft
in this deluge of blood that was fhed at this time
by foldiers, and fome gentlemen, that made it
their work to kill us where ever we could be
found, without either trial or fentence, or time
to prepare for death, or refpect to age or fex;
even women, fome of a very young, fome of an
old age being drowned in their fury. But in the
mean time of the height of this rage, the Lord
did remove the tyrant *Charles* II. which did put
fome ftop to it. Thereafter, when his brother
James duke of *York* was proclaimed, and a parliament convocated for eftablifhing him in his
ufurpation, we refolved upon a teftimony againft
the fame; and fo emitted another declaration at
Sanqubar, May 28. 1685. not only protefting a-
gainft the forefaid ufurpation, contrary to our

covenanted reformation and laws of the country; but giving our testimony against all kind of Papistry in general and particular heads, as is exprest in our National Covenants. This was done in the mean time of the earl of *Argyle's* expedition, with which we were much pressed to concur, and many embodied with us were drawn away with the importunity of some ministers and others of that association; yet we could not join with them, nor espouse their declaration as the state of our quarrel, because it was not concerted according to the ancient plea of the *Scottish* Covenanters, against both right and left hand opposites, in defence of our reformation, expressly according to our Covenants, National and Solemn League; because no mention is made of our covenants, nor of Presbyterian government, which was of purpose left the Sectarians should be irritate; because it opened a door for a confederacy with Sectarians and malignants, of which malignants they had some among them guilty of shedding our blood at *Airsmoss*. After the defeat of this expedition, in answer to the desire of some ministers, who came over with *Argyle*, we had a conference with them, *July* 22. 1685. in which, instead of allaying differences, the proposals that were made for union did heighten our breaches, both with them and among ourselves, as did appear by the consequents; herein though they offered accommodations, yet in conference to bring it about, they mentioned and did not disown that which bred alienation, to wit, a previous information they had sent to strangers, accusing us of heavy things, that we had not only cast off all magistrates in *Scotland,* but had constitute
among

among ourfelves all kinds of magiftrates, and were for cutting off all as open enemies, who did not acknowledge our imaginary government; that our focieties were only an erroneous faction, and have no power of calling paftors, &c. which information, fo full of calumnies, though they did extenuate, alledging that the copy of it which we produced was forged, yet they confeffed fome fuch information was written, and went on to profecute, in effect, the fame crimination; and .faid, they excerpted all out of our public papers:· and further challenged us, for falfely accufing them in our proteftation against the *Scottifh* congregation at *Rotterdam*;. where they with others were promifcuoufly charged with fundry things *in cumulo*, which they were not guilty of. We confeffed it was an overfight conjointly to accumulate thefe charges without diftinction; but taking them feparately, we offered to make out every thing there charged upon the names inferted. And further, in inveighing againft Mr. *Renwick's* ordination, they accufed the church of *Holland* of Fraftianifm,. and many other corruptions :. To which he only replied, that he had received his ordination from the Prefbytery of *Groningen*, and they being foreigners, and not chargeable either with our defections, or any declining from the teftimony of their own church, but advancing, and groaning under fome corruptions from which they were never reformed, would come under another confideration than minifters of our own church defending a courfe of defection; howbeit, as he protefted in the face of their prefbytery, when he received ordination, againft all things he knew among them diffonant to the work:

of reformation of the church of *Scotland*; so he told his purpose to inform that venerable presbytery how they were represented in *Scotland*; and if they could not clear themselves, at least, of some of the grossest of these things, he would be willing to acknowledge before such as were competent, that he had offended in meddling with them. The accommodation which they offered, was upon terms, which we thought, destructive to our testimony, to lay aside all debates, and let bygones pass, and go on in the public work; which we did not think was the way to heal our sore: But we offered, if differences and exceptions could be removed in a right and honest way, we would be most willing to join with them; which exceptions were given in, in these particulars following, *viz.* Their leaving the country and deserting the publick work, when it was so necessary to concur in the testimony, but condemning it in *Sanquhar* and *Lanerk* Declarations, even as to the matter of them; and not condemning the paying of the locality imposed for maintaining soldiers against the work and people of God; their countenancing the compliers of the time, while in the land, and when abroad; joining with the *Scottish* congregation at *Rotterdam*, and hearing the indulged preach there; then, informing against us, and aspersing us with slanders, such as these in the forementioned information; and then, concurring in the earl of *Argyle*'s association, against which we had so many things to object, as above hinted, Which exceptions (though among the least we have against many other ministers, with whom we have no clearness to join in our now circumstances, yet) we thought sufficient to demur upon;

upon; when, after many fruitless janglings, we
could receive no satisfaction about them, nor a
public testimony satisfyingly stated, wherein we
might both agree and concur; so the conference
broke up. And thereafter we were more unten-
derly dealt with by them; and also deserted by
many embodied with us in fellowship, who from
that time left off coming to our general meetings,
and to take separate ways, without respect to
our former consented agreements; and also did
hear, receive, and spread abroad some false reports
given forth against us, without premonishing us
about the same; and drew many off from our societies by such means. With some of which we
had a conference, *January* 28. 1686. who said they
had a verbal commission from some societies in
Carrick, &c. the effect whereof (whatever was
the intent of their coming) tended to a further
breach, though we were not conscious to ourselves of any untender dealing with them. For
first, we did endeavour to remove all supposed
grounds upon which they might stumble into
alienation from us, by clearing our minds about
all these things the ministers laid to our charge:
then several questions of weight about our present
differences were propounded to the meeting, about
a letter of accusation spread against us, which they
did not positively disclaim; and about *Argyle's*
declaration, which they would own or disown,
accordingly as it was diversely interpreted; a-
bout the exceptions given in against the ministers,
which they alledged were not valid; and finally,
we asked the foresaid persons, whether or not
they were clear to join with us in general and
particular fellowships, now when they had heard
us speak our minds so freely? this they refused to
answer,

anſwer, putting the queſtion back, Whether or not we would join with them? and generally in all theſe queſtions they declined freedom and plainneſs, and ſeemed averſe from ſatisfying us, and to be rather for contending, than a free communing for union; chiefly they ſtickled a-bout a general concluſion previouſly agreed to and reſolved upon among us, That nothing re-lative to the public, and concerning the whole of us, ſhould be done without the conſent, or at leaſt the knowledge of the whole; which con-cluſion, though formerly they agreed to, yet now they called an impoſition; alledging that hereby they might not hear a faithful miniſter when occaſion offered; though we told them, we did not take that concluſion in an abſolute ſenſe, as a reſtriction ſimply neceſſary, for all times, all places, all perſons, things and caſes; and in neceſſary duties, if the reſt ſhall ſinfully deny their concurrence, they propoping it, may lawfully without breach of the concluſion, do it for themſelves; but in points doubtful and con-troverted, it is neceſſary for adviſing and deſibe-rating, as a hedge againſt precipitancy and raſh-neſs, uſeful for preſervation of union, excluding confuſion, curbing petulent ſpirits, and for the right management of affairs. In fine, for the reſult of this conference, when we were urged as above, whether we would join with them as formerly, by way of retortion to our propoſals of the ſame to them; we told them, we could not anſwer in name of our ſocieties, having no di-rection from them for that effect; and that for our own parts, we would not refuſe accidental or occaſional communion with them as brethren and Chriſtians; but in the preſent circumſtances, we we could not be clear to concur with them as formerly, in carrying on the public work harmoniously, and habitually, until our exceptions were removed; which were, their breaking that conclusion of brotherhood formerly condefcended. to, in their calling ministers against whom we had exceptions unremoved, without acquainting us therewith; in their drawing together in arms without our knowledge, and contrary to what was concluded by themselves with our and their friends: their siding with other persons in points of disagreement against us. Whereupon, they broke away abruptly; and their carriage since hath been very disengaging, and discovered a great deal of alienation from us, by their labouring many ways to represent us unto the world to make us odious, in their informations given in to ministers against us, and by their protesting against and hindering Mr. *James Renwick* to enter their borders, yea, refusing to communicate with him so much as in family-worship, albeit it was sometime far otherwise, when they agreed with us in their testimony against Papists, malignants, Sectaries, and backsliders. But now we must bear many obloquies from them and others, waiting in dependance on the Lord's vindication, who will bring forth our righteousness, or rather the righteousness of his own cause by us maintained, as the light, and our judgment as the noon day; and in the mean time, carry ourselves abstractly, and let them be saying, we must always be aiming at doing.

Now, dear Brethren, we have thus far, with all unfeigned freedom, unboweled before you the naked account of our contendings, in short hints, without all prevarication, or taking advantage

vantage

vantage of your unacquaintedness to represent
our cause better than it is. We shall now shut
up our letter with a brief declaration of our testimony, which we now stand and suffer for, and
of our principles that we own and disown.

We do therefore testify our holding and adhering to the written word of God, as the only
rule of faith and manners, and all the received
principles of this reformed church, founded
thereupon, and consonant thereunto; as, our
Confession of Faith, Catechisms Larger and
Shorter, Covenants National and Solemn League,
Acknowledgment of Sins, and Engagement to
Duties, the Causes of God's Wrath, &c. We
adhere unto the doctrine, worship, discipline
and government of this reformed church, as we
are covenanted to maintain; and to all the acts
and proceedings of our general assemblies for
promoving the reformation. We own and adhere unto all the faithful testimonies of the
church, or of any of its faithful members or
officers, former, old or later, particular or more
general: against the public resolutions, Crom-
wel's usurpation, and toleration of sects and he-
resies in his time, before the overturning, and
since; against Prelacy, supremacy, or the compliances and defections of ministers and professors; particularly, we own the Rutherglen, Sanquhar, and Lanerk Declarations, and the late
Apologetical Declaration against intelligencers
and informers. We own all the duties professed and prosecuted by the faithful, for the pro-
moval and defence of these testimonies; as,
preaching in the fields, and defending the same
by arms, and appearing in a declared war against
the public enemies of this kirk and kingdom,
at.

at *Pentland, Drumclog, Bothwel,* and *Airſmoſs;*
and all ſuffering upon the account of theſe, or
any part of non-conformity, with the God-pro-
voking courſes of the time.

We diſown and obteſt whatſoever, in doctrine,
worſhip, diſcipline and government, is againſt,
beyond, or beſide the written word of God;
all damnable hereſy, as, Quakeriſm, Popery,
Libertiniſm, Antinomianiſm, Arminianiſm, So-
cinianiſm, and all other, under whatſoever de-
ſignation; together with the wild extravagancies of *John Gib:* as alſo, all kind of idolatry,
ſuperſtition and profaneneſs; all ſects upon the
right hand, as, Anabaptiſm, Independency, Mil-
lenarianiſm, and all other ſects and ſchiſms, and
diviſive courſes: and on the left hand, we diſown and deteſt Prelacy and Eraſtianiſm, and
whatſoever elſe is contrary to ſound doctrine
and the power of godlineſs; and all countenancing of or complying with Prelacy, ſupremacy, or tyranny, or any uſurpation upon church
or ſtate, made by this malignant enemy; all
hearing of curates or indulged, or paying either
of them ſtipends, enacted by iniquious laws, ſetting them up: all anſwering to the courts of
perſecutors, taking any of their oaths, as, the
Declaration, Teſt, the oath of Abjuration, or
any other oaths of ſupremacy or allegiance;
ſubſcribing any of their bonds, as, the Bond of
Peace, Bond of Regulation, the Bond of Com-
pearance, or any other of that nature; paying
any of their wicked impoſitions, as, militia-mo-
ney, ceſs, localiky, or fines or any thing that
may ſtrengthen the hands of ſuch evil doers. As
alſo, we diſcountenance all the ſteps of defection, declining from, or contradictory to our
fore-

fore-mentioned teſtimony; and diſown all aſſociation and confederacies with malignants or ſectaries.

But, more particularly, becauſe our principles are moſt ſuſpected upon the ordinances of magiſtracy and miniſtry, therefore we ſhall plainly unboſom our hearts about theſe alſo.

We profeſs then concerning magiſtracy, That as it is not founded ſubjectively upon grace, ſo it is a holy divine inſtitution, for the good of human ſociety, the encouragement of virtue, and curbing of vice, competent unto, and honourable among both Chriſtians and Heathens; and for ſuch magiſtrates as being rightful and lawfully conſtitute over us, do act as the miniſters of God, in a due line of ſubordination to God, in the defence of our covenanted reformation, and the ſubjects liberties, we will own, embrace, obey, and defend them, to the utmoſt of our power. In church matters we allow the magiſtrate a power over the outward things of the church, but not over the inward things, as doctrine, worſhip, diſcipline, and government. We allow him the cuſtody of both the tables of the law, and a power to puniſh corporally all offenders, even church officers, againſt the ſame; not under the conſideration of a ſcandal but of a crime: We allow him a power of ordering things for the wellbeing of the church; and in ſome caſes of convocating ſynods, *pro re nata*, beſides their ordinary meetings, and being preſent there, but not to precede in their debates; and of adding their civil ſanction to ſynodical reſults, but no power to reſtrain them in the power Chriſt hath given them: we allow him a cumulative power, to aſſiſt, ſtrengthen, and ratify, what
church

church officers do, by virtue of their office;
but not a privative power to detract any way
from the churches authority : we allow him an
imperative power to command church officers
to do their duties, but not an elective power,
either to do himself what is incumbent to church
officers, or to depute others to do in his name,
or by any ministerial power received from him.
Finally, we grant this to be the full extent of
the magistrate's supremacy in church affairs, to
order whatever is commanded by the God of
heaven, that it be diligently done for the house
of the God of heaven ; and what further he may
usurp, we disown and detest. But in things civil,
though we do not say that every tyrannical act
doth make a tyrant, yet we hold, that habitual,
obstinate, and declared opposition to, and overturning of religion, laws and liberties, and making void all contracts with the subjects, inter-
cepting and interdicting all redress, by suppli-
cations or otherways, doth sufficiently invalidate
his right and relation of magistracy, and warrant subjects, especially in covenanted lands,
to revolt from under and disown allegiance to
such a power : yet they may not lawfully arrogate to themselves that authority which the
tyrant hath forfeited, or act judicially, either in
civil or criminal courts ; only they may do that
which is necessary, for securing themselves,
liberty, and religion. But for the late tyrant,
as we did disown and do detest the memory of
his first erection, and unhappy restauration,
after, by many evidences, he was known to be
an enemy to God and the country ; of his nefa-
rious wickedness in ejecting the ministers of
Christ from their charges, and introducing ab-

M m   jured

jured Prelacy; his attrocious arrogance in rescinding all acts for the work of reformation;
his unparalleled perfidy and perjury, in-break-
ing, making void, and burning the Covenants;
his heaven daring usurpation, in arrogating to
himself that blasphemous supremacy; his auda-
cious and treacherous exerting of that usurped
power in giving indulgences to outed ministers,
to divide and destroy the church; his tyranny
over the consciences of poor people, pressing
them to conformity with the times abominations,
and imposing upon them conscience-debauching
oaths; his tyranny over the whole land, in levy-
ing militia and other forces, for carrying on his
wicked designs, of advancing himself to arbitra-
rian absoluteness, and imposing wicked exactions
for their maintainance, professedly required for
suppressing religion and liberty; his cruelty
over the bodies of Christians, in chasing, and
killing upon the fields, many without sentence,
and bloody butchering, hanging, heading, man-
gling, dismembering alive, quartering upon scaffolds, imprisoning, laying in irons, torturing
by boots, thumbkins, fire-matches, cutting pieces
out of the ears of others, banishing and selling
as slaves old and young men and women in great
numbers; oppressing many others in their e-
states, forfeiting, robbing, spoiling, pillaging
their goods, casting them out of their habita-
tions, interdicting any to reset them, under the
pain of being treated after the same manner:
So for the continued and habitual trade of these,
and many other acts of tyranny, we did disown,
and do yet adhere to our revolt from under the
yoke of his tyranny. And for the same reasons,
we disown the usurpation of *James*-Duke of
York,

York, fucceeding and infifting in the fame foot-fteps of tyranny, treachery and cruelty, and labouring to bring thefe lands in fubjection again to the yoke of Antichrift, being a profeffed Papift, and therefore by many laws of the land, incapable of bearing any rule. And here we ftand as to the point of magiftracy.

Concerning the miniftry, we own the lawfulnefs and the neceffity of that ordinance, againft Quakers, and all its other oppofers; and hold it our duty to obey and encourage all true and faithful paftors, and highly to honour them in love, for their work's fake, And we hold it unlawful for any man, though never fo well qualified, to take upon him the work of the miniftry without licence and ordination, by laying on of the hands of the prefbytery, or any competent number of thefe, to whom Chrift hath committed the power of the keys. And we hold, that power of church government and difcipline, and every part of the minifterial function, does not appertain to pope, prelate, magiftrate, nor multitude of believers, but only to the officers of Chrift's appointment, as the fubject and receptacle of all fuch power. We therefore profefs our fincere refpect unto, and will own, invite and imbrace all fuch minifters as are cloathed with Chrift's commiffion, in his orderly and appointed way; all fuch as are cloathed with righteoufnefs and falvation, confirming and a-dorning their doctrine by their practice; all fuch as are found, fpiritual, and orthodox in the doctrine, holding forth the word of life in incorruptnefs, gravity, fincerity, found fpeech, that cannot be condemned, and are faithful in the difcharge of their commiffion, *crying aloud,*

and

and not sparing, shewing Jacob his sins, and Israel his transgressions; constant and instant in their work, *in season and out of season, reproving, rebuking, exhorting with all long-suffering and patience,* making full proof of their ministry. Yea further, we profess, we will withdraw from no ministers, upon such insufficient grounds as their infirmities, their different judgment or practice in things that are either indifferent, or not material, or not contradictory to the testimony of the church of *Scotland;* their ignorance of the state of our testimony, having no occasion to be informed thereof, which hath made them heretofore stand back from concu.rence with us; and even their real scandals, not attended with obstinacy, but confessed and forsaken. But, we judge we have sufficient ground to withdraw from all who cannot instruct their being cloathed with Christ's call, in his orderly way; as the curates, &c. from all who have subjected their ministry to the disposal of strange lords, and taken a new holding from and upon a new architectonic and usurped power in the exercise thereof, by accepting a new grant, licence, and warrant from the usurper of their Master's crown; as the indulged, &c. From all such who pervert and corrupt their ministry, by preaching and maintaining errors, either in doctrine, worship, discipline or government, contrary to the Scriptures and our Confessions, and principles of our covenanted reformation, and contradictory to our present testimony founded thereupon, and agreeable thereunto; from all ministers guilty of gross compliances with the public enemies of this covenanted and reformed church, who have broken the covenant, destroyed the reformation.

mation, ufurped the prerogatives of Chrift, and are ftill, and by all means, feeking the extirpation of all the owners of the caufe of God; from fuch minifters who take the defence and patrociny of thefe courfes, and palliate and plaifter them, ftrengthening the hands, and hardening the hearts of thefe who are engaged in them; fo that none doth turn from thefe wicked things; from fuch minifters as are unfaithful in the exercife of their minifterial function, or in a fmooth, general, flattering way, applying, or rather mifapplying, their doctrine to the times; from fuch as are finfully filent, in deferting their duty, and lying by from the public work of preaching the gofpel, when the peoples urgent neceffity and preffing call doth make it indifpenfible, when people are deftitute of public warning, in the times when fnares are moft abounding, and the poor flock in the greateft hazard to be turned afide; from fuch as are fchifmatical and pragmatical dividers of the church, and wideners of the breaches thereof, already broken and divided, fowing difcords among brethren, and promoving their contentions: Finally, from all fuch as are fcandalous and diforderly, either in their minifterial or perfonal walk; from all minifters that deferve thefe characters, we think, we have fufficient grounds, from fcripture and acts of affemblies, to withdraw our communion. And therefore, as we hold ourfelves bound in confcience and duty, with all due refpect to the miniftry, and love to their perfons, to bear witnefs and teftimony againft the defections of the generality of the minifters of the church of *Scotland*, fince the overturning of our reformation, and intro-

ductions

duction of Prelacy; their fainting, and not giving a testimony for the church's liberties, against its destroyers, at their first introduction; their leaving their charges at their command; their deficiency in not giving a testimony when the covenant was broken and burnt, nor when the supremacy was established; their general lying by from their work, the poor people thereby wanting warning; some accepting of the indulgence, others not witnessing against it, but pleading for it, as no defection, or for union with the indulged; their meeting in presbyteries for the rebuking and censuring the more faithful, who did witness against that sin; their laying bonds on some young men, not to speak of it; their pleading for the Tyrant's interest at *Bothwel*; their accepting of the Cautionary Bond, to observe his orders in preaching after *Bothwel*; their persuading to, or not dissuading from taking many ensnaring bonds and oaths, imposed upon prisoners and others; their leaving the work of preaching the gospel in the fields, when they were mostly called to the duty, in a time of abounding snares from the right and left hand, and reproaching and condemning others, who did jeopard and loose their lives in that work; their complying with the enemies, in bonding with their courts, (some to that length, as to come under obligations to forbear the exercise of their ministry) and hearing of their curates; their joining with such confederacies and associations, that did open a door for the introduction of malignants and sectaries, contrary to our covenant engagements; and the like steps of defection, which we desire to mourn for: So, for these, and the like defections, we

must

must withdraw from, and difcountenance many of our ministers, whom otherwise we love and honour. And feeing in thefe times of diftempering confufions, we are now deprived of the remedy of thefe fettled judicatories, whereunto we might recur in the cafe, and yet are bound in our capacities to witnefs againft thefe defections, whereby the wrath of our God is fo much . kindled againft the land ; therefore, we judge it lawful, reafonable, and neceffary, in this declining and difordered ftate of the church, to leave that part of the church which hath gone aftray into fuch defections, whether ministers or profeffors, as to a joint concurrence in carrying on the public work (and let them return to us, but we not to them) and to adhere to the other part of the church, ministers and profeffors, though fewer and weaker, who are ftanding ftedfaftly to the defence of reformation, witneffing againft the declinings, until the defections of the backfliding party be confeffed and forfaken; wherein we altogether deny we can be charged with pofitive feparation from the church of *Scotland* ; yea, nor negative feparation, if it be confidered actively : We only acknowledge a feparation negative, paffively confidered, in our being left alone in the time of our greateft ftraits, and forfaken by the reft ; endeavouring, the mean while, with many failings and much weaknefs, to retain and maintain the covenanted work of reformation, in all its parts, as it was attained unto in our beft and pureft times; and choofing rather to ftand ftill and walk alone, than to go along with others in declining and offenfive courfes.

Now, having alfo given you, in all well-meaning

ing plainnefs, this declaration of our teftimony, we fhall not trouble you further, but conclude with a humble defire, That, as ye would weigh what we have faid in the ballance of truth and charity, fo you would acquaint us with your fentiments of the fame, and deal freely in admonifhing us, wherein you think we err, or go beyond, or come fhort of our duty. Your correspondence fhould be very acceptable and comfortable unto us: fo, recommending you to the grace and mercy of our Lord and Saviour Jefus Chrift, we reft,

Your affectionate friends and brethren in the Lord,

Subfcribed in our name, and by our direction, by the clerk of our general meeting,

MIC. SHIELDS.

LETTER XCI.

To the honourable Mr. Robert Hamilton.

Hon. and dear Sir,   *July* 6. 1687.

YOU may know from manifold experiences, that *through much tribulation we muft enter into the kingdom of God:* The way to the heavenly *Canaan* lieth through a wafte and howling wildernefs; our pilgrimage is through a valley of tears, and over mountains of difficulties: but as we have a good and comfortable guide, fo he can bring meat out of the eater, and fweet out of the ftrong, and make the flinty rocks give water to us; yea, he can make our bitter waters fweet unto us, and in abundance of forrow give fuperabundance of joy. We doubt not but you have
often

often found this, which helps and animates you, in obedience to the will of God, to undergo so many perplexities and discouragements.

We received your letters. In that which shows your purpose of travelling through other churches, we observe the various and singular troubles which you did meet with at *Lewarden;* your conflicts in that place have been sharp and multiplied; and we reckon it our part to be burden-bearers with you, though we be far short of this, as of all other duties. But we hope, you have both peace and joy in your lot, considering the precious and honourable cause for which you are redacted unto it. And we are greatly refreshed with the report of the tenderness, zeal and stedfastness of these few worthy friends at *Lewarden,* who have been encouraging to you, and took a share with you of all your afflictions. In the letter which gives a relation of your travels through some other churches, as we see your care to lay out unto them our pristine reformation and present sufferings; so also, to show us in what state affairs are amongst them; whereby we judge ourselves greatly obliged unto you, for that might be greatly to our advantage if we could improve it. Oh! we understand that hateful profanity, detestable carnality, vile superstition, deplorable defection, loathsome lukewarmness and infatuated security, are much abounding in these churches. The generality, both at home and abroad, seem to have conspired together to let go piety, and to cleave to policy: When policy is kept as piety's servant, it helps to secure it; but when it is advanced as master, it does much to undo it; the rule of scripture-simplicity and

car-

carnal wifdom are fquared very unlike to other.
O what can we expect but a defolation upon many lands! Chrift hath a great conqueft to make
in the earth,. and there muft be a ftrange fhaking
and overturning of kingdoms, that his kingdom
may get place, as *Hag.* ii. 6, 7.; in fuch a cafe
we fhould be careful to hold faft that which we
have, *Rev.* iii. 2.; we have a great word of
teftimony delivered to us, which (we are hopeful) fhall yet empty thrones and pulpits; O how
worthy is it, of all that we can witnefs and fuffer
for it! and how unworthy are we of it, if we fhall
defert it ? in fuch a cafe we fhould ftudy to be
wholly and only for the Lord God of hofts. The
profanity, carnality and indifferency of the generality fhould provoke us to holinefs, fpirituali-
ty and zeal; but alas! in the midft of all this,
we have our deep fhare of the fpiritual plagues
that are abounding in this day; it is not with us
as fometimes it hath been. O Lord pour out
thy fpirit upon us. In fuch a cafe we fhould be
mourning for all the abominations committed in
the earth, efpecially in the churches: O happy
fhall they be who fhall be found marked among
the mourners in *Zion,* for they fhall be fpared,
Ezek. ix. 6. O where is love to God? where is
zeal for his concerns? where is tendernefs now
to be found? when there is fo little holy indignation, fo little forrow and mourning for the
magnitude and multitude of the tranfgreffions of
this generation. In fuch a cafe, we fhould be
laying our own things amongft our feet, and preparing to meet our God, who is *coming out of his
place to punifh the inhabitants of the earth for their
iniquity,* Amos iv. 12. Ifa. xxvi. 21.

- The information which you give us of the fad
over-

overthrow, yea almoſt extirpation, of the ancient and famous *Waldenſes* in the valley of *Piedmont*, is very grieving and affrighting to us. O what may other churches expect, when ſuch things are done unto them! O that all churches would take warning from their ſad and lamentable coſt, of the ſin and danger of compounding with, or truſting enemies, whoſe offers are ſnares, and who know not to keep oath or promiſe either to God or man. We bleſs the Lord for any kindly acceptance you got in any place of your travels: We deſire, that in our name, you may thank theſe (whether in *Geneva* or *Switzerland*) who have received your information, or ſhewed you kindneſs. And when you write, ſignify unto them that we purpoſe (according to your deſire) to keep up a correſpondence with them, and to ſend them letters and informations; but apologize for the delay, conſidering our ſcattered condition, and the weighty affairs at preſent, among our hands, which we cannot defer.

We have few particulars to inform you of at the time; the adverſaries are reſtrained from that meaſure of outrage whereunto once they were given up; they change their methods, but they do not change their natures: the eyes of many are like to fail, with waiting for a liberty and free toleration, ſuch as is given to *England*, and we hear that the enemies are divided about it; they may be divided about the means, but they are united in the end and deſign. Many miniſters who formerly were lying by from their work, are now beſtirring themſelves more about it, and frequently preaching; but they do generally declare (or rather diſcover) themſelves

more

more fully than before, by loading us with false
imputations, and by preffing people in their letters and fermons, not only, not to concur with
us in our prefent teftimony; but to flee from
us. Yet the more that they are of this ftrain,
they gain not the more ground. We may fay,
by the good hand of the Lord, our number is
rather encreafing than decreafing: we are doing
our endeavour to have elders elected and admitted amongft us.

Now, worthy and dear Sir, we hope we need
not put you in mind to ftudy all neceffary freedom and tendernefs toward them of foreign
churches, and patiently to wait upon any of
them fo long as there may be hope; by your
frequent converfing amongft them, you will know
better what may be for their advantage and the
advancement of the kingdom of Chrift, than we
can tell you. The Lord be your leader and
guide, the eyes of many are upon you. O ftudy
that every word and action may be fo expreffed
and done, as you may not be afhamed to avow
it, if it were before the whole generation of
mankind, whatever be their different humours,
perfuafions and inclinations; and alfo, as you may
have peace in it before God. There lieth much
advantage to the caufe in our expreffing ourfelves
in fuch a form of found words as may pertinently
fignify the matter, faithfully declare our minds,
and not favour of prejudice, pride or paffion, or
in their own nature tend to irritate thefe who
do oppofe themfelves. We would feek the good
of every foul; and though as to many we mifs
our end, yet we fhould carry fo towards them
as may leave a conviction upon their confciences,
that it was their good we were feeking: whatever
others

others are in their way, we are the same by nature, and we should pity them, lament over them, and yet hate the garments spotted with the flesh, and carefully keep ourselves from partaking of their sins. Now we do heartily and jointly commend you to the all-sufficiency and faithfulness of your God, not ceasing to pray for you; and that any work you have been, or may be instumental to begin abroad, may be carried on by the good hand of the Lord. We are,

Honourable and dear Sir,
   Your sympathizing friends,
     and obliged servants in the Lord,

Subscribed in our name, and by our desire, by the clerk of the general correspondence,

MICHAEL SHIELDS.

LETTER XCII.

To Friends in Ireland.

Dear Brethren,   *Sanquhar, Jan.* 24. 1689.

YOur letter directed to our ministers was read to us, which affords matter both of joy and sorrow. Albeit we cannot but rejoice to see such ardent desires, as your letter demonstrates to be among you, to have the gospel faithfully preached, and the sacraments administered, by such ministers against whom we had no exception: Yet we ought to lament, with a sad lamentation, that in covenanted *Ireland* there are such defections from approven, received, and

N n   sworn

sworn to principles, and compliances with stated avowed enemies to truth and godliness, as gives you solid ground of withdrawing from ministers guilty of the same, whom, notwithstanding, ye, and we, and all, should reverence, respect and love. It is also grievous to us, when we consider not only your sad want of the faithfully preached gospel, from these against whom ye have no ground of exception; but likewise, that the same from hence cannot be so fully supplied, as yourselves and we both could desire; for tho' some other of our ministers intend shortly (if the Lord will) to give you a visit, yet, at this time, their absence from this land cannot be thought convenient. And we desire, as well as expect, that, upon their not coming, ye may put a more favourable construction, than to think the same proceeds from forgetfulness of you, or unconcernedness with you, seeing, as we have, though in weakness, so now we desire to have a brotherly affection to, and sympathy with you in all your trials for the cause of Christ. However, the Rev. Mr. *David Houston* is coming over to you, whose labours in the gospel among you we heartily pray may be crowned with success, to the glory of free grace. We hear it is reported with you, he and we should be separated one from another, which here we declare to be false. As formerly, so now, we much esteem him, though many (who had their tongues bended like their bows for lies, but they were not valiant for the truth upon the earth) have been at no small pains to load his name with reproaches and base calumnies; which, as they are grievous to us to hear, so we have endeavoured to search out the the truth of them; but after trial, (excepting
some

some sharp and too vehement expressions concerning the indulged party, which we wish and hope he will forbear) do find that the same hath chiefly flowed from prejudice in some, and ignorance in others; and all we shall say of them who have so done, shall be cordial wishes, that they may see the evil of it, and do so no more.

Dear friends, we hope it is needless to make apologies for our slackness in writing to you, seeing some of your number may know our share in the times confusions hath not been least, which proved oftentimes diverting from so necessary a duty. Though these few months bypast hath been a time of many confusions, great reelings, and strange overturnings, yet it hath been very fertile in bringing forth wonders; which as they are the Lord's doings, and should be marvelous in our eyes, so, at the time, though they be much admired and sought out by all the Lord's loyal lovers, and fearers of his great and dreadful name; yet, in after generations, they shall be more wondered at, to the praise of him who brought them to pass; when it shall be said, at such a time the Lord did great things for *Britain,* which it looked not for, yea for *Scotland* in particular, which it had little ground to expect; and that which makes it the more remarkable and worthy of observation is, the Lord's right hand that doth valiantly is so eminently seen in it, and the hand of men of high and low degree so little, so that none can say, their sword or their bow hath done it; to him alone who is the Lord of hosts belongs the glory; we may sing and say, *He hath triumphed gloriously, the horse and his rider hath he thrown into the sea: he hath poured contempt upon princes, and led kings away*

N n 2   *spoiled:*

spoiled: the wicked are snared in the work of their hands; and he hath brought to nought the counsel of the heathen, he hath broken the yoke of the oppressor, and made the oppressed to go free: Yea, what shall we say, he hath brought down in a great measure, the throne of iniquity in *Britain* and *Ireland,* under which his people hath been long groaning, and hath given a great dash to Popish idolatry. But though great and unexpected mercies call for great thankfulness, and much pains taken upon a people, should have more than ordinary fruitfulness following the same: Yet we cannot say our thankfulness is answerable to the mercies received, nor the fruit correspondent to the pains taken upon us. It might have been expected that mercies should have melted our hearts in kindly sorrow for sin, even after we had not been humbled under judgments, which for a long time had been lying upon us; yet alas! we are not so humbled, mourning, repenting and praying a people as we should be; and until we be such, it is presumption for us to expect that his anger will be turned away, but his hand will be stretched out still; so that we may fear we provoke the holy Lord to change his dispensations from manifestations of loving-kindness, to declarations of holy anger and indignation, and to stop the current of mercy which hath been for a time running, and in place thereof, that wrath, judgment and desolation shall run through this gospel-despising and mercy-contemning land. O pray for us, that we may be helped greatly to improve present mercies, and be preparing for future judgments.

Now, dear Brethren, as ye have begun, so hold on, in professing and contending for the

co-

covenanted work of reformation, which both ye
and we are bound in our covenants to the moſt
high God, to defend and maintain. Let not the
threatenings of men fear you, or their flatteries
entice you to abandon ſo noble a cauſe; remember that only theſe who endure to the end get
the crown. Let pins, hairs and hooves of Chriſt's
truths be precious unto you, although the generality of mankind deſpiſe them; the more they
are contemned, they ſhould be the dearer to us.
Beware, upon the one hand, of defection, and
upon the other, of running into unwarrantable
extremes and extravagancies. Let not ſecurity
ſeize upon you, under the preſent favourable
diſpenſation, as thinking _Zion's_ warfare is accompliſhed, the enemies fallen, and the church
delivered; if any think ſo, they are but dream-
ing: they are happy who are preparing for ſad
and evil days, which at the time are likely to be
near the door; for the report of theſe bloody
cut-throat Papiſts, the wild _Iriſhes_, their being
in arms are come to our ears, which is, at leaſt,
ſhould be very wounding and afflicting to us. As
your fathers and ours have experienced their
barbarous cruelty and helliſh rage formerly, and
all _Europe_ heard of the ſame; ſo, for former ſins
that land again may feel a little of the ſtroke of
their bloody and devouring ſwords: Yet tho' this
ſhould be, let not the forethoughts thereof prove
hand weakening and heart-fainting, but rather
alarming and upſtirring to you, to enter into
your chambers and ſhut the doors about you,
and _hide yourſelves, as it were for a little moment, until the indignation be overpaſt._ O fear
not _though the earth be removed, and the mountains caſt into the midſt of the ſea, for God is a_

refuge, a present help in the time of trouble' What though these wild and wicked creatures rage and roar, yet mind that they are bounded by him who set bounds to the sea, and said, *Hitherto shalt thou come, but no further, and here shall thy proud waves be stayed.* What though the floods lift up their waves, yet remember the Lord on high is mightier than the noise of many waters, yea than the mighty waves of the sea. Labour to have faith and patience in exercise, for this is a time that calls for it. Thus recommending you to the Lord, and heartily wishing his grace to be with you. We remain,

Your wellwishing and sympathizing friends and brethren in Christ,

Subscribed in our name, and at our desire, by the clerk of our general meeting,

MICHAEL SHIELDS.

LETTER XCIII.

To the honourable Mr. Robert Hamilton.

Crawfoord-John, February 14. 1689.

Right honourable Sir,

WE shall not much apologize for our long forbearance to write to you, but rather take with a fault in the same: However, as we may say, it is not the want of affection to you which hath hindered; so, since the last time we wrote, many reelings and confusions hath occurred, and our share thereof hath not been the

least

leaft, which oftentimes proved diverting from
fo neceffary a duty. We acknowledge indeed,
we are many ways obliged to you, and among
other things, for laying out yourfelf fo much
for procuring the ordination of Mr. *Thomas Linning* at *Embden*, now preaching the gofpel a-
mong us, we hope, with fuccefs, to the praife of
the riches of free grace. But as oft times we
are remifs in giving fignifications of our thanks
to them who well deferve the fame, efpecially
to you; and when given, they are infignificant:
fo we hope, though you want this from us, it
will not demur you from laying out yourfelf further in your ftation for propagating the teftimony of Chrift, nor make you repent of what you
have done already, for which you will not want
a reward.

Knowing you will be defirous to know how
matters have gone here thefe few months by-
gone, we fhall briefly relate only fome of the
moft memorable paffages which hath come to
pafs in and about this wonderful Revolution,
efpecially thefe things wherein we are more near-
ly concerned: To give a full and particular account of all the reelings and overturnings which
have been brought about this little while bygone,
would fo far exceed the bounds of a letter, that
it might fill a volume. However, by what is
here given, you may fee much of the Lord's
mercies towards this poor land, in his ftately
fteps of providence. Many, wonderful and
ftrange are the revolutions, thefe few months
have produced, whereat we ftand aftonifhed,
and adore the Lord's holy and infinite fovereignty in his way of working in and among the children of men; the Lord hath put a new fong in

our

our mouth, but alas we cannot fing it. He hath in a way very wonderful, difappointed the fears of his people, and hopes of his enemies, when they were ready to fpring their mines, and accomplifh their long intended and wicked enterprizes; behold, on a fudden their defigns are crufhed, and themfelves taken in the pit which they were digging for others, and they were enfnared in the work of their own hands.

In *September* laft, fome foldiers got fecret orders to go through the five weftern fhires, and take from the people all their arms; which was obeyed: whereby the country being difarmed, were unfit to defend themfelves againft the affaults of bloody Papifts: but fince, they are generally provided better than before. About this time, there were courts of inquifition to be kept in the weft, and fome of them begun, wherein fome profeffing lairds were to have a hand, in order to the finding out of thofe who had a hand in refcuing Mr. *Houfton*, and about going to field-meetings; which if they had gone on would have tended much to our bondage. But the news of the coming of the *Dutch* put a ftop to this threatened ftorm; whereby, and by the foldiers going to *England*, we got a little refpite. In this juncture, when nothing but wars was expected, we thought it duty to deliberate upon what was called for at our hands. Whereupon, after ferious deliberation and confideration, we refolved not to ly by, but to act againft the common enemy, yet in a diftinct body from others, with whom we could not affociate. But when nothing was looked for but wars and confufions, behold, in a way very ftrange, all turned to rumours of peace. The Lord, who is terrible to

the

the kings of the earth, and cuts off the spirits of princes, made the tyrant to tumble off his throne and run for it, and his army to desert him; whereby an eminent testimony was given against that absolute power arrogate by that poor mortal man. Likewise there was a testimony given against, and a dash unto Popery, yea more than had been for several years before: many monuments of idolatry were destroyed, and severals of them burnt in public places, in doing whereof severals of our number were active: the heads, hands and quarters of our martyrs were taken down and buried, and prisoners for truth set at liberty. When this was going on, there was a report spread through the country, of the *Irishes* being at *Kirkcudbright*, and raising fire and sword, which proved so alarming, that in a few days many hundreds were in arms in the west, especially many of our number appeared: But the report proving false, most part of us dismissed. However a part of us stood together some days in arms, and coming to *Douglas*, emitted a declaration (which is here sent) for their own vindication, and to make the intention of their appearance known to the world. After this, many of the curates were put from the kirks; so that at this time, there are few of them preaching in the west. These things, as they were strange, surprizing and astonishing, and much of the Lord's power, wisdom, mercy and faithfulness to be seen and observed in them; so they call aloud for great fruitfulness and thankfulness at our hands. But alas, our short-coming in this may make us afraid, that we provoke the Lord to change his way of dealing with us, and to
manifest

manifeſt his anger againſt us, as he hath of late
ſhown his mercy towards us.

There is one thing, worthy Sir, which oftentimes we know not to determine about, which
is, concerning your home-coming; when we
conſider how deſirable your company would be
to many here, and alſo your own deſire to come
home, we would gladly comply with it. But a-
gain, when we call to mind your uſefulneſs abroad,
wherein the Lord hath helped and honoured you
above others to lay out yourſelf for the advantage
and comfort of his followers; and not knowing
what larger door of acceſs may be opened for
you to be uſeful there, we dare not be poſitive
in our deſire to you to come home: ſo we leave
it wholly to yourſelf to be determined as the
Lord ſhall direct you; heartily wiſhing that where-
ever you are the Lord may be with you, leading
and guiding, protecting and preſerving, comforting and encouraging you. We earneſtly deſire you would refreſh us with a line, giving us
an account of the Lord's care of, and kindneſs
to you theſe months paſt. We remain

Your affectionate friends and wellwiſhers,

Subſcribed in the name, and at the deſire of
our general meeting, by

MICHAEL SHIELDS.

F I N I S.

SUBSCRIBERS NAMES.

Edinburgh

THe rev. Mr. James Hall minister of the gospel
Charles Brown druggist
Boswel Ross stud. of philosophy
John Arnot ditto
John Hall ditto
John Mosman ditto
James Liddle stud. in medicine
John Hutcheson ditto
Robert M'Michael student
James M'Cliesh bookbinder
Robert Currie merchant
William Taylor printer
Ebenezer Currie ditto
Robert Miln flax dresser
Michael Naismith mason
Moses Lothian staymaker
William Walker writer
James Paterson taylor
William Foord clerk
David Waldie staymaker
Alex Stewart mer Cannongate
Robt. Will merchant there
Ja Wauchop turner Caltoun
Geo. Cromar gardner Moultreeshill
Robert Morison coachwright
Y Plaisance
Ja. Bishop weaver, Causey-side

Duddingston

James Farningston mason
James Young ditto
William Yorkston ditto

Libberton parish

Christian Salmon
David Aitkin farmer

Laswade parish

The Rev. Mr. John M'Millan min. of the gospel Pentland
Charles Umpherston wright
Anabell Umpherston
William M'Niel wright
James Melrose taylor
George Johnston ditto
Walter Johnston collier
William Lietch ditto

Thomas Hall miner
William Innes wright
John Allen tenant

Dalkeith

Francis Eliot weaver

Collington parish

John Christy mason
John Mather ditto
John Clarkson ditto
Alexander Fleming wright
William Gibson quarrier
Rob. Thomson herd Kirkton
Archibald Keddie tenant Temple parish
Ja Grieve tenant Rinskinhope
Rob. Armstong herd Bowrhope
Miss Annie Laurie, Kerswell
Geo. Sommerville wright, Lenton, 12 copies

Calder parish

John Kirkland wright Garcosh.

Filashire

Ja. Balmain shoemaker, Kinghorn 12 cop.
William Forgan weaver, in Dunnykeir
Alexander Anderson ditto
John Wallace ditto
David Littlejohn, Shaws mill
William Shields in Sinclair
William Couper there
Robert Mathieson coalier, Kirkcaldy
Wil. Glass merchant Kinross

Glasgow

Andrew Galloway grocer
Alexander Bow
James Brown flax dresser
John Brash weaver
John Campbell weaver
John Donald distiller
Alexander Downy weaver
William Eaton hosier
Thomas Eaton wright
James Fulton workman
James George tobacconist
John Gilles shoemaker

John Gilles weaver
David Girdwood wright
Alex Hamilton tobacco-fpinner
Margaret Hamilton
James Hood cooper
John Kay weaver
Mrs. Lennox
Walter Lilburn taylor
Robert M'Lae fmith
Mary M'Nab
John M'Kindley workman
Mungo M'Farlane ditto
Robert M'Lintock fhoemaker
John M'Kinlay taylor
William Robertfon merchant
Thomas Rodger ftay-maker
Louifa Sharp
Archibald Simfon fmith
James Storie weaver
John Smith ditto
Mary Stirling
Widow Tod
Elifabeth Williamfon
John Wilfon fhoemaker
James Walker wright
Robert Waterftone
James Young printer
James Turnbull ⎫
David Turnbull ⎪
Matthew Turnbull ⎪
James Cherrie ⎪
John Fulton ⎪
John Jervey ⎬ weavers
Alexander Brown ⎪
Robert Nairn ⎪
John Thomfon ⎪
Andrew Brown ⎭
William Rodger taylor
Mary Campbell
David Miller, Calder bridge
John Anderfon, Airdrie, 2 cop.
Arch. Hamilton, in Cathkin

Paifley.

Ja. M'Quhae ftud. of divinity
Wil. Brown ftocking-weaver
John Bain merchant
Agnes Brown
Daniel Brown weaver
John Ballantyne taylor
James Laught taylor

Robert Beveridge ⎫
Thomas Beveridge ⎪
Robert Black
Robert Arthur
Robert Carfewell
William Carlifle
George Caldwell
John Craig
John Dreghorn
John Darling
John Gib
John Glasford
James Finlay
James Goldie
Richard Henderfon
Alexander Hill
Hugh Howie
John Hutchefon
James Keir
John Knox ⎬ weavers
John Lang
David Ligget
James Miller
James Mitchel
Michael Maltman
James M'Lintock
John M'Niel
Ebenezer Picken
William Robfon
James Simpfon
Samuel Smith
John Scot
William Thomfon
William Taylor
William Whyte
Jofeph Willie
David Willie
James Hodgert, Renfrew par.
Matthew Biggar weaver Pol-
    lockfhaws

Greenock.

Alex. Glafs tobacconift, 12 cop.
John Buchanan merchant
William Wallace grocer
James Zuill ftocking-maker
Archibald Shaw fhoemaker
James Carfewell ditto
John M'Carter couper
William Parker fmith
Ja. Park fhoem. Crawfordfdyke

Par Glasgow

William Morrison merchant
Alexander M'Pherson ditto
John Taylor junior taylor
Matthew Crawford porter
James Taylor ditto

Lochwinnoch

Mat. Aitken in East Barnock
James Armour in Turnershields
Patrick Robertson of Trees

Houston

William Dick merchant
Robert Shearer smith
John Bar wright
Mat. Bar farmer, Griefwries
William Galbreath smith at
Burns of Inchennan
George Bar in Kilbarchan

Kilmacolm parish

John Glen merchant
James Lang ditto
John Taylor ditto
John Boyd ditto
John Baird flax-dresser
Samuel Cuthbert couper
Alexander Laird taylor
Alexander Laird couper
James Laird clock maker
William Lyle weaver
Annabella Laird
Wil. Menzies stocking-maker
James Murray shoemaker
Alexander Semple clock-maker
Ja Laird maltman Romour
Alex. Lang farmer Everroun
Wil. Paterson farmer Branchlel
Wil. Andrew farmer in Gateside

Erskine

James Couper distiller
William Whitehill smith
Alex. Gardner farm. Middle-
penny
Tho. Inglis glazier, Langside

Killallan

Patrick Bar farmer Middleglen
Ja. Lindsay flax-dresser, Brig
of weir
Robert Kershaw dyster there
John Bar flax-dresser the

Galston parish.

Adam Brown weaver
John Brown wright
David Allan merchant
Hugh Bell
Andrew Campbell drover
Alexander Combs mason
John Gebbie shoemaker
Christian Graham
John Hunter mason
Alexander Kirkland
William Lambie weaver
Andrew Manson farmer
Alexander Meikle shoemaker
George M'Coul hedger
George Paterson malster
Archibald Piercie shoemaker
John Smith dyster
James Smith shoemaker
Hugh Wilson butcher
Andrew Woolock taylor

Parish of Kilmarnock

James Brown farmer
John Laurie bonnet-maker
John Kirkland calenture
Samuel Spier miller
Thomas Wright weaver
William Smith shoemaker
William Steven dyer

Parish of Loudon

John Dykes farmer
Andrew Mitchel bleacher
Jean Mair
Thomas Paton farmer
Archibald Salls weaver
Robert Woodburn farmer

Dumfries

The rev. Mr. John Courtas,
minister of the gospel at
Quarrelwood
William Thomson shoemaker
James Cowan portioner
William Cunningham taylor

Kirkpatrick durham

James Coats
John Coats in Town-head
Sam. Collin taylor Minniedow

John Coats travelling-chapman
William M'George weaver in Lairdlaugh
William Haighall shoemaker in Coalfad
John M'Connel miller in Kirkpatrick mill
William Gillefpie tenant in Lairdlaugh
John Kirk fhoem. in Moorwhirn
William Coupland fmith
R. Cunningham taylor weftland
John Canon travelling chapman 3 cop.

Kirkpatrick-juxta

Edward Thomfon tenant in Knockhill

Glencairn parifh

Walter Clark merchant in Minniehive
John Cunningham farmer Barbowie
John Edgar weaver Dalwinton
Samuel Grierfon taylor in Minnihive
James Grierfon taylor there
Thomas Gracie dyer there
William M'Whir there
Murdoch Murphie inkeeper there
Elizabeth Smith in Glenfan
Alexander Grierfon tenant in Loehenkitt

Lochruton parifh

Jofeph Laurie in Hills
Thomas Halliday there
John Carfon there
John Clark fchoolmafter in Betty-knows
Alex. Clark tenant Burnfide

Terregles parifh

Andrew M'Ghie in Kirkland
John Grierfon weaver there
John Sloan there
Samuel M'George in Bowfe

Dunfcore parifh

John Turner in Strawhan
William Waugh tenant in Fardenrufh

Kirkmahoe parifh

George Halliday weaver in Reddingwood
Wil. Brand wright Auchincairn
Wil. Beck tenant in Ruletown

Kirkmichal parifh

James Patie tenant in Nethernochenfhang

Balmaclellan parifh

Robert Cunningham tenant in Drumwhirn

Johnfton parifh

William Thorburn miller in Borland-mill

Parton parifh

Pat. M'George in Blackfhill
Samuel M'Michael in Upper-Corfock
Martin Beg weaver Blackfhill
George M'Lean weaver in Armannoch
James M'Connel miller in Corfock mill

Carfphairn parifh

John Hairftones
Sam. Harries tenant in Kilnair
Wil. Robfon weaver in Crofts
Samuel M'Keur farmer in Darngerroch
Mrs. M'George in Lary
Wil. Rowan in Stroanpatrick
Rob. Smith in Netherwhitefide
James Wilfon in Slengebar
James Wallet there
Agnes Hunter there
Hugh Smith fcoolmafter in Galloway
John Milligan chapman at Corfemichael-kirk
Robert Wright mafon at Coldftream, 12 cop.

Irvine

James Craig fhoemaker

Finwick parifh

John Howie farmer
John Boyd ditto
William Wilfon quarrier

Parish of Rickerton

George Goudie miller
Hugh Paton farmer
Hugh Pack coalhewer
James Adam taylor
James Wilson farmer
Thomas Wright
James Guilland farmer
John Morton farmer
David Sower

Hamilton parish

James Carmichael merchant
Thomas Weir weaver
James Lang merchant
William Cunningham merchant
Gavin Rowat wright
John Naismith stocking-maker
Ja. Morton taylor Garvelhead
Alexander Turnbull farmer Haughhead
Jo. Fleming Dunsystine carrier
James Rodger carter Laughup
Jo Smellie farmer Motherwell
Jean Cuthbert Mirriton

Bothwel parish

John Jamieson merchant Cleland
James Cleland miller.
William Smith wright
John Rodger carter

Airdrie

Ann Cleland merchant
Daniel Corse wright

Stonehouse

James Rowat wright
John Smith smith
Andrew Jack taylor
Sibylla Rowat
Isobel Craig
Robert Wilson farmer Watston
William Laurie weaver Hosenet
John Craig taylor Dervil

Dalserf parish

James Watt farmer Cannerside
James Muir shoemaker
Thomas Aitkin Coal-hewer
William Couper ditto
Robert Summers ditto
Alexander Bell ditto, Westburn

Carluke parish

William Nicol shoemaker
Susannah Muir
John Allan quarrier
Thomas Allan ditto
James Calderhead
William Calderhead
William Forest servant
Thomas Gray
John Gilchrist quarrier
James Lang weaver
William Newlands
John Pettigrew
William Storie

Murdieston

Ja. Inglis farmer, Westerhouse
Walter Paterson taylor
Thomas Steel
William Gowans
Alexander Gowans
Janet Nimmo
Mrs. Janet Meikison
James Watt
Thomas Willox gardener
Agnes Alexander
James M'Carter lint-dresser

Cambusnethan parish

John Sandilands smith
Thomas Pettigrew
Marion Bruce
Thomas Scot farmer
Robert Young
James Lindsay farmer
John Burns ditto Walston
Marion Shaddow
Marion Shots
Rob. Reid farmer in Foulburn
James Roger shoemaker
Thomas Johnston coalhewer
William Russel hammerman
Ja. Steel portioner in the Stone
Jean Muirhead
Jo. Hamilton farm. Calderhead
Wil. Dunse merch. Greenhead
James Young farmer
Thomas Smellie in Evertown
Rob Billie portioner in the More
William Mackie lint-dresser

Davie's Dykes

Thomas Ruffel portioner
John Ruffel
Thomas Ruffel
Robert Ruffel
Ja. Stewart farmer, Townhead
Mrs Gray in Auchterhead
Jo. Foreft couper in Kilhegie

Shots

John Reid farmer Windyage
William Brown lintdreffer

Crineldyke

Alexander Muirhead
John Dobie weaver
William Law
James Bell farmer Greenhead
William Robertfon
Patrick Nifbet wright
Margaret Kirkland
Gavin Laurie
George Carmichael taylor
James Scot
Robert Young
James Lindfay farmer in Walftonhead
John Smellie weaver
James Smith ditto
Archibald Prentice
John Cameron
James Davidfon
James Smith
James Melvin carrier
James Petticrew farmer in King'shill
John Dalziel
Daniel Bailie wright Middlehoufe
Robert Brownlee wright
Hugh Smith wright
Jo. Morton farmer Wefterhill
Ann Brownlee
Katharine Gilchrift Eafterhoufe
John Brodie in Heckler's-hall
James Johnfton lint-dreffer

Carnwath parifh

John Cameron
Daniel Simfon bookfeller
Thomas Curhtertfon merchant
George Law tenent

Lamington parifh

James Douglas fchoolmafter
Mary Wightmani
John Wightman miller
William Smith fmith
William Lindfay wright
Charles Ramfay clotier
Malcolm Wilfon
James Jackfon flax-dreffer
George Purdie weaver
Sufannah Johnfton
John Inglis in Cutter

Wanlockhead

James Ramage miner
John Ramage ditto
Alexander Robertfon ditto
Robert Tait wafher
James M'Millan miner
Thomas Watfon ditto
Alexander Lecky ditto
Charles Ramage ditto
Charles Lindfay
John Cuthbertfon miner
Robert Colthart fmelter
Archibald Rogerfon ditto
Nathaniel Paterfon ditto

Leadhills

Andrew Kennedy fmith
John Williamfon miner
Chriftian Brown
Mary Drips
John Young ftoremafter in Craikbridge-end
Mrs. Gordon there

Peebles

William Veitch mafon

Dunfe, &c.

Andrew Newton farrier
Andrew Newton merchant
Alexander Bruce lint-dreffer
John Bruce meal-feller
Robert Brown fhoemaker
William Boyd weaver
Alexander Cairns baxter
George Cochran wright
Thomas Gray merchant
John Hunter weaver

Robert Mitten weaver
John Ker dish-maker
William Mitchel dyer
John Paton chapman
George Ralph malster
Janet Redpath merchant
John Straughen weaver
Peter Darie weaver in Long-
town
David Smith grieve there
James Turner servant there
James Cockburn hedger there
Andrew M'Naught in Long-
town-mill
Thomas Henderson school-
master in Greenlaw
Robert Young taylor there
Ja. Cochran shoemaker there
George Johnston mason Black-
adder
Thomas Johnston hedger there
Robert Taylor in Whinridge
David Cockburn tenant Both-
wick
James Foreman in Chirnside
Thomas Thomson tenant in
Leadbrties
John Dods in Woodhead

Thomas Hedger in Allanbank
John Comb in Kimmerghame
Matthew Gibson in Hairhead
James Chirnside merchant in
West Reston
George Smith merchant in
Westruther
George Paterson in Pilridge
Katharine Redpath Ninilmains
Margaret Trotter Buttertown

Douglas

The rev. Mr. John Thorburn
minister of the gospel
The rev. Mr. John Fairly
minister of the gospel
Andrew Bell merchant
James Wilson there
James Begg schoolmaster
John Cowan farmer
Thomas Veitch carrier

Falkirk

Geo. Leishman mercht. 4 cop.

Bathgate

John Morten tenant

James Stewart miller, Westport
Leith.

ADVERTISEMENT.

There is in the Hands of some Wellwishers, a valuable Manuscript of the late reverend, learned and pious Mr. *John Brown's*, Minister of the Gospel at *Wamphray*, being an Exposition of *Paul's* Epistle to the *Romans*, which is promised, but not yet come to Hand, and for which Proposals will be published in a short Time, by the Printer of these Letters.

Edinburgh, June

PROPOSA

For Printing by Subfc

A New WORK, entitl

A

DICTIONARY

OF THE

HOLY BIBLE:

CONTAINING,

An hiſtorical and explanatory Account of the Perſons; a geographical Account of the Places; and literal and critical Deſcriptions of other Objeꞓts, whether natural or artificial, civil or religious, mentioned in the Holy Scriptures.

Alſo, unfolding the different Acceptations of the moſt expreſſive Appellatives; explaining Scripture Types; clearing the Meaning of many obſcure Paſſages; and reconciling ſeeming Inconſiſtencies.

The whole forming

A Body of Scripture Hiſtory, Chronology, and Divinity; and ſerving, in a great Meaſure, as a Concordance to the Bible.

Subſcriptions are received by DAVID PATERSON, the Publiſher, at his Printing-houſe, Lawn market, *Edinburgh;* where may be had Propoſals at large, with a Specimen of the Type and Paper.

CONDITIONS.

I. The book to be contained in two large octavo volumes, of about 600 pages each, to be printed on a fine demy paper, and an excellent good type; the price of each volume stitched to be only 3 s.

II For the conveniency of subscribers, a number, containing twelve sheets, will be published every six weeks, at 1 s. stitched in blue paper; the volume, altho' some sheets more, to be contained in three numbers

III. Subscribers for 12 copies shall have one *gratis*.

To the PUBLIC.

As this DICTIONARY of the BIBLE, or *Christian's Dictionary*, is undoubtedly a work of great trouble and expence, so also of great utility The design hereof is to diffuse that knowledge, and explain those subjects, which it is the indispensible duty of every one to be acquainted with; and certainly it claims the perusal of persons of every rank and condition of life It will contribute much to a right and distinct understanding of the Scriptures; and by the alphabetical order in which it is disposed, any person may, with the greatest ease, find out whatever article he desires

Here will be given an explanation of the scripture names of persons, together with a full account of their actions as recorded in the Holy Bible, and the periods wherein such actions were performed; the meaning of scripture types unfolded; the festivals, fasts, laws, ceremonies and solemnities of the ancient Hebrews illustrated; their money, weights, and measures reduced to the English standard; and the time when any particular occurrences took place distinctly related.

The whole collected from the best authorities ancient and modern, such as Josephus, Eusebius, Calmet, Buxtorf, Usher, Sir Isaac Newton, Grotius, Le Clerc, Wilson, Poole, Henry, Howel, Stackhouse, Ray, Prideaux, Cruden, &c. &c. &c.